Women Against Napoleon

D1995368

*Waltraud Maierhofer* is associate professor of German at the University of Iowa. *Gertrud Roesch* is professor of German as a second language at Heidelberg University. *Caroline Bland* is a lecturer in Germanic studies at the University of Sheffield, United Kingdom.

Waltraud Maierhofer, Gertrud M. Rösch,
Caroline Bland (eds.)

# Women Against Napoleon

## Historical and Fictional Responses to his Rise and Legacy

Campus Verlag
Frankfurt/New York

Distribution throughout the world except Germany, Austria and Switzerland by

The University of Chicago Press
1427 East 60th Street
Chicago, IL 60637

Bibliographic Information published by the Deutsche Nationalbibliothek.
Die Deutsche Nationalbibliothek lists this publication in the Deutsche Nationalbibliografie; detailed bibliographic data are available in the Internet at http://dnb.d-nb.de.
ISBN 978-3-593-38414-6

All rights reserved. No part of this book may be reproduced or transmitted in any form or by any means, electronic or mechanical, including photocopying, recording, or by any information storage and retrieval system, without permission in writing from the publishers.
Copyright © 2007 Campus Verlag GmbH, Frankfurt/Main
Cover illustration: Napoleon I., Le tyran démasqué, 1815 by Jean B. Gauthier. © akg-images.
Cover design: Campus Verlag

Printed on acid free paper.
Printed in Germany

For further information:
www.campus.de
www.press.uchicago.edu

# Contents

## Anti-war, Anti-Napoleon: Guardians of Material and Spiritual Welfare



## Forms of Aesthetics and Cultural-political Opposition



## Belated Nineteenth-century and Twentieth-century Opposition: Lessons of Nationalism

# Introduction: Women and Women's Writing against Napoleon

# Napoleon and Women? Women against Napoleon!

*Waltraud Maierhofer*

A grand exhibition, »Nelson and Napoleon« at the National Maritime Museum in London (2005), online events such as »Projekt Austerlitz 2005«, the »German-French year 2006« with a plethora of exhibitions and events promoted by the German National Tourist Board, not to mention the spectacular musical *Napoleon* (which premiered in London in 2000) – recently, it seems as if one Napoleon-related anniversary or commemorative event follows the other. The rise and fall of Napoleon were closely watched by his contemporaries and were the subject of animated discussions and analyses. Biographers, dramatists, novelists, historiographers, and historians continued to explore this phenomenon. Although in the beginning he had often been admired outside of France as a defender of freedom and a skilled leader, the opinions within Napoleon's subjugated neighboring countries generally turned into opposition to Napoleon, because he turned into a tyrant and aggressor. Writing about Napoleon seems to lend itself to reflection and reveals as much about the writer as about Napoleon. The study *Napoleon* by Robert S. Alexander surveys the changing image of Napoleon in historiography, literature, art, and popular culture in the nineteenth and twentieth centuries. Alexander characterizes his reputation as »a very complex work« (1) and demonstrates how passionate the debate about Napoleon's reputation was, both for and against, albeit restricted mostly to male-authored English-language works and a few in French, German, and Russian (with de Germaine de Staël as the standard exception and only woman author).

New biographies (such as the most recent one by Johannes Willms and the epic, four-hour, 2002 European feature film version, the most expensive European TV production to date) spend considerable effort depicting the women in Napoleon's life – his mother Letizia, his sister Caroline, his first wife Joséphine de Beauharnais, his second wife Marie Louise of Austria, his affair with the Polish Countess Marie Walewska, and his various mistresses. Admittedly, these women were significant in his life. But what about women who were not family or serving his love interests? Moreover, were there women in positions of influence or with celebrity status or female writers who opposed Napoleon, who spoke out publicly, acted or published against him? We find no trace of them in popular studies such as Frédéric Masson's *Napoléon et les femmes* (*Napoleon I and Women*, 1894) from the late nineteenth century or the recent *Frauen um Napoleon* (*Women around Napoleon*, 2001) by Stefan Gläser. Historians Susan Connor and Rebecca Rogers pointed out that Napoleon had little respect for women, and that his policies encouraged dichotomized gender roles, a return to pre-Enlightenment views of womanhood. He also excluded women from the »public sphere« and politics, although he established a system of girls' schools. Following up on this claim, Denise Davidson has written a historical monograph on women in the Napoleonic state, *Enacting the Social Order: Gender and Urban Public Space in Post-Revolutionary France.*

Prussia's beloved Queen Luise, who suffered hardship in the flight after the Prussian defeat at Jena and pleaded for lenient terms of peace in an audience with Napoleon in 1807, but was brusquely received, and the Swiss-born French aristocrat and writer Germaine de Staël, whom Napoleon expelled from Paris, are only his most well-known female opponents. According to her biographer Maria Fairweather, the exiled Staël who was a political activist, salon intellectual, and best-selling author of autobiographical novels, helped coordinate the European response that brought about Napoleon's downfall.

Women's writings on Napoleon and the Napoleonic wars were far more diverse. Scholars have only just begun to uncover and study this political and generic diversity. Napoleon and his admired principle of nationality continued to fascinate all of Europe far beyond his defeat and exile into the twentieth century. Johannes Willms and others traced how a powerful posthumous transfiguration of Napoleon's legacy helped shape European history in the nineteenth century and beyond. So far women's part in this discourse presents a gap in scholarship. »For German patriots the enduring tensions between France and Prussia perpetuated the need to resist his influence and commemorate those who had defeated him, a political discourse from which it has often been assumed that women were largely excluded,« writes Caroline Bland below. German-speaking women are therefore covered in a major part of this collection, but we also hear voices from France, Britain, Denmark, and Italy that reflect the wide geographical range of women's opposition.

In their important collection on British women's writings on the French Revolution, Adriana Craciun and Kari Lokke pointed out responses to Napoleon as one of the yet »largely unexplored fields of inquiry« (23), especially when one widens the perspective beyond Britain to women throughout Europe. The 1985 article by Emma Macleod, »British Women and the Debate on the Wars against Revolutionary France in the 1790s«, did not lead to further discussions and discoveries. Neither Simon Bainbridge's book, *Napoleon and English Romanticism*, nor Paul Michael Lützeler's article on Napoleon in European Romanticism analyze women's responses to Napoleon. The recent extensive study by Barbara Besslich on Napoleon and the Napoleon myth in German literature from 1800 to 1945 investigates more than 65 writers, philosophers, and historians from Goethe and Kleist to Thomas Mann, among them, however, there is only one work by a woman writer, Gertrud Kolmar. Individual essays and articles also cover mostly male authors such as Percy Bysshe Shelley (Cian Duffy). An article by Bernhard Spies on historical plays on Napoleon in German includes no women dramatists. A recent dissertation on the treatment of Napoleon by authors of the American Renaissance (William Daugherty) did not unearth spectacular female voices either. A noteworthy exception is the article by Kathleen Hallihan on the German Romantic writer Bettina von Arnim who wrote most enthusiastically about Napoleon. In her seminal article on British women writers and Napoleon, Jeanne Moskal hypothesizes that the writings of Helen Maria Williams »suggest a peak of enthusiasm similar to the one Bainbridge describes with male writers at about 1798–1802« after which he was considered the »destroyer of the Revolution« (185–6), as well as the destroyer of the hope for an end to superstition and despotism. We are thankful to Deborah Kennedy for following up on this thesis and exploring Williams and other English women writers in this present volume. The volume by Craciun and Lokke has restored »an important part of British literary and political history: women's contribution to the public sphere, and to the most heated debates of their day« and revealed »the extent to which women writers of the Romantic period did indeed write on those most ›masculine‹ of subjects: politics, revolution, and war« (9). I will discuss this intersection of gender and politics.

This present collection of essays has two main objectives: it broadens scholarship on literary representation and it contributes to recent groundbreaking scholarship on gender and military history. In the pioneering collection *Klio in Uniform?* (1997), historian Karen Hagemann first called attention to interrelated issues of nation, military, and gender in the Early Modern period, especially in Prussia during the anti-Napoleonic wars. Her chapter »Militär, Krieg und Geschlechterverhältnisse« was a groundbreaking study of inquiries, deliberations, and questions about the military history of the Early Modern Period that introduced issues of gender to military history and has since been developed in several publications. Most important for our context are her two other 1997 articles on the images of patriotic femininity during the Prussian wars of liberation (»Heldenmütter, Kriegerbräute und Amazonen«), and on nation, war and masculinity in the same period (»Of ›Manly Valor‹«). Her important publications on the discourse of female patriotism, culminating in her 2002 monograph (»*Mannlicher Muth und Teutsche Ehre*«) on nation, military, and gender during Prussia's anti-Napoleonic wars stimulated our research. Hagemann investigated the various possibilities for female patriots to participate actively in these wars. Those possibilities range from acts of charity to women's associations and press activity. In her recent article on »Female Patriots: Women, War and the Nation in Prussia during the Anti-Napoleonic Wars« she draws the following conclusion about the period of the Wars of Liberation against Napoleon between 1806 and 1815:

> »[It] proves to have been a central phase in the formation of a national political culture organised by gender. As a sort of catalyst, these wars accelerated and intensified the nationalisation of the gender order and the 'gendering' of the nation. They exerted a lasting influenced [sic] on the basic structures of the relationship between women, the state and the nation.« (»Female patriots«, 2004, 415)

Hagemann's monograph includes a chapter on the »Heroic Maiden and Amazon« who fought in the Prussian army, and how she was described by contemporaries (Hagemann 2002, 383-94). The perspective of gender aspects in the motivation of female soldiers and in their particular form of patriotism might be pursued further. Much of Hagemann's research has already been translated and is readily available, so a summary here will suffice.

In her chapter on heroic maidens and amazons Karen Hagemann investigates »female patriots« in Prussia and women's active involvement in the anti-Napoleonic wars 1806 to 1815. Hagemann reviews historical cases of a phenomenon often dealt with in literary texts, namely women cross-dressing as men in order to participate in the military cause of patriotic defense, which flourished for a last time during the anti-Napoleonic wars. She points out the following discrepancy: Women who carried arms and fought in armies were often stylized as heroines when their biological sex was discovered *after* their death in battle, while the ones discovered alive were simply dismissed and even publicly ridiculed for their transgression of gender roles. Hagemann places this discrepancy within the discourse on »amazons« in Prussia in 1813 and the women's demand to carry arms and participate in combat in the context of universal male conscription. As was the case earlier in revolutionary France, such demands were rejected (including overwhelmingly by other women) in favor of their duty to perform charitable and caring deeds towards the poor, wounded, orphaned, and widowed. Hence, polar gender roles were reinforced, prohibiting equality between men and women which was perceived as a threat to the social order.

Only one other historical study on women against Napoleon is available: historian John Lawrence Tone investigated »Spanish Women in the Resistance to Napoleon« in a 1999 publication on Spanish women's history, which is of great interest in our context and easily accessible. Tone compares the popular imagery of bellicose women who drove the French from the Peninsula with evidence of their actual participation in combat: this participation was one of the ways in which women influenced political processes and altered the highly gendered nature of politics.

## Warrior Men – Peace-loving Women?

About half of the articles in this collection examine fictional responses to Napoleon and the Napoleonic wars. A few remarks on the implication of biological sex and traditional gender roles in historical narratives that thematize war or have a wartime setting, suffice here to provide the theoretical background. Historical fiction, especially the more popular kind that is often turned into feature films, tends to perpetuate traditional social roles of men as warriors for the just cause and of women nurturing children, patiently awaiting the return of their heroic men, and tending to the wounded. The female fighter and soldier as a heroine was and continues to remain a rare exception, and often is, apparently, more of a sexualized curiosity and a device for suspense than a realistic depiction and encouragement of female participation in military conflicts. Images of erotic young women, faithfully waiting lovers and wives, and self-sacrificing mothers predominate. The portrayal of »masculine« matters of war continues to reinforce cultural constructs of the traditionally circumscribed and anti-bellicose woman.

The interrelation of women and war is much more complex than a simple dichotomy (men fight and lead wars, whereas women are victims of war, or in Margarete Mitscherlich's term are »the peaceable sex«). Women's relationship to and involvement in war is a growing field not only in literary scholarship, but also in a number of other disciplines and it has gained momentum in political debates as well. Joshua Goldstein's recent interdisciplinary collection of essays traces the effects of war on gender and the influence of gender on war across cultures. Goldstein concludes that killing in war does not come naturally for men or women, and that gender norms often shape men, women, and children to the needs of the war system. He observes that the image of a woman holding both a rifle and a baby is widespread among cultures as an image for liberation movements.

The anthology *War, Gender, and Literary Representation* by Helen Cooper theorized the intersections of research on gender and narratology of war, configuring the literary relationship between war and gender as early as 1989. The articles in that anthology pinpoint literature as being instrumental in perpetuating the ancient essentialist war myth. The essays examine the gendered mutual influence of war and literary representation from the Trojan wars to the Arab-Israeli conflicts and the nuclear age. The collection also investigates conventional war texts (texts that depict men who fight, and women who are keepers of the peace) and points out »that women's role in relation to war is much more complex and often complicitous« (XV). Not until World War I was there a wide variety of literary responses to war by women writers; in the 20th century, this array includes war perceived as liberation from the domestic sphere, as an embracing of war efforts, and, at the other extreme, women who abandoned the battle for feminist issues during times of war. While it is convincing that especially for twentieth-century texts, the dichotomy of the male fighter and the female peacemaker fails, our collection seeks to expand awareness of the nineteenth-century discourse of women and war, especially as it involves the discourse of the nation.

Already in the 1980s, feminist literary scholar Sandra Gilbert interpreted in »Soldier's Heart: Literary Men, Literary Women, and the Great War« the representation of masculinity in works on the two World Wars. Jean Elshtain, professor of social and political ethics at the University of Chicago, theorized extensively on women and war at around the same time. Her 1987 treatise *Women and War* confronts stereotypes of power and powerlessness deeply associated with the topic as mentioned above:

»We in the West are heirs of a tradition that assumes an affinity between women and peace, between men and war, a tradition that consists of culturally constructed myths and memories. Thus, in a time of war, real men and women – locked in a dense symbiosis, perceived as beings who have complementary needs and exemplify gender-specific virtues – take on, in cultural memory and narrative, the personas of Just Warriors and Beautiful Souls. Man construed as violent, whether eagerly and inevitably or reluctantly and tragically; woman as non-violent, offering succor and compassion. [...] These paradigmatic linkages dangerously over-shadow other voices, other stories: of pacific males; of bellicose women; of cruelty incompatible with just-war fighting; of martial fervor at odds – or so we choose to believe – with maternalism in women.« (4)[1]

In her book Elshtain demonstrates how these myths are undermined by the reality of female bellicosity and the imperatives of war. In her 1982 article »Women as Mirror and Other«, Elshtain offered an explanation which addresses why the image of women as peaceful, as the »other« to bellicose, remains so powerful, in spite of the actual increased number of women in the military. Traditional roles for women are built on characteristics that are antagonistic to everything inherent in war, namely destruction, chaos, and death (32). Thus, femininity guarantees the return to »normalcy« after war. Elshtain argues that readers embrace this promise, because it makes the topic of war more bearable. Since 1982, fiction and films such as the *Alien* trilogy (1979–92) or *G.I. Jane* (1997) have presented a notably expanded range of admirable tough women in the military; it remains to be seen, though, how influential they are for girls and women to overcome gender stereotypes.

In addition, romance was considered an essential part of a historical novel, especially since the publication of Walter Scott's influential *Ivanhoe* (1819). One cluster of articles in this volume studies fictional responses from the second half of the nineteenth century. These fictional responses were written during the heyday of historicism, when history and historical fiction were a staple of bourgeois education and at the heart of the Germans' search for a common national past and identity, as historian Thomas

Nipperdey describes in *Germany from Napoleon to Bismarck.* Occasionally, historical novels have a female protagonist, in most cases a fictional one, even when the subtitle emphasizes the historical component. These are usually »private« stories, mostly love stories. The »historical« element or background of the narratives is the war. The preconception is that war is made by men. In the traditional sense before the advent of Women's Studies and Gender history, women were not the agents of war and thus not the agents of history. The historian Leopold von Ranke (1795–1886) defined the goal of historiography as narrating »how it really happened.« Modes of modern and postmodern historiography are decidedly more skeptical about achieving objective insight into events and characters of the past. The school of New Historicism even states the contrary: that subjectivity and fictional elements are inevitable in even the most distanced and factual historical accounts. Moreover, such fictional elements may provide valuable insights into the past. This present collection is innovative in that it presents the research of both literary and historical scholars based on letters and diaries, as well as on historical fiction.

Hence, this volume seeks to expand our awareness of the range and diversity of women's responses to Napoleon by presenting an international spectrum of opposition to him that is both historical and fictional. The focus is on opponents to Napoleon, although several of the contributions chronicle changing views and attitudes over the course of time. Yet, the portrayal of women's opposition to Napoleon is not limited to women writers; we include a fictional account of opposition penned by Friedrich Spielhagen.

## Organization

The articles in this volume are grouped chronologically and by theme: major themes are war (first pro-war, then anti-war), aesthetics, and nationalism; erotic love and love-hate also play a role in several cases but are not separable from these themes. The contributions suggest that they are linked (although not exclusively, because there are overlaps) to spatial and historical proximity or distance. Women who suffered in the Napoleonic era turned to military aggression or took a stand for peaceful alternatives, while other contemporary women who knew of oppression and of war but who lived in secure circumstances, voiced their concerns in aesthetic or cultural-political terms. The second half of the nineteenth century represents yet another stance; it exploits opposition to Napoleon for the discourse of the German nation from a safe temporal and spatial distance. In the early twentieth century, Napoleon became a fictionalized object of desire and admiration. Parallels of Napoleon to Hitler, a dominant aspect in twentieth-century fiction, are mentioned in another chapter.

The first group of three articles is devoted to contemporary women who were directly affected by Napoleon's expansion and were involved in political opposition as royalty or who contributed to the public debate as writers. They supplement recent research on female soldiers in Prussia outlined above. Several of the writers lived in proximity to the battles and cheered on the fight against Napoleon's »tyranny«.

Deborah Kennedy examines the English writers Helen Maria Williams (1761–1827), Mary Berry (1763–1852), and Frances Burney (1752–1840). They published eyewitness accounts of Napoleon while on the Continent and in France. After he turned into a despot, they turned their pens against him. Indeed, Kennedy notes that the former revolutionary Williams became »as anti-Bonapartist as any British conservative,« including Hannah More, who mocked the First Consul in a poem and insisted on the superiority of the British constitutional monarchy. Early on, Williams diagnosed Napoleon's deep contempt for women. Frances Burney penned gripping accounts of the chaotic state of civilian life in Brussels and cheered for the English at the battle of Waterloo. Even writers who lived in safe distance from the war and who did not address the topic of war, were affected by it, as Kennedy points out in the cases of Dorothy Wordsworth (1771–1855) and Jane Austen (1775–1817). Kennedy's chapter affirms that the 1970s feminist slogan, »the personal is political«, is still valid for research on women's writings, especially in times of war.

Maria Carolina Queen of Naples (1742–1814), consort of Ferdinand IV di Borbone, daughter of Empress Maria Theresa, is far less celebrated for her opposition to Napoleonic expansionism than Luise of Prussia, and for good reasons. Although she had much less impact, she helps to round out the picture of resistance. Maria Carolina's leadership was decisive in Naples' alliance with England against Napoleon. Unfortunately, she was less successful in the later stages of her political struggle and lost her small kingdom to the French and British. She was a less »enlightened« representative of absolutism than Luise, not popular with the people, and not a

Neapolitan or even Italian herself. Thus, Maria Carolina did not lend herself to becoming a cult figure representing the Italian nation. Napoleon inspired the myth of the nation in the Italian people just as he had for the Germans after the official end of the Holy Roman Empire in 1806. In southern Italy, resistance against French rule changed into resistance against the re-instituted King Ferdinand after 1815. Her anti-French course provided *ex negativo* an important impetus for the struggle for Italian national unity in the later part of the nineteenth century. This chapter draws attention to how gender-biased criticism against Maria Carolina and her fight was carried over into historiography, biography, and fiction.

The last chapter in this section, by historian Dorothy Potter, explores the murky waters of a woman in love with and politically opposed to Napoleon as she was depicted in biography and twentieth-century fiction. In terms of discipline and genre, it ponders the boundaries of fact and fiction in the narration of history, a mix which some might call trivializing. The last third of our book is fully devoted to fiction; this chapter is mostly »historical.« It explores the life of Eugénie Désirée Clary, a French silk merchant's daughter who was engaged to the young Napoleon, married a future marshal of France, and later became Queen of Sweden. Potter includes in her study the depiction of Clary in the best-selling novel *Désirée* (1951) by the Austrian-born political journalist and emigrant to Denmark, Annemarie Selinko (1914–1986). The form of a diary justifies a highly subjective view of Napoleon, whose dangerous ambition Désirée recognizes early on. Potter's historical study affirms the historical accuracy of this novel and its depiction of the Swedish queen as a »discreet center of opposition«, although her earlier life had been entangled with his. The novel balances the memory of a woman of high standing and in opposition to the powerful usurper, while it also affirms and maintains post-World-War-II values of a woman's place in the family; possibly, this balance fulfilled a psychological need of those years and contributed to its international success.

Another important opponent representing a country besieged by Napoleon is Luise of Prussia (1776–1810), royal consort of Frederick William III, whose opposition to the yoke of Napoleon's reign is well-researched. Later in these pages we include a study of literary memorials to Luise which have received little attention so far. As Jennifer Askey writes in her chapter, »her early death was transformed in poetry and song to a rallying cry for revenge against the French.« Luise called for the study of

German history to revive the »noble German« spirit laid temporarily low by Prussia's defeat in 1806 and the end of the Holy Roman Empire.

The second group of essays explores women of various nationalities and standing who also were affected directly by the Napoleonic march across Europe. However, the women were anti-war and based their opposition to Napoleon on arguments for peace, tolerance, and economic and family welfare. Historian Denise Davidson investigates how »ordinary« French women – who were neither at the court nor writers – viewed the Napoleonic state and how they assumed a public political stance despite adverse legal and rhetorical restraints. Davidson studies mostly negative reactions by two women from different social groups and regions to Napoleon following his coronation. One was an upper-class independent monarchist in Marseille, the other a bourgeois business woman and matriarch in Rouen, who bequeathed us their views in journals and letters. Both women, Julie Pellizzone and Catherine Arnaud-Tizon, participated in city life and voiced their views on politics, economics, and military matters just like bourgeois men at the time. They believed that pursuing their individual and family interests would ultimately benefit the nation. Pellizzone opposed an illegitimate regime because it threatened well-being and wealth, and Arnaud-Tizon was most outspoken during the turmoil of the last years of the Empire. From additional memoirs Davidson suggests that even young women and girls participated in political discussions, both within the families and on the streets. Both men *and* women who resisted the military state, did not voice their opposition in different terms based on sex and gender.

On the basis of the letters of Rahel Levin (1771–1833), Gertrud Maria Roesch offers a study of the year 1813 and the discourses central to it. Not only do the military decisions which led to Napoleon's defeat 1813 intervene in Rahel Levin's private life, but she is also affected by social developments, marked as they were by romantically tinged nationalism and the emancipation of the Jews as a result of the edict of 1812. Applying a New Historicist approach, Roesch pursues a significant detail – namely charpie or lint from old linen, a material often used for dressing wounds at that time – in order to demonstrate how »meta-narratives« can be shown in the private history of the small and insignificant. In April 1813, while her future spouse Karl August Varnhagen von Ense (1785–1858), belonging to the staff of Colonel Tettenborn, defended the city of Hamburg, later having to clear the city out (whereby he experienced first-hand its devastation by the French), Rahel Levin took part in the planning of a large army hospital. After being ousted from this function, she took upon herself the tedious task of organizing food and clothing for the wounded soldiers from the front lines, returning from the first battles. The military preparations were accompanied by a wave of patriotic appeals which pointed at the problems besetting the project of emancipation. In order to avoid accommodating billeted soldiers and costly Berlin living, Levin finally relocated to Breslau in May 1813. The letters provide an atmospherically rich picture of everyday life there, which was characterized by a sociability more or less as in times of peace, remote from the fighting as it was. Finally, however, the reality of battle confronted the civil population, because countless wounded soldiers were transported into cities which could hardly provide for them. Roesch argues that Levin's charity work in Breslau was instrumental in liberating her from her familial ties and thus paved the way for a bond with Varnhagen. In this reading the War of Liberation, surprisingly becomes significant for a private life: it enables Levin's self-liberation.

The German-Danish writer Friederike Brun (1765–1835) lived in Rome during its occupation by the French and kept a record of her experiences. Only after Napoleon's defeat, in order to protect herself from negative consequences, did she publish her *Letters from Rome.* At the same time, she stylized herself as model historian in this publication. Brun opposes militarism and the growing nationalism of her era, advocating non-violent resistance and cosmopolitan thinking. Jeanne Moskal concludes in an earlier article that British writers like Mariane Starke, who also wrote from Italy, accorded Napoleon great religious and political significance without abandoning their own nationalism (Craciun and Lokke 12). In her article on Brun, Kari Lokke demonstrates that the role of religion in the context of Napoleon and his politics is even more complex: Brun portrayed Pope Pius VII as an »idealized *alter ego*« to Napoleon. Thus, she presented a radically new model of the »heroic«, a spiritual artist-hero, whereas Napoleon embodied the »heroic« in the traditional sense of successful military leaders. On the other hand, Pius comes to symbolize nascent Italian nationalism, free of military aggression, a »just« prince in Italian culture and art. Pius represents for Brun a cosmopolitan view of humanity. Just as Davidson found no gender-specific forms of resistance in the French men and women from the bourgeois class, so Lokke emphasizes that the attitudes to violence and love in war which Brun reported from Rome, were not gender-specific.

The third group of articles focuses on opposition to Napoleon concentrated on themes and arguments of aesthetics. Substantial scholarship has been devoted to the contemporary Swiss-French author Germaine de Staël (1766–1817) and her antipathy for Napoleon. However, Heather Belnap Jensen is the first to argue that Staël used art criticism as a mode of resistance to Napoleonic cultural practices. In the best-seller novel *Corinne ou l'Italie* (1807), detailed discussions of history paintings articulate Staël's opposing views on art and politics. Jensen poignantly argues that Staël questioned the »patriarchal ideologies« of the modern French school and the status Napoleon gave to culture. Jensen reveals how Staël criticized art »in the service of a corrupt regime.« Further, Staël's valorization of paintings of holy women takes on a new meaning in the context of Napoleon's »chauvinism«. Generally, the religious renaissance and Romantic aesthetic is adverse to Napoleon's artistic, cultural, and moral program.

Beatrice Guenther reveals a surprising disjunction between Staël and three German women writers: they shared her denunciation of Napoleon's politics, but criticized her book on Germany, *De l'Allemagne*, although it was confiscated in France as too germanophil. Guenther successfully builds on Benedict Anderson's recent cultural analysis of Staël's »imagined Germany« as one of the *Imagined Communities* in the context of the origin and spread of Nationalism. She helps us understand writings by Staël's German adversaries, Betty Gleim (1781–1827), Esther Gad (c. 1767–1833), and Caroline de la Motte Fouqué (1775–1831) as a defense of this imagined construct of Germany and a »correction« of it. Their defense was motivated by an anxiety that de Staël's »false« construct of Germanness would supplant the »true« Germany, even among Germans. While the aristocratic emigrant Staël emphasizes the art of conversation because it is constitutive of French cultural identity and typifies the classical ideal balance of sociability and individuality, her German counterparts make a case for German cultivation (*Bildung*) and defend their own forms of sociability (*Geselligkeit*). Gad in particular questions cultural stereotypes imposed on German identity and defends the non-centralism of German culture, while Betty Gleim, writing with the authority of a schoolmistress, points out errors in Staël's knowledge of German language, history, and literature. According to Guenther, the three critiques attempt to re-establish textual and linguistic authority over their own location, authority as readers of their own culture. The German opponents did not write from a safe haven:

Gleim and Fouqué also had first-hand experiences with French occupation, and the latter had a husband and a son in the army.

Caroline de la Motte Fouqué (1775–1831), one of the most prolific and popular writers of her time in Germany, was personally affected by the Napoleonic Wars, and shared at times the militant patriotism which was predominant in the German states that fought against Napoleon. She wrote several novels set against the background of the wars. *Edmund's Wege und Irrwege* (*Edmund's Ways and Meanderings*, 1815) is the only one that openly engages in ideological propaganda and that renders Napoleon's reign in negative terms. In the main part of her chapter, Silke Arnold-de Simine analyzes Fouqué's disillusionment in her hope for a national awakening after 1815 and her discussion of the role of women in the process of defining a national identity in writings on museums and their role in establishing a sense of national history and identity. The essay on the history of fashions between 1785 and 1829 defines fashions in a broad sense including political thought. Arnold-de Simine argues that Fouqué distanced herself from strategies of museal preservation, outlining instead communicative and cultural memory based on private recollections of everyday life and fashion. Fouqué develops a program for German identity based on literature and the concept of sociability, which would give women the lead in its construction.

The theme of national identity and nationalist propaganda is placed center stage in the following group of fictional and historiographical treatments of the Napoleonic era more than half a century later in Germany, a unified identity to which Napoleon paradoxically had contributed by founding the federation of the Rhine in 1806. Such writings from the second half of the nineteenth century when Historicism was en vogue, are bountiful if subjective. We present articles on a prolific female author of historical fiction, who also published a historical study of the Wars of Liberation; two examples of historical fiction for young adult readers, a very new area of research; one novel by a canonical male Realist, and finally a post-World-War-I cycle of poems by a German-Jewish woman author in an expressionist style. Positioned half a century later and against the backdrop of the German unification movement and the founding of the Second Reich in 1871, all of these works depict fictionalized or fictional women in central roles in the opposition to and defeat of Napoleon and beyond in the rise of the German nation.

Caroline Bland examines the depictions of the Napoleonic wars by Louise von François (1817–1893), proof that women participated in the political discourse of the time, in this case the liberal nationalist project which sought to legitimize Prussia's hegemony among the German states and drew on the wars against Napoleon for the construction of a German national identity. Bland analyzes François's portrayal of Napoleon in the narrative *Fräulein Muthchen und ihr Hausmeier* (*Miss Muthchen and her Steward*, 1859) and in the novel *Frau Erdmuthens Zwillingssöhne* (*Mrs. Erdmuthe's Twin Sons*, 1872). In both works Napoleon appears as a tyrant who is in total opposition to the principles François esteemed highly, namely brotherly love and the duty of the individual to work towards a common purpose. Bland's article rectifies another misconception about women's purported absence from the writing of history in the nineteenth century: François's historical study of the Prussian Wars of Liberation from 1813 to 1815 (1873), also published after the unification of 1871 and at times used as a textbook in military academies, presents Prussia's lead in the unification as predetermined.

Jeffrey Sammons's essay studies a woman character in a work of historical fiction written from a later perspective and for a Wilhelminian audience which eagerly absorbed the entertaining lesson in history. Sammons sorts out complex attitudes towards Napoleon and France in a work by Friedrich Spielhagen (1829–1911). His complex historical novel *Noblesse oblige* (1888) is set during the French occupation of Hamburg, which was remembered for the extreme atrocities committed. The central figure is a young woman, Minna Warburg, daughter of a senator and businessman who marries her off to another Hamburg-London business man, although she is in love with a Marquis in the French army. Minna performs her duties as loyal daughter and wife and joins the anti-French cause. She turns to active public engagement and cares for refugees. Minna is supported in her spirit of patriotism and civic duty by the publisher Perthes, who historically was active in uprisings against the French in Hamburg until the city was finally liberated. Spielhagen closely conformed major events of the novel to the historical record and employed a number of historical figures among the patriots in the background. Sammons considers possible sources Spielhagen may have used. From his decision to place a courageous and active female at the center of the novel, we learn that Spielhagen, although not openly supporting women's emancipation, developed remarkable sensibility for the issues when he portrayed women who sought to be equal with and and participated actively in this major historical event.

Jennifer Askey examines two fictional texts for girls and young women that center around the Prussian Queen Luise, who by the end of the nineteenth century was celebrated as »the paragon of German womanly virtue and as a secular Prussian saint.« Her life was fictionalized to guide young female readers in Wilhelminian Germany in their attitudes towards German culture and national belonging. Both Elisabeth Halden in *Königin Luise* (*Queen Louisa*, 1893) and Brigitte Augusti in *Die Erben von Scharfeneck* (*The Heirs of Scharfeneck*, 1889) introduce to the queen young female companions, who become her German history students and models of patriotic German women for the reader. In these narratives, Luise appears to conquer Napoleon in spirit, and his impact on German history is nearly erased, while Luise bridges the Old Empire and the Second German Empire. Askey makes apparent that the nationalist discourse in these historical novels is highly gendered; they teach girls and young women the importance of historical knowledge, loyalty to family, and raising children as part of a national effort to fight the Napoleons to come.

In our last article Napoleon is the object of a historical and fictionalized female character's split emotional response torn between love and hate, between erotic attraction and political resistance. Responses to Napoleon were not limited to contemporaries or even to the nineteenth century. Barbara Besslich provides an eye-opening perspective on a still under-researched author and her deliberations on women in history with a study of poems by the German-Jewish writer Gertrud Kolmar. The cycle of 19 poems by the young Kolmar entitled *Napoleon und Marie* depicts the Polish Marie Walewska (née Laczinska, 1786–1817), married without love to an older count. She is Napoleon's potential opponent. However, her resentment towards the upstart and usurper of her country is averted by erotic desire, self-sacrifice, and, moreover, a deep desire for the heroic, even the demonic, and for intense participation as a woman in an important historic period. Marie does not give in to Napoleon because of emotional weakness, but because of pressure from her own countrymen, including her husband, who see in her attractive body an instrument of politics and a sacrifice for the nation. Kolmar reminds us that historically an oppressed nation's – and a woman's – chance of influencing high politics frequently happened by marriage politics and in the bedroom. In the poems Marie's »fall« is not due to individual female weakness, but the conscious result of national martyrdom and sacrifice modeled on the Biblical Esther. The poems turn from Marie's political opposition and contempt for the ex-revolutionary to a description of love as war, as a woman's form of participation in the defense of her people and country.

## Open Questions

One important question remains to be addressed: Are biological sex and gender roles common factors for these women and their opposition to Napoleon? Are there other common factors, or do the differences outweigh them? Napoleon influenced the discourse of masculinity much more than that of femininity, as demonstrated in several recent and forthcoming studies (see Hagemann »Of ›Manly Valor‹« 1997, 2002). Several contemporary women, especially the German Gleim, continue to enforce their commitment to the education of women in spite of the *Code Napoleon's* limitations of women's legal rights. The list of reasons to be against Napoleon and his wars appears to be long and varied and thus similar to those of men, and gender was not the decisive factor. Friederike Brun, for example, wrote against war at the height of Napoleon's expansion in Rome, yet she points out that women are not always and naturally peace-loving and non-violent, but can show aggressive and evil behavior. Brun advocates love in wartime that ignores nationality, and she does so not by referring to gender roles, but as a writer living in a foreign country herself and being married to a member of another nation, and as a member of the Romantic generation with strong roots in Enlightenment beliefs in humanity, tolerance, and cosmopolitanism. Spielhagen's fictional heroine from Hamburg has to give up such Romantic transnational love and fight for her home city and its citizens instead. The fictional texts by Louise von François also present pleas for peace, but they were written for a middle-class audience in a powerful, unified Germany half a century after Napoleon and rely on dichotomized gender roles of martial males and peace-loving women, although this female writer shared liberal national thoughts much like the louder voices of her male contemporaries. Similar to Brun, who sought positive models of the non-aggressive heroic, François rejected the historicist search for great individuals who impersonated the nation and »made history«. Instead, she praised the middle-class as the foundation and strength of the nation, including women's gendered and subordinate role in it.

The only writer in our volume who reflects on the role of women in the making, writing, and memory of history is Gertrud Kolmar in the 1920s. Her choice of the lyrical genre is telling; it implies a rejection of epic totality. Her poems conflate images of the battle of the sexes with images of war. Besslich explicates that in the episode of the Polish countess and Napoleon Kolmar addresses an important factor in (Jewish) women's history since Biblical times, the model of self sacrifice for the sake of the nation. Besslich further reads the poem as a critical response to a »soldier song« written by the male poet Theodor Körner during the Napoleonic wars, which celebrated the heroic nature of masculinity, war, and death. Whereas Körner substituted the battlefield for love, Kolmar makes physical love a part of the Polish liberation efforts, a military endeavor, thus supplying a feminine model of the »heroic« in response to Körner's masculine one.

In our selection, Fouqué and Kolmar are the two writers most concerned with gender. The German Romantic Fouqué with her program of national identity, which would »not only include women, but give women the lead in constructing a collective identity« (Guenther) appears to be the most feminist. She adds a female voice and perspective to the cultural memory and the »museum«, similar to the Swiss-French émigré Staël in her critique of Napoleon's museum politics and the largely androcentric French art world. It is noteworthy that spirituality and religious beliefs – a major part of women's gender role in the nineteenth century and beyond – by themselves do not provide sufficient grounds for opposition to Napoleon's person and politics, but are intertwined with the major themes; for Brun, spirituality is heroic, Staël and those arguing for anti-French, anti-classicist art politics and aesthetics emphasize the moral code provided by Christianity, Spielhagen's female protagonist sees her selfless service for her fellow-citizens as Christian service, Kolmar's protagonist identifies with an exemplary woman in Judaism's central text.

A number of women are concerned with the nation and nationalism, and they connect these themes to issues of aesthetics, lessons from history, or women in history. The issue of patriotism and nationalism paradoxically seems of minor importance to the women soldiers unearthed by Hagemann. The Prussian »amazons« argued for equality with men, rather than for nationalism. It is noteworthy that when women writers participated in the discourse of nationalism later in the century, they did so in the context of writing German history in the light of Napoleon. A topic that certainly needs to be investigated in more detail is how nationalism is different for British and German women writers than for French women. It is interesting that the correspondence of two Berlin women during the Napoleonic wars suspends the discussion of nation and ethnicity in favor of such a small, but important detail like bandages for the wounded, whereas historical fiction at the end of the nineteenth century employs fervent lessons of nationalism supposedly learnt from the occupation and defeat by the French in favor of the formation of a German nation state in which the middle class takes pride and which is to be understood and underwritten by women. It is ironic that it was none other than the Napoleonic government which had taken steps towards the partial leveling of class discrimination and promoting Jewish emancipation. Our only contribution on the work of a male author makes a point from which we may conclude that gender was less decisive for the understanding of nation than other factors, for example, the importance of individualism. Spielhagen does not celebrate the liberation of Hamburg, but warns about unleashing popular forces; instead of favoring fanatic nationalism resulting from the French occupation, he supports ideas of cosmopolitanism and international understanding. By doing so, he is close to Brun's contemporary view and deviates strongly from »the main line of public opinion at the end of the century« (Sammons). If we may speculate, such an attitude would have faced much harsher criticism and condemnation from a female author at the time.

In conclusion, women opposed Napoleon and his regime for a wide variety of reasons. They were not a homogeneous group that spoke with one voice. With the passage of time, their focus shifted from those directly threatened by war, turmoil and/or an oppressive regime to those writing a century or more later who presented allegories of women in history or fascinating life stories with or without allusions to recent history.

The long line of women against Napoleon does not stop with Kolmar. Nor have we fully explored the range we introduce here. For example, two novels by the German author Friederike Helene Unger (1741[?]–1813), *Die Franzosen in Berlin* (*The Frenchmen in Berlin*, 1809) and *Der junge Franzose und das deutsche Mädchen* (*The Young Frenchman and the German Girl*, 1810), take place in French-occupied Berlin after the defeat of Prussia in 1806. A recent study by Regine Schwarzmeier suggests that with them the writer and business-woman Unger pleaded for German-French tolerance.[2] The historical dramas *Charlotte Corday* (1804) by Christine Westphalen and *Hildgund* (1805) by Karoline von Günderrode also deserve attention. Both plays are about women who assassinate a tyrant, and parallels with Napoleon are implied. We hope that further investigations will follow.

Caricatures are another venue of opposition to Napoleon not yet sufficiently explored from the perspective of gender. Caricatures, such as the two anonymous Italian ones dated 1799 included in this volume (figures 1 and 2), often peruse female allegories.

For this collection, we were not able to pursue Polish, Russian, or American historiography and fiction. To name just one example, in Sylvia Plath's poem »The Swarm« of 1962, Napoleon is the central figure (»A red tatter, Napoleon!«), and the poem portrays his genius and final defeat at Waterloo with the distinct absence of a »feminine« voice. Recent fiction and films should be examined, especially the film *The Emperor's New Clothes*, directed by Alan Taylor (Italy, UK, Germany, 2001) after the novel *La mort de Napoléon* (*The Death of Napoleon*) by Simon Leys, originally published in French. The film stars Ian Holm as the emperor Napoleon.

> »In this delightful romantic comedy, Napoleon escapes from St. Helena, leaving behind a double who had been a common seaman during the Napoleonic wars and who now enjoys a new-found life of leisure while merrily fabricating »his« memoirs, including salacious details about Marie Walewska and Joséphine de Beauharnais. Napoleon, meanwhile, assumes his double's name and identity when he returns to France to attempt a third coup d'etat – until he falls in love with a widow whose husband had spent the bulk of their married life as a soldier during the Napoleonic Wars and who hates (the historical) Napoleon for having filled France with widows and orphans.«[3]

We hope to stimulate further discussion and collaboration between students and scholars of European History, English, French, German Literary and Cultural Studies, and Women Studies.

–The University of Iowa

## Notes

1 Of course, many literary works break with this strict dichotomy; one might only mention Kleist's Penthesilea or Friedrich von Homburg, Goethe's Amazon-beautiful

soul Natalie, or Conrad Ferdinand Meyer's virago characters. However, these works never became part of mainstream culture.

2 Schwarzmeier's dissertation on Unger will soon appear elsewhere.

3 I am thankful to our anonymous manuscript evaluator for bringing this film to my attention and providing this intriguing information.

## Works Cited


Alexander, Robert S. *Napoleon.* (Reputations series.) London: Arnold, 2001.

Anderson, Benedict. *Imagined Communities: Reflections on the Origin and Spread of Nationalism.* London: Verso, 1982.

Bainbridge, Simon. *Napoleon and English Romanticism.* (Cambridge Studies in Romanticism.) Cambridge: Cambridge University Press, 1995.

Besslich, Barbara. *Der deutsche Napoleon-Mythos: Literatur und Erinnerung 1800–1945.* Darmstadt: Wissenschaftliche Buchgesellschaft, 2007.

Central European Napoleonic Society. *Projekt Austerlitz 2005*, <www.austerlitz 2005.com/de/projektausterlitz/>.

Connor, Susan P. »The Merveilleuse and the Coquette: Women during the Directory and First Empire«. *Proceedings of the Consortium on Revolutionary Europe* (1980). 49–57.

Cooper, Helen M., Adrienne Auslander Munich, and Merill Squier (eds.). *Arms and the Woman: War, Gender, and Literary Representation.* Chapel Hill: University of North Carolina Press, 1989.

Craciun, Adriana, and Kari E. Lokke (eds). *Rebellious Hearts: British Women Writers and the French Revolution.* (SUNY Series in Feminist Criticism and Theory.) Albany: State University of New York Press, 2001.

Daugherty, William C. *From the Sublime to the Ridiculous: The Image of Napolean Bonaparte in the American Literary Renaissance.* Diss. Texas A&M University, 2001.

Davidson, Denise Z. *Enacting the Social Order: Gender and Urban Public Space in Post-Revolutionary France, 1800–1830.* Cambridge: Harvard University Press, 2006.

Demandt, Philipp. *Luisenkult: die Unsterblichkeit der Königin von Preussen.* Köln: Böhlau, 2003.

Duffy, Cian. »The Child of a Fierce Hour: Shelley and Napoleon Bonaparte«, *Studies in Romanticism* 43 (2004). 399–416.

Elshtain, Jean Bethke. *Women and War.* New York: The Harvester Press and Basic Books, 1987.

Elshtain, Jean Bethke. »Women as Mirror and Other: Toward a Theory of Women, War, and Feminism«, *Humanities in Society* 5 (1982). 29–44.

Fairweather, Maria. *Madame de Staël.* New York: Carroll & Graf, 2005.

Geyl, Pieter. *Napoleon: For and Against.* New Haven: Yale University Press, 1949.

Gilbert, Sandra M.. »Soldier's Heart: Literary Men, Literary Women, and the Great War«, *Behind the Lines: Gender and the Two World Wars.* Edited by Margaret Higonnet et. al. New Haven Yale University Press, 1987. 197–226.

Gläser, Stefan. *Frauen um Napoleon.* Regensburg: Pustet, 2001.

Goldstein, Joshua S. (ed.). *War and Gender: How Gender Shapes the War System and Vice Versa.* Cambridge/New York: Cambridge University Press, 2001.

Hagemann, Karen. »Female Patriots: Women, War and the Nation in Prussia during the Anti-Napoleonic Wars«, *Gender & History* (2004). 396–424.

Hagemann, Karen. »Heldenmütter, Kriegerbräute und Amazonen. Entwürfe 'patriotischer' Weiblichkeit zur Zeit der Freiheitskriege«, *Militär und Gesellschaft im 19. und 20. Jahrhundert.* Edited by Ute Frevert. (Industrielle Welt 28.) Stuttgart: Klett-Cotta, 1997. 174–200.

Hagemann, Karen. »*Mannlicher Muth und Teutsche Ehre*«: *Nation, Militär und Geschlecht zur Zeit der Antinapoleonischen Kriege Preußens.* Paderborn: Schöningh, 2002.

Hagemann, Karen. »Militär, Krieg und Geschlechterverhältnisse: Untersuchungen, Überlegungen und Fragen zur Militärgeschichte der Frühen Neuzeit«, *Klio in Uniform? Probleme und Perspektiven einer modernen Militärgeschichte der Frühen Neuzeit.* Edited by Ralf Pröve. Köln: Böhlau, 1997. 35–88.

Hagemann, Karen. »Of ›Manly Valor‹ and ›German Honor‹: Nation, War and Masculinity in the Age of the Prussian Uprising against Napoleon«, *Central European History* 30 (1997). 187–220.

Hallihan, Kathleen M. »Following Bonaparte: Images of Napoleon in the Works of Bettina von Arnim«, *Colloquia Germanica: Internationale Zeitschrift für Germanistik* 36 (2003). 97–117.

Lützeler, Paul Michael. »The Image of Napoleon in European Romanticism«, *European Romanticism: Literary Cross-Currents, Modes, and Models.* Edited by Gerhart Hoffmeister. Detroit: Wayne State University Press, 1990. 211–228.

Macleod, Emma Vincent. »Women at War: British Women and the Debate on the Wars against Revolutionary France in the 1790s«, *Enlightenment and Dissent* 15 (1996). 3–32.

Masson, Frédéric. *Napoléon et les femmes; l'amour.* Paris: P. Ollendorff, 1894.

Mitscherlich, Margarete. *The Peaceable Sex: On Aggression In Women And Men*, translated from the German by Craig Tomlinson. New York: Fromm, 1987 (= orig.: *Die friedfertige Frau*, 1985).

Moskal, Jeanne. »Napoleon, Nationalism, and the Politics of Religion in Mariana Starke's *Letters from Italy.*« *Rebellious Hearts: British Women Writers and the French Revolution.* Edited by Craciun/Lokke. Albany: State University of New York Press, 2001. 161–90.

Nipperdey. Thomas. *Germany from Napoleon to Bismarck, 1800–1866*, translated by Daniel Nolan. Princeton: Princeton University Press, 1996 (= orig.: *Deutsche Geschichte 1800–1866*).

Rogers, Rebecca. »Competing Visions of Girls' Secondary Education in Post-Revolutionary France«. *History of Education Quarterly* 34 (1994). 147–170.

Sabiston, Andrew, and Timothy Williams. *Napoleon, The Musical.* Perf. Uwe Kröger, Anastasia Barzee, Nigel Richards, David Burt, et al. Shaftesbury Theatre. London. 22 Nov. 2000.

Schwarzmeier, Regine. *Weibliche Lebensentwürfe in den Romanen Friederike Helene Ungers: Eine sozialkritische Analyse.* Diss. phil. Vanderbuilt University, Nashville, TN/USA, 2005.

Simoneau, Yves (dir.). *Napoleon: An Epic Life/Le Tricorne de Napoléon* [videorecording]. Book Didier Decoin after the novel by Max Gallo. With Christian Clavier, Gérard Depardieu. France/Germany/Italy/etc., 2002. (Universal 905 337-1.) Universal Pictures and Beta-Film, 2003.

Spies, Bernhard. »Die Macht im Drama: Napoleon-Dramen von Schiller bis Dürrenmatt«, *Klassik-Rezeption: Auseinandersetzung mit einer Tradition.* Edited by Peter Ensberg and Jürgen Kost. Würzburg: Königshausen & Neumann, 2003. 243–55.

Tone, John Lawrence. »Spanish Women in the Resistance to Napoleon, 1808-1814«, *Constructing Spanish Womanhood: Female Identity in Modern Spain.* Edited by Victoria Lorée Enders and Pamela Beth. New York: State University of New York Press, 1999. 259–82.

Willms, Johannes. *Napoleon: Verbannung und Verklärung.* München: Droemer, 2000.

Willms, Johannes. *Napoleon.* München: Beck, 2005.

*Fig. 1: Anonymous Italian caricature, Roveredo 1799 (water color over copper engraving; 9,7 x 15,6 in).*
*Photo: Waltraud Maierhofer*

*Fig. 2: Anonymous Italian caricature, 1799 (water color over copper engraving; 10,0 x 16,1 in; private collection).*
*Photo: Waltraud Maierhofer*

# Contemporaries: With Scepter, Sword, or Pen – Forms of Resistance

# Englishwomen and Napoleon Bonaparte

*Deborah Kennedy*

Early in his life Napoleon Bonaparte began to earn his reputation as a young military hero whose success impressed a wider world beyond the borders of France. By 1797, as David Chandler observes, Bonaparte's name was »a household word throughout Europe« (130). The English public was fascinated by him, even though England and France had been at war since 1793. Everyone was talking about Bonaparte – men, women, and even children. This essay will explore the way that Englishwomen responded to Napoleon, from the heights of the late 1790s and the years that followed when he ruled Europe, until the time of his death in captivity in 1821.

Mary Berry (1763–1852), Frances Burney (1752–1840), and Helen Maria Williams (1761–1827) all lived through the three decades of his career and travelled from England to France for different periods of time. They published eyewitness accounts of Napoleon, and by bringing their viewpoints together, as well as comments from authors such as Jane Austen, Hannah More, and Dorothy Wordsworth, this essay aims to show what Englishwomen thought – and felt – about the much-mythologized figure. Some reviled him as a tyrant, plain and simple. As anti-Bonapartist sentiment grew, others had to fight against their attraction to Napoleon as a heroic figure. Napoleon's rise and fall was a subject of both common chatter and sober analysis, and it found a notable place in the published work and the private records of the Englishwomen of the time.

Of the women who wrote about Napoleon, Helen Maria Williams is the only one whose books were actually published at the different stages of his career. At the exact moment when he rose to power, she was living in France and writing books on European life and politics. Williams was a well-known English poet, who began publishing in 1782 with her first poem of sensibility, *Edwin and Eltruda.* Her mentor was the Reverend Dr. Andrew Kippis, a man of letters and the minister of the Princes Street

Presbyterian church, which her family attended in London. Williams and her mother and sisters visited France in 1790, and it was not unusual for women to travel to the Continent in this period (Dolan 3-13). Williams wrote a book in praise of the progressive changes of the French Revolution, which became the first of eight volumes called *Letters from France* (1790–1796). With good friends in Rouen and Paris, her family began what they thought would be a two-year visit in 1791. But by the time they planned to return in 1793, war had broken out between England and France, the Reign of Terror had begun, and many of Williams's moderate Girondin friends, including Madame Roland, were executed. Williams and her family expected that they would be allowed to leave the country (*Letters from France* 2.1.5), but all English were imprisoned, some for a few months, like the Williamses, and others for many years. Once released from prison in 1794, Williams's sister Cecilia married a Frenchman, Athanase Coquerel, and with travel to England now perilous, the family settled in Paris. Williams herself spent a few months in Switzerland, taking refuge from Robespierre. She completed her *Letters from France*, wrote several other books, and was a major figure in literary circles in Paris (see Kennedy).

During the late 1790s the French Republic had to recover from the outrages of the Terror, renew its idealistic objectives, and survive war against the rest of Europe. Bonaparte, now as a general, won impressive battles for France. He seemed different from other military leaders, who were agitated by »frantic ambition« and sought »profligate glory« (Williams, *Tour* 2, 54). Ironically, Williams would later say the same of Bonaparte too, but in her 1798 *Tour in Switzerland* she praised him as a great defender of liberty:

»It is not Buonaparte scaling the Alps, and chasing the imperial eagle back to its haunts [...] that claims the transport of admiration; his acts of valour may have been unequalled; the heroes of ancient and modern times may sink before him; [...] but these are not his loftiest honours; these are not his proudest claims to glory; what swells the heart with reverence, is not the hero standing in the breach, it is the benefactor of his race converting the destructive lightening of the conqueror's sword into the benignant rays of freedom, and presenting to vanquished nations the emblems of liberty and independence entwined with the olive of peace.« (Williams, *Tour* 2:55-56)

Here Williams justifies French militarism and creates a paradoxical image of Bonaparte as a conqueror turned peacemaker. People from all nations could admire him: »he belongs not exclusively to France, or her revolution;

like Homer, or Newton, Buonaparte belongs to the world« (Williams, *Tour* 2, 57). Worship of Bonaparte could not get higher than this.

In Williams's next book, the *Sketches* of 1801, she continued her reports on current events (from the actions of Admiral Nelson in Naples to constitutional matters in France), but she also devoted several pages to Bonaparte, remarking that »such a man as Buonaparte, will, no doubt, employ the pen of many an able historian, through all succeeding ages, over whom I can certainly boast of only one advantage, that of having been present at the scene« (Williams, *Sketches* 2, 2) Williams praised Bonaparte for his role in the peace negotiations of early 1800, and she noted that it was his practical experience on the battlefield that made him realize the need for peace:

»It is in truth the hero in the field, and not the statesman in the cabinet, who weeps over human miseries. While the conqueror supplicates for peace, it is the shielded metaphysical gowns-man who prates of war.« (Williams, *Sketches* 2, 186-7)

To demonstrate the softer side of the military leader, Williams described a particular incident involving Bonaparte and a barbet-dog or spaniel. A few years earlier, after the battle of Castiglione in September 1796 Bonaparte was moved by the sight of the dog sitting near the body of its dead master:

»where French and Austrians lay strewed in horrible profusion, [Buonaparte] perceived one living object amidst those piles of corpses, which was a little barbet-dog. The faithful creature stood with his two fore-feet fixed on the breast of an Austrian officer.« (Willimas, *Sketches* 2, 189)

Helen Maria Williams as the noted British poet of sensibility understands the power of this anecdote:

»The barbet-dog and Bonaparte have been associated in my mind ever since I heard the story; and were I to be the negotiator for peace, I should send with my dispatches to every cabinet, the portrait of the little dog at the battle of Castiglione.« (Williams, *Sketches* 2, 190)

Williams argues that the picture of the faithful dog would remind soldiers and statesmen, as it did Bonaparte, of a life outside of battle, where people have families, friends, and pets. The story of the barbet-dog is a curiosity of Napoleonic lore, which has been recorded in books such as A. G. Macdonell's *Napoleon and His Marshals*, and depicted in illustrations like the 1850 lithograph entitled *Napoleon the Great Rebuking His Officers at Bassano: »There, Gentlemen, that dog teaches us a lesson of humanity.«*

Not long after her book *Sketches* was published, Williams met her then hero. In 1801, she and her politician friend Nicholas Thiessé were out horseback riding when they met Napoleon. He complimented her on *Sketches*, which had just appeared in a French translation by Sophie Grandchamp, a friend of the late Madame Roland:

»Bonaparte had been First Consul only a brief time when I met him in the woods of Boulogne, one morning when I was horseback riding with one of my best and oldest friends, M. Thiessé, member of the Tribune. Bonaparte came directly to join us, put his horse to its paces, and made with us the tour of the woods of Boulogne, followed by a brilliant military officer. [...] The fact is that I saw only Bonaparte himself, that I attended to nothing but him. My enthusiasm was totally fervent. He was very polite because he had not yet attained that point of power in which, afterwards, only one of his glances would nearly make M. le Comte Volney disappear. He said to me that he had just read my description of the counter-revolution in Naples, and that he would answer for the truth of that which I reported. He said several things which were in reality quite ordinary; but my admiration accentuated the value of his words[...] .The error of my admiration for Bonaparte was not to last much longer.« (Williams, *Souvenirs* 132–133)

Events soon occurred that made her change her view of him. The revolutionary Williams would become as anti-Bonapartist as any British conservative, including another woman writer – Hannah More. On this subject – just as they had in their opposition to the slave trade – Miss Williams and Miss More could agree.

During the fourteen-month period from the signing of the Peace of Amiens in March 1802 to the resumption of war in May 1803, many British visitors to France were desperate to get a good look at the famed Consul, but other Englishwomen were brooking no such nonsense. Hannah More (1745–1833), known as a staunch and vocal defender of Church and King, has a unique role in English literary history because she was a prolific author who wrote popular pamphlets, stories, and poems promoting patriotism and morality. The importance of her work was widely recognized, and she was praised by people from all walks of life, whether clergymen, actors, or politicians such as Edmund Burke. Hannah More's friend Horace Walpole was so pleased by her counter-revolutionary pamphlet *Village Politics* (1793) that he remarked, »you will be more mistress of the subject than any man in England« (380). But neither Walpole nor Burke lived to see Napoleon's rise to power; they both died in 1797, and it was Hannah More who was to carry on fighting the French with her persuasive pen.

After 18 Brumaire in 1799, the new French system of government was devised as a Consulate, with three Consuls: Bonaparte, Sieyès, and Ducos (the latter two then replaced by Cambacérès and Lebrun) (Cronin 173-7). The powerful position of First Consul was held by Bonaparte, and Hannah More mocked this new form of government in her poem »A King or a Consul? A New Song«. More castigates Bonaparte for his craftiness and encourages her readers to face him with the strength of English pride:

> Come, all ye brave Englishmen, list to my story,
> You who love peace and freedom, and honour and glory!
> [...]
> No Corsican Despot in England shall rule,
> No Disciple avowed of the Mussulman school;
> A Papist at Rome, and at Cairo a Turk,
> Now this thing, now that thing, as best helps his work.
> [. . .]
> That Buoni's invincible, Frenchmen may cry;
> Let Sidney the brave give each boaster the lie;
> [. . .]
> One King did not suit them, three Tyrants they chose,
> And their God they renounce, while their King they depose;
> Then we ne'er will submit to the Corsican's rod,
> Britons want but one Wife, and one King, and one GOD.
> (More 2, 92-3)

In rousing verse, Hannah More defends British social and political stability in contrast to the newfangled French Consulate. She depicts Bonaparte as untrustworthy and vacillating: »Now this thing, now that thing, as best helps his work.« More alludes to controversies involving Bonaparte's campaign in Egypt, a period which also saw the victory of Nelson's English fleet at the Battle of the Nile (Lyons 23-8). She reassures the public that the British system is best, and her arguments echo those of Edmund Burke in his famous counter-revolutionary book *Reflections on the Revolution in France* (1790). As Burke had said,

> »instead of quarrelling with establishments, as some do, who have made a philosophy and a religion of their hostility to such institutions, we cleave closely to them. We are resolved to keep an established church, an established monarchy, an established aristocracy, and an established democracy, each in the degree it exists, and in no greater.« (188)

With this shared emphasis on English tradition, it is no wonder that Hannah More has been called »Edmund Burke in petticoats« (Goodwin 265).

When the war between England and France came to an end, Helen Maria Williams praised the peace negotiations in her poem »Ode to Peace« published in London in *The Morning Chronicle* in November 1801 and then in Paris in *Décade Philosophique* in December 1801. Apparently, though, Napoleon was offended that this English poet made no direct mention of him in her ode. Later, he had the police search her apartment, looking at all of her papers and even the toys of her nephews. She and her mother were imprisoned overnight, and after that her home was regularly under surveillance. This was for Williams a graphic personal instance of Napoleon's ambition:

> »However singular it may seem that he should have paid the slightest attention to such a circumstance, it is nevertheless true. The ambitious find time for every thing, and while they appear to be wholly absorbed by great objects, never lose sight of the most minute if connected with their own egotism.« (Williams, *Poems* xiii)

This was the early stage of what many historians have described as »the police-state character of the Napoleonic regime« (Bergeron 9).

As his own power grew, Bonaparte increased censorship, and in April 1802 he purged the government of liberal politicians like Thiessé, Williams's friend. But Bonaparte had great popular support, and in a plebiscite he was voted First Consul for life in August 1802. By that time, as Simon Bainbridge explains, many of his British enthusiasts had become disillusioned with him (17). H. T. Dickinson points out that French subjugation of neighbouring countries and threats of a British invasion meant that for many »Napoleon became synonymous with tyranny and military aggression« (64). In 1803, when Williams published her edition of the *Correspondence* of Louis XVI, Bonaparte had it seized, which caused her considerable financial losses (Woodward 153-68). He was made Emperor in 1804, and Williams later recalled how the »rapid successive gradations to the consulate for life, and thence to the imperial purple, dispelled all illusion« (Williams, *Narrative* 8). Williams published nothing more than a family poem until the fall of Napoleon, though she did begin her important English translation of the works of Alexander von Humboldt.

Williams was not the only famous British woman writer in France during the Napoleonic years. The renowned novelist Frances Burney moved to France in 1802 with her husband, the French emigré General Alexander d'Arblay. Burney was highly esteemed as the author of *Evelina* (1778), *Cecilia* ( 1782) and *Camilla* (1796), but she was equally gifted as a diarist, and her posthumously published journals and letters offer riveting accounts of the events of her time. Shortly after arriving in France she had a glimpse of Bonaparte during a military parade in Paris, and recorded her impressions in a letter:

»I had a view so near, though so brief, of his face, as to be very much struck by it: it is of a deeply impressive cast, pale even to sallowness, while not only in the Eye, but in every feature, Care, Thought, Melancholy, & Meditation are strongly marked, with so much character, nay, Genius, & so penetrating a seriousness – or rather sadness, as powerfully to sink into an observer's mind [...] he has by no means the look to be expected from Bonaparte, – but rather that of a profoundly studious & contemplative Man [...] The plainness, also, of his dress, so conspicuously contrasted by the finery of all around him, conspires forcibly with his countenance [...] to give him far more the air of a Student than of a Warrior.« (Burney, *Journals* 5, 313-4)

Burney was surprised to find that in person Bonaparte had the appearance of a serious and pale student. Helen Maria Williams too had remarked on how in these early years Bonaparte had conducted himself with modesty, shrinking from the »acclamations« of the crowd (Williams, *Narrative* 6). However, there was one way that Bonaparte would always dazzle onlookers, and that was when he rode a horse. Frances Burney was awestruck when she saw him:

»Buonaparte, mounting a beautiful & spirited white Horse, was closely encircled by his glittering Aid-de-Camps, & [. . .] holding his bridle indifferently in either hand [...] he only appeared to me a Man who knew so well he could manage his Animal when he pleased, that he did not deem it worth his while to keep constantly in order what he knew – if urged or provoked, – he could subdue in a moment.« (Burney, *Journals* 5, 314-5)

How telling are Burney's remarks: what she saw in 1802 as Bonaparte's horsemanship can be read as an apt metaphor for his skills as a leader. The writer Mary Berry, who was a frequent traveller to the Continent, made similar observations. A friend of Horace Walpole, and the editor of his works, Berry was a gifted social observer. She remarked years after Bonaparte's abdication that he had acted with »consummate prudence« in the first stages of his career (Berry 2:106). Like Frances Burney, Mary Berry also saw the First Consul at a parade in Paris in 1802: »But all I saw was a little man, remarkably well on horseback, with a sallow complexion, a highish nose, a very serious countenance, and cropped hair« (quoted in Melville 206). Writing some years later, Helen Maria Williams, even though no longer a Bonapartist, recalled how impressive it was to see Bonaparte on horseback:

»Bonaparte's presence excited no awe when he sat on his throne – he was even awkward in his gestures. [...] It was in the field and on horseback that his small figure, in a plain coat, cast a spell.« (Williams, *Letters* 1819, 128)

Bonaparte cast his spell over many of the British visitors to France, but soon relations between the two nations soured, and it was not long before war resumed. As Vincent Cronin has put it, »For the next twelve years, Europe was to reek with the acrid smell of gunpowder« (236).

Many British tourists had to escape France. Hundreds of men were detained in French prisons, some for a short period and others until the fall of Napoleon (Lewis 23-31). Helen Maria Williams wrote a poem to her friend James Forbes when he was released from Verdun in 1804 and preparing to return to the British Isles:

When severed from this hostile shore,
A weary captive now no more,
Home, cherished home, shall glad your sight
In blessedness of fresh delight. (Williams, *Poems* 251)

Having written several poems on how much she missed »her native Isle« while travelling on the Continent, Williams projects into the Forbes poem a nostalgic desire for her own return to England, which, it turned out, would never take place (Williams, *Poems* 229).

Frances Burney stayed in France for ten years, from 1802 to 1812, and she feared that war would make it impossible for her to leave. Her husband was not given his former position in the French Army because he would not agree to fight against the English, so the family was not well off during their years in France. They also feared that their son Alexander, Junior, would be forced by conscription to enter Napoleon's army. Finally in 1812 Burney arranged for secret passage across the Channel, only to have the ship seized by British authorities. When she and her son arrived in England, she literally kissed the ground, »in grateful joy at touching again the land of my Nativity, after an absence nearly hopeless of more than 10 Years« (Burney, *Journals* 6, 727). Although Burney was a prodigious letter writer and diarist, the difficulty of sending mail during a time of war and the problem of police surveillance restricted her, and she left few documents about her life in France under Napoleon. However, she did work steadily on her most political novel *The Wanderer* (1814), which was set during the French Revolution, and published when she returned to England.

After Napoleon's abdication, travel once again opened up between England and France. When the English poet Anna Laetitia Barbauld visited Paris in 1814, she remarked on how hypocritical it seemed to travel there at the first opportunity:

»Is there not something strange and rather revolting in speaking of the French, as most have done for these twenty years past, with the utmost abhorrence and contempt, – and pouring ourselves over their country the moment it is accessible, to mix in their parties and bring home their fashions?« (Quoted in Ellis 294)

Barbauld acknowledges the longstanding view of French culture, as a risqué blend of fashion, flirtation, and social freedom. Napoleon's own persona partook of this same »foreign« mystique. This was evident too in the earlier establishment of his Imperial Court, which Mary Berry described as »more expensive, and more magnificent« than that of any French monarch (Berrry 2,73). In Mary Berry's own history of the Napoleonic era *England and France: A Comparative View*, she uses an apt phrase to describe his conduct as Emperor: the »dazzling despotism of Bonaparte« (Berry 2, 130).

Once Napoleon had been transported to Elba, Frances Burney also ventured back to the Continent to visit her husband. Burney had the uncanny ability of always being in the right place at the right time (as seen in her journal accounts of King George III). She travelled across the Channel in 1815 only to learn that Napoleon had escaped from Elba. It so happened that she was living in Brussels, near the site of the Battle of Waterloo. Not only did she write letters at the time, but several years later she wrote her Brussels journals at the request of her husband, and these were published posthumously with her other diaries. So gripping were her eyewitness accounts that William Makepeace Thackeray is thought to have drawn on them for the Napoleonic scenes in his great novel *Vanity Fair* (1847–8) (Doody 372). Like a reporter on the ground, Burney recounts the state of chaos around her and admits that she could hardly believe the good news of the British victory at the Battle of Waterloo. In the days before cell-phones and the internet, the most she could imagine was having a hot-air balloon to ride through the air and tell her husband (still in Germany) the good news: »Why have I not a Balloon to be the first to tell you this enchanting news! Buonaparte has yielded to Lord Wellington!« (Burney, *Journals* 8, 255). As Joyce Hemlow noted of Burney, »the Englishwoman gloried in ›Wellington's tremendous charge‹« and cheered for »›Immortal Wellington! Vive! Vive! Vive! ‹« (Hemlow 371).

But Burney still lived the day-to-day reality, hearing rumours of Bonaparte's escape, and helping to make bandages for the wounded in Brussels, which she described as »a Walking Hospital« (Burney, *Journals* 8:273): »My hand shakes – & my spirits are agitated past all description, with an inward fear that all this will not be confirmed. O for an English Gazette!« (Burney, *Journals* 8:255). Only a few weeks after Waterloo, Burney had to try to make her way from Brussels to meet her husband in Trier, Germany. The journey was dangerous, with banditti and »rambling Buonapartists« at large (Burney, *Journals* 8:468). Like a recurring nightmare, transportation was hard to obtain, and when she »sent to order a Chaise [...] the answer was that no Horses were to be had!« (Burney, *Journals* 8, 479). What with a series of missed coaches, false directions, little money, and hostile bureaucrats, her travels were frustrated at every turn, but she gradually made her way to Cologne, Bonn, and finally Trier. It was with the greatest relief that Frances Burney reunited with her husband, and the two returned to England in October 1815.

For Burney, the dazzling Consul on a white horse that she saw in 1802 had long since become her nation's enemy, and yet she knew other women who continued to be impressed. She tried to explain the realities of Bonaparte's policies to her friend Lady Waddington:

> »How is it that my ever dear Mary can thus on one side be fascinated by the very thing that, on the other, revolts her? how be a professed & ardent detester of Tyranny; yet an open & intrepid admirer of a Tyrant? O had you spent, like me, 10 years within the control of his unlimited power, and under the iron rod of its dread, how would you change your language! [...] It was the choice of my Companion, not of my Taste that drew ME to such a residence [...] Corporal Liberty could only be preserved by Mental forbearance – i.e. subjection.« (Burney, *Journals* 8, 282-3)

To hate tyranny but to admire the »Tyrant« – Burney puts her finger on the paradoxical response that some people had to Napoleon. But she insists Napoleon would seem less glamorous if her friend had to live as Burney had in a state of »subjection«. The image of the »iron rod« that Burney uses to refer to his tyranny is ubiquitous in anti-Bonapartist discourse.

For another Englishwoman there was no question about how to view Bonaparte. From her home in the Lake District in northern England, Dorothy Wordsworth (1771–1855) followed the news of the Napoleonic wars. Her brother William Wordsworth had written about his disillusionment with Napoleon in 1802, in the sonnet, »I Grieved for Buonaparte.« Dorothy and William Wordsworth travelled to France in 1802 during the Peace of Amiens, when they visited his former love Annette Vallon, and Wordsworth's and Vallon's daughter Caroline. Dorothy Wordsworth was a patriotic Englishwoman but she also worried about the politics of France, partly because she was concerned for the welfare of her niece Caroline. For information on France, the Wordsworths had long depended on the books written by Helen Maria Williams, whom Dorothy described as a sweet woman, when they met years later (Kennedy 199). Dorothy Wordsworth kept constantly informed of events in France, and in 1811 she hoped Bonaparte was losing ground:

»God be thanked the tide is turned against Buonaparte and we shall see, I trust, the delusion speedily vanish which even in England has spread too widely, that he was a great genius and a great Hero.« (Wordsworth, *Letters* 2, 486)

Here she addresses the identical problem that Burney dealt with in trying to curb Lady Waddington's gushing attraction to Napoleon. Dorothy Wordsworth calls it a »delusion« to think of him as »a great hero«.

But the persistence of this paradoxical response continued to be a concern. It even affected how children were to be told the history of England and of the Napoleonic Wars. Barbara Hofland, a prolific writer from Sheffield, wrote a geography book called *The Panorama of Europe* (1813) which had a distinctly anti-Bonapartist slant (Grenby 13). The American author Caroline Howard Gilman found an interesting way to address the problem in her poem »Choice of Paintings«, written as a dialogue between the wise female instructor, named the Lady, and a group of children. In the poem, a child named Henry is thrilled by the picture of Bonaparte on a white horse crossing the Alps (the 1800 masterpiece by David):

Henry:
Give me the brave Napoleon,
    With his war steed thundering by,
Where the snowy Alps majestical,
    Look upward to the sky.
Lady:
Oh! boy, that conqueror leaped o'er hearts,

With reckless cravings too,
While his own was cold and tempest stirred,
As the mountain scene you view (Gilman 132)

The Lady explains to the boy that the hero on a horse is only part of the picture. Behind such a famous portrait are the realities of war, the »cold« heart, and the »tempest« of tyranny. Moreover, Bonaparte had actually used mules in the Alps, but the fictional steed makes for a more glamorous picture. During the Napoleonic Wars, there were many efforts to counter the popular idea of Napoleon's »greatness.« Books like Coxe's *The Exposé; or Napoleone* [sic] *Buonaparte Unmasked* attempted to do just that. Artists such as James Gillray produced unforgettable satirical prints. One Englishwoman who famously voiced her loyalty to Napoleon was Lady Holland, and she too was caricatured in the press (Lean 127-200). Even though Napoleon was of average height (5 foot 6 inches), British satirists depicted him in visual images as little – and therefore less threatening – Boney (Kelley).

This was certainly the way Dorothy Wordsworth wished others would view him. In 1814, responding to news of his abdication, she explains that though they may be tucked away in Grasmere, »every heart has exulted – we have danced for joy! But how strange! it is like a dream – peace peace – all in a moment« (Wordsworth, *Letters* 3, 142). This state of peace between England and France was also important to the Wordsworth family, because it meant that they could again visit Wordsworth's daughter. Dorothy in fact wanted to travel to France to represent the Wordsworth side of the family at Caroline's wedding to Jean Baptiste Baudouin. The news of Bonaparte's return from Elba ruined these plans and frightened Dorothy who said that she wished him to be »crushed at once, hanged and gibbeted« (Wordsworth, *Letters* 3, 217). After Waterloo, Dorothy continued to censure the popular interest in Napoleon, and she was appalled by the English who tried to see him when he was captured on board the ship the Bellerophon:

»Oh I am sick of the adulation, the folly, the idle Curiosity which was gathered together round the ship that held the dastardly spirit that has so long been the scourge of all whom he could injure.« (Wordsworth, *Letters* 3, 244)

While some English Napoleonists like William Hazlitt went around wearing mourning clothes as a public display of their continuing admiration for the conquered French leader, things were different in the Lake District, where the Wordsworth family enjoyed a celebratory bonfire and picnic organized by Robert Southey. With rum, roast beef, and plum pudding it was a truly English victory celebration (Gittings and Manton 206).

For another English view of Napoleon, one can turn to no better a representative than the best known woman writer of all time: Jane Austen. Austen (1775–1817) and Napoleon (1769–1821) were exact contemporaries, and both, in different ways, have gained a place in world history. Although Austen never left English soil, she had many family members who did. Two of her brothers, Admiral Francis Austen and Admiral Charles Austen, had long and distinguished careers in the Royal Navy, her family was related by marriage to the family of Admiral Nelson, and the Napoleonic Wars were topics of everyday conversation (Honan 163; 223).

It is well known that Jane Austen's novels centre on domestic life in small English towns and among the gentry class. She described her books as not being grand in scope, but concentrating on »domestic Life in Country Villages« (Austen, *Letters* 312). Her nephew said that her personal letters need not be published because they »treat only of the details of domestic life. There is in them no notice of politics or public events« (Austen-Leigh 312). In 1813, Austen joked that readers might find *Pride and Prejudice* »too light«, because it lacked more serious matter like »the history of Buonaparte«, but she could not add something so »unconnected with the story« (Austen, *Letters* 203). Austen was aware that readers were hungry for information about Bonaparte's life. As a comic writer and satirist, she simply could not accommodate a »history of Buonaparte« in her fiction (Cecil 145). Yet political events are relevant to the situations and the settings in Austen's novels.

Captains, colonels, and generals populate her books, even if the military action occurs off-stage. For example, in *Pride and Prejudice* the militia regiment has a key role in the plot involving Wickham. A long section of *Mansfield Park* is set in Fanny Price's hometown of Portsmouth, and Fanny's brother William eventually becomes a Lieutenant in the navy. The novel *Persuasion* especially pays tribute to the English navy. The heroine Anne Elliot marries Captain Wentworth, and his sister is the wife of an Admiral who served at Trafalgar. Early in the novel, when Anne Elliot's father Sir Walter is complaining about having to rent his house to a naval man, Anne ventures to state that

»The navy, I think, who have done so much for us, have at least an equal claim with any other set of men, for all the comforts and all the privileges which any home can give. Sailors work hard enough for their comforts, we must all allow.« (Austen, *Persuasion* 49)

In this passage, Anne Elliot speaks as the quintessential Englishwoman, articulating with quiet strength a sense of the honour due to those men who serve their country. One could say that Austen's novels are characterized by this firm patriotism. Her few surviving letters provide similar examples. After the British victory at Waterloo, Austen wrote of the pleasure she took in reading Robert Southey's poem »The Poet's Pilgrimage to Waterloo« (Austen, *Letters* 327). She also read Helen Maria Williams's *Narrative* of the Hundred Days. When Austen was in negotiations with John Murray for the publication of her novel *Emma* (1816), she was pleased to receive from him a loan of other books he had just published, including Williams's *Narrative*; and the poem *The Field of Waterloo* by Sir Walter Scott, who later wrote a biography of Napoleon (Austen, *Letters* 298).

Again British readers turned to Helen Maria Williams for her eyewitness account of important events in France. Her book on the Hundred Days (from March to June 1815), and its aftermath was published quickly in London, and a French translation appeared in Paris in 1816. Williams discusses the reaction in France to Napoleon's escape from Elba and to the proclamation of his return to power at the Field of May (Champ de Mai) and subsequent events that led to his second abdication, his surrender to the British, and departure for St. Helena. Her book is a colourful collection of personal and political anecdotes, rather than a military history, and she notes that others have already written in detail about the »memorable day of Waterloo«, a triumph for »English valour«, so she mentions it only briefly (Williams, *Narrative* 126).

The *Narrative* was well-received, and the *Quarterly Review* judged it to be the best book on the Hundred Days. Like many of her other books, this one is written in the form of letters to a friend in England: »I shall trace, as you desire, in a series of letters, the events which are passing before me, and which you will one day give to the public, if you consider my sketches as worthy its attention« (Williams, *Narrative* 3). She explains that she had stopped writing because of Napoleon's censorship: »the iron hand of despotism had weighed upon my soul«; and Bonaparte had gone from being heroic to being »the night-mare of the world« (Williams, *Narrative* 3).

With the return of Napoleon during the Hundred Days, shopkeepers had to change their signs from the lily to the eagle; and the »triumphant violet appeared glaring in the button-hole of every Bonapartist's coat« (Williams, *Narrative* 37). Williams did, however, grant that Napoleon had made some positive contributions to society. In a later book she wrote that he had introduced some social improvements through his Civil Code, and he had protected the rights of Protestants more than the Bourbons did, but she also states outright that »Bonaparte had a great contempt for women; he suffered indeed his contempt for the whole human race to be too apparent« (Williams, *Letters* 1819, 94, 124). Even though he established a system of girls' schools, it is often said that Napoleon had little respect for women, and that his policies encouraged a return to traditional views of womanhood (see Connor; Rogers). Helen Maria Williams asserts that »If Bonaparte could still boast of partisans among the men, it is at least certain that he found few among the women« (Williams, *Narrative* 44). Women who had lost so many sons in battle recoiled at the thought of his return. Williams felt that his militarism was inimical to feminine sensibility. Ultimately, for Williams, Bonaparte had become a political tyrant, and »every sentiment of female nature might [...] be averse to a system of tyranny and blood« (Williams, *Narrative* 44).

Such a response shows how much the Napoleonic wars took their toll on women. Moreover, any woman writing during this period of history had to deal with the effects of war, whether indirectly as in Austen's novels, or directly as in the works of Hannah More. Napoleon Bonaparte was inescapable and seemingly unconquerable until Waterloo. When the Allied troops entered Paris, Williams enjoyed meeting her countrymen and remarked that, »I hope my French friends will forgive me if I felt a little proud of being an Englishwoman« (Williams, *Narrative* 175). For her, it is the established English government that is the true model of liberty. The French, she writes, know only an »A B C liberty«; and »They have passed through many phases, from the wildest anarchy to the most oppressive despotism; and they now really know what is *not* freedom« (Williams, *Narrative* 205-206). A sense of weariness characterizes this book, and, like many of her contemporaries, Helen Maria Williams hoped that a period of tranquillity would follow years of devastation across Europe, for, as she affirms in one short sentence, »Bonaparte is fallen« (Williams, *Narrative* 253).

–Saint Mary's University, Halifax, Canada

## Works Cited

Austen, Jane. *Jane Austen's Letters.* 3rd. ed. Ed. Deirdre Le Faye. Oxford: Oxford UP, 1995.

Austen, Jane. *Persuasion.* 1818. Ed. D. W. Harding. Harmondsworth: Penguin, 1985.

Austen-Leigh, J. E. *A Memoir of Jane Austen.* In Jane Austen, *Persuasion*: 270-391.

Bainbridge, Simon. *Napoleon and English Romanticism.* Cambridge: Cambridge UP, 1995.

Bergeron, Louis. *France under Napoleon.* Trans. R. R. Palmer. Princeton: Princeton UP, 1981.

Berry, Mary. *England and France: A Comparative View.* 2 vols. London: Richard Bentley, 1834.

Burke, Edmund. *Reflections on the Revolution in France.* Ed. Conor Cruise O'Brien. Harmondsworth: Penguin, 1987.

Burney, Frances. *The Journals and Letters of Fanny Burney (Madame d'Arblay).* Ed. Joyce Hemlow et al. 12 vols. Oxford: Clarendon, 1972-1984.

Chandler, David. *The Campaigns of Napoleon.* London: Weidenfeld and Nicolson, 1967.

Cecil, David. *A Portrait of Jane Austen.* New York: Hill and Wang, 1978.

Connor, Susan P. »The Merveilleuse and the Coquette: Women during the Directory and First Empire.« *Proceedings of the Consortium on Revolutionary Europe* (1980): 49-57.

Anonymous [Coxe, Peter.] *The Exposé; or Napoleone Buonaparte Unmasked, in a Condensed Statement of His Career and Atrocities.* [sic] London: Miller, 1809.

Cronin, Vincent. *Napoleon.* Glasgow: William Collins, 1990.

Dickinson, H. T. *British Radicalism and the French Revolution.* Oxford: Basil Blackwell, 1985.

Dolan, Brian. *Ladies of the Grand Tour: British Women in Pursuit of Enlightenment and Adventure in Eighteenth-Century Europe.* New York: HarperCollins, 2001.

Doody, Margaret Anne. *Frances Burney: The Life in the Works.* New Brunswick: Rutgers UP, 1988.

Ellis, Grace A. *A Memoir of Anna Laetitia Barbauld, with Many of her Letters.* Boston: James R. Osgood, 1874.

Gilman, Caroline Howard. »Choice of Paintings.« *A Gift Book of Stories and Poems for Children.* New York: C. S. Francis, 1850: 131-134.

Gittings, Robert and Jo Manton. *Dorothy Wordsworth.* Oxford: Oxford UP, 1988.

Goodwin, Albert. *The Friends of Liberty.* Cambridge: Harvard UP, 1979.

Grenby, Matthew. »Politicizing the Nursery: British Children's Literature and the French Revolution.« *The Lion and the Unicorn* 27.1 (2003):1-26.

Hemlow, Joyce. *The History of Fanny Burney.* Oxford: Clarendon, 1958.

Honan, Park. *Jane Austen: Her Life.* London: Weidenfeld & Nicolson, 1987.

Kelley, Theresa M. »Turner, Napoleon, and Allegory«. *English Literary History* 58 (Summer 1991):351-382.

Kennedy, Deborah. *Helen Maria Williams and the Age of Revolution.* Lewisburg: Bucknell UP, 2002.

Lean, E. Tangye. *The Napoleonists.* London: Oxford UP, 1970.

Lewis, Michael. *Napoleon and His British Captives.* London: George Allen and Unwin, 1962.

Lyons, Martin. *Napoleon Bonaparte and the Legacy of the French Revolution.* London: Macmillan, 1994.

Melville, Lewis. *The Berry Papers: Being the Correspondence Hitherto Unpublished of Mary and Agnes Berry.* London: Bodley Head, 1914.

More, Hannah. *The Works of Hannah More.* 11 vols. London: Cadell, 1830.

Rogers, Rebecca. »Competing Visions of Girls' Secondary Education in Post-Revolutionary France«. *History of Education Quarterly* 34.2 (Summer 1994):147-170.

Walpole, Horace. *The Yale Edition of Horace Walpole's Correspondence.* Vol. 31. Ed. W. S. Lewis, Robert A. Smith, and Charles H. Bennett. New Haven: Yale UP, 1961.

Williams, Helen Maria. *Letters from France.* Intro. Janet Todd. Delmar: Scholars' Facsimiles & Reprints, 1975.

Williams, Helen Maria. *Letters on the Events which Have Passed in France since the Restoration in 1815.* London: Baldwin, 1819.

Williams, Helen Maria. *A Narrative of the Events Which Have Taken Place in France from the Landing of Napoleon Bonaparte on the First of March, 1815, till the Restoration of Louis XVIII.* 1815. Cleveland: Burrows, 1894.

Williams, Helen Maria. *Poems on Various Subjects.* London: Whittaker, 1823.

Williams, Helen Maria. *Sketches of the State of Manners and Opinions in the French Republic.* 2 vols. London: Robinson, 1801.

Williams, Helen Maria. *Souvenirs de la révolution française.* Paris: Dondey-Dupré, 1827.

Williams, Helen Maria. *A Tour in Switzerland.* 2 vols. London: Robinson, 1798.

Woodward, Lionel. *Une Anglaise Amie de la Révolution française: Hélène-Maria Williams et ses Amis.* 1930. Geneva: Slatkine Reprints, 1977.

Wordsworth, Dorothy. *The Letters of William and Dorothy Wordsworth.* 8 vols. Edited by Ernest de Selincourt; 2nd. ed. rev. Chester L. Shaver, Mary Moorman, and Alan G. Hill. Oxford: Clarendon, 1967-1993.

# Maria Carolina, Queen of Naples: The »Devil's Grandmother« Fights Napoleon

*Waltraud Maierhofer*

The »devil's grandmother« is a well-known stock character in German folk tales such as »The Devil With the Three Golden Hairs«, which the Grimms included in their famous early nineteenth-century collections. The figure illustrates how medieval beliefs manifested themselves in demonic characters. In Regensburg, for example, two small sculptures in the niches on opposite sides of the main entrance of the Gothic cathedral are known as »The Devil and the Devil's Grandmother«. Their significance is disputed in scholarship; they may have been placed there to remind the congregation that as soon as they left the safety of the church, evil and temptation awaited them.

Maria Carolina (Vienna 1742–1814 Vienna),[1] proud daughter of Maria Theresia (1717–1780), the ruling Empress of the *Holy Roman Empire* (since 1745), was queen consort to Ferdinando IV of Naples, who ruled the southern part of the Italian peninsula, including Sicily. Maria Carolina liked to use attributes and words such as »devil«, »Corsican bastard«, »Europe's scourge«, »wild beast«, or »arch scoundrel« for Napoleon. The opponent, in turn, payed her back in kind, referring to her as the modern version of the power-usurping, ferocious tyrannical ancient queen Athalia (Helfert, *Königin Karolina* 226), daughter of Jezebel and worshiper of Baal, or Queen Frédégonde of sixth-century France, or simply the »impersonation of crime« (Bonaparte, *Confidential Correspondence* 131). Dynastic politics by marriage was as important to Maria Carolina as to any of the Habsburg family – or any absolutist monarch. One of her many children – she endured eighteen pregnancies – Marie Thérèse (1772–1807), became the second wife of Maria Carolina's nephew Franz (Francis of Habsburg, 1768–1835). Franz was Emperor of the Holy Roman Empire until 1806 when Napoleon brought about its end and Francis had to dissolve it. Francis had already assumed the title of the first Emperor of Austria in October 1804. Marie Thérèse's oldest daughter Marie Louise (Vienna

1791–1847 Padua) was at the age of eighteen married to Napoleon after he arranged a divorce from his first wife. After Maria Carolina read of the wedding *per procurationem* of her granddaughter in Vienna in March 1810, she is said to have exclaimed, »[d]as war es, was mir in meinem Unglück noch gefehlt hat, des Teufels Großmutter zu werden« (quoted in Tamassino 341) [that is the last thing missing in my misery, to become the devil's grandmother].[2] The self-crowned French emperor Napoleon, the former anti-monarchist revolutionary, managed to divorce his first wife Josephine and marry into one of the powerful old European dynasties. Marie Louise was in the words of historian Jeremy Black a »spoil of war designed to cement Austria's new relationship with France« (Black 231). The marriage was to secure the peace in the East of Napoleon's vast empire. As Steven Englund writes in his Napoleon biography, the marriage »stupefied contemporaries as much as the coronation had done six years before. To kidnap and execute one Bourbon (Enghien), overthrow another (Spain), then proceed to marry a Habsburg, is a yarn few storytellers would dare to invent« (Englund 360). Austria's Foreign Minister Clemens Metternich encouraged the relation as a means of ensuring Austria's power against France. In 1809 Austria had been defeated and lost considerable amounts of territory and people to France and its client states. (In 1810, the year of the wedding, Austria rejected an approach by its distrusted rival Russia for an alliance.)

Whole monographs and biographies about Maria Carolina have been written under the attention-catching heading of her as Napoleon's adversary (Helfert, Bonnefons, Lacour-Gayet). The first was by the Austrian historian Joseph Alexander von Helfert who wrote two voluminous apologetic studies on Maria Carolina supported by archival documents, the first focussing on her *Kampf[ gegen die französische Weltherrschaft [fight against French world domination*] (Helfert 1878), the second subtitled *Anklagen und Vertheidigung* [*accusations and defense*] (Helfert 1884). On the other hand, the Queen of Naples plays only a minor role in Napoleon biographies, if she appears at all.[3] The 1980s saw several publications on Maria Carolina, and biographies appeared in German (Tamussino), Italian (Coletti), and French (Lacour-Gayet).[4] They would be interesting to compare, but this is not my goal. The following article will first outline Maria Carolina's struggle as Queen of Naples against Napoleon's expansions into her country, then it will examine a selection of significant passages in their correspondence.[5] Finally, it will reevaluate Maria Carolina's struggle and consider it in the broader context of women against Napoleon. Statements in her vast correspondence testify that she admired Napoleon's accomplishments and leadership very much and never underestimated him (even after the first expatriation). However, she certainly did not want him to extend his rule to her own sovereignty, and she definitely was not in favor of the upstart ruler becoming a member of the Habsburgs.

## I.

By 1810, the year of her granddaughter's wedding, Maria Carolina had fought against Napoleon for over a decade, above all by changing the course of Neapolitan politics. Her husband was a member of the Neapolitan Bourbons (while descendants of the French Bourbons ruled France until the French Revolution). Naples did not support the expansion of the Napoleonic empire. Under the threat of Napoleon's army and under Maria Carolina's leadership, Naples allied with the British and provided a base for Horatio Nelson and his fleet. Nevertheless the French army invaded Naples twice, and both times the court fled to its second residence in Sicily. Napoleon's brother Joseph, followed by his sister Caroline's husband Murat, were declared the new kings of Naples. In 1810, as she wrote to the anti-French general inspector of the Neapolitan army, Maria Carolina had lost everything, »Familie, Heimat, Leben, Existenz« [family, homeland, life, existence] (quoted from Tamussino 303).[6] She did live to hear of Napoleon's abdication on April 6, 1814 and his exile on Elba (from May 4 onwards); although she lived herself in exile near her hometown Vienna, there are letters that speak of her forgiving Napoleon and his staunch efforts to take away her kingdom. She died in September 1814 and thus not long enough to join her husband Ferdinando, who was reinstated as king (now named King of »The Two Sicilies« and therefore Ferdinando I) less than a year later, i. e. at the end of the Congress of Vienna. However, this had been her very goal until her death, and she never gave up hope. Without her anti-French course, Southern Italy may not have entered the struggle for Italian national unity in the latter part of the 19th century as easily.

Historical and biographical accounts have portrayed Maria Carolina in extreme terms. She has been condemned as ambitious, negligent of her people, responsible for the economic downturn of Naples, and above all as cruel, especially in her sentencing of the enemies of the monarchy in the 1790s. However, she also found defenders. Before we turn to her political struggle against Napoleon, we have to consider what her power consisted of and what the role of the state of Naples was in the eighteenth century and in Napoleon's empire.

In 1734, Southern Italy, or the Kingdom of Naples and Sicily, had become an autonomous monarchy ruled by the Bourbons. It faced many problems, above all the antiquated feudal system and the »backwardness of all southern Italian society« (Imbruglia I). Recent historical research has pointed out that »the life of the Kingdom of Naples shows us what it meant in the eighteenth century to construct and modernise a state in the age of Enlightenment« (Imbruglia I). In 1768 Maria Carolina, Archduchess of Habsburg, married Ferdinando di Borbone, who had been (as Ferdinando IV) King of Naples and Sicily since 1759. The marriage contract, probably negotiated by her powerful mother, provided that Maria Carolina »entered the council of state, the kingdom's ruling body, when she had given birth to a male heir« (Encyclopædia Britannica) which she did in 1777.[7] Securing the dynasty was her primary function and political role as a queen. The primary function of all queens in absolutist regimes was »to suggest in idealised form the symbolic harmony of male and female, the potency and fertility of the ruling male, and the continuity of the dynasty« (Orr 5). The eighteenth century was part of an »age which still invested monarchy with divine authority and derived legitimacy from the hereditary principle« (Orr 5).

Maria Carolina had no formal training, but she did have »a marked though ill-balanced talent for government« (Johnston, *Napoleonic Empire* I: 46) or, in more positive terms, at least a »partial understanding of political realities« (Sontag 180). Her husband Ferdinando was not exactly blessed with intelligence and diplomatic skills. Johnston calls him ignorant and immoral (Johnston, *Napoleonic Empire* I: 43, 45). His primary interests were hunting and other diversions. He did not change this attitude as the French threat to his kingdom grew, although formally he remained the head of the state. Maria Carolina presided over the Council during the King's frequent absences and made men of her choice (preferably with strong Austrian ties) ministers. However, she was never formally vested with the regency; Ferdinando kept formal authority as ruling head of the state and remained Commander-in-Chief of the army.

Prior to 1789, the royal couple ruled the small kingdom as absolutist monarchs and feudal landowners, though they did embrace moderate reforms and accepted Enlightenment philosophers as advisers and even as ministers in the *Supremo Consiglio*. The most important example is Gaetano Filangieri, who demanded »a complete reorganisation of society, the separation of politics and economies, and of public functions and private property« but also a virtuous monarch as sovereign (Rao 113). The royal couple favored Freemasonry, supported the reform of the university, and the founding of a Royal Society of Sciences and Arts. These were fundamental steps towards necessary economic reforms. The army and navy also underwent reforms for which the British statesman John Acton (1736–1811) was called upon in 1779. In the 1780s the people of the kingdom »had learned to trust in a monarch aided by philosophers« (Rao 114).

The court's support of Enlightenment reform radically ceased with the effects of the French revolution. Maria Carolina changed the court's pro-Spanish policy to pro-British. John Acton became Minister of Finance and Prime Minister (1785–1806 with brief interruptions). Under his influence and very likely motivated by the execution of her sister Marie Antoinette by the French, the queen took Naples into the first Austro-British coalition against the French Revolution, sent Neapolitan warships to join the British fleet near Toulon (1793), and allowed Naples to become a military base for England. These steps proved more than advantageous for the defeat of the French army in Egypt by the British in 1801.

Napoleon came onto the political scene in 1796. As Commander in Chief of General Schérer and his aggressive course into Italy, he began his first Italian campaign in April 1796, took Milan and drove the Austrians out of northern Italy. In 1798, under Ferdinando's command (and Maria Carolina's guidance) Naples joined the second coalition against France which was now under direct guidance of the Directory. The French continued southward, making Rome a Republic in February of 1798, which prompted the pope to flee the Vatican. In November, the small, neither very experienced nor competent Neapolitan army tried to occupy Rome to restore the monarchy, but was driven back by the French. Republican ideals did not have a strong base in Naples and spread slowly, but, as reforms were blocked, Naples saw its »passive revolution« (Rao 169) in that year. The royals fled to Sicily in early 1799 with the help of Admiral Horatio Nelson. The French Revolutionary army under General Championnet and liberal Neapolitans set up the Parthenopean Republic in January 1799, which they based on the French system. However, the revolutionary republic lasted only five months and was overthrown in turn by the *Lazzaroni,* the street people of Naples. A religious army, the *sanfedisti*, led by Cardinal Ruffo, fought for the reconquest of Naples, and the old order was by and large restored. By June of 1799 the monarchy was reinstituted in Naples, and thousands of republican partisans were executed in the cruelest reprisals – supervised by Lord Nelson. Terrible oppressions were imposed and the *philosophers* and revolutionaries were executed or intimidated, for which Maria Carolina bore at least part of the responsibility.[8] The Roman Republic fell a few months later, in September of 1799. The Bourbon monarchs from Naples took the opportunity to assert their authority over Rome with the same ruthlessness they had shown in Naples.[9] A new pope, Pius VIII, was elected in 1800.

The time in which Napoleon defeated Naples was also the phase when he had most control of »Italy« overall: The French dominated most of northern and central Italy, mostly in the form of »sister republics«, with constitutions modeled on the French, and Napoleon often chose the administrators himself.[10] After the *Coup d'état* of November 1799, Napoleon began as First Consul his second Italian campaign against Austria whom he would defeat. In March 1801, a treaty between France and Naples established peace, and the royal couple returned to Naples the following year.

When in 1803 Naples refused to give up its support of Napoleon's opponent England, his army occupied parts of the kingdom of Naples again. On July 29th, Napoleon wrote in firm language separately to the King and Queen of Naples that his policy was conciliatory to his neighbors, but as long as the kingdom of Naples was governed more by a foreign prime minister (namely Sir John Acton) than by its own court, he would have to treat it »comme un pays gouverné par un ministre anglais« (Bonaparte, *Correspondance* VIII: 422, no. 6951) [as a country governed by an English minister] (quoted in Asprey 461).[11]

In 1805 Maria Carolina once more engaged Naples in a war with France, calling the British and – secretly – the Russian fleets to her aid. When Napoleon found out about the alliance, he wrote to the Queen of Naples:[12]

»Votre Majesté, qui a un esprit si distingué entre les femmes, n'a-t-elle donc pas pu se détacher des préventions de son sexe, et peut-elle traiter les affaires d'État comme les affaires de cœur? Elle a déjà perdu une foi son royaume; deux fois elle a été la cause d'une guerre qui a failli ruiner de fond en comble sa maison paternelle; veut-elle donc être la cause de la troisième? [...] Quoi! Sa haine est-elle tellement jeune, et son amour pour l'Angleterre tellement exalté, qu'elle veuille, quoique assurée d'en être la première victime, embraser le continent, et opérer cette heureuse diversion pour l'Angleterre? [...] Que Votre Majesté écoute cette prophétie, qu'elle l'écoute sans impatience: à la première guerre dont elle serait cause, elle et sa postérité auraient cessé de régner; ses enfants errants mendieraient, dans les différentes contrées de l'Europe, des secours de leurs parents. Par une conduite inexplicable, elle aurait causé la ruine de sa famille, tandis que la providence et ma modération la lui avaient conservée.« (Napoleon à la reine de Naples, Paris, 12 nivôse an XIII [2 janvier 1805]; Bonaparte, *Correspondance* X: 103, no. 8255.)

[Your Majesty, whose mind is so distinguished among women, when will you detach yourself from prejudices of your sex and stop treating affairs of the state like affairs of the heart? Your Majesty has already lost her kingdom once, and twice has she caused a war that threatened to completely eradicate her paternal lineage; will she be at the source of a third one? [...] What! Is her hatred so young and her love for England so exaggerated that she is willing to cause a joyous diversion for that country even if she is assured that by setting the continent ablaze, she will be their first victim? [...] Through her erratic behavior, she will have caused her family's ruin whereas providence and my moderation would have saved it for her. May you heed this prophecy without impatience: at the first sound of a war that you cause, you and your posterity will have ceased to reign, and your children will wander like mendicants through the different countries of Europe, begging help off their relatives.][13]

Maria Carolina's response was fairly moderate (Corti 458). Napoleon restated his »unalterable« will about the end of the Bourbons several times to his brother Joseph (Bonaparte, *The Confidential Correspondence* 88 and also 83, 86). The war of the third coalition (Austria, Britain, Naples and Russia against Napoleon's army) of 1805 ended with Napoleon's victory at Austerlitz; the Peace of Pressburg stated among other changes that Austria had to give up all Italian possessions. Napoleon became »King of Italy« (the northern half of the peninsula, to be precise). Finally, the landing of an Anglo-Russian expeditionary force in 1805 gave Napoleon an excuse to depose Maria Carolina. On February 15$^{th}$, 1806, Joseph Bonaparte, upon his brother's order, invaded Naples at the head of a French army and proclaimed himself King of Naples after the conquest. Napoleon gave the order to conquer Naples in an army bulletin, written already in Schoenbrunn on December 27th, 1805. The bulletin names the King, even when aimed at his »advisor« Maria Carolina:

»Soldiers, for ten years I have done everything to save the King of Naples. He has done everything to ruin himself.

[...] I trusted him and treated him with generosity.

After the second coalition was broken at Marengo, the King of Naples, who had been the first to begin that unjust war, abandoned at Lunéville by his allies, stood alone and defenceless. He entreated, and I pardoned him a second time.

A few months ago you were at the gates of Naples. I had sufficient reason to suspect the treachery which was meditated, and to revenge the outrages which I had received. I was again generous: I acknowledged the neutrality of Naples, and directed you to quit that kingdom: for the third time the house of Naples was saved and re-established.

Shall we pardon a fourth time? Shall we trust a fourth time, a court without faith, or honour, or intelligence? No! No! The Neapolitan dynasty has ceased to reign, its existence is incompatible with the tranquility of Europe and the honour of my crown.

Soldiers, march; throw into the waves, if they wait for you, the weak battalions of the tyrant of the seas. Show the world how we punish treachery. Let me hear without delay that all Italy is subject to my authority or to that of my allies: that the finest of countries is relieved from the yoke of the most faithless of men [...].« (Bonaparte, *The Confidential Correspondence* 80, no. 110.)

The bulletin was widely published in Naples after its defeat and announced to all European courts.[14] Helfert, in his »apology« of Maria Carolina, called the bulletin a severe injury and offense, but also a calculated gesture that camouflaged Napoleon's real respect for the queen as a coequal adversary.[15] Helfert supports this claim by references to advice given by Napoleon to his brother Joseph; he should rule more strictly, more like Maria Carolina, and take her as »ein Beispiel« [an example], arguing, »*die* wisse was es heiße ihre Hoheitsrechte schützen; *der* sei kein Mittel zu rasch oder zu gewaltsam um damit zu ihrem Ziele zu gelangen, aber sie handle als *Königin*!« [*she* knew what it meant to protect sovereignty rights; *she* did not consider any means too quick or too violent that would achieve her goal, but she would act as *Queen*!] (Quoted in Helfert, *Königin Karolina* 244, no sources given.)

The royal family fled to Sicily for a second time in February of 1806. Napoleon dared to request from Maria Carolina, now reduced to queen of Sicily, to give one of her daughters to his viceroy Eugène de Beauharnais. Upon her refusal, the secretary of the Imperial Ambassador reported the following reaction by Napoleon:

»Sagen Sie ihr in meinem Namen, wenn eine Frau alt und häßlich wird, so bleibt ihr einzig nur übrig, sich der Frömmigkeit in die Arme zu werfen [...] Ich will ihrem

Haus nicht einmal so viel Land lassen, als für dessen Gräber notwendig ist.« (Reports by secretary Kruthoffer and Count Ferdinand von Bissingen, June 18, July 6 and 7, 1805; quoted from Tamussino 284.)

[Tell her in my name, when a woman becomes old and ugly, the only thing left to her is throwing herself in the arms of piety [...] I want to leave to her family not even as much land as is necessary for their graves.]

Nevertheless, Maria Carolina made plans to return to Naples and regain power. She is reported to have said to Prince Kaunitz[16] on July 3rd, 1806 that she was not willing to give up: »[E]s soll eine Dornenkrone sein was Napoleon seinem Bruder gegeben hat! « [[I]t shall be a crown of thorns what Napoleon gave to his brother!] (Quoted in Helfert, *Königin Karolina* 285, no source given.) It was indeed a crown of thorns, although – unlike in the rest of the Italian peninsula – most of the nobility in the kingdom of Naples cooperated with the new French King. The collaboration was prompted, as historian Desmond Gregory explains, »not merely by self-interest but because for the most part nobles shared the same enlightened values as the French« (Gregory 159). However, Napoleon admonished his brother repeatedly to rule in a less enlightened way, with less »kindness« and »softness« and instead with more »terror« and »vigour«, with the goal to be feared, and to enforce taxes instead of lightening them (Bonaparte, *The Confidential Correspondence* 103, 146, 95, 113, 97, 149) – that is, more like the absolutist Maria Carolina. Joseph did not strictly import French rule: »Neapolitans were awarded posts in the law courts, the police, the diplomatic service, the armed forces, the judicial commissions, as well as the council of state« (Gregory 163). Feudalism was abolished, but part of the nobility resisted this and other reforms. Especially landowners in the »disturbed provinces, particularly Calabria, [...] gave encouragement to bandit bands and looked to the return of the Bourbons« (Gregory 163). Others collaborated with both Joseph in Naples and Maria Carolina who was still Queen of Sicily.[17] There were a number of insurrections against Joseph's rule, and he did not find the country as rich as his brother kept telling him.[18] In the years from 1806 to 1811, the revolts in Calabria, a peninsula in Italy's utmost South, were among the most serious against Napoleonic rule in all of Italy (Gregory 170). Joseph Bonaparte tried in vain to conquer Sicily; instead the British occupied Sicily from 1806 to 1815. In 1812 the Sicilian parliament approved a constitution modeled on the English (Iachello 190). In 1808, Napoleon sent Joseph to the throne of Spain and replaced him in Naples with his own sister Caroline and her husband, the cavalry officer Joachim (»Gioacchino« in Italian) Murat. He was King of

Naples from 1811 to 1815. The people of the kingdom in general were »either hostile to Napoleonic rule or passively indifferent«, observes Gregory – except for a few Calabrian towns delivered from banditry and the Neapolitan *lazzaroni* whom Murat kept in good spirits with plenty of entertainment and food, as well as under control with strict law enforcement (165). Compulsory military service, poverty, and high taxation were the main reasons for discontent and rebellion; religion was also a factor in Naples. Reforms under the Napoleonic rule attempted to centralize and bureaucratize administration of the country, but they did not cure rural poverty (and banditry in its wake), but rather aggravated it (Gregory 167). Gregory's assessment of Napoleon's Italy is especially true for the Kingdom of Naples: »What is important to remember in assessing the unwillingness of the Italians to form a coordinated resistance movement is that the nobles and the bourgeoisie had no wish to encourage a peasant revolt that might threaten their own social position, which had benefited so substantially under Napoleonic rule.« (175)

In 1811 Maria Carolina was declared exiled from Sicily (by the British who occupied it), while her more cooperative husband and son were allowed to stay. Maria Carolina turned to her nephew in Vienna for asylum, the Austrian emperor Franz, while insisting that she would fight as long as possible.[19] And so she did; in spite of pressure by the British, she did not leave for Austria until June 1813 (Helfert, *Königin Karolina* 534). Even in Vienna, Maria Carolina did not give up her cause: As late as January 1814, she pleaded in a memorandum to Franz to have Naples returned to its legitimate king, her husband Ferdinando. She pointed out that now »all other legitimate monarchs return to their states« [alle andern legitimen Monarchen in ihre Staaten zurückkehren] (Helfert, *Königin Karolina* 561).

Maria Carolina lived to learn of Napoleon's defeat. She died on September 9, 1814 when the peace congress of Vienna was about to begin. She corresponded with the French representative Talleyrand and with the British foreign minister Lord Castlereagh about the future of Naples and the re-institution of the Bourbons as legitimate rulers. Half a year later, on May 20, 1815, at the convention in Casalanza, Ferdinando was re-instituted and political opponents were pardoned. In June 1815, the congress of Vienna confirmed Maria Carolina's husband Ferdinando as King of southern Italy, now no longer named Naples and Sicily, but »both Sicilies«. Critical voices pointed out that Ferdinando could only be re-instituted because Maria Carolina was no longer alive and thus there was less fear of oppression in Naples (Johnston, *Napoleonic Empire* I: 321, Acton 631). Ferdinando remarried a few weeks after her death. Naples was an exception to the many territorial changes that the congress brought about, that »helped mark the end of an era« (Black 239) and that determined the European agenda for the next century.

## II.

A few additional passages on Napoleon from Maria Carolina's vast body of correspondence may serve to further illustrate the tone and style of her judgement of her adversary. Andrew Martin argues that the rise and fall of Napoleon's empire were anticipated in his essays and his repeated attempts at a voluminous novel; while Napoleon failed in an essay competition he did succeed in imposing himself as the »archetype and inspiration of modern European culture« (Martin cover text). Maria Carolina's fictionalization and dramatization[20] of herself and others in her letters have yet to be more closely investigated. If scholars comment at all on her writing style, they characterize it as natural and see its function in relieving emotions (for example Acton 417), classifying it thus as writing typical for a woman, not a ruler. Especially when writing about her adversary Napoleon, it is evident how she clung to the claim to absolute power sanctioned by a divine mandate when in fact the authority of despots had been undermined by Enlightenment philosophy and economic developments even before the rise of Napoleon. She shared this view with most European monarchs, however.

When Napoleon first distinguished himself as general, and his army conquered Lombardy and other territories, shortly before the Peace of Campo Formio (October 17, 1797) Maria Carolina wrote to her ambassador to the Empire in Vienna, Marchese di Gallo:

»He is the Attila, the scourge of Italy, but I have a genuine esteem and deep admiration for him. He is the greatest man several centuries have produced. His force, energy, constancy, activity and talent have won my admiration. Happy the country with such a sovereign; for it need not fear conquest or defeat. Happy the prince with such a minister or general! [...] I admire him, and my sole regret is that he serves so detestable a cause. I should like the fall of the Republic, but the preservation of Bonaparte. For he is really a great man; ... But while I loathe his operations, I admire the man. I hope that his plans will miscarry and his enterprises fail;

at the same time I wish for his personal happiness and glory so long as it is not at our expense. [...] If he dies they should reduce him to powder and give a dose of it to each ruling sovereign, and two to each of their ministers, then things would go better.« (Acton 296) [Sic][21]

Blackly humorous remarks such the last sentence, of course, fed criticism of her as superstitious, brutal, and even cannibalistic. In another letter to Gallo after the Treaty of Campo Formio and the end of the Republic of Venice, she expressed general praise of Napoleon's personality and military achievements, but also with particular regard to her own country, the hope that Naples would be spared from his ambitions:

»Malgré tout le mal qu'il nous a fait en Italie je dois avouer que j'ai de lui une haute opinion et comme j'aime le grand en tout et partout, même quand je le trouve contre moi, je souhaite à cet homme rare, extraordinaire de réussir et de s'illustrer hors d'Italie. Je prévois que le monde retentira encore de son nom et que l'histoire l'immortalisera. En tout il sera grand, en guerre, diplomatie, politique, conduite, fermeté, talent, génie; ce sera le plus grand homme de notre siècle.« (Weil and Circello I: 497, no. 249)

[In spite of all the harm he has done to us in Italy, I must admit that I hold a high opinion of him, as I love the great in all things and everywhere, even when I find it turned against myself. I wish this rare and extraordinary man to succeed and distinguish himself outside Italy. I foresee that this world will resound with his name, and that history will immortalize him. He will be great in all things, in war, diplomacy, conduct, resolution, talent, genius: he will be the greatest man of our century. (Acton 296)]

Maria Carolina argues here not as a Habsburg defending the borders of the Old Empire or of Austria, but as Queen of Naples. She does not lament that the empire lost the left bank of the Rhine and Belgium to the French, the beginning of »what would result in the total collapse of the thousand-year-old Holy Roman Empire« (Schom 302), nor that the Habsburgs ceded Tuscany to the Spanish.

»Towards Bonaparte her dislike was tempered by extreme curiosity«, muses Johnston in his book on *The Napoleonic Empire in Southern Italy* (I: 59). She is reported to have said to Alquier, the French Minister of the Parthenopean Republic, in the year 1804: »You know that I detest your country. Yet I would willingly travel 200 leagues to see the First Consul. He loves glory and so do I.« (Quoted from Johnston, ibid. 59)

The French Senate proclaimed Napoleon Emperor of the French on May 18, 1804, and in December of that year Napoleon crowned himself with the crown of Charlemagne. Maria Carolina wrote about the proclamation to Gallo, June 6–7, 1804:

»[E]t de ce comble d'horreurs la nation acclame à être Empereur, lui, sa race de Corse bâtard, à être le chef d'à peu près la moitié de l'Europe, et cela ne doit pas révolter chaque être pensant. Point du tout, l'égoïsme, la faiblesse est telle qu'on étudie comment s'y plier, adorer l'idole et le souffrir.« (Weil and Circello I: 479, no. 480)

[[O]n top of all these abominations he is acclaimed as Emperor: he and his race of Corsican bastards are to dominate almost half Europe, yet every thinking person is not revolted. Far from it, their egoism and weakness are such that they study how low they can prostrate themselves before the new idol. (Acton 491) ]

Surprisingly, when exiled from her former country and dropped by her former British allies, she returned to a positive evaluation of Napoleon in a letter to her relatives in Vienna in April 1813:

»Ich glaube nicht zu irren daß ich bei meinem großen Feinde mehr Loyalität Edelmuth Seelengröße, mehr Rücksicht für mein Geschlecht, für meine Jahre, meine Gebrechlichkeit gefunden haben würde als bei unsern sogenannten Freunden denen ich und der König alles geopfert haben und die es jetzt darauf angelegt zu haben scheinen uns zu Tode zu quälen. Aber ich habe das nicht thun, mich an den Kaiser Napoleon nicht wenden wollen, weil man ohnedies Verläumdungen gegen mich gehäuft hat als ob ich mit den Feinden dieses Landes verbrecherischen Verkehr unterhielte.« (Helfert, *Königin Karolina* 533–34; no source given)

[I believe not to be mistaken that I would have found with my great adversary more loyalty, gallantry, greatness of soul, more respect for my sex, for my years, my fragility than with our so-called friends for whom I and the King have sacrificed everything and who now appear to intend to torture us to death. However, I did not want to do that, did not want to turn to the Emperor Napoleon, because calumniations against me have already been accumulated as if I entertained criminal relations with the enemies of this country.]

When Maria Caroline learned of Napoleon's abdication and exile to Elba she is reported not to have triumphed, but to have warned that the island was too close to Italy and that a man such as Napoleon could not be trusted even after his defeat.[22] Her granddaughter Marie Louise did not follow her husband into exile, but rather also sought refuge in Vienna. Maria Carolina is said to have confided to Marie Louise's secretary, Claude de Méneval, not only her disapproval of such unloyal behavior of a consort, but also of her own change of feelings towards Napoleon: »Ich habe in früheren Zeiten allen Grund gehabt, mich über ihn [Napoleon] zu beklagen, er hat mich verfolgt und in meiner Eigenliebe verletzt. Heute aber, wo er unglücklich ist, vergesse ich alles.« (Quoted from Tamussino 321)[23] [In earlier times I have had reason to complain about him [Napoleon]; he persecuted me and violated me in my holiest feelings. Today however, now that he is unhappy, all shall be forgotten.]

Maria Carolina's sympathetic biographer Tamussino maintains that Napoleon rightly considered her »seine unbeugsamste und durch nichts einzuschüchternde Gegnerin« [his most unrelenting adversary who could not be intimidated by anything (Tamussino 9)]. This biography portrays the Neapolitan Queen as intuitively correct about Napoleon and his fate. Her remarks from the year 1802, supposedly to the Russian ambassador in Vienna, Rasumofsky, characterize her not only as a good, but as a self-sacrificing queen:

»Seine ehrgeizigen Pläne sind maßlos und werden alle anderen entweder mit Gewalt oder gutwillig mitreißen [...] Ich aber habe den Willen, ihn zu bekämpfen [...] Ich sehe nach meiner Denkungsart das Glück nicht darin, nur eine Souveränin dem Namen nach zu sein und von Bonaparte und den sieben revolutionären Halunken aller Nationen abzuhängen, die um ihn leben und ihm den Hof machen. Wenn man so fühlt wie ich, kann man nicht glücklich sein.« (Quoted in Tamussino 266)

[His ambitious plans are exorbitant and will, either by force or willingly, carry along all others. [...] I have a strong will to fight him. [...] According to my way of thinking I don't consider it happiness being a sovereign only by name and depending on Bonaparte and the seven revolutionary scoundrels of all nations who surround him and court him. When one feels as I do, one cannot be happy.]

Many of these statements are second-hand recordings or anecdotal and may be tinted by the recorders' view of Maria Carolina; thus they cannot be taken as hard evidence. It is interesting in itself to observe who wrote down and passed on memories of her.

## III.

Historiography, biography, and fictional literature have described and evaluated Maria Carolina's power and its range and agency quite differently. Contemporary accounts of the Queen (such as Gorani, a French count, and his »critique of principal Italian courts«) were extremely negative, overstated the range of her power and her misuse of it, or exaggerated her sexual appetite.[24] In the eighteenth century, women rulers faced growing criticism for playing a visible role and stepping out of the domestic sphere deemed appropriate for women. As historian Joan Landes writes in her seminal study on women in public life in the eighteenth century: »The metaphor of ›the reign of women‹ signified the corruption of society at its heights. (By implication, only a corrupt and inadequately virile ruler would allow himself and his kingdom to be disarmed by the exercise of female power)« (Landes 27). Landes has examined how the middle-class intellectuals of France and Britain criticized women for exerting too much power in the old regime, often in devious ways, and by disenfranchising men of the middle class.

Maria Carolina has not been the protagonist in a historical romance.[25] Prominent American belletrist Susan Sontag came close in her unconventional novel *The Volcano Lover*, first published in 1992, which is set in Naples in the last two decades of the eighteenth century. Interspersed with reflections on revolutions and the discourse of women and power, Sontag depicts the love triangle of the British Ambassador to the Kingdom of Naples Sir William Hamilton, his celebrated wife of dubious background, Emma, and Lord Nelson, the British hero of the wars against Napoleon. Maria Carolina remains more in the background; she is portrayed not so much as a character, but in her role as the Queen. Sontag contrasts the evaluation of the power of the absolutist queen and of the low-born woman in the discourse of politics, revolutions, and the power of women in simple yet poignant terms:

> They were a family – a family doing wrong. And family was the model of rule, mostly misrule, that was being challenged by revolution. One consequence of the old model, in which eligibility for rulership was conferred by being born into a ruling family, was that women, a few women, had a visible and very real share in power. Occasionally monarchs themselves, often advisers to the monarch, who was a son, husband, brother – whatever the degree of their subjection, women cannot be entirely banished from family life. (The new model of rule, which revoked whatever legitimate claim women had to governance, was the assembly– composed only of men, since it derived its legitimacy from a hypothetical contract among equals. Women, defined as neither fully rational nor free, could not be a party to this contract.) (Sontag 299)

# IV.

Maria Carolina's nineteenth-century historian-advocate Helfert quoted her as writing to Theresia, one of her daughters, »je laisse mes justifications au temps et au ciel!« [I leave my justification to time and heaven!] (Helftert, *Königin Karolina* 83) How is Maria Carolina's struggle against Napoleon to be evaluated today? If the abolishment of Bourbon absolutist rule in Italy is considered a positive step towards Italian unification and national identity, how much more successful were Napoleon and his administrators in bringing progress to this country? Is gender a useful category for the case of a consort queen who is de facto ruling and striving to regain power, respectively?

Maria Carolina's evaluation of Napoleon has been confirmed by historical research, such as Jeremy Black's emphasis on Napoleon's personality, his strong will to dominate European international relations. As Black writes, Naples was one of the neutral powers that were »exploited and attacked by Napoleon« in »a politics of trickery and bullying« (Black 228). In 1803 it was occupied, just like Hanover, followed by the Hanseatic cities and much of the Papal States in 1806 and Rome in 1808.

Maria Carolina is a unique case in the range of female opponents to Napoleon presented in this book. She was one of few women with political power in late eighteenth-century Europe, although monarchs no longer had absolute power by her time. However, Maria Carolina thought in terms of absolutist monarchy and Habsburg *Hausmachtpolitik*. These were terms of the past, whereas the monarchical system under Napoleon I developed a new system of international relations and supported kindling an Italian national spirit in »his« kingdom of Italy.

While Maria Carolina did rule Naples de facto, she was not officially the ruling queen. She maintained harmony with her negligent husband, gave birth to a male heir and a herd of additional children (even during the years of crisis and the first exile) and was concerned about her children as her »dynastic capital« (Orr 5). By doing all this, she fulfilled her duties as absolutist queen consort. These duties were often contradictory to those of an effective sovereign. Maria Carolina could have been a better ruler had she lost her husband or disposed of him like Catherine the Great did. This is not an original thought; contemporaries such as Roger de Damas already commented that Maria Carolina depended on her husband's »intermittent credit« and »caprices« and struggled with juggling her many obligations and finding extra time for diplomacy (Acton 416, referring to memoirs by Roger de Damas). Would she have been a stronger opponent to Napoleon without a husband? It is impossible to say.

In memoirs and biographies Maria Carolina was much criticized for the emotional and personal component of her fight against Napoleon. Critics pointed out that she acted too much as a woman, not as a political leader. To name just one example, Napoleon biographer Englund writes that Marie Carolina was led by her feelings to »outright foolishness« and playing the »double game« of »formal relations with France while signing a secret alliance with Britain« (Englund 264). Historian Black corrects such prejudices: In the zeal with which she opposed the French, Maria Carolina was not unique. For example in the Tyrol, Portugal, Russia and Spain such opposition took »on the aspect of a crusade« (Black 248). Napoleon's foreign and military policies were driven by an – equally emotional – desire »to remold Europe, a cynical exploitation of allies, and a ruthless reliance on the politics of expropriation« (Black 220–21).

Maria Carolina was also not the only European monarch to make peace treaties with Napoleon and then break them. Her sentiment that Napoleon could not be trusted was not unique either; other rulers shared her attitude to his immoderate demands and his unwillingness to compromise (Black 223). Maria Carolina was often accused of being bloodthirsty and militaristic, of being responsible for Naples' prolonged involvement in the various wars and the economic suffering resulting from it. Again, her position was not exceptional among European monarchs who could not accept Napoleonic France as a hegemonic state and sought to bring it down, who saw war as »unavoidable and victory possible« (Black 222). Moreover, Maria Carolina was one of the minor opponents of Napoleon, but she was more prone to criticism because she was a woman.

Europe had a tradition of multipolarity, and in 1815 it returned to multiple kingship. Naples reemerged as a Kingdom ruled by the Bourbons. However, as in Germany and throughout Europe, French rule did assist the development of the Italian nation state. Napoleon's reorganization of the rest of Italy and resistance against French rule »provided momentum toward unification and stimulated national sentiment« (Grab 209).

When researching Maria Carolina, the category of gender appears most useful in investigating traditions of writing about her, how contemporary gender-biased criticism was carried over into biography and historiography – something this article has only begun to draw attention to. How Maria

Carolina was – and is – portrayed in historiography, biography, and fictional literature deserves further exploration.

–University of Iowa

## Notes

English translations of documents are my own unless printed translations or other sources are given.

1 The spellings »Marie Caroline« and »Marie-Caroline« are also common, especially in English and French scholarship. I will use original spellings of names in my article.

2 Tamassino ponders (note 28) that the saying may have been a clever invention of Castelot in his biography of Marie Louise's son Napoleon François Charles Joseph (Castelot 150).

3 Including for example the multi-volume French historical novel by Max Gallo, which has been translated into several languages and turned into a feature film and TV mini-series (Simoneau). Gallo appears to include women with strong political opinions only when they also show love-interests in Napoleon.

4 The only English-language biography – since Bearne and Jeaffreson around 1900 – appeared under the mysterious main title *In the Web of the Pink Spider* in 1967 (Bott).

5 Only a small part of Maria Carolina's correspondence has been published (Weil and Circello). She wrote in often shaky French, and nineteenth-century studies tended to smooth out the letters, or they provide inaccurate or no source information (Helfert, *Königin Karolina* and *Maria Karolina;* Acton). Johnston edited her memoirs from the autograph in the Biblioteca Nazionale in Naples (Johnston, *Mémoire*). In his study, *The Napoleonic Empire in Southern Italy*, he often refers to the memoirs as an important source – although »a jumble of fact, exaggeration, and fiction« (II: 146). Her diaries (Archivio Borbone, Archivio di Stato, Naples) were destroyed in 1945 (according to Tamussino 10).

6 Maria Carolina to Roger de Damas, May 8, 1810 (autograph copy in Archivio Borbone, Archivio di Stato Naples).

7 This paragraph after the anonymous entry, »Maria Carolina«, in the *Encyclopædia Britannica.*

8 Maria Carolina, who was at that time about to return to Naples from Sicily, instead traveled on to Vienna to present her daughters, who were of marriageable age, at the Imperial court. The British writer Cornelia Knight later journeyed with Maria Carolina; she reported the following defensive statement by the exiled queen: »They have represented me as cruel — after I had saved hundreds of ungrateful people! They have portrayed me as ambitious. Yes, so I am, if it is ambitious to defend the crown received from God. It is said that the reaction of 1799 was my doing. I deny this accusation; I disapprove of what happened then; in fact, I was not in Naples, I was in Vienna with my daughters at the time. Apart from which, if we had fallen into *their* hands, how would *they* have treated us?« (Quoted from Acton 612.)

9 Puccini's opera *Tosca* (based on the French play by Victorien Sardou of 1887) takes place against this historical background in Rome of 1800, although none of the main characters are historical ones. Napoleon and Maria Carolina (»the Queen«) are the only two historical references, and the queen's cruelty towards revolutionaries is hinted at.

10 For more details, see for example Moskal 164.

11 The letter to the King is a little shorter and does not contain this phrase; see Bonaparte, *Correspondance* VIII: 421, no. 6950.

12 Napoleon wrote to the King separately; this letter is a little shorter (Bonaparte. *Correspondance.* X: 102–03, no. 8254).

13 The sentence of the translation is quoted from Englund 264, and the rest of the translation is by Adrian Paredes-Velasco.

14 See the instructions by Napoleon to his brother Joseph in his letters (Bonaparte. *The Confidential Correspondence* 86).

15 See Helfert, *Maria Karolina* 243–4: »eine jener mit Berechnung herbeigeführten Scenen wobei es Napoleon darum zu thun war durch Einschüchterung der Andern seine Zwecke zu fördern. In seinem Innern unterschätzte er Karolinen keineswegs; sie war ihm eine *ebenbürtige* Gegnerin der er seine Achtung nicht versagen konnte.« [Emphasis by Helfert.]

16 The county Rietberg was among the many mediatized by Napoleon in 1806, and Dominik-Andreas of Kaunitz-Rietberg also lost his status as sovereign ruler. It became part of the kingdom of Westphalia which in December 1807 Napoleon gave to his brother Hieronymus (Jérôme).

17 Gregory 163 names examples.

18 For examples in his letters of March 6 and April 21, 1806 (see Bonaparte, *The Confidential Correspondence* 96 and 113).

19 See Helfert, *Königin Karolina* 484–5: Maria Carolina to Franz, letters of June 1, 10, 19, and 20, 1812.

20 Acton states: »The Queen dramatized herself when she picked up a pen. However ill or depressed she might be, this outlet seems to have given her relief.« (417)

21 Acton's translation of a passage from the long letter of October 15, 1797 leaves out a few sentences; see the original passage in the *Correspondance inédite* (with the omissions set in italics): »Il est l'Attila, le fléau de l'Italie, mais j'ai pour lui un sentiment de véritable estime et de profonde admiration. C'est le plus grand homme que des siècles aient produit. Sa force, son énergie, son ésprit de suite, son activité, son talent lui ont acquis mon admiration. Heureux le pays qui aurait un pareil souverain! Il n'aurait pas à craindre d'être vaincu ou conquis. Heureux le Prince qui aurait un tel ministre ou un tel général. *J'apprécie, j'estime, j'admire, je crains l'homme qu'on devrait imiter; mais pour cela il faudrait qu'on eût son talent, son caractère, sa volonté, son énergie, son génie. Je le préfère à Frédéric qui, à côté de ses talents, avait des petitesses et des ridicules. Chez celuici tout est grand.* Je l'admire et regrette seulement qu'il serve une si détestable cause. Je voudrais la chute de la République, mais la conservation de Buonaparte. Car c'est réellement un grand homme, *et quand on ne voit autour de soi et partout que des ministres et des souverains aux vues mesquines et étroites, on n'en éprouve que plus d'étonnement et de plairsir à voir s'élever et grandir un pareil homme, tout en déplorant de voir sa grandeur attachée à une si infernale cause. Cela vous paraîtra étrange.* Mais si je déteste ses opérations, je l'admire, lui. Je désire que ses projets avortent, que ses entreprises échouent et je souhaite en même temps bonheur et gloire à sa personne pourvu que ce

ne soit pas à nos dépens. *En un mot, je l'estime, je l'admire,* et je dis que s'il mourait, on devrait le réduire en poudre et en donner une dose à chaque souverain, deux à chacun de leurs ministres, et alors les choses iraient mieux.« (Weil and Circello I: 490, no. 248.)

22 Quoted from Tamussino 319; no source given.

23 Helfert, *Königin Karolina* 604 quotes a similar passage: »[...] elle ne parlai même de Napoléon qu'avec la noble franchise d'une ennemie, mais d'une ennemie qui ne fermait point ses yeux sur les grandes qualités de ce prince.« See also Méneval 144–5.

24 This is also pointed out by Sontag 302–3.

25 Alexandre Dumas père wrote a documented history of Naples, published in Italian, *I Borboni di Napoli* (1862–64). Only the first two volumes covering the years 1804 to 1815 have been found in French in Dumas's journal *Le Monte-Cristo* in 1863 (see Frank Wild Reed on the Alexandre Dumas père Web Site, <http://www.cadytech.com/dumas/work.php?key=660>, accessed April 6, 2005). Maria Carolina is, however, among the main characters in the historical novels *La San-Felice et Emma Lyonna* (1864/65), also by Dumas, and *Luigia Sanfelice* (1850) by Jeanne Marie von Gayette-Georgens; both take place in Naples in 1799 during the republic. Luisa Sanfelice (1764–1800), a Neapolitan aristocrat who discovered a pro-Bourbon plot and sided with the Republicans, was sentenced to death with the return of the Bourbons. The »actress« and mistress Emma Lyon, later Lady Hamilton, also lent herself more to »romantic« and fictionalized treatment than the Queen of Naples.

## Works Cited

Acton, Harold Mario. *The Bourbons of Naples, 1734-1825.* London: Methuen, 1956.

Asprey, Robert B. *The Rise of Napoleon Bonaparte.* New York: Basic Books, 2000.

Bearne, Catharine Mary Charlton. *A Sister of Marie Antionette: The Life-Story of of Maria Carolina, Queen of Naples.* London: T. F. Unwin, 1907.

Black, Jeremy. *European International Relations 1648–1815.* New York: Palgrave, 2002

Bonaparte, Napoléon. *Correspondance de Napoléon Ier.* 32 vols. Paris: Plon/Imprimerie Impériale, 1858–70.

Bonaparte, Napoleon [Napoleon I.]. *The Confidential Correspondence of Napoleon Bonaparte With his Brother Joseph, Sometime King of Spain.* Selected and translated [anonymously], with explanatory notes, from the Memoires du Roi Joseph. New York: D. Appleton, 1856.

Bonnefons, André. *Marie-Caroline, reine des Deux-Siciles: 1768–1814: Une ennemie de la Révolution et de Napoléon.* Paris: Perrin, 1905.

Bott, Ethlyn Wisegarver. *In the Web of the Pink Spider: The Story of Maria Caroline, Queen of the Two Sicilies.* New York: Pageant, 1967.

Castelot, Andrè. *Der Herzog von Reichstadt; Biographie.* Vienna: Neff, 1960.

Coletti, Alessandro. *La regina di Napoli.* Novara: Istituto geografico de Agostini, 1986.

Corti, Egon Caesar Conte. *Ich, eine Tochter Maria Theresias: Ein Lebensbild der Königin Marie Karoline von Neapel.* München: Bruckmann, 1950.

Englund, Steven. *Napoleon: A Political Biography*. New York: Scribner, 2004.

Gallo, Max. *Napoléon*. 4 vols. Paris: R. Laffont, 1997.

Gallo, Max. *Napoleon* [engl. translation]. 4 vols. London: Macmillan, 2004–05.

Gayette-Georgens, Jeanne Marie von (nee Johanna Sophie Marie Deinhard). *Luigia Sanfelice oder Die Revolution in Italien.* 3 vols. Leipzig: [s. n.], 1850.

Gorani, Giuseppe: Mémoires secrets et critiques des cours, des gouvernements, et des moeurs des principaux États de l'Italie. Paris, Lyon, and Marseille: Buisson / Allier et Leclerc / Mossy 1793.

Grab, Alexander. *Napoleon and the Transformation of Europe*. (European History in Perspective.) Houndmills, UK and New York: Palgrave Macmillan, 2003.

Gregory, Desmond. *Napoleon's Italy*. Madison: Fairleigh Dickinson University Press, 2001.

Helfert, Joseph Alexander. *Königin Karolina von Neapel und Sicilien im Kampfe gegen die französische Weltherrschaft, 1790–1814; mit Benützung von Schriftstücken des k.k. Haus-Hof- und Staats-Archives.* Wien: W. Braumüller, 1878.

Helfert, Joseph Alexander. *Maria Karolina von Oesterreich, Königin von Neapel und Sicilien: Anklagen und Vertheidigung mit Benützung von Schriftstücken des k. k. Haus-, Hof- und Staats-Archivs.* Wien: Faesn, 1884.

Iachello, Enrico. »Borbone e inglesi in Sicilia (1808–1815).« *I Borbone in Sicilia (1734–1860).* Ed. Provincia Regionale di Catania. Catania: Giuseppe Maimone, 1998. 190.

Imbruglia, Girolamo, »Introduction«. *Naples in the Eighteenth Century: The Birth and Death of a Nation State.* Ed. Girolamo Imbruglia. (Cambridge Studies in Italian History and Culture.) Cambridge and New York: Cambridge University Press, 2000. I–III.

Jeaffreson, John Cordy. *The Queen of Naples and Lord Nelson: An historical biography based on mss. in the British museum and on letters and other documents preserved amongst the Morrison mss.* London: Hurst and Blackett, 1889.

Johnston, R. M. [Robert Matteson] (ed.). *Mémoire de Marie Caroline Reine de Naples intitulé de la révolution du royaume de sicile [...] par un témoin oculaire.* (Harvard Historical Studies 16. Documentary Series 1.) Cambridge: Harvard University, London: Henry Frowde Oxford University Press, 1912.

Johnston, R. M. [Robert Matteson]. *The Napoleonic Empire in Southern Italy and the Rise of the Secret Societies.* 2 volumes. London and New York: Macmillan, 1904.

Lacour-Gayet, Michel. *Marie-Caroline, reine de Naples: 1752–1814: une adversaire de Napoléon.* [Reprint of original edition 1835.] Préface de Jean Tulard. Paris: Tallandier, 1990.

Landes, Joan B.. *Women and the Public Sphere in the Age of the French Revolution.* Ithaca: Cornell University Press, 1988.

»Maria Carolina«. *Encyclopædia Britannica.* 2004. Encyclopædia Britannica Online. 14 June 2004 http://www.search.eb.com/eb/article?eu=52132.

Martin, Andrew. *Napoleon the Novelist.* Cambridge: Polity Press, 2000.

Méneval, Claude François de. *Napoléon et Marie-Louise: Souvenirs historiques de M. le baron Méneval.* Paris: Amyot, 1843–45, vol. II.

Moskal, Jeanne. »Napoleon, Nationalism, and the Politics of Religion in Mariana Starke's *Letters from Italy*«. *Rebellious Hearts: British Women Writers and the French Revolution.* Edited Adriana Craziun and Kari E. Lokke. Albany: State University of New York, 2001. 161-91.

Orr, Clarissa Campbell. »Introduction«. *Queenship in Europe 1660–1815: The Role of the Consort.* Edited Clarissa Campbell Orr. Cambridge and New York: Cambridge University Press, 2004. 1–15.

Palumbo, A. *Maria Carolina, Regina delle Due Sicilie.* 8 vols. Napoli, 1877

Rao, Anna Maria, »The Feudal Question, Judicial Systems and the Enlightenment«. *Naples in the Eighteenth Century: The Birth and Death of a Nation State.* Ed. Girolamo Imbruglia. Cambridge, U.K., and New York, NY: Cambridge University Press, 2000. 95–117.

Schom, Alan. *Napoleon Bonaparte.* New York: Harper Collins, 1997.

Simoneau, Yves (dir.). *Napoleon* [videorecording]; screenplay by Didier Decoin; producers Jean-Pierre Guerin and Gérard Depardieu. 3 DVDs 480 min.) A&E Home Video, 2003 [originally produced for television 2002].

Sontag, Susan. *The Volcano Lover: A Romance.* New York: Farrar, Straus and Giroux, 1992

Tamussino, Ursula. *Des Teufels Großmutter. Eine Biographie der Königin Maria Carolina von Neapel-Sizilien.* Wien: Deuticke, 1991.

Ulloa, Pietro Calà. *Marie Caroline d'Autriche et la conquête du royaume de Naples en 1806.* Paris, 1872.

Weil, M.-H., and C. di Somma Circello (ed.). *Correspondance inedite de Marie-Caroline reine de Naples et de Sicile avec le Marquis de Gallo.* 2 vols. Paris: Émile-Paul, 1911.

# Marseilles to Stockholm – Bonaparte to Bernadotte: The unique life of Désirée Clary

*Dorothy Potter*

Even in the cycle of revolutions, empires, and restorations that marked the late eighteenth and early nineteenth centuries, Désirée Clary's life was remarkable. A Marseilles silk merchant's daughter, she became the wife of a Marshal of France, and in time Queen of Sweden and Norway. Cofounder of the Bernadotte dynasty which still reigns in Sweden she had also been Napoleon Bonaparte's fiancee. Most of the non-academic and non-Swedish world discovered her through Annemarie Selinko's best-selling novel *Désirée.* Published in German in 1953, it was eventually translated into more than twenty languages. Through the fictional device of Désirée's diary, Selinko interpreted many significant events from the end of French Revolution through the First Empire, and concluded with Désirée's 1829 coronation in Stockholm. The novel's popularity led to a 1954 film starring Jean Simmons, Marlon Brando (as Napoleon), and Michael Rennie as Jean Baptiste Bernadotte.

To analyze Désirée and her complex relationship with Napoleon as portrayed in this work, one must know something of the principal individuals and also the author herself. As we shall see, Selinko's own life was as dramatic as any novel, and her experiences during and after World War II influenced how she viewed the Bernadottes, Napoleon, and the nature of imperialistic tyranny.

Bernadine Eugénie Désirée Clary was born on 7 November 1777 in Marseilles, France, the youngest of thirteen children, ten of whom lived to adulthood.[1] Her father, silk merchant François Clary, married twice; Désirée's two half-sisters were adults when she was born. Her half-brother Etienne followed in his father's business. In 1759 François Clary married his second wife, Françoise Rose Somis. Two sons Nicholas and Justinien and five daughters Rose, Lucie, Honorine, Julie, and Désirée came from this union. Only the second Madame Clary, Etienne and his wife, Julie, Désirée, and their progeny are included in the novel. Madame Clary and her daughter-in-law have little character development, but Etienne plays a small but crucial role in the book's early pages. Julie is an essential character in *Désirée*. Interestingly, François Clary, deceased before the novel begins, remains a vital presence throughout; it was he who gave Désirée the diary, and imbued her with republican sentiments (Selinko, 3, 9-10; Bearne, 4-6). For the Clarys – in life or fiction – 1793-1794 was a dangerous time. Prior to the Revolution either François or Etienne had applied for *lettres de noblesse*. Though the request was denied, it became known to revolutionaries in Marseilles. Etienne was arrested on 17 September 1793. As Queen Désirée later recounted events to her court chamberlain Baron Hochschild, Etienne's wife Marcelle (»Suzanne« in the novel) learned a government official was visiting Marseilles. Marcelle asked Désirée to accompany her to the *Maison Commune* to ask for Etienne's freedom. (Bearne, 12-14, 19; Girod de L'Ain, 29-32; Selinko, 3-4, 18-23).

While Désirée dozed in a waiting room, Marcelle obtained Etienne's release and went to the prison with the necessary papers. Désirée awoke as an assistant was closing the office; he offered to escort her home, since it was dark. This man Joseph Bonaparte was the eldest son in a large family of Corsican refugees. While Joseph's connections with the Jacobins afforded the Clarys some protection, their troubles increased. Justinien Clary committed suicide in November, and François died on 20 January 1794 (Hochschild, 12-15).

Within months Joseph introduced his younger brother Napoleon to the Clarys. Though only twenty-five, Napoleon had been promoted to brigadier general after the siege of Toulon (1793), and had many ambitious plans. Initially Joseph considered marrying Désirée, but as she later recalled, Napoleon had other ideas:

»Dans un on ménage, il faut que l'un des deux cède à l'autre. Toi, Joseph, tu es d'un caractère indécis, et il en est de même de Désirée, tandis que Julie et moi nous savons ce que nous voulons. Tu feras donc mieux d'épouser Julie. Quant à Désirée, aujouta-t-il en me prenant sur ses genoux, elle sera ma femme. C'est ainsi que je devins la fiancée de Napoléon.« (Hochschild, quoted in Girod de L'Ain, 37)

[In a well-run household, one of the two yields to the other. You, Joseph, are of an undecided type, and it is the same for Désirée, whereas Julie and I know what we want. You would do better to marry Julie. As to Désirée, taking me on his knees, she shall be my wife. Thus I became Napoleon's fiancee].

Julie Clary married Joseph Bonaparte on 1 August 1794, and Désirée and Napoleon became engaged. Both were young and romantic; around 1795-1796 (the exact date is uncertain) Napoleon penned »Clisson et Eugénie,« a tragic romance influenced by Johann Wolfgang von Goethe's *Die Leiden des jungen Werthers* [*The Tribulations of Young Werther*] (1774). Admired throughout Europe, *Werther* was imitated by many lesser literary talents, including Bonaparte.[2] It is worth noting that after Napoleon left for Paris in April 1795, he complained in letters to Joseph that his fiancee did not often write. In 1796 Joseph was sent by the Directory to Genoa, taking with him Julie, Désirée, Nicholas, and Madame Clary (Girod de L'Ain, 61-74).

Napoleon's 1795 suppression of a potential coup against the Directory had given the young general new status in the eyes of those in power, and entree to the Paris salons. For the first time he met women of the world, sophisticated survivors of the guillotine completely unlike his provincial sweetheart. Among them was Josephine de Beauharnais, a widow six years older with two children. Napoleon quickly fell in love. He and Josephine were married on 9 March 1796, and after a brief honeymoon he left to command the Army of Italy.

According to various biographers, Désirée learned of her fiance's change of heart before the wedding but refused to believe it. Napoleon had written Joseph in September asking him and Julie to break the news to Désirée. She responded with a passionate letter that her heart was broken, and she wished to die. The Bonaparte women supported Désirée; neither his mother nor sisters made any pretense of liking Josephine (Dewes, 57, 59-60).

Concern Napoleon evidently felt over the broken engagement led him to send a subordinate General Léonard Duphot to Rome (where Joseph was transferred in August 1797) to seek Désirée's hand. She told Baron Hochschild while this was a goal of Napoleon and Joseph, she would not have married Duphot, who was killed on 27 December during anti-French riots in Rome. The mortally-wounded Duphot was brought to the embassy, a tragic scene that the Queen of Sweden said she never forgot, and which Selinko includes in the novel (Hochschild, 31-38; Selinko, 98-110).

In the spring of 1798 Madame Clary and Nicholas returned to Genoa, while Joseph, Julie and Désirée moved to Paris. Again one of Napoleon's friends, General Androche Junot, proposed to her, but she declined his offer (Hochschild, 39-40). By now she surely resented her former fiance's rather obvious matchmaking. The new man in her life – Jean Baptiste Bernadotte – appeared with no prompting from Napoleon.

Accounts agree that Bernadotte met Désirée at Joseph and Julie's Paris house and that their courtship was brief. Nor was this surprising; by 1798 Désirée had seen something of the world, experienced passion, disillusionment, and the violent death of a prospective suitor. Surrounded by Bonapartes, she probably wished to be mistress of her own house. While Bernadotte was friendly with Joseph and Lucien Bonaparte, he had no attachments to Napoleon.

Born in Pau in Gascony, on 26 January 1763, Jean Baptiste Bernadotte was the second son of attorney Henri Bernadotte and his wife Jeanne. His father died when Jean Baptiste was seventeen; joining the Royal-la-Marine infantry regiment in 1780, he spent eighteen months in Corsica, which had become a French possession in 1769. Bernadotte apparently did not meet Carlo or Letitia Bonaparte or any of their four children still on the island. (The two elder sons Joseph and Napoleon were in school in France) (Palmer, 6-8)

Returning to France in 1784, Bernadotte rose through the ranks to Sergeant and in the summer of 1789 was posted to Marseilles. Discontent filled France's third largest city; there were bread riots and talk about what the Estates General – called by Louis XVI after a 175-year hiatus – was accomplishing at Versailles. Prominent citizens asked the Royal-la-Marine commander the Marquis d'Ambert to maintain order. Years later, Désirée recalled:

»Un jour, un militaire se présenta chez nous, muni d'un billet de logement. Mon père, qui n'avait nullement envie de voir la tranquillité de sa maison troublée par le tapage que faisaient ordinairement les soldats, le mit amicalement à la porte avec une lettre pour son colonel, dans laquelle il priait celui-ce de lui envoyer plutôt un officier. Le militaire renvoyé était le fourrier Bernadotte qui devait plus tard m'épouser et devenir roi.« (Hochschild, quoted in Girod de L'Ain, 22)

[One day a soldier presented himself at our house, provided with a billet for lodgings. My father, who had no desire to see the tranquility of his house disturbed by the noise usually made by soldiers, politely sent him back with a letter for his colonel, in which he asked to rather be sent an officer. The soldier whom he sent back was the quartermaster-sergeant Bernadotte, who would later marry me and become king].

Bernadotte steadily advanced in rank, becoming *général de division* by October 1794 at age thirty-one. In 1795 he served in Germany; early in 1797 his division was sent to Italy to reinforce Napoleon's army. Having served under Bonaparte for two months, he was sent to Paris with captured Austrian flags and a letter for the Directory commending his efforts. These honors could have been a way to detach Bernadotte from his own men and potentially tie him to Napoleon's rising star (Palmer, 40-43, 50-51).

In January 1798 Bernadotte was appointed ambassador to Vienna but enjoyed a mixed reception in the homeland of Marie Antoinette. When he unwisely displayed the revolutionary tricolor, a mob sacked his house on 13 April; shortly thereafter he left Vienna, having been in residence only sixty-six days. By May he was in Paris where he met Désirée. They married on 17 August; she soon became pregnant and on 4 July 1799 gave birth to their only child, François Joseph Oscar. Napoleon in Egypt sent congratulations. The name Oscar was unusual; at St. Helena Napoleon said it was his choice, taken from the fashionable epic *Ossian*. Joseph also claimed to have suggested the name, but Désirée may have read *Ossian* and chosen it herself (Palmer, 66-69, 78-79; Selinko, 130, 139, 162-169).

Bernadotte was briefly Minister of War, but during a renewal of hostilities with France's neighbors, his political ambitions alarmed some Directors, and he was removed in September 1799. Napoleon's unexpected return from Egypt without his army the following month prompted Bernadotte to suggest he be arrested for desertion. Still Napoleon asked Jean Baptiste to support his coup d'etat of 18-19 *Brumaire* (8-9 November); Bernadotte declined but did not interfere. However he felt insecure enough to briefly go into hiding. Désirée supposedly accompanied him disguised as a boy, an episode not included by Selinko (Liverpool, 77-78).

The two men were reconciled by January 1800, when Bernadotte was appointed to the Consular Council of State and given command of the Army of the West in expectation of action against Britain. The Peace of Amiens in March 1802 ended that command. Several plots against Napoleon occurred during this time, and though Bernadotte's knowledge of them was never proved, the First Consul was anxious to be rid of him. Jean Baptiste accepted the ambassadorship to the United States but as he and Désirée awaited passage, word came of the sale of Louisiana to the Americans. Feeling his prestige undercut, Bernadotte resigned. Despite this, with the creation of the Napoleonic empire in May 1804, he was appointed a Marshal of France, seventh on the list of eighteen original Marshals (Chandler, 26-27).

From May 1804 to August 1805 Bernadotte was governor of occupied Hanover, where all accounts agree that he managed affairs well. He was at Austerlitz (2 December 1805) and in 1806 was given the title of Prince of Ponte-Corvo, formerly a Papal state. Désirée was relieved that she would remain in France, nor did Bernadotte ever visit his little kingdom (Palmer, 130-131).

In 1806, during France's war with Prussia and Russia, Bernadotte distinguished himself at Lübeck. There he accepted the surrender of a Swedish division; his courtesy to the officers played a part in events four years later. In January 1807 he was wounded in the neck at the battle of Spanden bridge, and Désirée journeyed to East Prussia to nurse him. This was fairly atypical for a marshal's wife, but not as unique as Selinko implies (Selinko, 282-289). Bernadotte was governor of Hamburg, Lübeck, and Bremen until war broke out with Austria in the spring of 1809. At the hard-fought battle of Wagram (5 July 1809) his Saxon corps was twice driven back; Bernadotte protested that Chief of Staff Alexandre Berthier had been undermining his efforts. Napoleon supported Berthier, and angry words were exchanged. Bernadotte resigned and returned home in disgrace. At this point as Fortune seemed to abandon him, a series of events changed Jean Baptiste's and Désirée's lives forever.

In March 1809 Sweden's ineffectual king Gustav IV Adolf was overthrown in a bloodless coup that installed his sixty-one year-old uncle on the throne. Charles XIII was elderly, simple-minded, and childless; thus an heir was essential. Complications ensued in May 1810 when the choice of the Royal Council, Charles XIII's cousin Christian August of Schleswig-Holstein, died unexpectedly. The King of Denmark and the brother-in-law of Tsar Alexander I were proposed but rejected. A pro-French group of Swedish officers then suggested a member of the Bonaparte family or even a Marshal. This idea surprised Napoleon, who had advocated the Danish candidate.[3]

Napoleon's stepson Eugène de Beauharnais was the pro-French faction's first choice, but he was unwilling to become Protestant. Of the Marshals, Bernadotte had several advantages: his former acquaintance with some Swedish officers, his experience as an administrator, his willingness to become a Lutheran, and his perceived closeness to the Bonapartes through marriage. No one in 1810 could have predicted that Napoleon's empire would implode within five years. It is also unlikely that the Swedish delegation knew of Bernadotte and Bonaparte's mutual antipathy.

Initially Napoleon had reservations about giving Bernadotte permission to resign from the army and leave France. However, despite Jean Baptiste's lack of a firm commitment, the Emperor assumed the former Marshal would support the Continental System. In August 1810 the Swedish Diet chose Bernadotte as Prince Royal. Taking the name Charles John, he left France on 30 September and arrived in Sweden on 20 October (Selinko, 335-341, 352-360). Princess Désirée and Oscar remained with Julie at Joseph's country estate. Other than regrets that the entire family had not arrived, relations between Charles XIII and Queen Hedvig Charlotte and their adoptive heir went well.

Désirée and eleven-year-old Oscar arrived in Stockholm on 6 January 1811. Some historians have speculated that Napoleon hoped to keep watch on Bernadotte via Désirée's letters to Julie and Nicholas. If so that plan was short-lived. Suffering from the cold, homesick for her family and her faith (she remained a Catholic), disliking court etiquette, and intimidated by the elderly royal family that had adopted her husband, the princess royal was miserable (Selinko, 378-381, 384-392). Oscar acquitted himself admirably, but Désirée did not impress her inlaws; Queen Hedvig Charlotte observed:

»La princesse est petite, nullement jolie, sans ancune tournure. Sa timidité la rend impolie. Elle est d'humeur inégale et ne se donne nulle peine pour être agréable. En somme, enfant gâteé mais douce, bonne, compatissante [...]« (Girod de L'Ain, 202)

[The princess is petite, not pretty, without any figure. Her timidity makes her impolite. She has an uneven temper and takes no pains to be agreeable. In sum, a spoiled child, but sweet, good, and compassionate [...]]

It must be remembered that while Charles John was forty-eight, Désirée was in her early thirties. In their correspondence, he sometimes resembled a schoolmaster or a father, encouraging her to conquer her shyness and pursue intellectual matters in which she had little interest. This paternalism must have carried over into their life together (Bearne 109-113). The fact that Désirée did not seem strong-willed made her departure from Sweden even more remarkable.

Convincing her husband that the climate had undermined her health and that she needed a rest-cure in France, Désirée took the title Countess of Gothland and left for the waters at Plombières on 4 June, accompanied by her companion Élise de Flotte (a minor character in the novel). Julie was Queen of Spain and lived in France – why should the Princess Royal of Sweden be different? Even separation from her son did not deter her; Oscar, now Duke of Södermanland, was Sweden's child. Julie joined her at Plombières until autumn; then insisting that she was too unwell to attempt a cold journey across Germany and a sea crossing, Princess Désirée returned to her Paris house in the Rue d'Anjou (Girod de L'Ain, 208-210. Palmer, 183-184. Selinko, 405-406).

Both of the men who were such vital forces in her life were discomforted by her choices. For Charles John his wife's absence was an embarrassment that continued more than a decade – she did not return to Sweden until 1823. For Napoleon any influence his former sweetheart might have had on the man he reluctantly respected but distrusted was now moot. Conservative in matters of male authority, Napoleon disapproved of Désirée leaving her husband; nor had she asked permission as a foreign royal to enter France. In response, Désirée wrote a letter on 6 September 1811, pleading ill-health. She took care to maintain a minimal household with only her companion, a majordomo, and a few servants. Important men like Talleyrand and Fouché were invited to her entertainments, but everything was done discreetly (Girod de L'Ain, 208-210. Hochschild, 63-64. Selinko, 417-422).

Sweden's disengagement from Napoleon's economic policies had led to the occupation of Swedish Pomerania in 1811. Even before France's invasion of Russia in 1812, the Swedes had come to terms with their powerful neighbor through a series of treaties that guaranteed their respective borders and opened Swedish ports to all nations, in defiance of the Continental System. By 1813 Sweden and Britain were allies, and Charles John commanded the Army of the North against France. He was present (though late) at the »Battle of the Nations« at Leipzig (16-18 October 1813), that spelled the beginning of the end for Napoleon's regime.

After crossing the Rhine into French territory on 10 February, Charles John issued a proclamation at Cologne, in an effort to justify himself to his former compatriots. Neither the French, nor the Prussian, Russian, and Austrian victors were impressed by this high-flown directive. Any tentative aspirations Bernadotte might have had about replacing Napoleon as a constitutional king of France did not materialize.[4] Arriving after the Russians and Prussians marched through Paris, Charles John spent less than a month with Désirée and then returned home. To be viewed as an ex-Marshal of France by many of his former countrymen, rather than Crown Prince of Sweden, was not comfortable. Désirée remained in Paris; with the collapse of the Bonaparte kingdoms, Julie and her family were her first concerns (Girod de L'Ain, 236-237, 247, 252-256. Selinko, 496-505).

Norway, long controlled by Denmark, had supported France. As a reward for Bernadotte's services in defeating Napoleon, the Allies in the treaty of Kiel (14 January 1814) gave their blessing to the acquisition of Norway by Sweden in exchange for Russia controlling Finland. The Norwegians who were not consulted in these reworkings of the map drew up a constitution on 17 May 1814 which made the *storting*, or National Assembly their chief instrument of government. Charles John briefly invaded Norway but preferred to negotiate. The solution was for Norway to be a free nation, with the Swedish king as its sovereign. Charles John became Charles XIV John, King of Sweden and Norway on 7 February 1818. Still citing delicate health, Désirée did not return for either his coronation in Stockholm on 11 May 1818 or in Norway on 7 September at Trondheim. Queen Dowager Hedvig Charlotte died on 20 June, but Queen Désirée chose to take the waters at Aachen (Palmer, 227-228).

Although he never mastered Swedish, Carl XIV John became a successful, well-respected monarch. Still so prolonged a separation led to rumors; Désirée was at one point romantically linked to Armand, Duke de Richelieu, Louis XVIII's chief minister. Bernadotte at various times was reputed to have had affairs with Jeanne-Françoise Récamier, Germaine de Staël, Mariana Koskull (a lady-in-waiting to Queen Hedvig) and a few other court ladies. Oscar was still a bachelor and had a mistress. It was necessary to secure the Bernadotte dynasty (Palmer, 231-232. Selinko, 453, 548-553).

Both Désirée and Carl John were interested in Josephine, daughter of Prince Eugène de Beauharnais, Napoleon's stepson who had married Augusta, daughter of Maximilian Joseph, King of Bavaria. Initially Oscar was not enthusiastic about a wife chosen for him; moreover Josephine was not yet sixteen and a Catholic. He agreed to go on a Grand Tour of Italy, the Netherlands, and various German states where he would see a number of potential brides. After eleven years of separation Oscar and Désirée met at Aachen in June 1822, a reunion touchingly recreated in the novel. They then visited relatives and friends, including Julie in Brussels, and Josephine and her parents at Eichstatt (Girod de L'Ain, 290-294. Selinko, 546-554).

In May 1823 Josephine accompanied by Désirée sailed for Sweden, and on 19 June she and Oscar were married. Désirée planned to go back to Paris, but Charles John persuaded her to remain with him. Having lived apart, both had their own routines, and as her Court Chamberlain noted, the Queen missed her friends and her Paris house. The births of four grandsons and a granddaughter helped fill her time. Having agreed to remain in Sweden, Désirée asked to be crowned. On 21 August 1829, the nineteenth anniversary of her husband's election as heir to the throne, she was proclaimed »Queen

Desideria of the Swedes, Goths, and Vandals« in an elaborate ceremony. On this high point the novel ends.[5]

Carl John died on 8 March 1844, after suffering a debilitating stroke on his eighty-first birthday. What probably distressed Désirée more was the untimely death of Oscar I in 1859 after a lingering illness. She did not long survive him, dying quietly on 17 December 1860. She had lived thirty-seven years in Sweden, but those decades in a country whose language she never mastered and whose climate she found trying, were pale reflections of her days in France. As her Chamberlain Hochschild noted, »The early part of the life of Queen Désirée is full of interest; the last is barren of it [...]« (Hochschild, 77). Thus Annemarie Selinko was wise to end her novel with Désirée's coronation, and her symbolic transformation to Queen Desideria, the »desired one.«

Events in Ms Selinko's youth mirrored the trauma of those who managed to survive the French Revolution and experienced the war-weariness of Napoleonic Europe. Born in Vienna, Austria in 1914 shortly after the commencement of World War I, she became a journalist and began writing in the late 1930s. *Désirée* was her fourth and most popular novel. In 1938 Selinko married a Danish diplomat and later joined the Danish resistance. She and her husband Erling Kristiansen escaped Nazi-occupied Denmark to Sweden in 1943; her sister Liselotte, to whom *Désirée* is dedicated, died in a concentration camp.

In Sweden Ms Selinko worked with Red Cross relief headed by Count Folke Bernadotte. The second son of King Oscar II's second son, Count Bernadotte arranged exchanges of disabled prisoners of war, and aided survivors of the Nazi concentration camps. In May 1948 under the auspices of the United Nations, he traveled to Palestine to attempt to arrange a truce between Arabs and Jews but in September was assassinated by Zionist extremists (Palmer, 255).

Ms Selinko's association with Count Bernadotte sparked her interest in his family and particularly in Désirée, a non-royal whose life was interwoven with an emperor and a king. However, her admiration for Count Bernadotte led to the weakest part of the narrative, for his ancestor is depicted as a nearly flawless character. Whether general, marshal, or king, Bernadotte is constantly engaged in self-improvement, inevitably makes the correct moral choices, and says all the right things.

While Selinko avoids the crudely obvious comparison of Napoleon to Hitler, the corroding effects of unlimited power and the triumph of human freedom – exemplified in the »Declaration of the Rights of Man« – are themes that resonate throughout her narrative. She is too skillful an author to couch her story in simplistic terms of evil versus good, but readers experience through Désirée's diary Napoleon's gradual corruption by ambition and essentially limitless power. Faced with similar lures of domination and prestige, Bernadotte resists temptation.

In the early twentieth-first century we may miss the subtle thrust of Selinko's comparisons of a nineteenth-century tyrant to a twentieth century monster and madman. But for those in their teens or older in 1953, the themes of invading armies, small countries overrun, and a dictator out of touch with reality were unpleasantly familiar, especially for her European audience.

Many of the novel's specifics are confirmed by accounts of the historical Désirée. The most obvious fiction is the diary itself; while Désirée recounted some of her experiences to others, she did not apparently keep a systematic record of her life. Relevant details may be found in her letters, acquaintances' reminiscences, and anecdotes after she became queen. Some Selinko employed, others she ignored; this was a work of fiction, not a scholarly biography.

Apart from the diary, Selinko's major invention is Désirée's secret visit to Paris, where she dramatically confronts Napoleon and Josephine as their engagement is being announced. She then flees the salon and attempts suicide in the Seine, only to be saved by Bernadotte. A rescue from a watery death creates a more dramatic story line than being introduced to one of your brother-in-law's friends. It also initiates the comparisons and contrasts of Napoleon to Jean Baptiste. Napoleon's abandonment of Désirée is a sign of his growing callousness to human feelings as he pursues his ambition. Bernadotte's instinctive sympathy for a girl whose name he does not even know leads him to observe her flight from the engagement party, and shortly thereafter save her life. While Désirée refuses to divulge her identity to her rescuer and returns to Marseilles, the two recognize each other immediately, when they are later introduced by Joseph (Selinko, 79-95, 130-133).

In fact, as in fiction, Désirée experienced conflicted feelings for the two men she had loved, and although Napoleon chose another wife, he continued to have feelings for his former sweetheart. He singled her out for special attentions, including a priceless sable coat, one of three given him by the Czar. The first he kept for himself, the second went to his favorite sister Pauline, and the third was given to Désirée. In the novel, Sweden's chilly climate provides the excuse for his gift, as Princess Désirée is leaving France (Barton, 215; Selinko, 365-366).

Though Bernadotte during most of his tenure in the French army was under Napoleon's command, Désirée's choice as a husband became her supreme act of defiance. As she explained to Baron Hochschild, »I consented to marry him when I was told that he was man enough to withstand Napoleon.« (Hochschild, 41). When Jean Baptiste is chosen heir to the throne of Sweden, initially Désirée leaves all that is dear and familiar and reluctantly travels to a strange country where she does not conform to the conventions of royalty.

Females – usually wives – found unsuitable for various reasons have been part of historic subtexts for centuries; generally they adapt, become essentially invisible, or are replaced by a mistress. Some, like Catherine of Aragon and Josephine, are divorced. In fact and in fiction, Désirée committed a radical act for the most conventional of reasons: she left Sweden and returned home for her health and to be with her sister. Such basic motivations appear throughout the novel. Désirée uses illnesses to avoid the showy Court functions Napoleon required his subordinates and their wives to attend. While not a prisoner in a physical sense after returning to Paris in 1811, her tenuous position – when Sweden joins the coalition against France – and her verbal sparring with Napoleon are powerfully depicted.

A confirmed Jacobin, Bernadotte's rivalry with Napoleon began as early as 1799; both played a major role in the evolution of republican France. The question of his skills as a commander can be left to military historians. It is certainly true that along with his extraordinary good fortune, Bernadotte was a self-made man. However Selinko came close to undermining the counterpoint of Bernadotte versus Bonaparte by portraying him as a nearly flawless hero. She does not make the same error with Désirée. Désirée make mistakes and is not infallible. Thanks to the interruption of her convent education by the Revolution, she appears ignorant of geography, and is relatively uninterested in self-improvement (Selinko, 257-258, 263, 291, 348-351).

Unlike Napoleon and Bernadotte, the Désirée of the novel remains committed to the ideals of the Republic, symbolized by a broadside of the Rights of Man given her by her father. In fiction as in fact she was a reluctant royal, without power yet willing to defy Napoleon and allow her house to become a discreet center of opposition. Unlike Prussia's Queen Luise, Désirée Clary did not become a legend or a martyr – the novel ends with her reunion with her husband and son and acceptance of her role as Queen of Sweden.

–Lynchburg College, Lynchburg, VA

## Notes

1 Most historians rely on the reminiscences of Queen Désirée's court chamberlain Baron Hochschild, who gave her birth date as 8 November 1781; however Gabriel Girod de L'Ain thinks this an error and makes a good case for the earlier date. Girod de L'Ain, 21-22.

2 In appendix III, 401-408, Girod de L'Ain reprints what survives of the manuscript, with notes by various authors.

3 For the complex situation regarding the succession, see Palmer, 164-172.

4 After the Russians entered Paris in March 1814, Tsar Alexander broached the subject of Bernadotte as constitutional monarch of France to Talleyrand, at whose home he was staying. Ever the witty survivor Talleyrand who had served France in various capacities since Louis XVI responded: »Why choose a soldier when you have just discarded the greatest of them all?« Palmer, 212.

5 Hochschild, 73-77. An account of the coronation in the Moniteur universel [8 September 1829] is quoted by Girod de L'Ain, 321-322. Selinko, 555-557, 570-575.

## Works Cited

Barton, Sir Dunbar Plunket. *Bernadotte and Napoleon: 1763–1810*. London: John Murray, 1921.

Barton, Sir Dunbar Plunket. *Bernadotte: Prince and King: 1810–1844*. London: John Murray, 1925.

Bearne, Catherine. *A Queen of Napoleon's Court. The Life-Story of Désirée Bernadotte*. London: T. Fisher Unwin, 1905.

Chandler, David G., ed. *Napoleon's Marshals*. New York: MacMillan, 1987.

Dewes, Simon. *Sergeant Belle-Jambe*. London: Rich & Cowan, 1943.

Girod de L'Ain, Gabriel. *Désirée Clary*. Paris: Librairie Hachette, 1959.

Hochschild, K. F. L. Baron. *Désirée Queen of Sweden and Norway*. Trans. Mrs. M. Carey. New York: Dodd, Mead & Company, 1890.

Liverpool, Lord Russell of. *Bernadotte: Marshal of France & King of Sweden*. London: Butler & Tanner, 1981.

Palmer, Alan. *Bernadotte: Napoleon's Marshal, Sweden's King.* London: John Murray, 1990.

Selinko, Annemarie. *Désirée.* London: Heinemann, 1953 [paperback, London: Phoenix Press, 2002].

Koster, Henry (dir.) *Désirée* (USA, 1954). Videorecording VHS 20th-Century Fox 1998. Starring Jean Simmons, Marlon Brando [as Napoleon], Michael Rennie [Bernadotte], and Merle Oberon [as Josephine]. Writing credits Daniel Taradash after the novel by A. Selinko.

# Anti-war, Anti-Napoleon: Guardians of Material and Spiritual Welfare

# French Women Respond to Napoleon

*Denise Z. Davidson*

During and immediately after the French Revolution, women in France became associated with the counter-revolution. Their assumed attachment to the Catholic Church and their king made them seem more likely to fight against the Revolution than for it. And women did indeed fight alongside men in the uprisings of the Vendée in western France, and in other regions where resistance to the Revolution was widespread. Once Napoleon took power, and especially after the 1801 Concordat with the Pope, which ended much of the religious strife that had resulted from the de-Christianization efforts of the Revolutionaries, these uprisings calmed. External warfare replaced civil war, and internal disputes calmed, if only because Napoleon was so successful at building an administrative and policing system that left little space for dissent – for men or for women.

Historians have examined how Napoleon and his regime viewed women, particularly through analysis of the Civil Code and other legal and literary expressions of women's prescribed roles. These studies imply that Napoleon's efforts to limit women's involvement and influence in politics and the »public sphere« succeeded in their goals.[1] However, because they focus on legal discourse and literary representations, these studies do not give an indication of how women responded to arguments that they should not »meddle« in public affairs. More work needs to be done exploring how »ordinary« French women viewed the Napoleonic state, how their activities brought them into contact with the state, and how, despite all the legal and rhetorical efforts to separate them from the »public« and from politics, French women could indeed play roles within the state during the Napoleonic period. By »ordinary«, I mean women who were not well known during their lifetimes, as opposed to the women who participated in the Napoleonic Court and literary women whose musings on Napoleon and his empire have been discussed by scholars in various disciplines.[2] Here I focus on negative (or only weakly positive) reactions to Napoleon and his policies by such »ordinary« women, but that is not to say that all women rejected Napoleon's Empire. Small numbers of women were convinced Bonapartists willing to take risks by shouting Napoleonic slogans in public or hiding Napoleonic souvenirs in their homes once the Bourbons returned to the throne, for example.[3] However, most French women and men were probably ambivalent to the regime, as was the case with one of the three women I examine here. It appears that the vast majority of the French population loved Napoleon when his armies were successful and when peace and prosperity reigned at home; when that was no longer the case, they were quick to realign their allegiances.[4]

This essay makes use of letters and memoirs by three women holding different political perspectives and representing diverse social groups to reflect on their responses to Napoleon and his regime. First is Julie Pellizzone (1768–1837), an upper-class woman from Marseille whose unhappy marriage to an Italian aristocrat left her largely on her own during the First Empire and Restoration. She circulated among artistic and literary types (her father was an artist), and was a convinced monarchist. Her recently published journals, written between 1811 and 1824 but going back in time as far as 1787, include lengthy tirades against Napoleon, as well as accounts of the anti-Napoleon sentiment she observed among the inhabitants of Marseilles. The second woman's reflections contrast sharply with the first. Catherine Arnaud-Tizon (c. 1764-c. 1830) was a bourgeois matriarch in Rouen who oversaw a large family and assisted in the family's business, a textile factory. A collection of over 300 letters she wrote to her daughter and son-in-law in Paris between 1805 and 1816 includes a great deal of information on bourgeois life under Napoleon as well as this woman's reflections on the war and the economic effects of the Empire, both on her family and on the people she observed around her in Rouen. The third woman, Adélaïde Bauche (1797–1869), who began writing her memoirs in 1837, was from a profoundly Catholic and monarchist family of small-scale, but successful, textile producers in Rouen. Deeply resentful of Napoleon and all that he stood for, she expressed her views forcefully. Like men, women who opposed Napoleon had limited options available to them to voice their opinions or to take action against the state. How they did so, in what context, and under what terms are the focus of this essay.

## An Intellectual Against Napoleon

Julie Pellizzone believed that only the monarchy could provide stability. She hated Napoleon, whom she viewed as a usurper and a tyrant. As his regime began to crumble, Pellizzone hoped that she would see an end to the suffering he had caused in France and beyond. Her account of how the inhabitants of Marseille received the news of Napoleon's eminent defeat in spring 1814 makes clear her own beliefs:

»La crainte et l'espérance agitent tous les individus, et chacun forge ou débite des nouvelles suivant le sentiment qui l'anime.... Nous sommes dans une crise terrible, tout est suspendu, on se couche chaque soir sans savoir si on passera la nuit tranquil.[...] Le 8 avril [...] (after officials announced fall of Paris) les uns s'affligent et les autres se réjouissent de cette nouvelle. J'ose même croire que ces derniers forment le plus grand nombre [...] Cela amène une réflexion toute naturelle, c'est qu'il faut qu'un peuple soit bien malheureux pour désirer l'enemi! [...] On dit que les coalisés [ne] sont venus en France que pour mettre Louis XVIII sur le trône et qu'il est rentré à Paris avec eux, où il doit être proclamé à present. Et voilà ce qui fait extravaguer ce bon peuple, toujours français, malgré ses erreurs et les crimes affreux qu'on lui a fait commettre«.[5]

[Fear and hope have everyone stirred up, and everyone is inventing or spreading news reflecting their own sentiments. We are in a terrible economic situation, everything has come to a halt, we go to bed each evening unsure if we will have a peaceful night [...]8 April [...] (after officials announced the fall of Paris) some grieved while others celebrated the news. I dare even believe that the latter comprised the greater number. This leads to a natural reflection: it is necessary for a people to be very unhappy to desire the enemy! They say that the allies have come to France only to put Louis XVIII on the throne and that they brought him back to Paris, where he will be proclaimed king. And it is this that causes celebration among this good populace, always French despite its errors and the horrific crimes it has been compelled to commit.]

For Pellizzone, the French people were not to be faulted for the atrocities of the previous regimes, but rather their leaders who had pushed them onto the wrong path. Once Napoleon was gone, the »good populace of France« would return to their natural state, and the bloodletting would finally come to an end.

Among the reactions she observed, Pellizzone drew particular attention to women of the popular classes, whom she depicted as loving their king, as in this account of women's excited response to a messenger:

»13 avril 1814 [...] On a cru que les autorités avaient pris leur partie et qu'on allait proclamer qu'il fallait se soumettre à Louis XVIII. Une foule immense s'est attroupée autour de cet homme, des femmes du peuple l'ont entouré pour l'embrasser: il a failli être étouffé. [...] Des cris réitérés de »Vive le Roi!« se sont fait entendre ... Enfin il a lu une proclamation de Sa Majesté l'Impératrice, datée de Blois du 3 avril 1814, signée Marie-Louise, par laquelle elle annonce qu'elle est réfugiée à Blois, que son mari est sur les murs de Paris pour tâcher de la reprendre et qu'elle espère que les Français le seconderont.

A la lecture de cette pièce, l'enthousiasme a fini tout d'un coup, les cris de joie ont cessé et tout le monde s'est séparé assez tristement. Pauvre peuple, ton ivresse a été bien courte!« (364).

[13 April 1814 [...] It was believed that the authorities had made up their minds, that they were going to proclaim the necessity to submit to Louis XVIII. An immense crowd formed around this man; women of the popular classes surrounded him to embrace him; he was nearly suffocated. Repeated cries of »Vive le Roi!« were heard. Finally he read a proclamation from Her Majesty the Empress, dated 3 April 1814, [and] signed Marie-Louise, in which she announced that she had taken refuge at Blois, that her husband was at the walls of Paris trying to take it back, and that she hoped the French would support him.

With the reading of this announcement, the excitement came to an abrupt halt, the cries of joy ceased, and everyone walked sadly away. Poor people, your rapture had been very short-lived.]

According to Pellizzone, the population of Marseille, especially women, wanted their king back, not more warfare. Although her political sympathies make her a far from objective observer, historians too have found the population of Marseilles to have been less supportive of Napoleon than those in some other cities and regions.[6] Her emphasis on the women's reactions confirms both historians' findings and contemporary assumptions about women's tendencies toward monarchism; and they were unafraid to make their sentiments known in public, on city streets.

As to her own feelings, Pellizzone was far from ambiguous. She went out of her way to find examples of people who suffered because of Napoleon. On 18 June, three thousand men who had been prisoners of war in Spain were quarantined in Marseille, attracting

»une multitude de gens du peuple, surtout des femmes [...] C'était une chose à la fois hideuse et pitoyable de voir ces pauvres gens, maigres comme des squelettes, nus ou à moité couverts de lambeaux pourris [...]. Ils ont été huit ans prisonniers en Espagne et les Espagnols, justement indignés de la guerre atroce et cruelle qu'on leur faisait, ont fait souffrir à ces infortunés tout ce qu'il est possible d'imaginer.[...] Et celui qui les a guides en Espagne et qui a causé tous leurs maux, celui qui a perdu l'armée de Moscou et celle d'Allemagne existe encore! [...] Et il a six millions de revenues et un asile sur la terre!... Ô Providence! Je me prosterne devant toi [...]« (403).

[a multitude of the popular classes, especially women […] It was at once hideous and pitiful to see these poor people, thin as skeletons, naked or half covered by rotting rags […] They had spent eight years as prisoners in Spain, and the Spanish, justly indignant at the atrocious and cruel war made on them, made these unfortunate men suffer as much as it is possible to imagine […] And he who brought them to Spain and who caused all their suffering, he who lost the armies of Moscow and Germany, still lives and he has six million [francs] in [annual] revenues, and a refuge on this Earth! Oh! Providence, I prostrate myself before you […]]

For Pellizzone, »Bounaparte«, as she always insisted on calling him, deserved much harsher punishment than he had received in light of the cruelty and loss of life he had unleashed across the continent. Pellizzone was a woman with uncompromising political views; her observations of Marseilles and of the events taking place around her always reflected those views. When she saw people expressing opinions that meshed with her own, she made sure to record it. She also no doubt shared her feelings and recounted her observations with friends and family, in addition to recording them in her journal. As demonstrated by Pellizzone's own views and her observations of others around her, women could be as deeply concerned with politics as men.

## The Pragmatic Concerns of a Bourgeois Woman

In contrast, the Arnaud-Tizon family was not particularly engaged politically. Like many, they flowed with the times, accepting succeeding regimes in France after 1789 with little apparent difficulty. They seem to have supported the Revolution, and then participated in social events organized by both Napoleonic officials and those who replaced them when the Bourbons returned to the throne in 1814 and again in 1815. Catherine Arnaud-Tizon, our bourgeois matriarch in Rouen, followed current events with great interest. She read newspapers and used familial and social contacts to get the most up-to-date and reliable information possible. In November 1805 she wrote to her son-in-law: »En ce moment toutes les cloches sont en branle, le canon resume, cela anonce bonnes nouvelles, j'attends les journaux avec impatience.«[7] [At the moment, all the bells are ringing, the cannons have started again, this is to announce good news, I am waiting impatiently for the newspapers.] She enjoyed reading about and celebrating France's successes on the battlefield. A few days later she wrote:

»Parlons des grandes nouvelles. En verité nos armées fond (sic) des choses bien ettonnantes. Un seul combat prive nos ennemis de 45 mille hommes, encore un de cette espece et je crois qu'il ne seroit plus a leur choix de faire la paix ou la guerre. Il me tarde de savoir combien nous avons perdu de monde, et si notre pauvre general n'est point victime [...] Enfin il faut toujours esperer [...] que les François se couvrent de gloire dans cette campagne.« (22 frimaire an 14/13 December 1805).

[Let us speak of the big news. Our armies are truly accomplishing astonishing feats. One battle caused our enemies to lose 45,000 men, another one like that and I think they will no longer be able to choose whether to make peace or war. I am anxious to know how many men we lost, and if our poor general is safe [...] Well, one must always hope that the French will bath themselves in glory with this campaign.]

Sounding like a true patriot, she cared enough about military matters to pay attention to every detail. Her reference to the general (she presumably meant the Marshal Suchet, with whom her family was connected by marriage) suggests that her concern was partly due to knowing someone who was directly involved. However, her patriotic language at the end reflects larger issues, namely a desire to see France as a glorious and powerful nation, a goal clearly shared by the Napoleonic regime.

She paid close attention to current affairs. When things were going well, she expressed pride and enthusiasm, wanting to know all she could about France's triumphs. In late 1806, she wrote: »Au moment ou j'ecris les cloches nous annoncent un cinquieme Bulletin; nous faisons vraiement des prodiges" (7 October 1806). [At the moment that I am writing, the bells are announcing a fifth Bulletin; we are truly performing prodigiously.] Napoleon's successes represented »our« successes in the eyes of this woman. »J'ai bien de la curiosité d'entendre la lecture de la relation ecrite par [illegible] sur le triomphe de nos armées, il y donne surement des détails que nous n'avons pas vu dans les journaux« (10 December 1806). [I am curious to hear about the written account by [illegible] on our armies' triumphs. He must surely give details there that we have not seen in the newspapers.] Proud of her nation and its accomplishments, she always wanted more details, on military exploits as well as other issues. When things turned bad for the French armies, she still wanted to remain *au courant*, as though knowing what was happening was preferable to uncertainty. With defeat on the horizon the presence of her family and access to news helped her cope. In January 1814 she wrote:

»Vous ne pouvez vous faire une idée de la consternation qui regne ici. Chacun est avide de nouvelles; on en cherche partout, on en fait même, et le fait est qu'on ne sai (sic) rien. Les journaux ne disent absolument rien. On est reduit a attendre et esperer un meilleur tems [...] On se perd en conjecture. L'assurance que vous ou Ludovic [her son] m'ecrirez sil il y avoit quelque chose de nouveau est la seule idée qui me tranquilise un peu« (3 January 1814).

[You cannot imagine the consternation that is reigning here. No one has any information; everyone is trying to find out the latest news; people are even making things up. But we know nothing. The newspapers tell us nothing. We are reduced to waiting and hoping for better times [...] We lose ourselves in conjecture. The certainty that you or Ludovic [her son] would write to me if there was anything new is the only thing that calms me down a bit.]

The desire to know what was happening caused her to rely even more on family members living elsewhere. Napoleon's dangerous exploits left her feeling uncertain about her family's future, and she confided those concerns to those who were close to her.

Military issues mattered to this woman not only because she loved her country and hated to see her friends, family, and fellow French suffer, but also because war and instability affected the family's economic position. In December 1805 she wrote:

»On nous dit ici la paix signée. Cela ne peut manquer d'aprais l'enormité de nos suxès (sic). Je croix qu'on a pas d'exemple d'une campagne aussi courte et aussi glorieuse. Nous avons bien besoin d'un tems de calme pour le commerce, qui est dans une crise bien facheuse; on parle ici comme à Paris de faillittes« (2 nivôse an 14/23 December 1805).

They say that the peace [treaty] has been signed. This had to happen after the enormity of our successes. I think there has never been a campaign that was as short or as glorious. We desperately need a period of calm for the sake of business, which has been in an awful situation; we talk here, as in Paris, of bankruptcies.

Happy to hear of France's military successes, she was happier still to think that the economy would turn around once peace arrived. With the warfare of the last years of the Empire, and worrying about the future, she again followed events closely:

»Il part chaque jour d'ici des dettachements de garde nationale. Les soldats on (sic) la facultée de ce faire remplacer, et a voir la foule de remplaçants qui se presentent on a peine a croire a la disette d'homme. A verité toutes les fabriques sont dans l'inaction et les ouvriers qui non (sic) pas de paint (sic) se vendent« (16 January 1814).

[Detachments of the national guard leave here everyday. Soldiers are permitted to have someone substitute for them, and when one sees the crowd of replacements who present themselves it is difficult to believe that we are short of men. In truth, all the factories have stopped running, and the workers who have no bread are selling themselves.]

Military and economic issues coalesced in this woman's mind. Workers were so poor that they jumped at the chance to replace wealthier men who had been drafted.[8] She appeared to be grieving at the suffering she observed around her, that of the nation as a whole as it struggled to hold on militarily, and that of her downtrodden countrymen. Arnaud-Tizon wanted glory for France, but she desired peace and economic prosperity even more. She appeared ready to support any regime that managed to accomplish these goals, and switched allegiances effortlessly in spring 1814.

»Le commerce attend ici avec une impatience mellez (sic) de crainte de connoitre les conditions de paix que chacun range a sa maniere. Il est ettonant qu'on permette aux journaux d'avancer a ce sujet leurs opinions. Enfin il faut croire que nous ne seront pas long-tems dans l'incertitude et que bientôt on pourrat travailler avec securité; demain on celebre ici un service pour Louis seize. Les dames se dispose a aller embellir l'assemblée [...] Dimanche on distribue a la garde urbaine a cheval l'ordre du lis. On dit qu'aprais la ceremonie il y aurat un banquet; car dans ce regime comme dans tous les autres, il faut bien finir par manger« (26 May 1814).

[The business community is waiting with impatience mixed with fear to know the peace terms, which everyone imagines in their own way. It is astonishing that the newspapers are permitted to express their opinions on this subject. Well, we must hope that the lack of certainty will not last long, and that soon we will be able to work [perhaps she means »invest«?] with security. Tomorrow they are holding a memorial service for Louis XVI. The ladies [she means the women of her family] are planning to embellish the gathering [...] Sunday the urban guard will be receiving medals. They say that a banquet will follow the ceremony, since in this regime, as in all the others, one must always end up eating.]

In addition to underlining the close attention this woman paid to the press and the astonishing sequence of events taking place around her, this letter gives insight into Arnaud-Tizon's political views. Having seen regime follow regime since 1789, she seemed to view all political systems with equal skepticism. All would hold festivities; all would stage banquets for the local elite. In the end, pragmatism was her political philosophy, an attitude that served her overarching goal of seeing her family prosper in every sense of the term. In all probability the vast majority of the French population held similar views – though again vehement monarchists like Pellizzone could be found everywhere as could unflinching supporters of Napoleon.

## Remembering an anti-Bonapartist youth

In her memoirs, which she began writing in 1837, Adélaïde Bauche expressed fiercely anti-Bonapartist sentiments. Bauche was deeply religious, taking a vow of celibacy in 1818, which she observed throughout her life.[9] She spent much of her adult life living in the household of her brother-in-law, helping to raise her two nephews after her sister died in 1832. Her memories of her youth include her strong aversion towards Napoleon, stirred up by his visit to Rouen in 1810 when she was thirteen years old. In April of that year Napoleon married Marie-Louise, daughter of the Emperor of Austria; several months later he took her on a tour around France and they visited several cities with great fanfare. Bauche described the large crowds that filled the boulevards of her city, hoping to catch a glimpse of the Emperor. When he finally arrived, his carriage careened so quickly through the streets, that no one could see any of the passengers inside:

»La foule qui étoit sur pieds depuis trios jours fut péniblement désappointée. On comparait l'entrée de Bonaparte Ier Consul à celle de Napoléon, Empereur, et l'on murmurait et j'étais enchantée de ces murmurs. Car quoique ma curiosité n'eut pas été plus satisfaite que celle des autres, je goutais une certaine satisfaction à voir le peuple mécontent de son Empereur.« (Bauche, *Souvenirs*, 155-156)

[The crowd, which had been on its feet for three days, was horribly disappointed. Comparisons were made between the arrival of Bonaparte, First Consul, and that of Napoleon, Emperor, and people were grumbling and I was delighted by this grumbling. Despite the fact that my curiosity had been no more satisfied that anyone else's, I found satisfaction in seeing the people unhappy with their Emperor.]

Apparently when he visited Rouen while still holding the title of First Consul, Bonaparte had deigned to mingle with the populace of the city. By 1810, he was more interested in wooing local elites with luxurious balls and a court-like lifestyle than in mingling with the common people who lined the streets hoping to approach him. Bauche ridiculed Napleon's efforts at mimicking traditional royalty, too, as she described the rules requiring men to appear in old-fashioned dress to satisfy the Emperor's wish to »faire revivre l'ancienne etiquette« [bring back to life old-style etiquette] (Bauche, *Souvenirs*, 160).

Bauche's whole family were ardent royalists, evidenced by the fact that they turned down an invitation to attend the ball held in honor of Napoleon's visit. They had no interest in demonstrating their support for the Napoleon and Marie Louise. In addition to her family's political leanings, Bauche had another reason to dislike both the Emperor and his new wife: like many women of her age and class, she felt great sympathy for Josephine when Napoleon divorced her. »Elle était généralement aimée. Tout le monde plaignit son sort. Pour moi, je pris cette affaire à cœur comme si elle eût été personelle. J'aimais Joséphine avant son malheur, je l'aimais bien davantage après et l'Empereur me devint odieux.«[10] [She was generally loved. Everyone pitied her. For me, I took this affair to heart, as if it had been personal. I loved Josephine before her misfortune; I loved her even more afterwards and the Emperor became odious to me.] Her language of »taking the affair to heart" and it becoming »personal« suggests that she closely identified with Josephine and her suffering. Such »personal« matters may have had more of an effect on women's opinions of the Emperor than on men's. Bauche gives the impression that Napoleon's treatment of Josephine solidified the negative opinion she held of him based on her upbringing and her emerging political and religious sentiments. As we saw in the other examples, the personal and the political mingled in this woman's mind.

Like Arnaud-Tizon and Pellizzone, Bauche was aware of the difficulties faced by poorer inhabitants of her city, particularly the weight of conscription. Looking back on the year 1813 and the aftermath of the Russian campaign, she described one common practice to avoid the draft. »Une foule de jeunes gens se hâtèrent de se marier, afin d'échapper aux nouvelles lois qui les appelaient sous les drapeaux. On entendait à chaque instant des jeunes filles à peine sorties de l'enfance que l'on mariait pour éviter à un jeune homme les dangers de la gloire.« (Dubuc 357) [A crowd of young people rushed to marry to avoid the new laws calling them to serve under the flag. At every instant we heard about young girls barely out of childhood who were being married to a young man hoping to avoid the dangers of glory.] Bauche's recollections give the impression that »glory« had lost its appeal by 1813. The willingness of Frenchmen to rally behind Napoleon once again, even after his return from exile on Elbe during the Hundred Days in 1815, suggests that Bauche may have been seeing only one side of the story. She chose to ignore the diehard supporters of Napoleon and to emphasize the ways in which she saw people working to oppose him. Still, we can imagine her and other anti-Bonapartists expressing outrage at Napoleon's excessive drive for glory, with its concrete effects taking shape in the marital practices she went out of her way to describe.

## Conclusion

The personal and the political, private matters and public affairs, necessarily meshed for these women. Napoleon's wars caused devastation on many levels, and Pellizzone's and Arnaud Tizon's comments about the suffering they observed around them proves that they saw the connection. Whether it was French prisoners of war returning from Spain or poor workers lining up to risk their lives by offering themselves up as replacements for wealthier conscripts, they wanted to see an end to these ramifications of Napoleon's search for glory through battle. Although differing social positions and political perspectives impacted their interpretations of the state and the world-changing events they were observing, these women hoped for the same thing: peace, prosperity, and happiness. Their view of the state depended in part of its ability to accomplish these goals. They hated to see their cities' poorer inhabitants suffer from food shortages, economic crises, and the weight of conscription. In addition, neither Pellizzone nor Arnaud-Tizon was willing to accept a purely »domestic existence.« Both participated in city life – attending theaters and social gatherings – and they voiced their views on politics, economics, and military matters when they did so.[11] They may not have joined political parties or given speeches, but no one (male or female) could do these things due to the repressive nature of the regime (Sibalis). Instead, they used their influence on family and friends to push for what they believed would benefit themselves individually and ultimately their nation as well.

For Pellizzone, that meant returning the rightful king of France to the throne, and for Arnaud-Tizon, ending the turmoil of the last years of the Empire. The example provided by Adélaïde Bauche functions differently. First, as a woman who chose not to attend theaters, which she viewed as immoral, and who never married but instead devoted her life to raising her nephews, she led a much more »domestic« lifestyle (Dubuc 352 and 360).

She also wrote about her experiences during the Empire twenty years after the fact; we cannot assume that the opinions she expressed in 1837 accurately reflect her feelings when she was living through the events of 1810. Still, her enjoyment of the »grumbling« she heard when the Emperor's carriage passed through the streets at a fast trot seems quite vibrant and very real. Her political opinions were already well-formed when barely in her teens, suggesting that girls, too, were not completely excluded from political discussions that took place in the household and on city streets.

Women who opposed Napoleon, like men, operated within narrow limits imposed by what has been termed a police state – limits that had little to do with gender or concepts like the public and private »spheres«. They crossed such imagined boundaries without reflection, acting and speaking as they saw fit. One can imagine each of the three women examined here commenting to friends, neighbors, family members, or anyone else who might listen to them, about their dissatisfaction with the Emperor and his decisions. They were no more, or less, silenced than the men around them as they sought to accomplish their personal goals while living under a repressive military state.

–Georgia State University

## Notes

1 Hesse 32-33 summarizes this body of work; as does Alexander 189-191. A valuable discussion of assumptions about women's religiosity and political bent appears in McMahon 134-138. For a recent discussion of the Civil Code and its revolutionary precedents with regard to family law, see Desan chap. 8.

2 One of the most recent discussions appears in Kale, chap. 3.

3 Examples of such behavior appear in police records held by the Archives Municipales de Lyon, I 2 33. Kroen, chap. 4, discusses the existence of Bonapartist souvenirs and other practices of political opposition during the Restoration.

4 On shifting public opinion under Napoleon, see Tulard 131 and Ellis chap. 6.

5 Pellizzone, *Souvenirs I*, 361-63. All translations are my own.

6 The entry for Marseille in Fierro, Palluel-Guillard, Tulard eds. explains that »Si l'opposition marseilliaise ne se rallie jamais vraiement à l'Empire, la crise économique en est la veritable raison. Le grand commerce maritime est mort à cause de la guerre avec l'Angleterre et ne subsiste plus qu'un mediocre cabotage avec l'Italie« (940). [If the Marseillaise opposition never really rallied to the Empire, the economic crisis is the explanation. Maritime commerce died because of the war with England, except for some small-scale trade with Italy.]

7 AML Fond Vitet, 84 II 12, letter dated 6 frimaire an 14 (28 November 1805). The fact that she used the Revolutionary calendar, even in personal correspondence, suggests that she accepted the changes brought by the Revolution, at least in part. The letters include many errors, using mostly phonetic spelling and rarely punctuation. I have provided punctuation to facilitate reading and mention »sic« only when an error might hinder comprehension. Remaining references to these letters come from the same collection. Hereafter, I will provide only the letter's date.

8 On the issue of conscription and the hiring or replacements, see Woloch, chap.13. Average costs for hiring replacements appears on Table XIII-2, p. 402.

9 Biographical material on Bauche comes from Dubuc. A copy of her memoirs, which she entitled *Souvenirs*, is held by the Archives Départementales de la Seine-Maritime in Rouen, code 1M1 1137.

10 Dubuc 356. Pellizzone expressed similar views towards Josephine: »Elle a prouvé qu'un mari scélérat peut avoir une digne et vertueuse femme.« [She proved that a villainous husband can have a worthy and virtuous wife.] Pellizzone, *Souvenirs I*, 394.

11 On Arnaud-Tizon's social life, see Davidson.

## Works Cited


Alexander, Robert S. *Napoleon*. (Reputations series.). London: Arnold, 2001.

Bauche, Adélaide. *Souvenirs*. Archives Départementales de la Seine-Maritime, Rouen, code 1M1 1137.

Davidson, Denise Z. »Pleasure and Politics in Rouen: Bourgeois Provincial Sociability, 1805–1816«, *Proceedings of the Western Society for French History* Vol. 28 *Selected Papers of the 2000 Annual Meeting* (2002): 264-271.

Desan, Suzanne. *The Family on Trial in Revolutionary France*. Berkeley: University of California Press, 2004.

Dubuc, André. »Une Rouennaise de 1837 face à son passé«, *La Femme en Normandie: Actes du XIXe congrès des sociétés historiques et archéologiques de Normandie*, Archives Départementales du Calvados, 1986: 349-361.

Ellis, Geoffrey. *Napoleon*. London: Longman, 1997.

Fierro, Alfred; Palluel-Guillard, André; Tulard, Jean eds. *Histoire et Dictionnaire du Consulat et de l'Empire*. Paris: Robert Lafont, 1995.

Hesse, Carla. *The Other Enlightenment: How French Women Became Modern*. Princeton: Princeton University Press, 2001.

Kale, Steven. *French Salons: High Society and Political Sociability from the Old Regime to the Revolution of 1848*. Baltimore: Johns Hopkins University Press, 2004.

Kroen, Sheryl. *Politics and Theater: The Crisis of Legitimacy in Restoration France, 1815 1830*. Berkeley: University of California Press, 2000.

McMahon, Darrin. *Enemies of the Enlightenment: The French Counter-Enlightenment and the Making of Modernity*. Oxford: Oxford University Press, 2001.

Pellizzone, Julie. *Souvenirs I (1781–1815)*, transcribed by Hélène Échinard, presented and annotated by Pierre and Hélène Échinard and Georges Reynaud. Paris: Indigo & Côté-femmes, 1995.

Sibalis, Michael. »The Napoleonic Police State«, *Napoleon and Europe*, ed. Philip G. Dwyer. London: Longman, 2001: 79-95.

Tulard, Jean. *La Vie quotidienne des Français sous Napoléon*. Paris: Hachette, 1978.

Woloch, Isser. *The New Regime: Transformations of the French Civic Order, 1789–820s*. New York: Norton, 1994.

# The Liberation from Napoleon as Self-Liberation: The Year 1813 in the Letters of Rahel Varnhagen

*Gertrud Maria Roesch*

Biographical accounts of Rahel Levin's (1771–1833) life in 1813 unanimously speak of her self-sacrificial commitment to wounded soldiers. According to such accounts, her care for the soldiers almost exhausted her finances, and she overstrained herself physically to such an extent that she broke down completely afterwards. No account, however, questions the reasons for her actions; they seemed to have been inevitable and, in view of the things that took place on the battlefield, a simple necessity. Heidi Thomann Tewarson, one of Rahel Levin's biographers, summarizes her role as »Organisatorin einer Hilfsaktion« (Thomann Tewarson, 1988, 96) [the organizer of a relief operation] and further elaborates how scrupulously she kept track of her spending and the use of the funds entrusted to her.[1] Much more biographical relevance is attached, however, to her baptism, on the occasion of which Rahel Levin adopted the name Antonie Friederike, and to her marriage on September 27th, 1814 to Karl August Varnhagen von Ense (1785–1858), fourteen years her junior. Instead of glossing over the year of 1813 simply as an interim of suffering, the following study aims to reconstruct – to the extent that this is possible – the reasons for the almost excessive humanitarian aid rendered by Rahel Levin not only in Berlin in the spring, but also in Prague in the autumn. Thomann Tewarson finds »eine große Anzahl […] zeit- und kulturgeschichtlicher Themen« [a large number of topics relating to contemporary and cultural history] in the letters from this year (Thomann Tewarson 1988, 99). In the following, these topics will function as sources for the reconstruction of a woman's war-time quotidian history.

By focussing on one detail, i.e. charpie (the dressing material of the time when caring of the wounded), a »récit en miniature« will be attempted, i.e. a narrative constructed around insignificant details, as in accordance with the theoretical position of New Historicism. Rejecting »totalisierend[e] Gesamtbehauptungen und Metanarrationen« (Baßler, 19) [totalizing global assertions and meta-narrations], New Historicism emphasizes the details and the plurality of small-scale stories that allow the wider picture to become visible in the smaller one. It is in such a procedure that the master narrative finds its antipode antithesis and its abstractions become undone. The historical snap-shot of the year 1813 offers a synchronous account of military developments (Napoleon's defeat), social upheaval (the emancipation of the Jews), and literary discourse (Rahel Levin's relationship to the Romantics). This simultaneous network is to be reconstructed here by using the example of Rahel Levin's letters. As a Jewish woman, Rahel Levin was implicated in all of these discourses and her letters offer evidence of her decisive steps towards self-liberation in this year.

## Berlin, April 1813: Plans for an Army Hospital vs. Germanophile Publications

On March 16th, 1813, with Prussia's declaration of war on France, the fighting recommenced. Wilhelm von Humboldt (1767–1835) was a Prussian ambassador living in Vienna at the time. It was his duty to persuade the imperial court to form an alliance with Prussia and Russia against Napoleon. Only in June would Austria finally join.

In the spring, Varnhagen was in Hamburg and belonged to the staff of Colonel Tettenborn; there he was responsible, among other things, for the selection of army doctors and for the provisioning of the army hostipals. His letters from May to July highlight General Davoust's occupation of Hamburg and the devastation of the city by the French. As an eye-witness, Varnhagen gives impressive testimony[2] of the historical events that supplied Friedrich Spielhagen with the backdrop for his novel *Noblesse oblige* (1888) (see also the essay by Sammons in this volume).

At this time, Caroline de la Motte Fouqué (1775–1831) had her *Ruf an die deutschen Frauen* [A Call to German Women] released by her publisher Julius Eduard Hitzig.[3] Both the content of this appeal and Rahel's reaction to it in her letter to Varnhagen from April 5th reveal the initial reasons behind her humanitarian action during the course of the year. Since it meanders repeatedly around the same themes, it is difficult to boil down Motte Fouqué's appeal to its central points. The most important point made, however, is clearly the duty of women to send men to the impending battle and to take their place at home: »Keine von allen deutschen Frauen möge durch feige Thränen des Mannes Entschluß wankend oder ihm den ernsten Schritt schwer machen.« [Of all German women, may none allow the man's resolve to waver through her cowardly tears or render his grave step more difficult to take] (Motte Fouqué 168). In order to make the heroism she demanded believable, Motte Fouqué took recourse to examples from Germanic history and tradition: »Der Riesengeist der alten Germania schreitet durch unsere Provinzen, er ist es, der unsern Männern, unsern Söhnen, unsern Brüdern die schimpflichen Ketten unwürdiger Knechtschaft löst.« [The giant spirit of Germania strides through our provinces, it is that which frees our men, our sons, our brothers from the ignominious chains of unworthy servitude.] (Motte Fouqué 165)

This historical reassurance leads her finally to the constitution of a national character which, on the one hand, is generated by reflecting back on the history and supposed characteristic attributes of the German people:

»Uns ist unser Vaterland fremd geworden; die Entwicklung der Zeit hat so viel daran verschoben, gerührt, beschnitten und hinzugethan, dass aus dem, was man National=Charakter nennt, ein Ding entstanden ist, von dem man nicht weiß, ob man darüber weinen oder lachen soll. Es thut uns daher Noth, das Eigenthümliche deutscher Natur aufzusuchen.« (Motte Fouqué 174)

[Our Fatherland has become foreign to us; time's progression has displaced so much of it, stirred it up, cut from and added to so much of it, that a thing has emerged from what we call national character about which we do not know whether to cry or to laugh. It is thus necessary for us to seek out that which is particular to the nature of the Germans.]

On the other hand, this national character expresses itself in the personal behavior of each individual woman – to whom the appeal is indeed directed:

»Für die Freiheit und Ehre des deutschen Landes soll deutsches Blut fließen, [...] Sie ist da, tief in der Wurzel deutschen Seyns da; das äußerlich Hemmende soll das Schwerdt vertilgen, das innerlich Lähmende die leise, sichere Hand der Frauen wegräumen. Einmal und hauptsächlich durch die Behauptung eigenthümlicher Würde, sodann durch den Geist, der von dieser ausgeht in häusliche und gesellige Verhältnisse, sich offenbart in Tracht, Sprache, und als Gipfel von allem, in der Bildung der Kinder.« (Motte Fouqué 173-174)

[For the freedom and honor of the German country, German blood should flow, [...] She (i.e. freedom, GMR) is there, deep in the roots of German being;

outward impediments should be destroyed by the sword, inner hesitations should be swept away by the gentle, assured womanly hand. It is mainly through the assertion of our particular dignity, then through the spirit emanating from this in domestic and social circumstances, and through the social standards revealed in habit, in language, and, as the pinnacle of all, in the education of children.]

Motte Fouqué reminded her readers to meet the requirements of the present, a reminder motivated by her view that all domains of life were interconnected. This comprehensive cultural and historical view makes her writings – if one ignores the political manifesto – a beyond–by valuable source of everyday history of her time. The *Ruf* and the *Die Geschichte der Moden* [1829-30, History of Fashion] share the same educational purpose and illuminate each other mutually; in both, the author tries to represent apparently marginal everyday phenomena as important indications of social development (Kabus, in: Motte Fouqué 26).

However, whenever she comes to speak of the determination of women, her innovativeness suddenly wanes. In such cases, one finds her confining women to conventional behavior (»the gentle, assured womanly hand«) and to legitimate margins of womanly activity (»domestic and social circumstances«, »the education of children«). In the concluding appeal, in which she makes the female essence and person the starting point of reform, the gender-political codification finds its culmination:

»Edle germanische Frauen! Unsern Händen ist das künftige Loos deutscher Geschlechter anvertrauet! Ich wiederhole es, laßt uns in Sprache, Tracht, geselligem Verkehr und einfach edler Haltung uns selbst bewahren, und die Ehre unserer Nachkommen retten. Von uns gehet das Licht aus, laßt es still, bescheiden, fromm und sicher leuchten.« (Motte Fouqué 178)

[Noble German Women! To our hands is entrusted the future fate of generations of Germans! I repeat: Let us remain true to ourselves in our language, habit, social intercourse and simple, noble bearing, and so save the honor of our offspring. The light emanates from us; let it shine calmly, modestly, piously and clearly.]

The cultural norm of passivity and immobility to which women were bound in educational texts and fiction between 1770 and 1830 could hardly allow any other pattern of behavior. If they were to remain cut off from all possibilities of active engagement, their bodies had to become the residual guarantee of reform, figured here in salvational terms. One must read the emphatic metaphor of the hands in this sense – the hands which preserve »the future fate of generations of Germans« and »the light«. The form of address »Noble German women!« and, even more so, the series of epithets of feminine virtues both point to the definition of an exclusive circle within an elevated social class. Incipient signs of the »Regenerierung des Adels« [regeneration of the nobility] (Ueding 53), which belonged to the basic Romantic idea of the state, are present in Motte Fouqué's appeal; not only Adam Müller (1779–1829), but also Achim von Arnim (1781–1831) and Friedrich Schleiermacher (1768–1834) would identify themselves with the notion of a class-based society which met (in the form of a constitution, for example) the demands of the bourgeoisie (Ueding 53-54).

Rahel Levin, however, rejected the *Ruf* with utter disdain: »Hier schicke ich Dir Frau von Fouqué ihren Aufruf. Gott im Himmel! wie durchaus erbärmlich! sie wußte absolut nichts, als daß sie einen schreiben wollte [...]« [I'm sending you Frau von Fouqué's Appeal. God in the heavens, how pitiable! She knew nothing except that she wanted to write one.][4]

Levin accuses Motte Fouqué of drawing upon »alle Mythologien der Welt« [all the mythologies of the world], which however is a simple exaggeration; Motte Fouqué preferred to make reference to Germanic tradition, however complicated the results of her contextualization. One must call to mind here, for example, the *christlich-deutsche Tischgesellschaft* constituted in Berlin on January 18th, 1811 (Berghahn 284-292) in order to understand the nature of the connection made at the time between Christianity, patriotism, Teutonic spirit, and anti-Semitism. Fouqué's allusions are embedded in the literary patriotism of the Wars of Liberation; one finds many (frightening) examples of this prevalent discourse, which – with few exceptions (e.g. Heinrich von Kleist's dramas *Die Hermannsschlacht* [The Battle of Hermann] and, in mythologically deferred mode, *Penthesilea*) – were very influential at the time but are now only of interest to literary historians.[5]

In order to contradict this sort of implication, Rahel Levin introduced on her part another model of national identity:

»[D]aß wir Deutsche heißen und sind, ist eine Zufälligkeit; und die Aufblaserei, dies so groß hervortreten lassen zu wollen, wird mit einem Zerplatzen dieser Thorheit endigen. *Jedes* zu Verstand gekommene Volk soll brav sein; und die Freiheit haben, es zu sein. [...] Dies muß jedes europäische, christliche, Gott in sich selbst erkennende Volk; und jedes solches muß dies allen anderen Völkern gönnen und wünschen: und nicht sich prahlerisch *allein* dazu ernennen, ausschreien und brüsten.« (Varnhagen, GW 5, 32)

[The fact that we are Germans and are so called is a coincidence; and the puffed-up vanity of attaching prominence to this circumstance will end with this folly bursting asunder. Every people which has found reason should be good; and it should have freedom to be so. [...] This is the obligation of every European, Christian people which recognizes God in itself; and every such people must grant this to and wish it for all other peoples, and should not arrogantly name itself alone as deserving of this, proclaiming it loudly, and boasting about it.]

The choice of Christian Europe as standard, implicitly negating the Germanophilia inherent in Motte Fouqué's text, represents a rejection of the patriotically motivated demarcation from the French and the polemics directed against their culturual influence; Motte Fouqué, in Levin's view, takes recourse to an all too easy argument by attacking the French language.[6] In this point, Rahel Levin defended her own existence, one part of which lay in the past, i.e. her salon, whereas the other – i.e. her christening – would become an integral part of her social future. All representations of the salons of the Romantics emphasise the influence of French salon culture (most recently: Berghahn 236). The work of integration done by just this sort of social intercourse to reunite the »getrennten Sphären von Religionen und Ständen« [the separate spheres of religions and classes] (Berghahn 248) was implicitly endangered by a renaissance of political and cultural nationalism. With 1806, a phase of renewed social exclusion began which was caused by a mixture of the military-political catastrophe following the battle of Jena that year, the political as well as cultural nationalism of the time, of which the Romantic variety is the most important here, and also the growing influence of religion. These were all taking place at the time of the Edict of Emancipation of 1812, which stipulated mainly that the special laws applied to the Jewish population (among others, special taxes and vocational limitations) were to be suspended. They were now given the right to settle both in the city or in the country and to be appointed as schoolteachers and municipal administrators. Access to state offices and to the military followed in 1814 in a separate military service act. Through this edict, the Jews became »Einländer und preußische Staatsbürger« [subjects and citizens of the Prussian state] (Thoman Tewarson, 1988, 73).

Even Humboldt had a role in the prehistory of the edict; before being signed on the 21st of March, 1812, it had to pass through various ministries and departments, in the process of which it was also presented to Wilhelm von Humboldt. The latter made his case confidently for consistent, unqualified equality. The consistency of his position was a result of his conviction that the emancipation and immediate suspension of the special legal status of the Jews would usher in their assimilation and integration into the Christian state (cf. Berghahn 270-276). However, while the Edict of Emancipation of 1812 was effective on a formal level, it failed to alter the »Macht der Majorität« [might of the majority] (Barnouw 93), which is something clearly apparent in statements made by Humboldt and his wife in their letters.

It must have struck Rahel Levin even more, however, that Motte Fouqué turns her attention so thoroughly to married women and mothers, as in the following:

»An uns ist es jetzt, zu entbehren, das Unterbrochene zu ergänzen, den getheilten Hausstand zusammen zu halten, Ordnung, Ruhe und Klarheit überall zu verbreiten, in gläubiger Zuversicht die Fähigkeit bewahrend, großen Widerwärtigkeiten begegnen zu können.« (Motte Fouqué 171)

[It is now we who must do without, complete that which was left unfinished, hold together a divided household, spread order, calm and clarity, preserving in pious confidence our ability to confront great tribulations.]

What resonates all too clearly in this statement are the existential conditions of the land-owner and mother of four and thus the prerequisites of the sort of life from which Rahel, although her alimony was abundant, had to remain excluded. Motte Fouqué's appeal struck at the very core of her endeavors, since she had just experienced a disappointment of great consequence which may be considered as one of the catalysts of her reaction. Her efforts to organise an army hospital stood in stark contradiction to the manifesto's requirement of passive womanhood:

»Als im Anfang durch einige Herren der Stadt bei mir zuerst ersonnen war, daß Frauen hier ein Lazareth stiften sollten, wozu wir dreißig Vorsteherinnen aus allen Ständen und Religionen gewählt hatten, welche die Prinzessinnen um ihr Präsidium bitten sollten, faßte ich das ab, was diese Dreißig in die Zeitungen sollten setzen lassen. [...] Die Prinzessinnen und ein Konseil von Herren haben alles umgestoßen zu einer Einrichtung, die mir nicht gefällt. Geld kommt aber viel zusammen.« (Varnhagen, GW 5, 33)

[When the idea came to me at first by way of a few gentlemen of the town that the women here should found an army hospital, for which we had chosen 30 directors from all classes and religions who were to request of the princesses that they yield their executive powers, I composed the text that these 30 were to have printed in the newspapers. [...] These princesses and a council of gentlemen overruled everything, creating an establishment I do not like. Much money is nevertheless being collected.]

The Jewish woman must have felt cheated in more than one way: Not only was the initiative wrenched from her; in addition, the organization – which in its integrating function was meant to embrace all classes – became appropriated by a circle of noble ladies and gentlemen for whom overcoming class boundaries could hardly have been of any interest. This episode should be seen as providing the background for her own hectic form of charity, which she mentions in the same breath:

»Diesen Morgen muß ich noch nach Hemden laufen, die Markus giebt: ich muß es, weil ich mich keine Mühe, kein Klätern, keinen Weg, keine Anrede, und Rede mit gemeinen Leuten verdrießen lasse: weil ich denke, je schneller die Hülfe, desto mehr ist die Hülfe [...].«[7]

[This morning, I must go and fetch some shirts that Markus will give me. I must do this, because I will not allow myself to be distressed by the effort, by idle chatter, by the length of the journey, by the greetings and speech of the common folk, because I believe that the faster the help arrives, the more help it will be.]

Rahel Levin's action neither required legitimation, nor was it selective; it was based solely on the immediate need, following the principle of »bis dat cito dat« (the faster the help, the greater the help). Furthermore, it was conceived as an integrative action with the »common folk«.

For her, the sabotage of her work for the army hospital represented an insult which could be only slightly compensated by the fact that the subsequent bad management of the hospital created a scandal:

»Unser großes Lazareth war in einem *schrecklichen* Zustand!! wegen unordentlicher Einrichtung und Deprädation. Kaum erfuhr es aber die Stadt, so war ein General=*Aufstand. Jeder* schrie, lief, und gab. [...] Wäsche aller Art, Betten, [...] Essen, wo immer hundertundfünfundzwanzig Frauen kochen ließen; keine schlief, keine ruhte mehr; [...] Die Herz ist unendlich thätig: ich sporne sie noch mehr. [...] Gäben doch die Christen so wie die Juden! dann wäre hier wenigstens keine Noth.« (Varnhagen, GW 5, 48)

[Our great army hospital was in a horrific condition because of disorderly maintenance and depredation. As soon as the town caught wind of this, there was a general uprising. Everyone cried out, and hurried to give. [...] All kinds of clothing, beds, [...] food, wherever it was possible to arrange for 125 women to cook; no one slept, no one rested any longer; [...] – Herz is untiringly active: I spur her on still more. [...] If only the Christians gave like the Jews do! Then there would be nothing wanting here.]

The vividness and attention to detail conveyed by this letter is only truly apparent in juxtaposition with other reports from these months. »Die Herz ist unendlich thätig: ich sporne sie noch mehr.« [Herz is untiringly active; I spur her on still more..] (GW 5, 48) – this sentence reappears in a long letter from April 20$^{th}$, 1813, to Varnhagen in Hamburg. Upon an investigation of the memoirs of Henriette Herz (1764–1847), who is mentioned in the letter, all one finds regarding her impression of the situation is the laconic remark: »Ich erzähle nicht von den Zeiten der Freiheitskriege, und wie Mann und Weib, Alt und Jung, Arm und Reich seine Pflicht tat, und vielfach noch weit über diese hinaus, und mit welcher Freudigkeit.« [I haven't related anything about the time of the Wars of Liberation, and how man and woman, old and young, rich and poor did their duty, many of them going well beyond this, and with such joy.] She forbids herself »in die Einzelheiten [...] einzugehn« [to go into the particulars] of how everyone »mitwirkte und mitlitt« [acted and suffered together] at the time so as not to injure the »bescheidene Anspruchslosigkeit« [modest selflessness] that they all showed back then.[8]

In view of such a cursory glossing over of everyday realities by Herz, Rahel Levin's account simply seems more valuable as a documentation of daily life. Also, Rahel Levin's letters call into question the universal charity emphasised by Henriette Herz; it is clear that the stronger commitment lay on the side of the Jews. Above all, the Berlin letters provide an explanation of Rahel Levin's later rapid action in Prague, where she received an opportunity to put the knowledge she had gleaned into practice.

## Breslau, May 1813: The Flight from Familial Ties

After the French troops' evacuation from Berlin and Prussia's declaration of war on its former ally France, Rahel Levin left Berlin and settled in Prague with her brothers Moritz and Ludwig. There, she hoped to live more securely and cheaply and to avoid the expenses of billeting,[9] although she was certainly not without means, and thus could have held out in Berlin. The journey from Berlin via Breslau like all travelling by women was considered an unwomanly activity.[10] In a more concrete way, the journey also represented a large expenditure on her part: »Ich esse gut mit Dore und vollauf, für etwas weniger als zwölf Münzgroschen. Spare wo ich kann. Doch Reisen – Koffer ausbessern, Unvermuthetes, Zölle, Trinkgelder, Stricke, Mauthen, alles kostet Unberechenbares.« [I eat well with Dore, and plentifully, and for somewhat less than 12 pennies. I save whenever I can. But travel – mending the bags, unexpected occurrences, customs, gratuities, ropes, tolls – it all costs an amount one cannot predict]

(Varnhagen, GW 5, 82). Considering the physical hardship she underwent on top of that, for example the completely unfurnished room she took on the way in Reinerz (a town near Breslau), in which she was forced to sleep in a bed of straw (Varnhagen, GW 5, 82, 85), one must ask why she did nothing to avoid such extremes. A close reading of the letters can provide the answer.

Her financial situation became urgent when she relinquished the silver she had taken with her from Berlin to her elder cousin in Breslau.[11] Shortly afterwards, she had a severe quarrel with her elder brother Markus, who reproached her for not having turned to him instead of informing another relative about her lack of money. What her brother feared the most was that the old silver would have been melted down along with their parents' monogram. For this reason, Rahel would then explicitly ask the uncle in a letter not to sell the silver to a third party. This confrontation gives a poignant example of her twofold dependency. Not only was the sister dependent on the support of her brothers; she was also becoming repeatedly dragged back into the cultural mold and set of interests espoused by the Levin family. In a letter to Varnhagen, she describes the burden of her familial affiliation:

»So eben hatte ich einen harten Strauß mit Markus, der ganz empört ist, daß ich dem Onkel meine Armuth durch das Silber entdeckt habe: ›*Das* hast Du doch bei Gott! nicht nöthig, ich oder Moritz hätte Dir doch auch hundert Thaler darauf geliehen!‹ [...] Ich soll noch die *Reiche*, die besorgt wird, *spielen*, für seine Ambition.« (Varnhagen, GW 5, 85-86)

[I just had a bad fight with Markus, who is rather angry that I revealed my poverty to my uncle through the silver: ›That you did not need to do, by God! I or Moritz could have lent you another 100 talers on top of that!‹ [...] For his ambition, I am obliged to play the rich woman who is provided for.]

Barbara Breysach gives a very vivid account of the everyday effects of this familial bond; the family remained »eine kulturelle Insel« [a cultural island] of Jewish culture within the dominant German one, albeit one »ohne verbindliche Orientierung an neuen Verhaltensmustern« [without a binding orientation to new models of behavior].[12] In the course of 1813, the ambivalence would intensify. On the one hand, the sister was being let down financially; directly before this time, i.e. in the fall of 1811, her brothers had reduced her annual income from 1200 to 800 Reichsthaler (cf. Thoman Tewarson, 1988, 94); on the other hand, she was trying to find independent financial means which would allow her to distance herself from her family:

»Noch sprach ich nicht reinen Wein: aber ich fühle, es kommt. […] Den Onkel nannte er einen *fremden* Mann! Wenn *der* fremd ist! […] Siehst Du! das ist mein größtes Leid: wär' ich *Einmal* von deren Interesse geschieden! Aber Gott giebt es mir! So wie er mir Dich so spät gab!« (Varnhagen, GW 5, 86)

[I haven't spoken my mind as yet, but I feel it coming. […] He called my uncle a stranger! As if he were a stranger! […] You see, that is my greatest woe! If I could one day just be cut off from their concerns! But this is given to me by God, just as He gave you to me so late!]

## Prague, June to August 1813: Everyday Life in the Anticipation of War

Rahel Levin arrived in Prague with her brother Ludwig Robert (1778–1832) on 1 June 1st after failing to find accommodation in Breslau.[13] There she shared lodgings until September 1814 with the actress Auguste Brede[14] at 681 Fleischhackergasse. At the time, Prague was a center of both diplomatic and military action against Napoleon; simultaneously, it had become a refuge for many of her Prussian contemporaries who had fled for various reasons. Ludwig Tieck, for example, was in Prague and, with Rahel, frequented the theater in which Auguste Brede performed (Varnhagen, GW 5, 143). Carl Maria von Weber lived in the same house as Rahel Levin, so they saw each other often (Varnhagen, GW 5, 130).

A delicate situation was occasioned by her meeting with Clemens Brentano (1778–1842), who was involved in a row with Varnhagen. The two had met in Halle in 1806; in the course of an encounter in Teplitz in 1811, an insulting statement was made about Rahel Levin, and her reactions to this in the letters represent a substantial, if indeed partial source for this dispute. On April 24th, 1812, Varnhagen had given Brentano two slaps in the face, retaining the manuscript of the tragedy *Aloys und Imelde* as a forfeit (as Varnhagen noted on the manuscript). Such was the backdrop for their meeting in 1813. Brentano had, with Tieck's help, sought out Rahel Levin in Prague and – if one is to credit the letter from June 10th – attempted, in long conversations marked by strong emotions on his part, to explain his standpoint. In Rahel's words:

»Ich sah ihn, ohne die *geringste* Emotion. Er kam in die allerheftigste. Erzählte mir seine Katastrophe mit Dir ganz genau, bis zu Thränen. [...] Er erzählte mir von allen seinen Frauen, Schwestern, Freunden, Ehen, Achim, Schlegel; *von allem*. Ich *ihm von nichts*.« (Varnhagen, GW 5, 126, 127)

[I looked at him, without the slightest emotion. He was seized by increasingly strong ones. He related his catastrophe with you to me quite exactly, during which he broke down in tears. [...] He talked about all his women, sisters, friends, marriages, Achim, Schlegel; about everything. I told him about nothing.][15]

In addition both to daily meetings with old acquaintances like Friedrich von Gentz and Wilhelm von Humboldt and to her regular correspondences, Rahel re-established contact with Caroline von Humboldt, who was in Vienna with her five children.[16] The family was separated from 1809 to 1810, Wilhelm having been engaged in service for the Prussian government as Director of the Section for Public Worship and Education [Sektion für Kultus und Unterricht], only being reunited with his family in 1810 upon becoming ambassador at Vienna. During the decisive final phase of the war of the Allies against Napoleon, Caroline stayed behind for the most part as Humboldt spent time at the Prussian headquarters and in the vicinity of State Chancellor Hardenberg. Only in November 1814 would the family move back to Berlin, this in order to avoid the household costs raised by the Congress.[17]

Caroline von Humboldt shared the same social stance and personal life as Caroline de la Motte Fouqué whose ideas Rahel resented clearly. With Humboldt, however, Rahel found a common level of understanding – at least temporarily. The exchange between Rahel Levin and Caroline von Humboldt in 1813 is genuinely unique; its contents are reflected, but with quite different accents, in the letters between the Humboldts and in Rahel's correspondence with Varnhagen. Still, all the letter exchanged share the common context of the war and its results for daily life between the sites of battle.[18]

In a long letter sent from Prague to his wife, Caroline, dated July 25th, 1813, Humboldt described the political process, especially addressing the question of whether and when the war with the French might be redeclared. In this context, he mentions some of the refugees who were in the city, including Rahel Levin:

»Die kleine Levi [...] ist ziemlich unverändert. [...] Sie hat mich sehr agaciert, allein was soll man mit der Judenmamsell? Gentz versichert zwar noch immer, sie sie die geistreichste Frau auf Erden. Man muss auch des Geistes entbehren können. Ich bleibe also unerbittlich.«[19]

[Little Levi […] is rather unchanged. […] She has aggravated me much, but what is one to do with the Jewish mam'selle? Gentz still assures me that she's the most brilliant woman on the earth. One must also be able to do without the wit. Thus I remain inplacable.]

The scornful tone that Wilhelm strikes here is astonishing considering their past acquaintanceship in Paris.[20] After severing contact with Finkenstein in the Summer of 1800, Rahel Levin had travelled to the French capital as the companion of Countess Karoline von Schlabrendorff. There, she often met the Humboldts, whom she had first encountered in Henriette Herz's Berlin salon. Breysach calls the letter »einen plumpen Versuch sozialer Degradierung, der seine Ursachen auch in einer Abwehr ihrer Präsenz als Frau im männlich dominierten Geistesleben haben kann.« [a crude attempt at social degradation which could also be attributed to a rejection of her presence as a woman in male-dominated intellectual life] (Breysach 135). Anti-Semitic reservations were nothing extraordinary in the circles in which she moved; both of the personal scandals discussed above are proof of this.

But there is more to Humboldt's comment than that. Rahel Levin used the years 1813 and 1814 in a pragmatic, determined manner to secure her future husband's chances in the redistribution of political power and to legitimize and consolidate the legal status she had just gained. The provocation thus had less to do with her Jewish background and more with her own character, which enabled her to establish herself anew, i.e. to build up stable relationships outside of the family and to compensate successfully for the limitations of class by virtue of her personality alone. It is at this point that her self-perception had to collide with conventional gender roles present in the Humboldts' letters. Wilhelm's letters to his wife in these tension-filled months bespeak this in clear terms: again and again, he assures her of how highly dependent he is on her as the resting point of his life and the legitimation of his action. Certainly, such passages in the letters are moving even today, but they reveal nevertheless the rigid, dichotomous division of gender roles.[21] One finds a corresponding reflection of this attitude towards women and the female sex in Humboldt's essays *Über den Geschlechtsunterschied* [On the Difference between the Sexes] (1794) sowie in dem *Plan einer vergleichenden Anthropologie* [Outline of a Comparative Anthropology] (begun 1794, but unpublished), in which he made a case for the complementarity of the sexes and succinctly captured and codified the static, pre-individual ideal of femininity.[22]

Caroline, for her part, took up the topic of Rahel Levin once again on August 10th:

»Die Levi schreibt, wie sie zu der Gräfin Schlabrendorff zurückgekommen sei, sitzt Herr v. Humboldt da. ›Er behandelte mich äußerst gleichgültig, bekannt und nicht unhöflich, war sehr launig, und wir mussten in der kurzen Zeit lachen. Doch finde ich ihn anders als sonst. Er sieht sehr wohl aus, und wenn es sich für einen Menschen seines Alters schickte, so würde ich sagen, er hat mehr Aplomb wie ehemals, selbst sein Scherz ist ihm gleichgültiger, und wenn er ihn sonst mit einer gewissen Schnelle sagte, die diese Gleichgültigkeit dramatisch darstellen sollte, so ist es jetzt reine Natur, und nun ganz graziös.‹

Diese letzte Bemerkung habe ich erstaunend hübsch gefunden.« (Humboldt, 1910, 91-92)

[Levi writes how Herr v. Humboldt was sitting there when she returned to Countess Schlabrendorff. ›He treated me with the utmost indifference, familiarly and not impolitely, was very jocular, and we had to laugh after little time had passed. I find him, however, to be different than usual. He looks very well, and if it were proper for a man of his age, I would say that he has more aplomb than ever, he is more indifferent even to his jokes, and if he did tell them before with a certain swiftness which was supposed give dramatic expression to this indifference, it is now purely natural, and indeed quite graceful.‹

I found the last remark to be astonishingly well-put.]

The last sentence in particular gives evidence of the contradictory reactions which Rahel Levin's conversation provoked. The »social degradation« of her birth was counterpoised by the involuntary respect exacted by her gift for observation and her ability to express herself. Even if some ulterior motive may have ultimately been at play, the »astonishingly« superior ability displayed by Rahel Levin won Caroline over, at least to the extent that she found the passage worth citing to her husband.

These letters exchanged between the married couple should be borne in mind, so that one can appreciate the shift in focus revealed by the letters exchanged by Rahel Levin and Caroline Humboldt in the fall of 1813. The strategic ulterior motives recede temporarily as the war and its impact on humanity begin to impose their all-dominating presence.

## Prague, September and October 1813: Care of the Wounded and Patriotic Identification with Prussia

The care of wounded soldiers of the time was centered around a then common dressing material, charpie, which receives continual mention in the letters. Caroline referred to it on October 1st: »Ich schikke dir, Liebste, eine kleine Quantität Charpie, ich hoffe die größeren Quantitäten Charpie und Bandagen sind dir richtig zugekommen« (Leitzmann 115). [I will send to you, dearest, a small quantity of charpie, hoping that you have correctly received the larger quantities of charpie and bandages]. Rachel Levin wrote back on October 18th: »Auch will ich dir sagen habe ich alle 5 Sendungen Binden *charpie* etc: richtig erhalten.« (Leitzmann 123) [I also want to mention that I have correctly received all five parcels of bandages, charpie etc.]. The German »Scharpie« goes back to the French term »charpie« and refers to linen which is plucked or torn into strips and pieces to serve as surgical wool, albeit one which was by no means aseptic.[23] The repeated mentioning of charpie in Rahel Levin's letters serves as a »leitmotif« for tracing the daily life in battle zones or in the cities and countryside near to them. It would be an inaccurate simplification, though, to say that women restricted themselves to the negotiation and organisation of humanitarian support without simultaneously sharing the patriotic rhetoric. On the contrary, the letters of both women show a constant alternation between the two discursive modes. Both features – the participation in patriotic discourse and the communitive charitable engagement – occur in their correspondence with remarkable frequency. To Rahel, these activities offered a release from her familial and social frustration, one which she embraced, as she herself emphasized, with unusual vigor. This rarely experienced robustness of constitution left her again in the moment in which this assistance was no longer required.

In a letter sent to Caroline von Humboldt from Prague on September 7th, 1813, following the Battles of Katzbach and Kulm, Rahel mentions all aspects of her charitable activity:

»Du mußt, du kannst durch deinen Einfluß, ich kenne ihn ganz; durch deine ausgebreitete Bekandschaft und dein Gewicht in Wien, bey den Damen eine Einsammlung, schnell bewirken; mit all deinen Kräften. Sehen sie, die Damen auf uns Preußinnen was wir thaten: mit keinem Stolz, mit recht kann ich wir sagen. Kurtz: auf den Straßen, im Koth, liegen unsere – der alliirten alle – Verwundete umher. Die Stadt thut was sie vermag an geben und thun; Ärzte, Hebammen, Judenmädel die man besonders lobt und nennt, verbinden auf den Wagen die sie bringen in den Straßen. Zu 100 solcher Wagen stehen hintereinander: man kann nicht gehen. wir schiken Essen, Wäsche, was wir vermögen. Diese Menschen waren das Bollwerk mit ihren Leibern dieser, eurer Prowinz [sic].« (Leitzmann 96-97)

[You must, you can, with the help of your influence – I know it so well – in the wide circles of your acquaintance und through your social impact in Vienna, quickly start a collection among the ladies of society; with all your might. Look at us, [Viennese] ladies, at us Prussian women and what we did: and it is not out of pride, but with full justification, that I can say us. In short: on the streets, in the dirt, the wounded soldiers are strewn about – the wounded soldiers of all allied armies. The city does what it can to give and to help: surgeons, mid-wives, Jewish girls, who receive particular mention and praise, bandage their wounds in the streets, upon the carts on which they are transported. About a hundred such carts stand in a row: no one can pass through. We send food and linen and whatever else we can afford. With their bodies, these men formed the bulwark of this – your – country.]

The entire chaos taking place in the streets of Prague is represented by a series of enumerated hardships and impressions. She tries to capture the sheer bulk of wounded soldiers in their thronging physical presence both numerically (»100 solcher Wagen« [a hundred such carts]) and metaphorically (»das Bollwerk mit ihren Leibern« [the bulwark with their bodies]). At the same time, she singles out two groups from this picture of general confusion: firstly, the »Preußinnen« [Prussian women], among whom she counts herself (»mit recht kann ich wir sagen« [with full justification can I say we]), and secondly the »Judenmädel die man besonders lobt und nennt« [Jewish girls, who receive particular mention and praise]. The image mirrors her own situation; in it we see simultaneously the two groups spanning the transition between »Jewish mam'selle« to Prussian woman, a transition which Rahel finally succeeds in making.

This patriotic identification pervades Rahel Levin's letters, replete as they are with emotional outbursts as in the letter from September 15th, 1813, sent to Vienna: »Blücher und Bubna sollen wieder gesiegt haben. Mir schaudert! die Boten: ach! ich kann Gutes immer nicht glauben. Und immer unsere Preußen. Karoline wenn ich einen sehe, und einer sagt ik bin en Preuße; *vergehe* ich. Ach! das gefühl kennst du nicht.« (Leitzmann 106) [It is said that Blücher and Bubna have once again achieved victory. I shudder! The messengers: alas, I am still unable to believe that good things can happen. And always our Prussians. Caroline, whenever I see one, and he says ‚I'm a Prussian,' I could die. Alas! You don't know the feeling.]

Neither food nor dressing material were available, and for this reason we see Rahel Levin entreating her friend to render assistance:

»Schikt, ich bitte euch! weder das *gouvernement* noch die Stadt allein vermögen die *Zahl* zu bestreiten: das *Land* muß helfen: *wie bey uns*! Heute regnet's auf den Wunden Menschen mit Wundfieber! [...] Sie liegen hungrig schmachtend im *Koth*. Werffe dich in den Wagen, und fahre umher. [...] Du sihst meine *agitation*. Es ist nicht Schwäche allein: wenn du gesehen hättest, die 8 Tage; wenn du *sähest*. [...] Und so lange der Frieden nicht proclamirt ist, bereitet euch *vor* in Wien, auf Verwundete! Leider ist das hier *nicht* geschehen.« (Leitzmann 96-97)

[I beg you, do send something! Neither the government nor the city people themselves can take care of the sheer multitude; the entire nation must help, as we did! Today the number of the soldiers' wounds is compounded by streams of men with wound fever that endlessly pour in. [...] They lie in the dirt, languishing in hunger. Throw yourself into your carriage und drive around. [...] You can see my agitation. It is not only frailty: If you had seen it those eight days – if you were to see it now. [...] As long as peace has not been proclaimed, you should prepare yourself in Vienna to take in wounded soldiers! Unfortunately, this has not been the case here [i.e. in Prague].]

Having profited from her experiences with the badly organized army hospital in Berlin, she overtook the leadership for provisioning and care.[24] In the process, she came in very close proximity to the wounded, as her letter from September 15$^{th}$ shows. She took constant action in order to alleviate their distress:

»[S]o will ich ihnen kochen lassen: und ihnen Hemden und Soken [sic] spenden. *Das* ist zu nothwendig für arme kranke Geplünderte Abgerissene. [...] Es geht ihnen ohnerachtet sie sehr bedürftig und beklagenswerth sind etwas besser: es ist mehr Ordnung schon; sie haben Madratzen. Stroh, Lappen doch was man nur in den Straßen siht muß Einem was man nur besitzt abloken und Thränen und Herz und Seele. Gestern ging ich gebend in der Sonne umher: und als ich Einem gab, kam eine Bauersfrau mit einer schwehren Butte auf dem Rücken, und gab dem selben einen Kreutzer: recht Mutter: sie antwortete mir viel auf bömisch, und wischte sich Thränen ab. So geht's immer weg. man möchte vergehen. Sag Karoline! wird uns Gott diesen Vertheidigungskrieg nicht gewinnen lassen?« (Leitzmann 101).

[And so I'm going to arrange someone to cook for them; and donate some shirts and socks. That is all too necessary for the poor, sick, plundered, down-and-out people that they are. [...] Although they are very needy and pitiful, they are doing somewhat better: Things are already more ordered; they have mattresses. Straw and rags, but what one sees in the streets must move one to give everything possible and tears, heart, and soul to boot. Yesterday, I ran around in the sun, giving things, and as I was giving to one person, a farmer's wife came by with a heavy vat on her back, and she gave him a kreutzer. You were right, mother: she answered me at length in Bohemian, wiping away her tears. And so it goes on. It makes one want to die. Tell me, Caroline! Will God not let us win this defensive war?]

Althought this account, like many other of her letters, is punctuated by patriotic remarks, the physical reality nevertheless remained the focus of its author. The identificatory and emotionally unguarded behavior she exhibits becomes particularly clear in comparison with a description given by Wilhelm von Humboldt. After the battle near Leipzig, he rode over the battlefield in the company of Hardenberg, writing about his experience to Caroline on October 20th, 1813:

»Es war dies das erste Schlachtfeld, das ich sah, und ich habe nun erst einen Begriff davon. Es liegen noch eine Menge von Toten darauf, die meisten halb oder ganz nackt ausgezogen, oft mehrere übereinander. Die meisten lagen mit ausgestreckten Armen auf dem Gesicht, wo man erst das Homerische ›die Erde mit den Zähnen nehmen‹ recht versteht und einsieht. Ein armer Hund suchte immer an einer Stelle herum und war nicht wegzubringen. Man sah keinen Toten, aber er hatte gewiss irgendeine Spur seines Herrn. Wie wir an einem Ort waren, wo mehrere Tote lagen, bemerkte ich, dass ein scheinbar Toter noch eine Hand rührte. Wir ritten heran, er hatte eine starke Kopfwunde, aber zuckte noch. Wir ließen Leute herankommen, und obgleich er gar kein Zeichen gegeben hatte, dass er unsere Bemühungen für ihn hörte oder achtete, so fühlte er nicht so bald, dass man ihn anfasste und ihm half, als er alle Kraft zusammennahm und sich mit aufhalf. Wir brachten ihn ins Dorf, er sprach aber gar nicht und ist vermutlich doch gestorben.« (Humboldt, 1910, 149-150).

[This was the first battlefield that I saw, and only now do I have an idea of how it really is. A multitude of dead bodies are still lying here, most of them either half-naked or fully unclothed, often many atop each other. Most lay with arms extended over their faces, and only by the sight of them can one truly appreciate and understand Homer's phrase ›biting into the earth with one's teeth‹. A poor dog kept searching around in one area and wouldn't be removed. There was no sign of a dead man there, but it most certainly had discovered a trace of its master. When we were at a place where many dead men were lying, I noticed the hand of one who appeared dead still stirred. We rode up to him, he had a severe wound to the head, but he was still twitching. We summoned men to come to help, and although he gave us no sign that he heard or noticed our efforts, as soon one took hold of him and helped him, he gathered all his strength and tried to raise himself up. We brought him to the village, but he uttered not a word and probably he died after all.]

Humboldt adopts a distanced attitude in the face of suffering. His elevated position on horseback protects him and gives him an aesthetic perspective that allows him to view his immediate environs through the medium of an antique text. At this time Humboldt was working hard at a translation of Aeschylus; involuntarily and unexpectedly, the view before him supplied the artistic reality of the text with real experience »where one [...] truly appreciates and understands«. He was elevated over the situation both intellectually and physically, and was able to maintain this distance, for help was provided by his and Hardenberg's having »men come to help«. Later too, in the city, the encounter with the injured men in St. Thomas' Church transformed before his eyes into an atmospheric »sight« and a »spectacle«. He registers bodily details, but remains aloof from both the bodies and the people:

»Den Nachmittag ging ich in der Stadt bei den Verwundeten und Gefangenen herum. In der Thomaskirche liegen an 700 gefangene und verwundete Franzosen, von denen heute abend seit dem 16. und 18. noch keiner verbunden war. Von dem lugubren Anblick der halbdunklen Kirche mit dem dumpfen Gewinsel und Gestöhn hat man keinen Begriff. Die Gefangenen herdenweise von den Kosaken wegtreiben zu sehen, ist auch ein eigenes Schauspiel.« (Humboldt, 1910, 150)

[In the afternoon I went into town, circulating among the injured and the captives. About 700 captive and wounded Frenchmen lie in the St. Thomas' Church, among which this evening, since the 16th and the 18th (October, i.e. the dates of the Leipzig battle) none were bandaged. One cannot conceive of the dismal sight of the half-darkened church and the muffled whining and moaning. To see the Cossacks driving the captives away in great herds is also a spectacle in its own right.]

As Caroline von Humboldt wrote to Varnhagen on October 23rd, 1813, Rahel was at the same time tirelessly active in Prague[25] and experienced her bodily strength as a personal victory:

»Gott giebt mir eine *besondere* Gesundheit hier, zu den Erschütterungen, und zur Thätigkeit. Du glaubst es vielleicht nicht: aber ich habe nicht einen *Augenblik* Zeit seit ich den Soldaten helfe. Aber wie glüklich bin ich! Ich kann helfen: womit habe ich das *verdient*? Warum helf' ich ihnen, Sie nicht mir? [...] *Große große* Gnade hab ich schon in diesem Kriege erfahren; auch schon zu Hause: ich konnte sehr Gutes wirken, mit meinen beschränkten mittlen, und elendem Rahmen.« (Leitzmann 106-107)

[God gives me a particular sort of health here, to cope with the shocks and for activity. Perhaps you don't believe it, but I have not one moment of free time since I've been helping the soldiers. But how happy I am! I can help; how did I deserve this? Why do I help them, and they not me? [...] I have already experienced great, great grace in this war, at home already too: I could do great good with my limited means and under wretched circumstances.]

## Conclusion

In March 1814 this charitable activity came to an end – an end Rahel Levin herself would define with considerations of where she would go next. She consulted Caroline in long letters not only about this question, but also about a possible meeting and treatment by David Ferdinand Koreff, whom Caroline met in Vienna and who also treated her. Then Rahel married Varnhagen, and Caroline visited a spa for her health. In a further extant letter from June 5th, 1818, they address each other with the formal »Sie«. The closeness of the weeks of common aid never returned.

In the correspondence of these two couples, who experienced the fighting in different places, the private and simultaneously political perspective of the year 1813 becomes apparent. During the couples' respective conversations, one question was raised again and again: How and where should Humboldt/Varnhagen engage himself after the war? In the letters written between the women, however, such questions remained unraised or lingered below the communicative threshold; they refer rather to the immediate present and the demands placed by it.

Achieving a place in the »kultivierten gesellschaftlichen Elite« (Barnouw 98) [cultivated social elite], of which the Humboldts could claim to be the spokespeople, was not a certain prospect for Rahel Levin, but she came closer to achieving this aim. The chance was given to her by the short, anarchic year of 1813, with the misery of war which temporarily loosened otherwise rigid class limitations. The end of the war also meant the end of the legitimizing contexts for action she had created for herself with her engagment in charity work; but she knew how to take advantage of the acquaintances she had made in the time of need in order to mediate a position for Varnhagen, which in turn would facilitate their marriage and life together; Rahel wrote to Varnhagen on April 26th, 1814 (Varnhagen, GW 5, 332): »Gehe nur zu Humboldt; mache ihm ja die Kour! Sie schreibt mir sehr lieb und theilnehmend, und setzt voraus, Du gehst zu ihm.« [Just go to Humboldt; court him! She writes very nicely and sympathetically to me, and assumes that you will go to him.]

About ten years later, in her educational text »Frauen in der großen Welt« [Women in the Wide World] (Berlin, 1826), Caroline de la Motte Fouqué would complain about the social development which, in her eyes, was responsible for bringing about »immer größere Individualität und Egozentrik« [ever greater individuality and egocentrism] (Kabus, in: Foqué,

24). Her insistence on a renaissance of more conventional forms of social contact reveals her strongly negative reaction to the cataclysms of the Napoleonic Wars and a desire to strengthen the old class order anew.[26] An exemplary provocation of this order is provided by the irrevocable integration of a woman like Rahel Levin, who by her own efforts was able to secure a position in society as Frau von Varnhagen. Considering this, the term »Wars of Liberation« takes on a highly ambiguous meaning.

–University of Heidelberg, Germany

This article has been translated by Eric Kuchle, Heidelberg.

## Notes

1 Thomann Tewarson, 1988, 98; this volume also includes a facsimile of one of the extant letters.

2 Being in Tettenborn's staff, Varnhagen's perspective is unavoidably subjective; in addition, he also contributed to the *Deutscher Beobachter*. The letters from July 13th and 22nd, 1813, especially report on the devastation of the city and the treatment of its inhabitants, Varnhagen, GW 5, 133: »In Hamburg sieht es schrecklich aus, man presst Geld und Geld, und zeigt es unverhohlen, dass einem nichts daran gelegen ist, nachher in zehn Jahren aus dieser Stadt keine Einkünfte ziehen zu können. Wer kann, wandert aus. Die reichsten Leute müssen persönlich an den Schanzen arbeiten, alle prächtigen Alleen vor den Thoren sind umgehauen und die Stämme zu Pallisaden gebraucht.« [It looks appalling in Hamburg. They collect ever more money, and make no secret of the fact that the last thing they want is to be unable to make revenues from the city in ten years. Those who can, emigrate. The richest people have to work personally at the entrenchments, all the splendid avenues before the gates have been laid waste, the trunks of their trees used as palisades.]

3 The appeal must have appeared between April 3rd and 5th; this can be ascertained from a letter from April 3rd, 1813, Varnhagen, GW 5, 25-26: »Apropos! heute ist, für vier Groschen Kourant, auch zum Landesbeitrag, von Frau Fouqué ein Aufruf für Frauen bei Hitzig angekündigt.« [Apropos! Today, an appeal to women by Frau Fouqué has been announced at the price of four pennies courant, and the proceeds shall be a contribution to the state.] The title page noted explicitly: »Die Einnahme fürs Vaterland« [proceeds for the Fatherland], i.e. the profits earned were conceived as a contribition to the mobilization. – Also, »Landesbeitrag« [contribution to the state] referred to the additional donations and proceeds for military campaigns which were collected in varying ways, e.g. the benefit concerts Rahel Levin mentioned to Varnhagen in a letter from April 20th, 1813, cf. Varnhagen, GW 5, 50-51.

4 Varnhagen, GW 5, 32. Kabus (in: Motte Fouqué 39) mentions Rahel's contemptuously horrified reaction, however without pursuing the further implications of this and, above all, failing to recognize the status of this letter as a first-rate example of reception on her

part. In spite of Fouqué's »patriotically tinged nostalgia« in this manifesto, Kabus grants Fouqué a mediate stance between the progressive and the restorative, but Rahel's letter shows that at least her Ruf an die deutschen Frauen was rather understood as a disavowal of women's claims to participation in the public sphere. Cf. also the essay by Arnold-de Simine in this volume.

5 Schulz offers both a thematic overview and a selection of texts by Ernst Moritz Arndt, Theodor Körner, as well as Heinrich von Kleist. Essen shows how the battles against the French represented a major influence both thematically and in terms of the conception of individual characters using the example of Kleist's *Die Hermannsschlacht*. The most important genre, because of its wide circulation, was poetry, whose function is investigated by Weber.

6 Motte Fouqué was not alone in this opinion; Henriette Herz, too, devoted much attention to the notion of the dominance of the French as one in which little national sentiment was manifested, cf. Schmitz 174: »Bei der ohnehin so gesunkenen Kraft des Vaterlandsgefühls vollendete die Macht und der Zauber der Sprache des Feindes den Sieg derselben. Jetzt strafte sich die Torheit, dass man mit Hintenansetzung der schönen vaterländischen Sprache die französische zur Modesprache, zu derjenigen gestempelt hatte, in welcher allein man sich mit Feinheit und Anmut auszudrücken vermöge, und dass die französische Literatur vorzugsweise die geistreiche sei.« [In the already so reduced strength of feeling for their Fatherland, the might and the magic of the language of the enemy sealed their victory. It was now that the foolishness of disregarding the beautiful language of the Fatherland and making French the fashionable language, so that the latter was stamped as the only language in which one could express oneself with refinement and grace and that French literature was seen especially as the literature of wit, punished itself.]

7 Varnhagen, GW 5, 48; here, »klätern« means »reden, schwätzen«. The often mentioned Marcus Robert (1772–1826) is the eldest brother, who had taken over the family business after his father's death in 1790.

8 Schmitz 193. Henriette Herz wrote her memoirs between 1823 and 1829; these notes were added by the Berlin writer Joseph Fürst, along with recorded accounts of conversations, to a corpus of memoirs, which was first published in 1850. Cf. Schmitz 435-436.

9 Cf. the letter to Varnhagen from April 3rd, Varnhagen, GW 5, 26, 27: »Die Noth kann doch kommen, und dann habe ich kein Reisegeld mehr, also muß ich vor der Noth weg. Könnt' ich kalkuliren, was ich hier mehr brauchen muß, als meine Einnahme, so blieb ich: ich reise nicht gerne durch marschirende Truppen, nicht gerne ohne sehr sichere Begleitung, nicht gerne, wenn ich meine Heimath für eine ganz reizlose unsichere neue aufgeben muß [...].« [The need could always still come, and then I'll have no more travel money, so I must leave before this happens. If I could calculate what I will need beyond my income, I would stay: I don't like to travel through marching troops, without a secure escort, or if I have to give up my homeland for a rather charmless, unsafe new one.]

10 Until well into 18th century, travelling was the privilege of wealthy aristocrats, whereupon and because of that travelling became an emancipatory, social-revolutionary gesture on the behalf of the bourgeois bound up with both the desire to appropriate the world beyond that of book-learning and, when the journey was documented, satisfying

the autobiographical needs of the traveller. Women did travel, as well, but only in exceptional cases or for urgent reasons. With the expansion of the institution of the post, travelling became safer for women and lent itself better to planning; inside the carriage, women were again domesticized and protected while still having left their homes; cf. the excursus on female travel in Krug 323-326.

11 Varnhagen, GW 5, 84: »Als ich in Breslau war, sagte ich dem Onkel, ich hätte noch zwanzig Louisd'or und fünfzig Thaler Kourant; und sechzehn Paar silberne Messer, Löffel, Gabel, und einen Vorlegelöffel bei mir: die hätte man mir im bloßen Silber, ohne Facon, schon hundertundzehn Taler taxirt: ich möchte sie gerne hierlassen, ob er mir hundert Thaler dafür geben wollte, so verlöre er gewiß nichts dabei.« [When I was in Breslau, I told my uncle I still had 20 louis d'ors and fifty talers in Prussian currency; I also had 16 pairs of silver knives, spoons, forks, and a serving spoon with me. These had been taxed in pure gold to the amount of 110 talers, without the ornaments. I would like to leave them with him. If he would like to give me 100 talers for them, he would certainly lose nothing by it.]. The »Onkel« actually refers to a cousin, Lipmann Meyer, who was the same age as her father; he finally gave her 150 talers for the silver, whereby it remains unclear whether the cutlery was thus sold or rather simply left behind as a pledge. A Friedrichsd'or was a gold coin (exchange value: 5 talers und 3 pennies); a reichstaler/taler/kourant was a silver coin (exchange value: 90 kreuzers or 24 pennies). On the currencies cf. Varnhagen, 2001, 602-603.

12 Breysach 106. The most telling occasion motivating Breysach's representation is a family festivity held on the first wedding anniversary of her sister Rose, which Rahel Levin described in detail in a letter from February 9th, 1802, addressed to this very sister.

13 As a result of a lot-drawing, Ludwig Robert was supposed to enlist in the universal militia (Landwehr). This he circumvented by fleeing to Breslau and Prague., cf. Varnhagen, 2001, 919-920.

14 Auguste Brede was a friend of Count Bentheim, who was in turn a friend of Varnhagen; he stayed on the Count's estate during the Winter of 1811, and in 1812 they were together in Prague for another Winter. It was thanks to Varnhagen's mediation that they were provided during these months with an amply furnished and comfortable room in an otherwise overrun Prague.

15 For a biographical chronology cf. Varnhagen, GW 12, 323-337. In the revised form of the play, Brentano lent features of Varnhagen to both Comingo and Lussan and had them get into a fight over family papers, cf. Schulz, 292-325. On the basis of this communication, Varnhagen gave back the manuscript in the fall of 1814. This conflict bore an unfortunate similarity to the one between Achim von Arnim (1781–1831) and the young Moritz Itzig (1787–1813) when the latter, challenged by mocking speeches, challenged Arnim to a duel. When Arnim refused, Itzig attacked him and was sentenced to a minor punishment. The case was discussed widely in Berlin, serving Ludwig Robert as the inspiration for his bourgeois tragedy *Die Macht der Verhältnisse* [The Might of Circumstances]. Both scandals are characteristic of the anti-Semitic sentiment of those years. For more on the clash between Itzig and Arnim and on Robert's encrypted representation of the scandal in his bourgeois tragedy *Die Macht der Verhältnisse* cf. Rösch 413-414.

16 Wilhelm von Humboldt and Caroline von Dacheröden had married in Erfurt on June 29th, 1791, living at first on the Dacherödens' estates; their first two children were born

in this period. Upon Wilhelm's and his brother's becoming economically independent with the death of their mother on November 1st, 1796, they both went to Paris, where Theodor was born in January 1797; in May 1800, their daughter Adelheid followed; in May 1802, Gabriele was born. Humboldt's position of Prussian envoy to the Papal Court necessitated relocating in Italy, where their son, Wilhelm, died of fever on August 15th, 1803. Their stays alternated between Germany and Italy, constantly overshadowed by the developments of European politics, as well as by the birth of two more children (Louise in 1804; Gustav in 1805; both died within two years after birth).

17 For more details, cf. (among other sources) Humboldt, 1991, 259-271.

18 On the data and the military decisions between the first encounter in August 1813 (Battle of Katzbach) and the final battle near Leipzig on October 16th, 1813, cf. Nipperdey 82-101.

19 Humboldt, 1910, 80. Rahel Levin sensed the rejection very well; she wrote about her encounter with Humboldt in a letter to Varnhagen on July 30th, 1813: »Wilhelm Humboldt boudirt mich; ich sah ihn nur einen Augenblick bei Gräfin Schlabrendorf, die Dich grüßt [...].« [Wilhelm Humboldt is ignoring me; I saw him for only a moment at Countess Schlabrendorf's, who sends you her greetings.] cf. Varnhagen, GW 5, 141., cf. Sanders vol.1, 166.

20 The condescending tone was an integral part of the behavioral code held by the couple; during the same period, i.e. on July 28, 1813, Caroline wrote from Vienna to her husband, cf. Humboldt, 1910, 73: »Die kleine Levi will, wie ich höre, in Prag die Auflösung der Dinge abwarten. Sie soll sehr herunter an ihrer Gesundheit sein.« [Little Levi wants, I have heard, to wait for things to resolve themselves in Prague. Her health is supposedly going rather downhill.] And in another letter to Humboldt from August 6th, Humboldt, 1910, 87: »Die arme kleine Levi! es wird sie doch schmerzen, dass Du so unerbittlich gegen sie bist. […] Von Dir schreibt sie wunderhübsche Sachen.« [Poor little Levi! It probably pains her that you're so adamantly against her. […] She writes wonderfully nice things about you.]

21 When Wilhelm informed Caroline on August 11, 1813 that after Prussia, Austria too – and at his own instigation – had now declared war on France, he announced his intention to make a short stay in Vienna. His letters to his wife show how strongly dissociated the relative realms of action of man and woman had become, however emotionally sensitive they remained to each other as partners, cf. Humboldt, 1910, 96-97: »Sonst aber kann ich in acht bis zehn Tagen, vielleicht früher, bei Dir sein. Ich freue mich unendlich darauf. Wir machen dann alle Vorkehrungen gemeinschaftlich. […] Ich muß hier schließen, süßes, teures Wesen. Ewig mit ganzer und inniger Seele Dein H.« [Otherwise, I will be able to be with you again in eight to ten days, maybe sooner. I look forward to this infinitely. We will make all provisions together. […] I must close here, sweet, dear creature. I remain eternally with the wholeness and the depths of my heart, your H.] – On August 21st, he announced his intentions to travel to Vienna, cf. Humboldt, 1910, 105: »Ich schreibe Dir, liebe Li, heute nur zwei Worte, aber ich bin unendlich glücklich, denn ich reise morgen abend unfehlbar um 8 Uhr zu Dir ab. Wie ich mich freue, kann ich Dir nicht sagen. Mein besseres Leben ist nur bei Dir, und Dich einige Tage lang wiederzusehen, Deine süße, liebe Stimme zu hören, die teuren Augen zu küssen, wird mich unendlich glücklich machen.« [I'm writing only two words to you today, dear Li, but I am infinitely happy, for tomorrow I'm leaving without fail at

8 o'clock in the evening to go back to you. I can't tell you how much I look forward to this. My better life is only with you, and to see you again for a few days, to hear your sweet, beloved voice, to kiss your dear eyes will make me infinitely happy.]

22 Cf. Humboldt, 1903, 311-334: *Über den Geschlechtsunterschied und dessen Einfluss auf die organische Natur* (1794) [On the Difference between the Sexes and its Influence on Organic Nature]. In this work, Humboldt differentiated between male and female qualities, e.g. reason vs. fantasy, productive vs. receptive powers, »in the former a striving which is keenly productive, in the latter an effort to conserve through bonding«, cf. 326; he finally stressed however the unity of nature in the interdependence and complementarity of both powers. The article *Über männliche und weibliche Form* [On Male and Female Form], also published in the Horen in 1795 (cf. Humboldt, 1903, 335-369), uses these categories in the contemplation of antique statues; the last essay, *Plan einer vergleichenden Anthropologie* (cf. Humboldt, 1903, 377-410), which wasn't published, rests in its argumentation on the differentiation between woman and man he had already expounded.

23 Charpie was extracted by means of picking apart broad bands of linen. After 1870, it was replaced by loosly woven cotton (gauze). One could sterilize the dressing materials through steaming them at a temperature of over 100 degrees Celsius or by using iodoform. Cf. Brockhaus Konversations-Lexikon, vol. 4, 112. – One of Rahel Levin's contemporaries, i.e. the Dresden painter Wilhelm von Kügelgen (1802–1867), described this activity in his much-read memoirs with ironic distance, cf. Kügelgen 149.

24 For a particularly gripping description, see the letter of September 2nd, 1813, Leitzmann 109-110.

25 Cf. Leitzmann 124-125: »Von unsrer lieben Freundin Rahel empfange ich jezt öfter Briefe. Sie hat das seltne Glük gehabt einen theuren Freund zu pflegen, und selbst unmittelbar thätig für die HülfsBedürftigen sorgen zu können.« [I now receive letters more often from our dear friend Rahel. She has the rare fortune of caring for a dear friend, and of being able to provide help directly to those who need it.] The friend whom she took care of especially was Alexander von der Marwitz (1787–1814), whom she had known since 1809. He died in action on February 11, 1814 in the battle of Montmirail.

26 Motte Fouqué admonished women in *Die Frauen in der großen Welt* [Women in the Wide World] to combat society's egotism and the compulsion for women to gain status through their conversational and harmonizing abilities. She was also outspoken in her demands for the cultural reorientation of the Germans to their own heritage. Cf. Wägenbaur 68-77.

## Works Cited

Arendt, Hannah. *Rahel Varnhagen. Lebensgeschichte einer deutschen Jüdin aus der Romantik*. 4. Aufl. München: Piper 1983 (zuerst 1959).

Barnouw, Dagmar. »Einzigartig. Rahel Varnhagen und die deutsch-jüdische Identität um 1800«, *Rahel Levin Varnhagen. Studien zu ihrem Werk im zeitgenössischen Kontext.* Ed. Sabina Becker. St.Ingbert: Röhrig 2001 (Sofie 13), 81-117.

Baßler, Moritz (ed.). *New Historicism. Literaturgeschichte als Poetik der Kultur.* 2. Aufl. Tübingen: Francke 2001 (UTB 2265).

Becker, Sabina (ed.). *Rahel Levin Varnhagen. Studien zu ihrem Werk im zeitgenössischen Kontext.* St.Ingbert: Röhrig 2001 (Sofie 13).

Berghahn, Klaus L. *Grenzen der Toleranz. Juden und Christen im Zeitalter der Aufklärung.* Köln, Weimar, Wien: Böhlau 2000.

Breysach, Barbara. *›Die Persönlichkeit ist uns nur geliehen‹. Zu Briefwechseln Rahel Levin Varnhagens.* Würzburg: Königshausen und Neumann 1989 (Epistemata: Literaturwissenschaft 44).

*Brockhaus Konversations-Lexikon.* 16. vols. 14. Aufl. Leipzig, Berlin, Wien 1892.

Essen, Gesa v. »Römer und Germanen im Spiel der Masken. Heinrich von Kleists ›Hermannsschlacht‹«, *Kleist-Jahrbuch* 1999, 41-52.

Humboldt, Wilhelm v. *Briefe an Karl Gustav Brinkmann (1839).* Ed. Albert Leitzmann. Leipzig: Ernst Siegfried Mittler 1839.

*Wilhelm und Caroline von Humboldt in ihren Briefen.* Ed. Anna v. Sydow. Vol. 4: Federn und Schwerter in den Freiheitskriegen. Briefe von 1812 bis 1815. Berlin: Mittler 1910.

Humboldt, Wilhelm v. *Werke.* Ed. Albert Leitzmann. Vol. 1: 1785–1795 (Gesammelte Schriften 1). Berlin: Behr 1903. Nachdruck Berlin: de Gru b yter 1968.

Humboldt, Caroline v. *Ein Leben in Briefen.* Ed. Gunther Tietz. Frankfurt, Berlin: Ullstein 1991.

Kemp, Friedhelm (ed.). *Rahel Varnhagen im Umgang mir ihren Freunden (Briefe 1793–1833).* München: Rösel 1967.

Kügelgen, Wilhelm v. *Jugenderinnerungen eines alten Mannes.* Ed. und mit einem Nachwort by Sigfried Asche. Frankfurt/M.: Weidlich 1963.

Leitzmann, Albert (ed.). *Briefwechsel zwischen Caroline von Humboldt, Rahel Varnhagen.* Weimar: Böhlau 1896.

Motte-Fouqué, Caroline de la. »Ruf an die deutschen Frauen. Die Einnahme zum patriotischen Zwecke«. Berlin, bei Julius Eduard Hitzig (1813), *Ausgewählte Werke.* Ed. Petra Kabus. Vol. 3: *Texte zur Stellung der Frau in der Gesellschaft.* Hildesheim, Zürich, NY: Olms 2005, 163-178.

Nipperdey, Thomas. *Deutsche Geschichte 1800–1866. Bürgerwelt und starker Staat.* 5. durchges. Aufl. München: Beck 1991 [zuerst München 1983].

Rösch, Gertrud Maria. »Geschichte und Gesellschaft im Drama«, *Zwischen Restauration und Revolution (1815–1848).* Eds. Gert Sautermeister, Ulrich Schmid. München, Wien: Hanser 1998, 378-420 (Hansers Sozialgeschichte der deutschen Literatur 5)

Sanders, Daniel. *Fremdwörterbuch.* 2 vols. 2. Aufl. Leipzig: Wigand 1891.

Schmitz, Rainer (ed.). *Henriette Herz in Erinnerungen, Briefen und Zeugnissen.* Frankfurt/M.: Insel 1984.

Schulz, Gerhard. »Von der Verfassung der Deutschen. Kleist und der literarische Patriotismus nach 1806«, *Kleist-Jahrbuch* 1993, 56-74.

Thoman Tewarson, Heidi. *Rahel Levin Varnhagen. Mit Selbstzeugnissen und Bilddokumenten.* Reinbek b. Hamburg: Rowohlt 1988.

Thoman Tewarson, Heidi. *Rahel Levin Varnhagen. The Life and Work of a German Jewish Intellectual.* Lincoln: University of Nebraska Press 1998.

Ueding, Gerd (ed.). *Klassik und Romantik. Deutsche Literatur im Zeitalter der Französischen Revolution 1789–1815.* München, Wien: Hanser 1987 (Hansers Sozialgeschichte der deutschen Literatur 4).

Varnhagen, Rahel Levin. *Briefwechsel mit Ludwig Robert.* Ed. Consolina Vigliero. München: Beck 2001 (Edition Rahel Levin Varnhagen).

Varnhagen, Rahel. *Gesammelte Werke.* Eds. Konrad Feilchenfeldt, Uwe Schweikert, Rahel E. Steiner. München: Mathes und Seitz 1983.

Wägenbaur, Birgit. *Die Pathologie der Liebe. Literarische Weiblichkeitsentwürfe um 1800.* Berlin: Erich Schmidt 1996 (Geschlechterdifferenz und Literatur 4).

Weber, Ernst. *Lyrik der Befreiungskriege (1812–1815). Gesellschaftspolitische Meinungs- und Willensbildung durch Literatur.* Stuttgart. Metzler 1991.

# Friederike Brun's *Briefe aus Rom* (1816): Cosmopolitanism, Nationalism, and the Politics of *Geistlichkeit*

*Kari Lokke*

With the wisdom of hindsight provided by historical perspective, many nineteenth-century women writers offered powerful critiques of Napoleon Bonaparte's political career and military campaigns. In her lyrical and autobiographical novel *Die Günderode* (1839), Bettine von Arnim, for example, describes him as an »Ungeheuer der Mittelmäßigkeit« (637) (»monster of mediocrity«) who held sway over a blind and intoxicated mob. And Mary Shelley's *Valperga, or The Life and Adventures of Castruccio, Prince of Lucca* (1823) delineates, in the form of its title character, a clear-sighted portrait of the death and destruction brought about by a ruler possessed of the fatal combination of seductive charisma and ruthless will to power. From an earlier generation, the German-Danish writer Friederike Brun (1765–1835), on the other hand, like her more renowned friend, Germaine de Staël, experienced the effects of Napoleonic tyranny first hand. Furthermore, unlike Goethe, Stendhal or the canonical English Romantics, who, as Simon Bainbridge has shown, all expressed admiration for and sometimes even identification with Napoleon, Brun's religious sympathies, her personal experiences in both Denmark and Italy, and perhaps her gender as well, precluded any admiration whatsoever for the French ruler.[1]

Most significantly, Brun's beloved city Copenhagen, where she had lived since infancy when her father became pastor of the German Lutheran congregation there, had been devastated by the English's fleet's 1807 bombardment in response to Denmark's alliance with France. In her autobiography *Wahrheit aus Morgenträumen* (1824), she writes movingly of the fiery destruction of the settings of her dearest childhood memories – homes, churches, and gardens, even a favorite willow tree.[2] And from 1808 to 1810, during Napoleon's Italian campaigns, Brun lived in Rome and witnessed the occupation of that city by French troops, describing this historical drama first in daily diaries and then in a series of letters sharing her responses with her brother, Friedrich Münter, a Lutheran bishop in Denmark. In 1816, a year after Napoleon's defeat at Waterloo, Brun published these letters as *Briefe aus Rom*. She waited to publish her letters till after Napoleon had lost power because, as she claimed in her Introduction, immediate publication would have constituted a declaration of war and she had no desire to become a martyr (1). Her friendship with Staël, whom Napoleon had expelled from Paris, had made only too clear to her the French emperor's willingness to persecute outspoken opponents of his policies. Similarly, the English expatriate Helen Maria Williams virtually ceased publication during the empire; her Parisian house had been searched and she and her aging mother imprisoned for a twenty-four-hour period after her 1802 *Ode to Peace* had offended Napoleon by refusing to mention him (Kennedy 178).

Furthermore, invoking the »incorruptible« Clio, muse of history, Brun implies that a historical distance of nearly a decade allowed her, in reworking the letters for publication, a healthy detachment from the events she described. Thus, her historical proximity to the French emperor's military campaigns endowed her observations with what she termed »der frischesten Lebendigkeit des Eindruckes« (2) [the liveliness of the most immediate impression], while they gained objectivity by virtue of the later perspective of their editing for publication. Indeed, through her unique combination of objectivity and enthusiasm, Brun claims for herself the role of ideally qualified historian of the Napoleonic occupation of Rome. If it is true, she writes, that »das reine Resultat der Geschichte« [the pure result of history] can only be comprehended by foreign observers rather than by actively involved, native participants,

»[S]o war die Verfasserin, durch ihr fernes Vaterland, durch ihre dem Süden vielfach entgegenstehende Nationalbildung und ihr politisches und religiöses Glaubensbekenntniß vielleicht von allen damals in Rom anwesenden Nichtrömern am meisten geeignet, mit ungetrübtem Blick zu beobachten and mit dem einzigen Enthusiasmus, der auch dem Geschichtschreiber erlaubt ist, mit jener Begeisterung, die aus der Liebe zum unwandelbaren Recht entspringt und durch die heilige Indignation [...] das Beobachtete auf der Stelle mit dem frischesten Lebendigkeit des Eindruckes niederzuschreiben.« (2)

[So the author, through her distant fatherland, through her nation's *Bildung*, in many ways opposed to that of the South, as well as her political and religious profession of faith, was perhaps, of all outsiders present in Rome, the best suited to observe with unclouded eye and with that particular enthusiasm that is also allowed the historian, with that inspiration that springs from the love of immutable justice and through sacred indignation, to record observations on the spot with the liveliness of the most immediate impression.]

In this portrait of herself as model historian, Brun prefigures the ideal of European citizenry and its subjectivity that she develops throughout her *Briefe aus Rom* – a subjectivity that is cosmopolitan yet aware of its national heritage, Christian but ecumenical, and open to an inspiration that, Brun claims, aligns it with universal right and justice. This essay examines the manner in which Brun seeks to portray Pope Pius VII as embodying this ideal and explores the tensions between Italian pride, nascent nationalism and cosmopolitan humanitarianism, Christian principle and universal compassion, heroic action and non-violent resistance that both create and threaten this ideal. If, as Simon Bainbridge asserts, »Napoleon was the supreme embodiment of the hero in an age in which the artist was increasingly seen as heroic« (2), then Brun's spiritual conception of the artist-hero in *Briefe aus Rom* clearly constitutes a radical departure from this prevailing model.

Brun's letters are of value to the twenty-first century reader as a lively record of the immediate responses of a well educated and well traveled northern European woman to the presence of French troops in nineteenth-century Rome. Brun was fluent in written and spoken German, French and Italian and spoke Danish and Spanish. Married to, and soon estranged from, an international financier, Johann Christian Constantin Brun, she spent significant portions of her adult life in Italy and Switzerland. A member of Staël's Coppet circle, Brun also presided over her own salons in Copenhagen and Rome and was close personal friends with a number of the most significant intellectuals and artists of her day, among them Simonde de Sismondi, Caroline and Wilhelm von Humboldt, Angelika Kauffmann, Karl Victor Bonstetten, and Bertel Thorvaldsen. More specifically, the *Briefe aus Rom* testify to the cultural and political significance of religious thought for this woman writer of the Romantic era, as Brun seeks to address, through a model of universalized spirituality (*Geistlichkeit*), the tensions common to her historical moment between subjectivity and objectivity, Romantic individualism and Enlightenment universalism, nationalism and cosmopolitanism, allegiance to the status quo and reform or revolution. For Brun, it is above all else blind nationalism and partisanship that are the enemies of truth and justice.

Perhaps surprisingly for us today, it is Christianity that she identifies as the antidote to these destructive forces. In her autobiography, she explains that because she herself left Germany for Copenhagen when she was barely four weeks old, she never really knew to what people or nation she belonged. Her complete lack of »ausschließende Vaterlandsliebe« (5) [exclusive love of fatherland] enabled her, she claims, to approach other lands and peoples with an open mind and heart. Quoting her father, Brun anachronistically takes the New Testament, in particular, as exemplifying enlightened cosmopolitan consciousness: »Christus habe gegen nichts früher und anhaltender gearbeitet, als gegen die ausschließende Vaterlandsliebe, and den noch ausschließendern Vaterlandsstolz; und nichts eifriger zu befördern gesucht, als offenen Weltbürgersinn. Auch mir scheint dies aus allen Evangelisten klar hervorzugehen« (5). [There is nothing Christ worked earlier and more continuously against than exclusive love of fatherland and the even more exclusionary pride of country; and he sought to foster nothing more zealously than the openminded consciousness of the citizen of the world. And this seems to me to follow clearly from all of the gospels.] In her internationalist perspective and her praise of the open minded citizen of the world (»offenen Weltbürgersinn«) Brun joins dissenting Protestant supporters of the French Revolution like the Reverend Dr. Richard Price who in his famous *Discourse on the Love of Our Country* delivered to the Revolution Society in 1789, counseled his fellow Britons against exclusive love of their own country: »We ought to seek [our country's] good, by all the means that our different circumstances and abilities allow, but at the same time we ought to consider ourselves as citizens of the world, and take care to maintain a just regard to the rights of other countries« (quoted in Kennedy 56). Yet Brun is writing twenty years later, with a still vivid horror of the French Terror and a deep distrust and fear of Napoleon and his troops whom she terms »Söhne der Revolution« (10) [sons of the revolution]. Thus she turns away from the realm of politics for her model citizen of the world. Accordingly, Brun makes the Pope the hero of her *Briefe aus Rom*, a Pope who, stripped of all his worldly power and exiled to Savona by the end of her narrative, becomes an emblem of pure *Geistlichkeit*.

Though it would seem from our contemporary, secular perspective that Brun is taking an arch-conservative stance here in defending the Pope against such Napoleonic reforms as the liberalization of divorce law and the abolition of the requirement of priestly celibacy, her position is in fact much more complex and nuanced once one moves beyond these domestic social issues. Indeed, as Angela Keane has shown in the case of Hannah More's educational efforts amongst Britain's laboring classes and Jeanne Moskal with reference to Marianna Starke's Italian travelogues, ostensibly conservative Romantic era women writers often take political positions that are notoriously difficult to categorize in their effects and implications. In fact, as Marlon Ross has pointed out, even to put pen to paper and speak out publicly about political events is in a sense an act of opposition to the status quo: »During the early Romantic period, women's political discourse – across the ideological spectrum – occupies a position of dissent. Simply to speak about politics is to place oneself against the political establishment, where women's role is normatively defined solely by silent obeisance« (92). Brun's hesitation to publish her *Briefe aus Rom*, for fear of retaliation against such a »declaration of war«, despite the fact that they were couched in the semi-private form of letters to her brother, suggests that she was well aware of the risks involved in such public self-assertion.

As we have seen, Brun furthermore takes full rhetorical advantage of her identity as a foreigner in Rome and as a woman outside of existing political power structures to emphasize her privileged capacity to envisage ideals of truth and justice and to assert a kind of moral authority beyond the corrupting influence of political struggles and partisanship. Again this position is to a certain extent universal to European women of her era and as Ross asserts common to Britain's dissenting tradition of women writers as well:

»The woman who dares to dissent, however, finds herself in an ironically fortuitous position, possessing a political voice without the drawback of belonging to the corrupt interests of established power. For her to speak politics is automatically to assault the status quo. Her primary problem is how to speak politics without being contaminated by the moral compromises which characterize mainstream politics.« (92)

Like the British writers Ross describes, Brun's reliance on moralized sentiment distances her commentary from topical satire and from political factionalism and discourages her readers from viewing themselves as members of any political party.

Nowhere is this effort to escape politics or, perhaps more precisely, to clothe a political stance in moral garb clearer than in Brun's story of the family of Lucian Bonaparte, Napoleon's brother. This narrative constitutes the central sub-plot of the letters and portrays the family as a kind of ideal domestic unit set in opposition to the political machinations of Lucian's ruthless and infamous brother. According to Brun, Lucian's wife had, as a young woman, been the object of both brothers' desire. She chose the more »liebenswertheren« [worthy of love] brother Lucian with whom she was now happily married; consequently, Napoleon had tormented them ever since. His cruelty took the form of relentless pressure to accept offers of rulership of various territories on the condition that Lucian's »bourgeois« marriage be dissolved. Both Lucian and his wife steadfastly rejected these offers and remained loyal to each other and their marriage, in contradistinction, of course, to Napoleon's manipulation of his own marriages for political ends. Early on in her first letter she recounts this history of Lucian's marriage and nuclear family and returns to it repeatedly at crucial moments in her narrative. Indeed, as if to signify Lucian's effort to distance his loved ones from political controversy, Brun concludes *Briefe aus Rom* with the news that this family has fled the war-torn continent of Europe.

At the beginning of her second letter, Brun again presents their family as a paragon of domesticity and high culture persecuted by a cruel tyrant and compelled to exile in the bleak, winter countryside:

»Ihr fast ganz isoliertes harmloses Leben in Florenz, wo beide nur für die Erziehung ihrer Kinder lebten, und er sich noch außerdem ämsig mit einer Uebersetzung der Gerusalemme liberata (sic) beschäftigte, konnte die finstere Seele des kaiserlichen Bruders nicht beruhigen! Denn im November erscholl die Nachricht, die unschuldige Familie habe Florenz, eben so plötzlich wie Rom verlassen müssen, und sei auf eine ihr zugehörige Besitzung in der romischen Campagna, am See von Bracciano, geflüchtet; welche den Namen Canino mit großem Rechte führen soll, da dies Gut durch Oede der Gegend, Abgelegenheit und Verfallenheit der Wohngebäude beinahe unbewohnbar ist.« (26)

[Their almost totally isolated, harmless life in Florence where both lived entirely focused on raising their children, and he in addition to that had worked diligently on a translation of *Gerusalemme liberata*, could not soothe the dark soul of his imperial brother. For in November the news went out that the innocent family had had to leave Florence just as suddenly as they had left Rome, and had fled to their property in the Roman countryside on Lake Bracciano; it most appropriately bears the name Canino, for this estate is nearly unlivable because of its deserted, out of the way location and the disrepair of its dwellings.]

Brun concludes this vignette by glorifying Lucian's rejection of politics and material gain in favor of the private sphere. The rhetorical and ideological nature of Brun's glorification of companionate marriage stands out in relief when one recalls that her own marriage was little more than an empty form and that she maintained a decades-long close relation with the love of her life, the Swiss philosopher Karl Victor Bonstetten.[3] Indeed, she suggests that Lucian's choice to eschew political power and to suffer the resultant persecution by his brother accords him a kind of transcendent spirituality that is analogous to the inner spiritual realm she praises in her introduction to the letters: »[N]ur durch seine Leiden steigt Lucian jetzt über die verhaßte Dynastie empor, zu welcher er gehört, so wie durch die edle Wahl des Privatlebens, deren Weisheit aber auch die Zeit immer mehr enthüllen wird« (26). [Through his suffering, Lucian now mounts high above the hateful dynasty to which he belongs, as well as through his noble choice of private life, the wisdom of which time will increasingly reveal.]

It is the Pope whom Brun holds up as the ultimate model of moral authority and spiritual purity, opening her letters with the assertion »Der brave Pabst hält sich wie ein Held, mein theurer Bruder« (3). [The brave Pope behaves like a hero, my dear brother.] She creates in Pope Pius VII, as she does with Lucian Bonaparte, a feminized model of otherworldly power, an idealized alter ego. In part this choice has clear autobiographical roots. She is addressing these letters to her brother, a Bishop of the Lutheran Church. And she is the daughter of a German pastor who served a Lutheran community in Denmark. Her autobiography leaves no doubt as to her idealization of and identification with this beloved patriarchal figure whom she describes as loving and deeply loved by the citizens of his adopted country:

»Allein herzlich innig liebte er das Land seiner Wahl, das liebe Dänemark, herzlich ist er von dem gütigen Volke wieder geliebt worden. [...] Aber er verdiente es auch; denn er war milden Herzens, ohne Stolz, mit offenem Sinne das Gute erkennend, wo er es fand, und durch sanften Einfluß um sich ausströmend den Geist des Friedens, der heiteren Erkenntniß und Liebe.« (*Wahrheit* 5)

[He loved the country of his choice, beloved Denmark, sincerely and profoundly; he was loved by this good people heartily in return. [...] But he also deserved it, for he was a gentle soul, without pride, who acknowledged goodness openly, wherever he found it, and through his gentle influence exuded a spirit of peace, cheerful intelligence and love.]

Her childhood was marked by her father's melancholy at the dismissal from the Danish court of his close circle of distinguished artistic and intellectual friends, among them Klopstock, Cramer and the Stollbergs, as part of a power play by Count Struensee to take control of the Danish cabinet. In place of these »hellleuchtenden Sterne«, (*Wahrheit* 12) [bright shining stars] whom Brun associates with such liberal reforms as the abolition of serfdom, Struensee's power, she asserts, instituted a government in defiance of both religion and morality (13). It is easy to see her transposition of this scenario onto the Italian conflicts, with Napoleon playing the role of

Struensee and the Pope standing in for her father and his beloved circle of absent or »exiled« friends. Indeed Brun suggests that this experience of identification and sympathy with her father's loss constituted perhaps *the* formative influence on her future character: »Mein Vater blieb lange sanft traurig und ich mit ihm, und es entwickelte sich in mir mit seltner Energie die Schmerzensfähigkeit, und das tiefe Gefühl des Vermissens der Geliebten, welche den eigentlichen Grundaccord meines Wesens auszumachen bestimmt waren« (*Wahrheit* 13). [My father remained sad for a long time and I with him, and a capacity for suffering developed with unusual energy in me along with the deep feeling of missing absent loved ones that were destined to become the fundamental chord of my being.]

As a sign of her enduring bond with her father, as well as her independence from her husband, she used the name Friederike Brun *geborene Münter* for all of her publications (Keith-Smith 1987, 146).

Beyond her personal motivations, Brun's response to Pius VII also typifies and was perhaps instrumental in forming that of her European contemporaries. According to Brian Keith-Smith, *Briefe aus Rom*, which he terms »a minor masterpiece [...] history seen from a reporter's view«, was a »best seller in its time« (Keith-Smith 1987, 27-8). It was immediately translated into several languages and went into a second edition in 1820. As Roberta Olson emphasizes,

> »[I]n studying the events of Pius' life, his quiet heroism, tenacious commitment to his mission, and his penchant for passive resistance emerge as the ideal character traits for an individual in his time and position. They enabled him to become a quasi-saint in the eyes of all Europeans regardless of faith, except for committed Bonapartists.« (77)

Modern papal historian E. E. Y Hales describes him as monklike and otherworldly, »a gentle and pious Benedictine, with hidden reserves of strength and a smile that bewitched the painter Louis David« (*Duel* 329). Or again, »It was the quiet spiritual courage shown by Pius VII, held in power of Napoleon, and possessed of no States, that had moved the mind of Europe to admire him« (*Consalvi* 622). Similarly, the *New Catholic Encyclopedia* continues to foster the legend of Pius's »apolitical« politics and suggests that Pius's firm focus on spiritual issues combined with his avoidance of overt confrontation with Napoleon were keys to the survival of the Church in a post-revolutionary world. »For the monk become pope, detached from all temporal interests, what counted was above all else the spiritual, which he lived intensely. He was courageous, lucid, and although averse to administrative minutiae, able in critical moments to frame major decisions to orient the Church. He deserves to be called ›the pope of the new age‹« (381). Thus unlike Pius VI before him, who had died after his imprisonment by soldiers of the French Directory, Pius VII was not identified with the *ancien régime*. In fact, during Bonaparte's 1797 campaign, the future pope had issued a homily that had shocked his conservative colleagues and earned him the title of »Jacobin«. In an effort to reconcile Christ's teaching and Revolutionary aims, he had written: »The form of democratic government that you have chosen does not clash at all with the Gospel; on the contrary, it demands every sublime virtue which can only be learned at the school of Jesus Christ. [...] Be good Christians, and you will be good democrats«. (Hill 165) Such a position accords well with Brun's moderate republican politics, signified by her friendships with Staël and Sismondi and her admiration of the Swiss republics.

As previously mentioned, Brun opens her *Briefe aus Rom* with an unequivocal declaration that Pope Pius VII is the hero of her narrative: »[d]er brave Pabst hält sich wie ein Held, mein theurer Bruder« (3). Emptied of his overt political power by Napoleonic usurpation, the Pope becomes a repository for her ideal of pure spirituality as an agent of sociopolitical transformation on a European and perhaps even global scale. Linked to Brun's concept of spirituality are her opposition to militarism and aggressive nationalism as they are manifested by both sides in the Napoleonic wars and her concomitant belief in the effectiveness of nonviolent acts of resistance in the face of oppressive power. Early on in her first letter, Brun makes it clear that, as a historian, she writes not just for the present, but also for the future, in order to demonstrate the power of the spirit to vanquish the power of the sword: »Wie leicht in der Wagschaale der richtenden Nachwelt der Tyrann, der einen wehrlosen Greis fesselt, dessen festen Sinn er nie wird beugen können! Wie erhaben hingegen der moralische Widerstand dieses Einzigen, gegen die Ungeheuerste Obermacht [. . .]« (4).[4] [How light in posterity's scales of justice this tyrant who chains a helpless old man, whose firm mind he will never bend! How sublime on the other hand the moral resistance of this single individual against this immense supreme power.] Thus, when the Papal troops are rounded up and compelled to swear allegiance to Napoleon or be shot, Brun exclaims, »Wie recht hatte der Pabst, nicht auf diese Elenden zu rechnen? Sein Einfluß kann kein weltliches Militair bilden, allein sein Militair ist seine Geistlichkeit« (10). [The Pope was so right not to count on these wretched men. His influence can create no worldly army; his sole army is his spirituality.] And Napoleon is compelled to rescind his order that Roman cardinals born in Naples travel to that city to pay tribute to his brother Joseph Bonaparte. Midway through their journey, the cardinals are returned to Rome as the French come to see that such highhanded treatment of honorable elderly churchmen would not only create a public relations nightmare but would also fail of its purpose. »Man hatte zu spät bedacht, daß man doch die bepurpurten ehrwürdigen Greise, die Gegenstände der allgemeinen Verehrung, nicht mit der Knute zum Schwören zwingen könne. [. ..]« (13). [They realized too late that the purple clad venerable old men, objects of universal reverence, could not be forced with whips to swear oaths of loyalty.] Once again, the mind takes precedence over brute force.

Brun's portrayal of the Romans' loyalty to their Pope in the face of French occupation bears comparison to present day depictions of the Tibetan peoples' devotion to the Dali Lama as a symbol of national, cultural and spiritual independence in the face of Chinese aggression. In this context, loyalty to a priestly caste takes on emancipatory potential. And her account of the refusal on the part of the Roman populace to celebrate Carnival represents this refusal as a particularly effective act of non-violent resistance and protest against the French occupation. Efforts to compel the Romans to participate in Carnival festivities against the express wishes of the Pope are ridiculous and futile because a people cannot be forced into enjoying themselves! »[D]as Lächerliche desselben in der Progression der Kraft besteht, welche man aufwendet, um ein ganzes Volk zur Freude par force zu jagen« (26). [The ludicrousness of the progression of events is to be found in the power that they wield in order to force an entire people to enjoy themselves.] The Romans completely disregard the French governing General Miollis's command that Carnival take place, such that streets and boutiques are glaringly empty and deathly still, resulting in what Brun terms the »Allgemeinheit [des] Nichtkarnavals« (31) [universality of the not-carnival]. In the end the French troops, who, Brun claims, would rather face bullets than disdain, are the object of Roman scorn as they are ordered to attend hollow festivities that are boycotted by the natives. And the Romans' resistance becomes an act of moral courage and ultimate victory: »Dieser stille Kampf aber ist merkwürdiger, als die Frivolität des Gegenstandes es glaublich macht; denn er zeigt, wo wenigstens einer der Marksteine des Despotismus gesetzt ist, und wo seine ganze Macht scheitert? An der kindlichen, leichtgeflügelten Freude!« (29). [This silent battle is more remarkable than the frivolity of the subject would seem to allow, for it shows where at least one of the boundary-stones of despotism is set and where its power fails entirely: with childlike, light winged joy!] In particular, Brun praises the poorest classes who do not want to accept payment for their forced labor on these Carnival days. Among them, she writes, »Nichtsthun [ist] wahre Großmuth« (30) [to do nothing is true magnanimity]. *Briefe aus Rom* deserves to be read alongside Percy Shelley's grim *Mask of Anarchy* as a lighter meditation on the power of collective, popular non-violent resistance.

Just as the Napoleonic troops cannot *compel* the Romans to celebrate their beloved Carnival in a city under occupation so they also cannot *prevent* the universal honoring of the Pope during his coronation feast days at the end of March, 1809 in a silent show of lights that Brun terms [eine] »glänzende Fest der Liebe« (37) [a brilliant festival of love]. The collective social element in this spiritual experience is clearly central for her. Brun also shares the sublime experience of this transfiguring illumination of the city's most prominent monuments with her countryman the sculptor Bertel Thorwaldsen who exclaims, »Ist's nicht Göttlich?« (38) [Isn't it divine?]. Thorwaldsen would later carve Pope Pius's tomb in St. Peter's, an exceptional and scandal-provoking choice, given his Protestant faith.[5] Even in his death, then, Pius VII was associated with a transcendence of sectarian limitations. Brun furthermore portrays the lighting of the buildings and plazas by street vendors and porters as well as illumination of the smallest homes and poorest huts by their inhabitants as courageous acts of resistance on the part of these Roman citizens who have reclaimed their Promethean fire from Napoleon:

»So hat keine Hauptstadt Europens, in diesen Zeiten wo Kraft und Gewalt (wie in Aeschylos Prometheus) die liedende Menschheit fesseln, seine Liebe zu einem der mißhandelten rechtmäßigen Souveraine gezeigt, und keine so muthig; denn Muth gehört dazu, erzt ein ganzes Sieggekröntes Militair so zu verhöhnen, als es das französiche am ersten Carnavalstage ward: und dann in einer von feindlichen Truppen stark besetzten Stadt einem gefangenen Souverain so glänzende und allgemeine Beweise der ungetheilten Liebe zu geben, daß selbst der Feind sich gezwungen sieht, in dieselben einzustimmen. Ich erinnere mich nicht, in den Revolutionsjahren, etwas ähnliches gehört zu haben.« (40)

[In these times when power and violence chain suffering mankind (as in Aeschylus's Prometheus) no European capitol has shown its love this way for a mistreated legal sovereign, and none so courageously; for it takes courage, first to scorn a military crowned by victory as was done to the French that first day of Carnival and then, in a city heavily occupied by enemy troops to give an imprisoned sovereign such splendid and universal proof of undivided love that even the enemy feels compelled to join in. I don't remember having heard of anything similar during the French revolutionary years.]

The lights hold emancipatory potential as symbols of Roman and Italian pride that suggest a constructive nationalist impulse in this popular resistance to foreign occupation. Brun pointedly privileges these impulses over French Revolutionary fervor.

Brun, then, associates Pope Pius VII not just with Enlightenment cosmopolitanism but also with nascent Italian nationalism. Indeed, Roberta Olson calls him the first Risorgimento hero who was depicted, especially by Italian artists, through »pregnant and politically ideological works in which Pius symbolized the resurgence and unity of Italian civilization« (78-9). This cultural pride is clearly to be distinguished from the exclusive and excessive love of country that she condemns at the beginning of her letters and that she associates with military aggression and the desire to impose foreign will on other peoples. As a poet and *salonnière*, Brun is particularly horrified by Napoleon's plundering of Italian art, architectural monuments and libraries (the Vatican library and archives in particular), thefts she terms »Barbarenthaten« (65) [acts of barbarism]. Describing French authorities in Rome as »Instrumente in der Hand des Bösen« [instruments in the hands of evil], she writes, »Kurz, kein Pallast, kein Museum, keine Privatsammlung unter den Nahmhaften, haben Zwang oder Noth verschont!« (66) [In short, no palace, no museum, no notable private collection has been spared compulsion or force.]. Fittingly, when Pius VII returned from exile, he played a key role in repatriating such treasures as the Apollo Belvedere and the Laocoön from France and undertook an intensive building and restoration program in the Vatican and the city of Rome. According to Olson, these restorations, as well as impressing foreign visitors to Rome, also »increased Italians' sense of pride in their heritage and thereby created a national consciousness that helped to set the tone for the Risorgimento« (90). In her critique of the Napoleonic plundering of Rome, Brun seems to distinguish between justified pride in Italian cultural accomplishment and aggressive, militant nationalism that claims superiority over other nations and cultures. Yet such distinctions can be slippery and treacherous. Pius VII was celebrated by the sculptor Canova as an international peacemaker in his bust-length portrait that highlighted the word PAX in the papal coat of arms (Olson 90). At the same time, depictions of his return to Rome from exile sought to equate him with triumphant Roman emperors, just as Brun herself celebrates imperial Rome as »die glücklichsten Zeiten, welche die Herrscherin Rom der Erde gegeben« (37) [the most fortunate times that Rome as ruler gave the earth].

Brun furthermore repeatedly emphasizes Pius's role as a peacemaker who abhors violence and finds much more effective nonviolent means to achieve his spiritual and political ends. She acknowledges that the Pope would only have to say the word for the armed Roman populace to rise up against the foreign occupation, but the Pope wisely refuses to match »Gewalt mit Gewalt«; »er will nur sein geistiges Reich behaupten« (40) [Violence with violence; he intends to claim his spiritual realm only].

»Denn eben dies Gefühl, daß es, bei Behauptung seines Willens, um etwas höheres gilt, als um Land und Gut: dieser Gedanke des Unsichtbaren ist es, welcher ihn seinen Unterthanen als den darstellt, daß Reich eigentlich nicht von dieser Welt ist, und dem sie also mehr durch Liebe und Gehorsam, als durch gewaltthätige Aeußerungen, die Innigkeit und Festigkeit ihrer Anhänglichkeit zu beweisen haben.« (40-1)

[Because it is precisely this feeling that in the assertion of his will something more is at stake than just land and property; it is this idea of the invisible that makes his subjects represent him as one whose realm is not of this world and one to whom they must show the depth and firmness of their attachment through love and obedience rather than through violent actions.]

Here the popular will meets and mirrors that of their spiritual leader. Indeed, Brun emphasizes that history has accorded past warlike and aggressive Popes nothing but mistrust, disapproval and scorn.

The immediate occasion for Napoleon's invasion of Rome and the Vatican was the Pope's refusal to take sides with the French against England, a product of his desire to distance and protect the Catholic Church as much as possible from violent partisan conflict. Similarly, the most moving and timeless passages in Brun's correspondence, by exposing the wartime brutalities perpetrated by both sides, communicate a powerful anti-war message. Of battles between Calabrese insurgents and German soldiers compelled to fight on the side of the French who have conquered their lands she writes: »Die bei diesem Partheikriege vorfallenden Grausamkeiten machen die Menschlichkeit schaudern; und Calabrien ist wie Spanien ein offnes Franzosengrab! Aber ach! Auch Deutsche müssen (o Schmach und Schande, daß sie es müssen!) gegen die tapfern Calabresen fechten!« (8-9) [The atrocities accompanying this partisan war make humanity shudder; and Calabria, like Spain, is an open grave for the French! And ah! The German must [o shame and disgrace that they must!] also fight against these brave Calabrese!]. War (which she explicitly and pointedly terms »partisan«) is the ultimate affront to her ideal of humanity (*Menschlichkeit*). She finds horrific both the slaughter of her enemies, the French, by these Italian rebels and the fact that the complexities of European politics compel her German compatriots to fight on the side of these enemies. Above all else she bemoans the fate of the young men on both sides of the conflict who are sent into war as cannon fodder and refers to military draft as »jugendmordende Conscription« (25) [conscription murderous to youth].

Brun is particularly intrigued by women's relation to wartime violence, revealing women to be anything but mere passive spectators of male aggression and emphasizing extremes of behavior, both demonic and angelic. The Calabrese women, she recounts, searched through deserted battlefields, like »furchtbaren Rachegeister« (9) [terrible avenging furies] for wounded enemy soldiers whom they executed on the spot. She has learned of these atrocities from an officer who had been severely wounded in the battle. Witnessing the fate of his compatriots, he had dragged himself into the nearby woods to escape certain death, only to be followed by his faithful dog whose barking risked giving away his hiding place. In the end he was forced to use his last strength, before losing consciousness, to strangle his beloved companion. In contrasting the loyalty of the officer's dog with the ruthless inhumanity of the Calabrese women, Brun shows that war has the potential to strip those blinded by partisanship of common decency and compassion, to render them less than human, indeed less than animal.

Brun also insists, with the counterexample of a young Spanish woman, that women also have the capacity to transcend the atrocities of war through an allegiance to common humanity and compassion. This young woman rescues an enemy French soldier who is near death from her murderous female compatriots by dragging him to the altar of a local cathedral. Here she watches over him until she can take him home, bind his wounds and feed him. For six weeks she is his sole caretaker, even playing the guitar and singing for him when depression overwhelms him. Brun, who has heard this tale from the French/Genevan officer himself, makes clear that she believes the young woman has fallen in love with the »junger wunderschöner französischer Offizier« [beautiful young French officer] who soon is well enough to return home. Here Brun celebrates not just Agape but also Eros as powerful forces in the battle against partisan blindness, cruelty and inhumanity. Her sympathies in this tale are clearly with the young French soldier despite the fact that he has served as an agent of Napoleon's army. As for the young Spanish girl, Brun asks »Wird daß Bewußtseyn einer schönen That das jugendlich glühende Herz nicht beruhigt haben?« (9) [Will not the consciousness of her good deed have soothed the young, burning heart?]. It is as if her courageous selfless act embodies the spirituality or *Geistlichkeit* that for Brun is a reward in itself. And literally loving one's enemy is perhaps the highest good.

In this the Pope once again sets the tone. Even when he is dragged by the French in the middle of the night from the Quirinal palace where he has been imprisoned for seven months to be transported against his will into exile, he stops to bless the enemy troops, forgetting his own decree of excommunication, »dem sanften Zuge des Herzens folgend« (60) [following the gentle tendencies of his heart]. Brun is horrified by this »gewaltsame Schandthat« (60) [violent, infamous act] on the part of the French and her response reflects her ever present awareness of historical record and legacy:

»Der französische General, welcher den Pabst entführt hat, heißt Radèz, sein bis jetzt unbekannter Name wird nur zu seiner Schande in der Geschichte genannt werden; wie tief sind die Franzosen gesunken, wie tief!! Ein General der sich von einem Diebe anführen läßt, um einen wehrlosen Greis, selbst wie ein Dieb einbrechend, aus seinem Schlafgemache zu stehlen!« (61)

[The French general who kidnapped the Pope is named Radèz; his name, until now unknown, will go down in history as a disgrace; how low the French have stooped, how low! A general lets himself be led by a thief and breaks in like a thief upon a defenseless old man to steal him away out of his bedchamber.]

Whereas she excoriates Radèz, Brun takes her cue from the Pope and offers a generous and sympathetic portrait of the French general in charge of Rome, Generalgouverneur Graf Miollis, seeking when she can to find the good in a political enemy, at the same time condemning his willingness to serve tyranny and his moral complicity with evil:

»Er ist sonst immer gleich sehr mit Militairorden und mit Wunden bedeckt, denn so habe ich nie einen Menschen vom Kriege zugerichtet gesehen; dabei hat er ein so treues gutes Gesicht, und etwas so gerades gutmüthiges in seinem Wesen, daß man ihn nicht ansehen kann ohne zu bedauern, daß er diesem Herrn dient, und fur eine so üble Sache sein Blut verschwendet hat. […] Miollis ist wirklich zu bedauern. Man sagt, er habe die Stelle nur angenommen, weil er Italian überhaupt, und Rom insbesondere, so sehr liebe, und Schlimmeres verhüten wolle. So sanft und schonend wie möglich ist er, – allein wenn sich keine ehrlichen Leute gebrauchen ließen, so würde das Maaß eher voll, und der letzte Tropfen, der überall noch fehlt, machte es bald überschäumen! Nun geschieht doch das Böse, nur leidlich guter Art, und die Völker dulden nun einmal so lange sie können.« (19-20)

[He is otherwise so thoroughly covered with military medals and wounds, that I have never seen a man so marked by war; at the same time he has such a good honest face and something so straightforwardly good natured in his manner that one cannot look at him without regretting that he serves this master and has shed his blood for such an evil cause. [...] Miollis is really to be pitied. People say he only took the position because he loves Italy, Rome especially, and wanted to prevent worse from happening. He is as gentle and mild as possible, – except if no honorable people allowed themselves to be thus used then the cup would rather be full and the final drop that is now missing everywhere would soon make it overflow. But thus evil does indeed occur, in a tolerably decent fashion, and the people bear it as long as they can.]

Brun's efforts to represent a transcendent humanity beyond the boundaries of nation and country culminate in her portrait of another Frenchman, one Chevalier d'Agincourt, whom she terms »die Krone und das Herz meiner hiesigen Bekanntschaften« (47) [the crown and heart of my acquaintances here]. This elderly gentleman in his eighties functions as a kind of accessible double for the deceased father and the inaccessible Pope who, Brun laments, does not receive women! »Kindlich hangen wir an ihm, und werden väterlich von ihm wieder geliebt« (47) [we are attached to him like children and are loved paternally by him in return], she writes of this aged member of the French nobility. In her portrait of d'Agincourt, we witness Brun's acknowledgment of, respect, and appreciation for what might be termed national character in its complex relation to her conception of universal humanity:

»Dieser ernste Gelehrte verbindet in sich alles was dans la vieille bonne France die Individuen seiner Nation im Alter am vortheilhaftesten auszeichnete: Lebendige Munterkeit, reges Zartgefühl: jene Galanterie des Herzens, im Umgange mit Frauen, welche überhaupt den südlichen Nationen eigen, durch die Franzosen am zartesten ausgesprochen wurde.« (47)

[This serious scholar unites in himself all that distinguished individuals of his nation most advantageously in *la vieille bonne France* – lively cheerfulness, active delicacy of feeling, that gallantry of the heart in their relations with women that is absolutely unique to southern countries and that is expressed most delicately by the French.]

At the same time, her portrait moves beyond these national traits to transform this aging Chevalier into an emblem of pure humanity and otherworldly spirituality:

»Dies ist er als Franzose; was er allein als Mensch ist – das ist weit höher, und gehört keinem Völke ausschließend an; d'Agincourt hat jene hohe, allen Entweihungen unerreichbar gebliebene Reinheit und Klarheit der Seele; jene sanfte Gott geweihte Frömmigkeit des Herzens [...]welche diese seltnen Palmen unter den weisesten Menschen, mit einer Morgenröthe der Unsterblichkeit, schon hienieden umglänzt.« (47)

[This he is as a Frenchman; what he is as human being alone is much higher and belongs to no people exclusively; d'Agincourt possesses that purity and clarity of soul that has remained out of reach to all desecration; that gentle piety of the heart consecrated by God that surrounds these rare palms among the wisest of men with a dawning light of immortality here below.]

For Brun the Chevalier's spiritual clarity is furthermore inseparable from his opposition to his nation's imperial policy under Napoleon and thus accords with her condemnation, in her autobiography, of exclusive love of country, as well as her association of cosmopolitanism and spiritual enlightenment. The above image of the Chevalier as a rare palm among wise men transfigured by the dawning light of immortality has an eastern or orientalist flavor as does her subsequent playful reference to him as her Brahmin because of his vegetarian diet and his meditative, secluded life.

Here the question of the limits of Brun's cosmopolitanism inevitably arises for the twenty-first century reader. Is it exclusively a pan-Europeanism based in Western Christian values or does it encompass all peoples of all faiths, as her portrait of the French Chevalier seems to hint? In many ways, Brun's *Briefe aus Rom*, in its idealization of the Pope, seems a strangely contemporary text in 2005 following on the heels of the overwhelming mass adoration and the cries of »santo subito« that accompanied Pope John Paul's recent funeral. Furthermore, the question of Brun's pan Europeanism/ Eurocentrism is a particularly troubling one today, given the recent votes in France and the Netherlands against the European Union constitution, votes clearly influenced by anti-Turkish sentiment among voters. At the conclusion of her third letter, Brun describes »ein seeliges Gefühl allgemeiner Bruderliebe« (51) [a holy feeling of universal brotherhood] as her response to the Roman celebration of Ascension Day attended by »[eine] Menschenflut von allen Altern und Geschlechtern, und aus allen Ständen [...] Bekleidete und halbnackte, bleiche Elende, Krüppel, Verlassene von der ganzen Menschheit« (49) [a flood of humanity of all ages and sexes and from all stations […] clothed and half naked, pale wretches, cripples, forsaken by all of mankind]. Ultimately, this brotherly love seems reserved for, or at least focused upon, fellow Christians, as Brun imagines the day when all the world's Christians are united in an ecumenical, embracing faith, when »einst in der Fülle der Jahrhunderte alle Bekenner des Christenthums, nicht durch Tyrannenmacht in eine formlose geistlose Masse amalgamirt, sondern durch das Gefühl der hohen Einheit des christlichen Bekenntnisses […] in eine Liebe, eine Hoffnung, und eine Seeligkeit vereint zusammenströmten« (51) [In the fullness of the centuries, all those who profess Christianity will come together, not amalgamated through tyrannical power into a formless, spiritless mass, but joined through the feeling of the higher unity of Christian confession in one love, hope and spirituality].

Given the current global tensions between nominally Christian and Islamic nations since 2001 and the US invasion of Iraq, it is both striking and distressing to turn to Brun's later poem entitled *Lieder für Hellas* (Songs for Hellas), written as Keith-Smith observes, »in a spirit of Christian crusade« (Keith-Smith 2000, 156). The wisdom, both subtle and profound, of Brun's antimilitaristic, pacifist stance in *Briefe aus Rom* as well as her clear understanding of the power of non-violent, spiritual resistance are glaringly absent in this fanatically Christian diatribe. Instead *Lieder für Hellas* begins on a bloodthirsty note: »O Hellas, Hellas im blutigen Kampf/ Wie bist du schön« (273) [O Hellas, Hellas in bloody battle/ How beautiful you are]. Patriotic stanzas drawing parallels between Germany and Greece as well as stanzas entitled *Gebet für Griechenland* [Prayer for Greece] and meant to be sung to the tune of *God Save the Queen* follow. The same labels that Brun applied to Napoleon and his troops – barbarians and tyrants – are now applied to the Turks. But whereas Brun sought to counteract her opposition to French policy by finding the humanity in individual French citizens of her acquaintance, she demonizes the Turks as enemies of God. Algerians are »Hunde der Hölle« (280) [Hounds of hell] and the entire continent of Asia condemned as weak and enervated. And her subtitle »Niedergelegt auf den Altar der Menschlichkeit« [Laid on the Altar of Humanity] suggests that perhaps only Christian Europeans belong in this privileged category and that all Others are relegated to the category of the sub-human. Finally, Brun concludes her poem with the refrain »Gott ist mit Euch« (292) [God is with you], rendering unequivocal her faith that God has taken sides with the Europeans and Christians against the Islamic world. Byron's hopes notwithstanding, this war of mutual extermination was less about Greek independence than it was about assuring European control of the region and about »saving« Greece for Western civilization, as the final victory of England, France and Russia and their installation of a Bavarian king suggests. In conclusion, then, Brun's ideals of cosmopolitanism, pan-Europeanism and *Geistlichkeit* as developed in *Briefe aus Rom* represent a remarkable model for non-violent resolution of conflict, resistance to abusive power and the balancing of national and international claims. Their implementation in the militaristic *Lieder für Hellas*, however, as exclusively Christian and Western, should offer us a warning today of their potential for devastatingly destructive influence.

–University of California, Davis

## Notes

All translations of Brun in this paper are my own.

1 Bainbridge asserts that Napoleon became crucial to British Romantic poets' ideas of »their own roles and their acts of self-conception« (1). »They both identified with him, appropriating him as a figure of power, and used him as an Other against which they could define themselves« (1-2). Clearly gender plays a key role in such processes of identification, appropriation and opposition.

2 »Aber auch gegen die frühesten geliebtesten Schauplätze meiner Kindheitserinnerungen, wütheten die Bomben der Engländer! Petrikirche und Kapelle; die beiden Häuser so wir bewohnten, die Gärten an denselben, alles ist noch eine Ruine! « (83).

3 Though critics frequently call this a platonic relationship, the intensity of their correspondence would suggest otherwise. Marie-L. Herking perhaps puts it best when she writes: »On se demandera, très probablement, si les rapports entre Mme Brun et Bonstetten ne furent platoniques. Il est permis de s'en douter, bien qu'aucun document nous enseigne à cet égard« (219).

4 Here Brun echoes the ideas of Swiss German historian Johannes von Müller (1752–1809) whom she also quotes in her Introduction as emphasizing that it is the Pope's detachment from military force that grants him the moral authority to speak truth to political power (2). Müller was associated with the Staël circle and was an acquaintance of Brun and Bonstetten.

5 According to Olson, »Thorvaldsen was the first Protestant commissioned to carve the tomb of a Pope. This commission understandably caused a great deal of controversy« (92). Thorvaldsen also carved the tomb (1824–25) of Pius VII's great Secretary of State Cardinal Consalvi in the Pantheon »where Consalvi is depicted as restoring the Papal Provinces to Pius VII.« (92).

## Works Cited

Arnim, Bettine von. *Die Günderode. Werke und Briefe.* Ed. Walter Schmitz and Sybille von Steinsdorff. Vol. I. Frankfurt: Deutscher Klassiker Verlag, 1986. 3 vols.

Bainbridge, Simon. *Napoleon and English Romanticism.* Cambridge: Cambridge UP, 1995.

Brun, Friederike. *Briefe aus Rom.* Intro. and ed. Brian Keith-Smith and Herman Moens. German Women Writers. Vol. 12. Lewiston, NY: Edwin Mellen, 2000.

Brun, Friederike. *Lieder für Hellas* in *Wahrheit aus Morgenträumen* und *Idas aesthetische Entwickelung.* Aarau: Sauerländer, 1824: 271-93.

Brun, Friederike. *Wahrheit aus Morgenträumen.* Intro. and ed. Brian Keith-Smith. German Women Writers. Vol. 11. Lewiston, NY: Edwin Mellen, 2000.

Hales, E. E. Y. »Cardinal Consalvi: The Tragedy of Success«. *History Today* 10, No. 9 (1960): 616-622.

Hales, E. E. Y. »Napoleon's Duel with the Pope«. *History Today.* 8, No. 5 (1958): 328-36.

Hales, E. E. Y. *Revolution and Papacy, 1769–1840.* London: Eyre and Spottiswoode, 1960.

Herking, Marie-L. *Charles-Victor de Bonstetten, 1745–1832: sa vie, ses oeuvres.* Lausanne: La Concorde, 1920.

Hilt, Douglas. *Ten against Napoleon.* Chicago: Nelson-Hall, 1975.

Keane, Angela. »The Anxiety of (Feminine) Influence: Hannah More and Counterrevolution«. *Rebellious Hearts: British Women Writers and the French Revolution.* Ed. Adriana Craciun and Kari E. Lokke. Albany: SUNY, 2001. 109-34.

Keith-Smith, Brian. »Friederike Brun, (1765–1835): in tears there is joy«. *Sappho in the Shadows: Essays on the work of German women poets in the age of Goethe (1749–1832).* Ed. Anthony J. Harper and Margaret C. Ives. Bern: Peter Lang, 2000. 145-88.

Keith-Smith, Brian. »Friederike Brun and her contemporaries«. *Women Writers of the Age of Goethe.* Vol. I Ed. Margaret C. Ives. Occasional Papers in German Studies, 1. Lancaster: U of Lancaster, 1987. 8-35.

Kennedy, Deborah. *Helen Maria Williams and the Age of Revolution.* Lewisburg: Bucknell UP, 2002.

Leflon, J. »Pius VII, Pope«. *New Catholic Encyclopedia.* 2nd Edition. Farmington Hills, MI: Gale Group, 2003.

Moskal, Jeanne. »Napoleon, Nationalism, and the Politics of Religion in Mariana Starke's *Letters from Italy*«. *Rebellious Hearts: British Women Writers and the French Revolution.* Ed. Adriana Craciun and Kari E. Lokke. Albany: SUNY P, 2001.

Olson, Roberta J. M. »Representations of Pope Pius VII: The First Risorgimento Hero.« *The Art Bulletin* 68, No. 1 (Mar., 1986): 77-93.

Ross, Marlon. »Configurations of Feminine Reform: The Woman Writer and the Tradition of Dissent«. *Re-Visioning Romanticism: British Women Writers, 1776–1837.* Ed. Carol Shiner Wilson and Joel Hafner. Philadelphia: U of Pennsylvania P, 1994: 91-110.

# Forms of Aesthetics and Cultural-political Opposition

# Diversionary Tactics: Art Criticism as Political Weapon in Staël's *Corinne, ou l'Italie* (1807)

*Heather Belnap Jensen*

At the height of the Napoleonic Empire, Germaine de Staël published *Corinne, ou l'Italie* (*Corinne, or Italy*, 1807), a widely popular novel that forcefully engaged contemporary issues of aesthetics, cultural patrimony, and the state of the European community. Discussions of art objects form a critical component of the novel in that these map out the unsettled territory of post-Revolutionary culture. Declaring that her critical activity was merely an »aimable adresse« [pleasant stratagem] and an »innocentes ruses« [innocent ploy] (Staël 1985, 215),[1] Staël's protagonist, Corinne, guides her lover through various museums and sites in Rome, as well as through her personal collection of paintings housed in Tivoli. What I will argue is that the ways in which this picture gallery is framed and discussed belie these protests of inconsequentiality and indicates that Staël carefully calculated this construct as a means of articulating her anti-Napoleonic views on art and politics.

While there is significant scholarship devoted to this author's antipathy for the Emperor, her use of art criticism as a mode of protest against Napoleonic cultural practices is a surprisingly overlooked component of her work. Within this discourse, Staël declares her distaste for Napoleonic cultural practices, such as the transportation of Europe's finest art collections to France and the reification of the Neoclassical paradigm, as a means of thwarting cultural authenticity. Moreover, the valorization of those aspects of German Romantic aesthetics and modes of art criticism voiced within this section reveals yet another layer of her anti-Napoleonic sentiment. Close examination of the contents of Corinne's imaginary collection, which includes paintings from the modern school of French painting, Italian Renaissance masters, and contemporary British and German artists, as well as the manner in which these works are discussed, reveals Staël's adversarial position toward Napoleon.

Consideration of Staël's aesthetic theory and criticism in the novel *Corinne, or Italy* within the framework of contemporary theory and practice in early nineteenth-century French art criticism demonstrates that her contributions to this area were manifold. Her interest in introducing Romantic aesthetics to the French public, her explication of central issues in contemporary French art criticism, and her desire to add a female voice and vision to the traditional male discourse in this field are truly significant. Moreover, her questioning of the patriarchal ideologies imbued in paintings of the modern French school illustrates her desire to question the social order under Napoleon. These discussions also testify to Staël's commitment to effecting change in Napoleonic society, and her recognition of the role cultural criticism could play in that process.

Staël's approach of cloaking subversive political ideas under the guise of art criticism followed conventions established before the Revolution and maintained throughout the Napoleonic period in popular discourse. With a public well accustomed to reading politicized art criticism, these critics could condemn state-sponsored art in aesthetic terms, thereby covertly critiquing Napoleonic policies (Siegfried, 1994; Fort, 1998). This phenomenon also occurs in the literary criticism of the Coppet circle (Staël and her entourage), where the debates over the Classical and Romantic models in literature masked an indictment of Napoleon's regime: Classicism was framed as a sterile vehicle for despotism, whereas Romanticism was fashioned as an vital means of emancipation (Tenenbaum, 1980). The writer knew well the necessity of masking anti-Napoleonic critiques. Exiled in 1802 by the French leader, who chafed at the sway Staël held in political and cultural circles, the author was condemned to live in exile for more than ten years afterward.[2] Cultural criticism was perhaps the safest medium to use as a means of protest against the current status of both French art and society; thus, in her art discussions Staël could voice her opinions without much fear of reprisal.

It is in *Corinne, or Italy* that Staël fashions a work that is deeply committed to art, thereby staking a claim for her place in the early nineteenth-century realm of aesthetics and art criticism. Her novel, staged between 1794–1803, centers around the ill-fated romance between the handsome and sensitive Englishman Oswald, Lord Nelvil, who, while grieving over his father's recent death, is touring Italy; and Corinne, the most illustrious woman of that country. While in Rome, Oswald sees Corinne being honored at the Capitol and is immediately smitten with her, as she is with him, and the two quickly become lovers. Importantly, the heroine is a woman of genius who is endowed with extraordinary artistic abilities. In addition to her inimitable talents as an *improvatrice*, Corinne is also a superlative poet, actor, dancer, and painter (Dehon 1-9). A significant aspect of this novel is the ways in which the heroine fashions herself as a cultural interlocutor for her lover, Oswald. The climax of their excursions is reached in Book VIII, »Statues and Paintings«, the section in which Corinne invites Oswald to accompany her on a tour of the art of Rome, a pivotal moment in both establishing the nature of the protagonists' relationship and revealing Staël's aesthetic agenda. They will see the ancient statues and Renaissance masterpieces of the Vatican and other art sites, visit Antonio Canova's studio by torchlight, and tour Corinne's private gallery at Tivoli. While Staël comments on art and architecture throughout the novel, it is within Book VIII that the author most ardently converses on issues and ideas central to contemporary art criticism, in which she expresses an antipathy to Napoleonic cultural policies. On the surface, the discussion between Corinne and Oswald involves nothing more than a conversation on the merits of a handful of paintings, or a »pleasant stratagem« or »innocent ploy« intended merely as a diversion for her troubled lover. This articulation of the insignificance of the upcoming narrative may be seen as a revelation of Staël's anxiety of authorship – or as a strategy for preventing the subversive elements of her cultural criticism from garnering notice. And although Corinne will remark, »elle ne prononçait que des paroles indifférentes« (Staël 1985, 232) [her words were inconsequential], what her aesthetic discourse demonstrates is Staël's abilities as an interlocutor on the arts, as well as her desire to critique the current state of contemporary Europe.

The conversation between Corinne and Oswald begins in the Vatican, where they encounter sculptures from antiquity that invite consideration of the differences between the classical and modern worlds. In the discussion of ancient sculpture in *Corinne*, the *Laocoön, Niobe*, the *Medici Venus*, and the *Dying Gladiator* are mentioned. All of these works were on display in the Musée Central in 1803; while it is possible that Staël saw several of these works in Paris prior to her exile in 1802, it is certain that the works this author viewed on her trip to Italy in 1804 were merely plaster casts created by Canova. The excursion of Corinne and Oswald into the Vatican sets the stage for her incisive criticism of Napoleonic cultural policy. The description of these halls, filled with antiquities, constantly refers to the inapproachable perfection of the ancients. The narrator explains:

»La douleur dans nos temps modernes, au milieu de notre état social si froid et si oppressif, est ce qu'il y a de plus noble dans l'homme; et, de nos jours, qui n'aurait pas souffert, n'aurait jamais senti ni pensé. Mais il y avait dans l'antiquité quelque chose de plus noble que la douleur, c'était le calme héroïque, c'était le sentiment de sa force qui pouvait se développer au milieu d'institutions franches et libres.« (Staël 1985, 216-17)

[In our modern day, society is so cold and oppressive that suffering is man's noblest aspect, and any man who has not suffered has neither felt nor thought. But in earlier times, there was something nobler than pain; it was heroic equanimity, the sense of strength that could develop among unequivocally free institutions.]

Thus, contemporary institutions – the state and its enterprises under Napoleon – limit the freedom of the individual. The narrator continues in this vein, writing: »L'encouragement, l'émulation étaient le principe des beaux-arts comme de la politique; il y avait place pour toutes les vertus, comme pour tous les talents« (Staël 1985, 218) [Encouragement, emulation: these were the principles of the arts as of politics; there was room for all virtues as for all talents]. Given Staël's combative relationship with the Emperor Napoleon, who seemed intent on squelching the author's every enterprise, the remark reads as pointed.

As a means of testing some of these theories, Corinne has created an extraordinary gallery of paintings, located on her estate in Tivoli. Filled with both original works of art and copies of contemporary masters' work, this collection is carefully crafted to not only further her narrative goals within the novel, but also to enter into aesthetic discussions on those issues particularly germane in the early nineteenth-century art world, and ultimately, to critique Napoleon's use (or abuse) of the arts and the cultural domain. In many ways, this section of the novel works as a kind of »permanent verbal museum«, to borrow Bernadette Fort's phraseology (Fort 1998, 150), in which the carefully selected works foreground those issues central to aesthetic debates in Napoleonic France. In this formative stage in the creation of institutions like museums[3] and practices such as art criticism, Staël's creation of an imaginary collection-owned and explicated by Corinne, the female spectator *par excellence* – empowers the female viewer in significant ways.

The dialogue format of Staël's critiques in »Statues and Paintings« follows conventions established in the late eighteenth century and continued well into the nineteenth century, and reflects a commitment to the dialectical task of educating the public through such discourse. As an adherent to the idea that art criticism reflect the myriad issues and voices involved in the creation of the new public art sphere, Diderot wrote in a conversational mode (Crow, Diderot's *Salons*, 1995, xiii). Salon pamphlets abound in examples of the dialogue format. This kind of conversational approach is also used in Friedrich Schlegel's journal *Europa*, to which Staël referred in her notes in the novel, and in the Schlegels's dialogue, »The Paintings«.[4] The novelist's stratagem of organizing her tour through the gallery as a debate exemplifies the recognition of the obligation of the art critic to educate the public on various issues associated with a particular topic or artwork.[5] That the novelist wishes to educate her readers is suggested in the note she provides within this section on the specific artists and artworks that figure into Corinne's gallery. She writes:

»Les tableaux historiques qui compasent la galerie de Corinne sont des copies ou des originaux du Brutus de David, du Marius de Drouet [sic], du Bélisaire de Gérard. Parmi les autres tableaux cités, celui de Didon a été fait par M. Rehberg, peintre allemand; celui de Clorinde est dans la galerie de Florence; celui de Macbeth est dans la collection anglaise des tableaux pour Shakespeare, et celui de Phèdre est de Guérin; enfin, les deux paysages de Cincinnatus et d'Ossian sont à Rome, et M. Wallis, peintre anglais, en est l'auteur.« (Staël 1985, 591, note 21)

[The historical paintings that make up Corinne's gallery are copies or originals of David's *Brutus*, Drouet's [sic] *Marius*, Gérard's *Belisarius*. Among the other paintings cited, *Dido* is by M. Rehberg, the German artist; *Clorinda* is in the gallery in Florence; *Macbeth* is in the English collection of paintings for Shakespeare, and *Phaedra* is by Guérin; the two landscapes showing Cincinnatus and Ossian, done by the English artist M. Wallis, are in Rome.]

I maintain that the selection process for the art works in this gallery was neither arbitrary nor facile. While I agree with Simone Balayé, who asserts that the primary motivation for the author's choice of artworks had to do with the relationship between these and Staël's aesthetic principles, I do not think Balayé explored the full implications of these selections. I believe that it was fashioned as a means of emphasizing the disparity between her vision of cultural plenitude and the reality of the arts under Napoleon's regime. Significantly, many of key works discussed in this section were among the spoils of his Italian conquest that were relocated to Paris and on display in the Musée Napoléon when *Corinne* was published.

The gallery tour begins with a statement aimed at undermining Napoleon's pillaging of Italian art, where the protagonist reminds the reader that »[l]es chefs-d'oeuvres de la peinture étaient alors réunis à Rome, et sa richesse, sous ce rapport, surpassait toutes celles du reste du monde« (Staël 1985, 221) [the masterpieces of painting were collected in Rome at the time, and in this respect, she was vastly more wealthy than the rest of the world]. Given that the novel is set in the mid-1790s, this was a true statement indeed; however, Napoleon's armies had impoverished Italy of its art treasures by 1807, the year in which *Corinne* was published, and the works had become part of the Musée Napoleon (see Gould, Boyer). This plundering was an event much commented upon throughout Europe.[6] Thus, these paintings had a particular cultural valency for the readers of the novel, as this transportation of artistic treasures was a major event that had important ramifications. Napoleon's attempt to make Paris the center of the art world was achieved, but by so doing, he created a false pan-European museum that was built on a haphazard and coercive collecting strategy. Corinne counters this model with a gallery that offers works by European artists in a variety of genres that spanned several centuries. Staël's imaginary collection becomes a sort of laboratory for considering the central aesthetic issue in early nineteenth-century Europe: what was the current state of contemporary art?

Several of the paintings under discussion were well known and esteemed works from the modern French school that were often used in discussions of this very question. Corinne enters into the debate on the development of the school of David by asking: »La nature des sujets que les grands artistes d'Italie ont choisis se prête-t-elle à toute la variété, à toute l'originalité de passions et de caractères que la peinture peut exprimer?« (Staël 1985, 221) [Do the subjects chosen by the great Italian artists lend themselves to all the variety, to all the originality of passion and character that painting is capable of expressing?]. On this point, the two lovers disagree. Essentially, Corinne feels that religious subjects were the most suited to painting, whereas Oswald espouses the belief that historical events are more appropriate topics. Corinne claims:

»les faits historiques, ou tirés des poëmes, étaient rarement pittoresques. Il faudrait souvent, pour comprendre de tels tableaux, que l'on eût conservé l'usage des peintres du vieux temps, sur un ruban qui sort de leur bouche. Mais les sujets religieux sont à l'instant entendus par tout le monde, et l'attention n'est point détournée de l'art pour deviner ce qu'il représente« (Staël 1985, 222)

[events drawn from history were rarely pictorial. Painters from earlier times wrote the words their subjects were to speak on ribbons issuing from their mouths; often, historical paintings would be comprehensible only if this practice had been retained. But religious subjects are immediately understood by everyone, and attention is not diverted from art to the problem of guessing what it means]

This observation echoes the emphasis given by contemporary critics to the issue of an artwork's accessibility; these writers often stressed that a viewer should not have to consult a *livret* or label in order to identify with the subject (Wrigley, 373-74).

Essentially, Corinne's antagonism toward Neoclassical French painting, and the ideologies these promote, along with her valorization of religious painting in the vein of the German Romantics, should be viewed as a means of protest against the Napoleonic regime. She spurns imitative Classicism, as promoted by the Emperor, as it is used to inculcate an ideology that places duty to the state above all others and reduces the freedom of the individual. In Napoleon's attempt to establish legitimacy and to reaffirm patriarchal ideals, he appropriated the ancient Roman republic as a model for contemporary French society – an era that Corinne characterizes as one in which »la gloire n'attiraient que le malheur et l'insulte« (Staël 1985, 233) [talent and glory attracted nothing but insult and misfortune]. His unabashed exploitation of the arts, in which he embraced the Neoclassical style, in part explains Staël's disdain for the school of David (as named after the eminent French painter Jacques-Louis David) that the Emperor so fervently supported. We must be mindful that history painting remained the preeminent genre in painting throughout the Revolutionary and Napoleonic era. In a memo to Pierre Daru, Intendant-General of the Imperial Household, Napoleon declared: »I want you to know that I intend to direct the arts particularly toward those subjects which will help to perpetuate the memory of the events of the past 15 years.« (Napoléon 1862, No. 9050, as quoted in Eitner, 15.) That the vast majority of the historical works produced in this genre were androcentric is abundantly evident (Landes, 2001; Crow, 1995); Solomon-Godeau, 1997).

In *Corinne*, Staël expresses her dislike for contemporary French history painting, a reaction that should be construed as anti-Napoleonic. Corinne owns three contemporary history paintings: Jacques-Louis David's *The Lictors Returning to Brutus the Bodies of his Sons* (1789), Jean-Germain Drouais's *Marius at Minturnae* (1786), and François Gérard's *Belisarius* (1795). We should not characterize their inclusion as an indication of approval of the style or subject matter exemplified in these works.[7] Indeed, I maintain that Staël included these well known works from this school of painting for pedagogical purposes: she intended to reveal the inadequacies of painting placed in the service of a corrupt regime to her reading audience. Importantly, all three of these paintings deal with the subject of civic virtue, a key issue in Revolutionary and Napoleonic debates concerning the nature and role of the citizen in the new French state.

David's *The Lictors Returning to Brutus the Bodies of his Sons* (fig. 3), the first historical painting Corinne discusses, is perhaps the quintessential example of French Neoclassicism, both formally and ideologically. Corinne owns a copy of this work, which was executed in Rome but exhibited in Paris in the Salon of 1789. This acclaimed work, which represents the Roman leader Brutus and his family in the aftermath of his sons' executions, which he ordered, has been the object of numerous analyses, many of which comment on how it constructs gender ideology.[8] Indeed, such a work was readily identified with not only the political issues of the day, but with the valorization of the law of the fathers. The vocabulary used to describe the *Brutus* canvas in the 1789 Salon displays that contemporary critics saw its gendered character as well; it was hailed as »male, severe, terrifying« (Mattick 1995, 35). In *Corinne,* the author recognizes the public/domestic dichotomy David has set up within the painting, noting that the stoicism of the Roman leader Brutus and the slaves which are carrying away his sons' bodies is in sharp contrast to »l'autre côté du tableau ou la mère et les soeurs s'abandonnent au désespoir; les femmes sont heureusement dispensées du courage qui fait sacrifier les affections du coeur« (Staël 1985, 232) [the other side of the painting, [where] the mothers and sisters give way to despair: fortunately, women are not bound to the courage that makes people sacrifice the affections of the heart]. Of her selection of this canvas, she explains, »J'ai choisi ce sujet, parcequ'il rappelle la plus terrible action que l'amour de la patrie ait inspirée« (Staël 1985, 233) [I have chosen this subject because it recalls the most fearful act ever inspired by love for the land of one's fathers]. This comment strongly indicates Staël's antagonism toward a political system that relegates all personal feelings to public duty. Indeed, the painting emblematizes this form of morality, for women react out of interest for others rather than for any abstract ideal.[9] It is important to remember that images such as Brutus were used as political propaganda during the French Revolution and that Napoleonic art reflected similar sentiments regarding the sanctity of those male virtues of civic duty, as well as the marginalization of women in French society.

Corinne also criticizes the subject matter of David's *Brutus* on the grounds of its incompatibility with meaningful visual representation. Her comment that »les faits historiques, ou tirés des poëmes, étaient rarement pittoresques« (Staël 1985, 222) [events drawn from history or poetry were rarely pictorial] clearly illustrates her position. She finds the accessory details of the statue of Rome and the city off in the distance helpful, but she objects to the painting on the basis, »mais vous auriez pu le voir, sans en deviner le sujet. Et cette incertitude, qui existe presque toujours dans les tableaux historiques, ne mêle-t-elle pas le tourment d'une énigme aux jouissances des beaux-arts qui doivent être si faciles et si claires?« (Staël 1985, 233) [you could have seen it without guessing the subject. And that ambiguity is almost always found in historical paintings. Does it not mix the tension of a riddle with the pleasures of the arts which are meant to be so easy and so clear?]. As Thomas Crow points out, the belief that »painting, alone among all the arts, could and therefore should offer itself to immediate, instantaneous apprehension by any viewer whatever represents an idealization of what goes on in the public exhibition space [...] [is reiterated] over and over in the criticism and aesthetic theory of the period« (Crow 1978, 450). Her condemnation of this ambiguity she sees as inherent in history paintings in general and in this painting specifically, an undesirable characteristic in the minds of most contemporary critics, reflects Staël's courage to question the status quo in French art and society and suggest new directions for its development.

Corinne continues this line of thought in the second work she critiques, Drouais's *Marius at Minturnae* (fig. 4), a painting whose subject, although taken from Roman history, clearly resonates with Staël. Exiled for his political beliefs, Marius is forced to wander alone and abandoned, an abject figure cast out by the society he had sought to defend his whole life. This scene highlights how, upon his capture, he is ultimately spared execution. The parallels to both Staël's situation, and that of her father, Jacques Necker, former Minister of Finance to Louis XVI, who was also exiled and never recompensed for his loss of status and property, are suggestive of why she selected this work for Corinne's gallery.[10] This subject is taken from the later Roman Republican period, when, as Corinne notes, »les lois n'existaient plus, mais quand le génie exerçait encore un grand empire sur les circonstances« (Staël 1985, 233) [there were no longer any laws, but genius still held great influence over events]. Using cultural criticism to cloak political dissent, Staël here undermines the current imperial regime.

The last historical painting that Corinne describes is Gérard's *Belisarius* (fig. 5), a work that underscores the protagonist's contention that historical subjects are not the most conducive for pictorial representation. In this painting, the major success of the Salon of 1795 and shown amid acclaim in the Salon of 1802 as well, the now blind Belisarius is carrying his poisoned guide. Corinne clearly admires Gérard's artistic abilities; she will proclaim: »Cette figure de Bélisaire est admirable, et depuis les peintres anciens on n'en a guère fait d'aussi belles« (Staël 1985, 233) [That face of Belisarius is splendid, and since the days of antiquity, scarcely any so beautiful have been done.]. However, Corinne questions the efficacy of treating such subjects in painting, asking: »[M]ais qui nous dit que c'est Bélisaire? Ne faut-il pas être fidèle à l'histoire pour la rappeler; et quand on y est fidèle, est-elle assez pittoresque?« (Staël 1985, 233) [But who tells us that Belisarius is the subject? To bring that fact to the mind, must not the painter be faithful to history, and if he is, will his work be sufficiently faithful to the aesthetic of painting?]. For the author, paintings that are based on historical events are not easily recognizable and are thus not accessible to the viewer.

Corinne concludes her exegesis on these key works of the modern French school by reiterating the fundamental flaw of the approaching historical subjects pictorially. Indeed, she thinks »[L']expression des peintres modernes, en général, était souvent théâtrale« (Staël 1985, 222) [the expressions of modern painters, generally speaking, are often theatrical,][11] and claims that »tous ceux qui ne savaient pas caractériser cherchaient les ornements accessoires, réunissaient tout le prestige d'un sujet brillant aux costumes riches, aux attitudes remarquables« (Staël 1985, 223) [those who did not know how to portray character compensated with incidental embellishments, combining all the prestige of a splendid object with rich costumes and striking poses]. Her remarks seem aimed at the modern-day artists of Davidian Classicism, against whom such criticisms were levied.

However, her qualms with these paintings clearly transcend the aesthetic and moves into the political. She sums up these three paintings in derogatory terms, stating »dans Brutus les vertus qui ressemblent au crime; dans Marius, la gloire, cause des malheurs; dans Bélisaire, les services payés par les persécutions les plus noires, enfin toutes les misères de la destinée humaine que les évènements de l'histoire racontent chacun à sa manière« (Staël 1985, 233) [in Brutus, these pictures show virtues that are the very image of the crime; in Marius, glory as the source of misfortune; in Belisarius, service paid for by the foulest persecution – in a word, all the woes of human destiny with each recounted by history in its own way]. Indeed, all three paintings highlight individuals who have, in one way of the other, been victimized by the state. Staël's discussion poses an important question: If art's primary function is to inspire greater morality, as most contemporary critics contended, can the current French school of art encourage the nation's true progress? It is on this issue that this debate ultimately turns. Toril Moi is right to point out that in *Corinne*, aesthetics and ethics are inextricably connected (Moi 2001, 144). Clearly, the author conceives of morality in terms of the personal responsibility to individuals rather than in terms of one's duty to the state. Indeed, one of Corinne's chief contentions against history painting is that it reflects and engenders a morality divorced of all compassion; in the works she critiques, one's obligation to society supersedes all else. Staël's exegesis proposes that such an ideology is not only restrictive, but also unethical.

Ultimately, the heroine's eloquent expressions of aversion to history painting, and its championing of patriarchal ideals, deride the practices of contemporary French painting and deny the validity of androcentric values. By focusing on artists who were closely associated with Napoleon – David was knighted by Napoleon in 1803 and appointed First Painter in 1804; Gérard was appointed First Painter to the Empress Josephine in 1806 – Staël boldly stakes a subversive position. As Jean Ménard understates, »En jugeant sévèrement la peinture historique que l'on prisait tant au début du XIXe siècle, Corinne se montre assez novatrice. « (Ménard 1970, 258.) [In severely judging the history painting that was valued at the beginning of the nineteenth century, Corinne shows herself to be quite an innovator.]

She reserves her utmost admiration for the religious paintings of the Italian Renaissance, admiring the »la composition sans artifice des tableaux de Raphaël, surtout dans sa première manière« (Staël 1985, 222) [artless composition of Raphael's painting, particularly his early manner] as seen in works such as his *Mass at Bolsena* (1512) and *Saint Cecilia* (1513-14) (fig. 6). According to Staël's protagonist, religious paintings do not need embellishments, rich costuming, and striking poses, as frequently relied upon in modern painting, for a

»simple vierge tenant son enfant dans ses bras, un vieillard attentif dans la messe de Bolsène, un homme appuyé sur bâton dans l'école d'Athènes, sainte Cécile levant les yeux au ciel, produisaient, par l'expression seule du regard et de la physionomie, des impressions bien plus profondes. Ces beautés naturelles se découvrent chaque jour davantage; mais au contraire, dans les tableaux d'effet, le premier coup d'oeil est toujours le plus frappant.« (Staël 1985, 223)

[simple virgin holding her child in her arms, an attentive old man at the Mass of Bolsena. . .[and] Saint Cecilia looking up to heaven made a far deeper impression through the expression of their eyes and countenances alone. This natural beauty is revealed more fully with each day, but for ostentatious paintings, the first glance is always the most striking.]

Here, the author refers to works by Raphael, whose reputation in France had waned during the Revolution. Under Napoleon, French critics such as Eméric-David, Lavallée, and Landon dutifully praised the Raphael paintings confiscated by Napoleon in terms of its Academic qualities; however, they tended to view Raphael through the lens of French aesthetics and the auspices of the Academy, and thus they had a biased approach to his work (Rosenberg 1985–86, 185; Rosenberg 1995). It was with the German Romantics, such as Wilhelm Heinrich Wackenroder and Friedrich Schlegel, that the »Romantic« qualities of Raphael were introduced and these were the aspects that drew Staël to his works. Perhaps this author felt the French embrace an artificial one, as their version of the artist had been polluted over several centuries, and that Raphael's place in their art world had been obscured during the Revolution.

In Corinne's gallery, the works she esteems most highly are those that are Italian Renaissance religious paintings – works which laud qualities of the female subject that Staël finds most worthy of emulation, such as compassion and maternal devotion. Her discussion of works outside of this historical period occur not because of the author's inability to stay on task, as suggested by Geneviève Gennari (Gennari 1947, 172), but are motivated by desires to create a more pan-European aesthetic rooted in liberalism and to assert the autonomy of the individual. When we compare Staël's aesthetic ideas and critiques of history paintings to those she expounds in relation to religious paintings, it is evident that she prefers religious subjects because of their timelessness, their ability to evoke powerful emotions, and their non-exclusionary approach to women. While she criticizes contemporary French history paintings and the implications of its Neoclassical style, she praises Italian religious paintings of the Renaissance, with their »Romantic« qualities and preoccupation with the female subject, such as the Madonna or female saints. Paintings that draw inspiration from religion evoke »idées pures« [pure ideas] and »jamais épouser l'émotion« (Staël 1985, 234) [emotion... [that] is never exhausted]. In the course of this discussion, Corinne makes a powerful case for the superiority of religious works of the Renaissance – and those heralded by the German Romantics – to those history paintings currently in vogue in France. The author reminds us: »Enfin Corinne trouvait que les tableaux pieux faisaient à l'ame un bien que rien ne pouvait remplacer, et qu'ils supposaient dans l'artiste un saint enthousiasme qui se confond avec le génie, le renouvelle, le ranime et peut seul le soutenir contre les dégoûts de la vie et les injustices des hommes.« (Staël 1985, 223) [Ultimately, in Corinne's view, nothing could replace the benefit of religious painting for the soul. In her judgment, they suggested a holy enthusiasm in the artist, that, blending with genius, renews and quickens, and alone has the power to sustain genius in the face of life's discouragements and man's injustice.]

The valorization of holy women, as emblematized in the art discussed in Staël's *Corinne*, is one of the most significant aspects of this author's criticism and serves as a gesture of defiance to the Emperor's notorious chauvinism. Staël was drawn to various manifestations of spiritually powerful women. While in Italy, Staël became quite attracted to the cult of the virgin, believing it »il semble s'allier de quelque manière à ce qu'il y a de plus pur et de plus sensible dans l'affection pour les femmes« (Staël, 1985, 260-61) [united in some way to all that is purest and most sensitive in our affection for women]. Marianism certainly enjoyed a resurgence in popularity during the nineteenth century, a phenomenon which some have perceived as a reassertion of the female principle in religion and culture (Pope 1985). Corinne's many references to paintings of the Madonna attest to this attraction. In addition, Staël elevates the figure of the sibyl, who was a priestess publicly worshipped in pre-Hellenic times. Corinne is often compared to a sibyl; our first glimpse at this character reveals a woman »vêtue comme la Sybille du Dominiquin« [dressed like Domenichino's Sibyl] (1616–17) (fig. 7) who seemed »une prêtresse d'Apollon« (Staël 1985, 52) [a priestess of Apollo]. We know that this character was modeled after the Erythraean Sibyl, who supposedly brought the Sibyline books of prophecy to Italy (Vallois 1987, 269, note 13). Here, Corinne is charged as an interlocutor who is transmitting not only Italian, but also English and German cultural values to her European audience. Marie-Claire Vallois deems Staël's decision to compare Corinne with such women an act of provocation in Napoleonic France, for it was Roman gods and patriarchs who were praised in this society (Vallois 1991, 83).

Staël felt that it was only through Christianity that cultural union could be achieved, for it offered a moral code and a firm philosophy on which to base the laws of a free and productive society (Polowetzsky 1993, 40). Significantly, she did not believe that she was introducing a new element into French society. The religious renaissance that Staël hoped to advance in such works as *Corinne* or *De l'Allemagne* (*On Germany*, 1810) was indigenous to her country. As Maurice Cranston points out, in Staël's writings, she tried to show

»that she was not advocating anything foreign to France, but was simply appealing to an older tradition which the French had once shared with the Germanic nations, to a world the French had lost, the medieval world of Christianity […] Romantic art, she pointed out, took its standards from that world, just as Classical art took its standards from the ancient world. […] It was Classicism, she protested, which was the alien presence in a France that belonged to Christian Europe.« (Cranston, 80)

Although Staël found in this Romantic, religious aesthetic a validation of her own agenda, she also had a strong conviction that it was her duty to encourage the progress of French culture and that this could be accomplished only by obedience to Christian codes.

While Staël commends the accomplishments of Renaissance painters in her novel, the aesthetic that she is championing is essentially Romantic and thus inimical to Napoleon's artistic program. By privileging feeling and enthusiasm above all else, as she does in her discussion of these religious painters, she expresses the emerging Romantic emphasis on emotion. When Staël suggests that the disagreements over aesthetic issues »tenait à la diversité des nations, de climats et des religions« (Staël 1985, 221) [had to do with differences in nations, climates, and religions], she was introducing a relativism into aesthetic issues that was distinctly Romantic. It was the religious focus, the purity of vision and »the stamp of genius« found in these Italian works that appealed to Staël's sensibility. That is not to say that she wholeheartedly rejected Classicism in art; she merely questioned its contemporary appropriation. She, along with other German Romantics, found something very appealing about the Renaissance artists who attempted »to fuse the Romantic spirit and Classical form in most beautiful harmony.«[12] Staël also embraces the notion of art as a vehicle for personal expression, thereby asserting her Romantic leanings. An indication of her Romanticism is the declaration, given by Corinne, that

»il nous est impossible de créer dans leur sens, d'inventent pour ainsi dire sur leur terrain. L'on peut les imiter à force d'étude; mais comment le génie trouverait-il tout son essor dans un travail où la mémoire et l'érudition sont si nécessaires? Il n'en est pas de même des sujets qui appartiennent à notre propre histoire ou à notre propre religion. Les peintres peuvent en avoir eux-mêmes l'inspiration personnelle; ils sentent ce qu'ils peignent, ils peignent ce qu'ils ont vu.« (Staël 1985, 223)

[it is impossible for us to create the way [the ancients] did, to invent ideas in what might be called their territory. They can be imitated by dint of study, but how could genius soar where memory and erudition are so vital! The situation is different for subjects belonging to our own history or to our own religions: painters can tap into their own personal inspiration, feeling what they paint, painting what they have seen.]

With this declaration, Staël urges a shift from the imitative mode of Classicism to the expressive mode of Romanticism.[13] This signifies her divergence from those aesthetic ideals institutionalized under the Emperor.

It is significant that the specific paintings Staël lauds in her art discussion are not those executed by French artists; rather, she champions those created by Italian masters, for in the novel, Italy is associated with art, the female, and plenitude. It was here that Corinne was allowed to explore her intellectual and artistic potential. In her last address, she sings of the freedom she found in Italy:

»Vous m'avez permis la gloire, oh! vous, nation libérale, qui ne bannissez point les femmes de son temple, vous qui ne sacrifiez point des talents immortels aux jalousies passagères, vous qui toujours applaudissez à l'essor du génie: ce vainqueur sans vaincus, ce conquérant sans dépouilles, qui puise dans l'éternité pour enrichir le temps.« (Staël 1985, 582)

[You have allowed me glory: you, the liberal nation that does not banish women from its temple, you who do not sacrifice immortal talents to fleeting spite, you who always applaud the soaring flight of genius: that victor of the vanquished, that conqueror without the spoils, who draws on eternity to enrich the domain of time.]

By heralding the works of Italian masters, the novelist declares the superiority of a nation that validates powerful women and their public presence over those that oppress women of genius. This embrace of the spiritual in art was contrary to the state-sponsored cultural production in Napoleonic France. It is true that the artists Staël singled out in both her *Travel Notebooks* and *Corinne* were fashionable objects of veneration in the early nineteenth century; indeed, the author's interest in Raphael, Michelangelo, and Dominichino were not especially forward thinking per se (Balayé 1971, 183; Ménard 1970). However, the ways in which she contrasts these Renaissance artists to those of the contemporary French school is a significant gesture of cultural criticism. This valorization of sacred art was not in keeping with larger cultural trends in France at this time. Although religion experienced a renaissance in France during the early years of Napoleon's reign, this did not carry over into art. Religious painting had been largely replaced by secular art in the Salons of late eighteenth-century

France, and by the mid-1790s (the time frame for the novels under discussion), there was a noticeable decline in the production of sacred art (Conisbee 1981, 108).

Two of Corinne's most prized paintings are »de l'ancienne école« (Staël 1985, 233) »of the old school«,[14] »Francesco Albani's« (but probably Cristofano Allori's) *Christ Sleeping on the Cross* (n.d.) from the seventeenth-century Florentine school, and Murillo's *Christ Carrying the Cross* (c.1665–75), which was then attributed to Titian; these are works that »soulagent un peu l'ame oppressée« (Staël 1985, 234) [soothe the depressed soul]. This Mannerist work sharply contrasts the Classical style so readily embraced in France. The other painting, then attributed to Titian but now known to be of Murillo, exemplifies her ideal of virtue. Commenting on the mother's reaction to seeing her son's suffering, Corinne exclaims:

»Admirable respect d'une mère pour les malheurs et les vertus divines de son fils! Quel regard que celui du Christ! quelle divine résignation, et cependant quelle souffrance et quelle sympathie par cette souffrance avec le coeur de l'homme! Voilà sans doute le plus beau de mes tableaux. C'est celui vers lequel je reporte sans cesse mes regards, sans pouvoir jamais épuiser l'émotion qu'il me cause.« (Staël 1985, 234)

[How splendid a mother's respect for her son's misfortunes and heavenly virtues! What an expression there is on the face of Christ! What divine resignation and yet what suffering; and through that suffering, what compassion for the heart of man! Of all my paintings, this is surely the most beautiful. It is the one my eyes always go back to, and yet the emotion it brings is never exhausted.] (Staël 1991, 154–55.)

One cannot ignore the focus on Mary and the love she conveys for her son; contrast this to Brutus's condemnation of his sons to death. Her sensitivity to spiritual feeling, a characteristic Staël valued perhaps above all others, and the emotion this subject encourages in the viewer, attest to the superiority of religious subjects in our author's opinion. Mary's devotion is to her son, not to the Roman state that ordered his crucifixion. Analysis of Corinne's responses to various works suggests not just an aesthetics of sensibility, but one in which empathy, even pity, plays a primary function. Lori Jo Marso has suggested that it is through pity – through the ability to see the subjectivity of other individuals – that Staël creates an alternative politics in her post-Revolutionary writings (Marzo, 1999).

While Staël is particularly interested in religious painting and its contrast to paintings drawn from historical subjects, she is also at pains to include in her pan-European gallery paintings executed by artists outside of Italy and France that deal with extra-historical subjects. This constitutes an anti-Napoleonic move as well. Corinne displays German artist Friedrich Rehberg's *Aeneas Encountering Dido in the Underworld*, a work which never has been located, and a painting of Macbeth, which is variously attributed to Henry Fuseli or Joshua Reynolds; I believe that she may have had in mind the *Macbeth and the Witches* painting (1765) by Francesco Zuccarelli, R.A., a wildly popular artist in late eighteenth-century England.[15] Also, she includes two literary paintings by the Scotchman Georg Wallis, a historical landscape known as *Cincinnatus* and a representation of the Ossianic tale of Caïrbar sleeping on the tomb of his father; both of these works are known today only through contemporary travelogues. The inclusion of these painters' works may be ascribed to their Northern European connections, as Staël was intent to illuminate these cultures to her French readers; also, these serve as examples of extra-historical paintings and are thus conducive to the author's aesthetic enterprise of inclusiveness. We should acknowledge that Staël's innovative means of presenting art works created in different historical periods and cultures and from various genres works – as well as her preference for religious paintings that promote a morality of compassion and connection – ultimately serve to promote her primary agenda: freedom for the individual. Staël's project of creating a more holistic European community in which cultural differences are recognized, celebrated, and then integrated so as to form a space conducive to the realization of individual potential is furthered by the conception of Corinne's gallery. It is a goal that is distinctly at odds with the aims of the Emperor Napoleon, whose cultural program was seen as stultifying. In her *Considerations of the French Revolution* (1818), Staël laments how the youth of France failed to receive a liberal education under Napoleon's rule. She writes: »Eh! juste ciel! quoi donc penseront-ils, ces jeunes gens élevés sous le régime de Bonaparte, seulement pour aller se battre, sans aucune instruction, sans aucun intérêt pour la littérature et les beaux-arts? « (Staël 1830, 255). [Ah! just sky! Of what do they think, these young people raised under Bonaparte's regime – only of going into battle, without any instruction, any interest for literature and the fine arts?]

We should recognize the significant work performed by Staël in fashioning this gallery, an experimental space in which issues – aesthetic, political, and cultural – are entertained with erudition and enthusiasm. The art discussion in the section »Paintings and Statues« demonstrates Staël's engagement with contemporary French and German aesthetic theory while simultaneously proposing the consideration of innovative approaches to art. Analysis of her work in these arenas also illuminates this novelist's desire to assert a woman's voice in the largely androcentric French art world. Perhaps most significantly, it also reveals how Staël deployed cultural criticism in *Corinne, or Italy* in her ongoing battle with the tyrannical Emperor. Indeed, the author used these seemingly innocuous conversations on art as a diversionary tactic, which was meant to disarm the censors but ultimately to disable the cultural regime of Napoleon.

–Brigham Young University

## Notes

Translations are mine, unless otherwise noted. A Kress Travel Fellowship and grants from the College of Fine Arts and Communications and the Women's Research Institute at Brigham Young University facilitated the researching and writing of this article. A special thanks to Michael J. Call, who introduced me to Germaine de Staël, Nanette Le Coat, for inviting me to participate in roundtable, ›Self-Censorship from the Revolution to the Empire‹ at the 2005 American Society for Eighteenth-Century Studies conference in Las Vegas, where I presented a shortened version of this paper, and to Karyna Szmurlo, the respondant for this session, who offered insightful comments on my material

1 All citations from Simone Balayé's authoritative 1985 edition of *Corinne ou l'Italie*. The English translations of this text follow Avriel H. Goldberger, *Corinne, or Italy*, unless otherwise given.

2 Besser's *Germaine de Staël Revisited* details the animosity between Napoleon and Staël, which began soon after his ascension to power. When Bonaparte dismissed the Tribunate in January 1802, she referred to him as an »idéophobe«; infuriated by this, Napoleon told his brothers to »warn that woman not to try to bar my way or I will smash her, I will crush her« (quoted in Besser, 12). Staël continued to publish veiled attacks against the Emperor in places like her novels *Delphine* (he responded with a harsh condemnation of the work in the *Moniteur*) and *Corinne*, which assured that her exiled status would remain unchanged while he was in power. She returned briefly to Paris in 1814, and then again in 1816 (after Napoleon's deposition), but ill health necessitated that she return to Switzerland, where she died in 1817. In her book *Dix années d'exil* [*Ten Years in Exile*], she summed up her feeling for Napoleon, saying: »He came to exchange their [The French] tranquility, independence, language, laws, blood, and children for the misery and shame of being destroyed as nations and despised as men« (quoted in Besser, 132).

3 This aspect – Napoleon, the museum, and memory politics – is discussed with regard to the German writer Caroline de la Motte Fouqué in the chapter by Silke Arnold-de Simine.

4 I maintain that there is an extremely important source in the conception of Corinne as an art critic, and in particular in the section of the novel, »Statues and Paintings«, and

this is the art conversation titled »The Paintings« published in the *Athenaeum*, the short-lived but highly influential periodical produced by the Schlegels. This is the subject of an article in progress, »Beyond the Lover's Quarrel: Art Conversations in the Schlegels' *Athenaeum* and Staël's *Corinne, or Italy*.«

5 On the place of art in the formation of the public sphere, see Habermas 40-42.

6 For example, in 1810, sculptor Antonio Canova purportedly said to the Emperor, in relation to the continued transportation of art out of Italy, »De grâce, Sire, laissez ces choses en Italie [...]« (quoted in Boyer 1959, 25) [Have mercy, Sir, leave these things in Italy].

7 While Marie-Hélène Girard thinks it would be imprudent to deduce a complete embrace of the Davidian aesthetic based upon the contemporary French works Corinne discusses, she suggests that it does seem to suggest a predilection for it. I disagree. Fundamental to Staël's enterprise is a critique of the regime that embraces this style, and the inclusion of these works is for pedagogical purposes. See Girard 1988, 246.

8 While there are many noteworthy analyses of the *Brutus*, the gendered issues attending this painting frame the discussion in Gutwirth 1992.

9 On the subject of women's morality, particularly as it pertains to the Revolutionary period, see Outram 1989, 46-48.

10 This observation is made by Simone Balayé in her chapter, »Du Sens Romanesques de Quelques Oeuvres d'Art dans *Corinne*«, (Balayé 1994, 126).

11 This is my translation – Goldberger's translation that »modern painting is often theatrical« (146) does not quite capture the essence of this critique, in my mind.

12 As characterized by Friedrich Schegel in his discussion of Italian Renaissance writers in *Dialogue on Poetry and Literary Aphorisms* (1968, 101).

13 M.H. Abrams brilliantly characterized the move from the classical viewpoint to the romantic by the metaphorical shift from viewing art as a mirror to viewing art as a lamp. In the former concept, the artist passively imitates reality; in the latter, the artist illuminates the world through personality and imagination. See Abrams 1953.

14 This is the same descriptor used by Friedrich Schlegel in his *Descriptions de Tableaux*.

15 Corinne describes an image in which the artist attempts to compress several elements of the play into one painting; in my opinion, Zuccarelli's *Macbeth* fits this description far better than the other proposed representations.

## Works Cited

Abrams, M.H. *The Mirror and the Lamp: Romantic Theory and the Critical Tradition.* New York: Oxford University Press, 1953.

Balayé, Simone. »Du Sens Romanesques de Quelques Oeuvres d'Art dans *Corinne*« Madame de Staël: Écrire, Luttre, Vivre. Paris: Droz, 1994. 111-35.

Besser, Gretchen Rous. *Germaine de Staël Revisited.* New York: Twayne, 1994.

Boyer, Ferdinand. *Le Monde des Beaux-arts en Italie et la France de la Révolution et de l'Empire.* Turin: Società Editrice Internazionale, 1970.

Boyer, Ferdinand. »Napoléon et les Collection d'Antiques en Italie.« L'Information Historique 21.1 (1959): 22-25.

Conisbee, Philip. *Painting in Eighteenth-Century France*. New York: Cornell University Press, 1981.

Cranston, Maurice. *The Romantic Movement*. Cambridge: Blackwell, 1994.

Crow, Thomas. *Emulation: Making Artists for Revolutionary France*. New Haven: Yale University Press, 1995.

Crow, Thomas. »Diderot's Salons: Public Art and the Mind of the Private Critic.« *Introduction to Diderot on Art: The Salon of 1767*. Ed. and trans. John Goodman. 2 volumes. New Haven: Yale University Press, 1995. ix-xix.

Crow, Thomas. »The Oath of the Horatii in 1785: Painting and Pre-Revolutionary Radicalism in France.« *Art History* 1.4 (1978): 424-71.

Dehon, Claire L. »Corinne: Une Artiste Heroine de Roman.« *Nineteenth-Century French Studies* 9 (1980-81): 1-9.

Eitner, Lorenz, ed. *Neoclassicism and Romanticism 1750–1850. Sources and Documents*. 2 volumes. New Jersey: Prentice-Hall, 1970.

Fort, Bernadette. »The Visual Arts in a Critical Mirror.« *›The Mémoires Secrets‹ and the Culture of Publicity in Eighteenth-Century France*. Jeremy D. Popkin and Bernadette Fort, eds. Oxford: Voltaire Foundation, 1998: 143-74.

Fort, Bernadette. »Voice of the Public: The Carnivalization of Salon Art in Pre-Revolutionary Pamphlets.« *Eighteenth-Century Studies* 22 (1989): 368-94.

Gennari, Geneviève. *Le Premier Voyage de Madame de Staël en Italie et la Genèse de ›Corinne‹*. Paris: Boivin, 1947.

Girard, Marie-Hélène. »Corinne Collectionneur, ou le Musée Imaginaire de Madame de Staël.« *Art et Littérature, Actes du Congrès de la Société Française de Littérature Générale et Comparée*, Aix-en-Provence, 24-25-26 septembre 1986. Aixen-Provence, Université de Provence, 1988. 241-61.

Gould, C. *Trophy of Conquest: the Musée Napoléon and the Creation of the Louvre*. London: Faber and Faber, 1965.

Gutwirth, Madelyn. *The Twilight of the Goddesses: Women and Representation in the French Revolutionary Era*. New Brunswick: Rutgers, 1992.

Gutwirth, Madelyn. *Madame de Staël, Novelist: The Emergence of the Artist as Woman*. Chicago: University of Illinois, 1978.

Habermas, Jurgen. *The Structural Transformation of the Public Sphere: An Inquiry into a Category of Bourgeois Society*. Trans. Thomas Burger. Boston: MIT Press,1996.

Landes, Joan B. *Visualizing the Nation: Gender, Representation, and Revolution in Eighteenth-Century France*. New York: Cornell University Press, 2001.

Marso, Lori Jo. *(Un)Manly Citizens: Jean-Jacques Rousseau's and Germaine de Staël's Subversive Women*. Baltimore: Johns Hopkins University Press, 1999.

Mattick, Paul, Jr. »Beautiful and Sublime: ›Gender Totemism.‹« *Feminism and Tradition in Aesthetics*. Eds. Peggy Zeglin and Carolyn Korsmeyer. University Park: Penn State University Press, 1995. 27-48.

Ménard, Jean. »Mme de Staël et la Peinture.« *Madame de Staël et l'Europe*. Colloque de Coppet, 18-24 juillet 1966. Paris: Klincksieck, 1970. 253-264.

Moi, Toril. »A Woman's Desire to Be Known: Expressivity and Silence in Corinne.« *Bucknell Review* 45.2 (2001): 143-75.

Outram, Dorinda. *The Body and the French Revolution: Sex, Class, and Political Culture.* New Haven: Yale University Press, 1989.

Polowetzsky, Michael. *A Bond Never Broken: The Relations Between Napoleon and the Authors of France.* Toronto: Associated University Press, 1993.

Pope, Barbara Corrado. »Immaculate and Powerful: The Marian Revival in the Nineteenth Century.« *Immaculate and Powerful: The Female Sacred Image and Social Reality.* Eds. Clarissa W. Atkinson, Constance H. Buchanan, and Margaret R. Miles. Boston: Beacon, 1985. 173-200.

Rosenberg, Martin. *Raphael and France: The Artist as Paradigm and Symbol.* University Park: Pennsylvania State University Press, 1995.

Rosenberg, Martin. »Raphael's *Transfiguration* and Napoleon's Cultural Politics.« *Eighteenth-Century Studies* 19.2 (1985–86): 180-205.

Schlegel, Friedrich. *Descriptions de Tableaux.* Ed. Bénédicte Savoy. Paris: École Nationale Supérieure des Beaux-Arts, 2001.

Schlegel, Friedrich. *Dialogue on Poetry and Literary Aphorisms.* Trans. Ernst Behler and Roman Struc. University Park: Penn State University Press, 1968.

Siegfried, Susan. »The Politicisation of Art Criticism in the Post-Revolutionary Press.« *Art Criticism and its Institutions in Nineteenth-Century France.* Ed. Michael R. Orwicz. New York: Manchester University Press, 1994. 9-28.

Solomon-Godeau, Abigail. *Male Trouble: A Crisis in Representation.* New York: Thames and Hudson, 1997.

Staël, Germaine de. *Corinne, or Italy.* Trans. Avriel H. Goldberger. New Brunswick: Rutgers University Press, 1991.

Staël, Germaine de. *Corinne ou l'Italie.* Ed. Simone Balayé. Paris: Gallimard, 1985.

Staël, Germaine de. *Les Carnets de Voyage de Madame de Staël.* Ed. Simone Balayé. Geneva: Droz, 1971.

Staël, Germaine de. *Oeuvres Complètes de Madame de Staël.* Vol. 14. Bruxelles: Louis Hauman, 1830.

Tenenbaum, Susan. »The Coppet Circle: Literary Criticism as Political Discourse.« *History of Political Thought* 1.3 (1980): 453-73.

Vallois, Marie-Claire. »Old Idols, New Subjects: Germaine de Staël and Romanticism.« *Germaine de Staël: Crossing the Borders.* Eds. Madelyn Gutwirth, Avriel Goldberger, and Karyna Szmurlo. New Brunswick: Rutgers University Press, 1991. 82-97.

Vallois, Marie-Claire. »Voice as Fossil: Madame de Staël's *Corinne, or Italy*: An Archaeology of Feminine Discourse.« *Tulsa Studies in Women's Literature* 6.1 (1987): 47-60.

Wrigley, Richard. *The Origins of French Art Criticism from the Ancien Régime to the Restoration.* New York: Oxford University Press, 1993.

*Fig. 3: Jacques-Louis David, The Lictors Returning to Brutus the Bodies of his Sons, Musée de Louvre, Paris.*

*Fig. 4: Jean-Germain Drouais, Marius at Minturnae, Musée de Louvre, Paris.*

*Fig. 5: After François Gérard, Belisarius, Bibliothèque nationale, Paris. Engraving by Auguste Boucher Desnoyers.*

*Fig. 6: Raphael, Saint Cecilia, Pinocoteca nazionale, Bologna.*

*Fig. 7: Domenichino, The Cumaen Sibyl, Galleria Borghese, Rome.*

# Rewriting the National Paradigm: Staël's *De l'Allemagne* (1810) and the »German« Defence of Sociability

*Beatrice Guenther*

Mme de Staël's *De l'Allemagne* (1810) is a well-known example of cultural studies *avant la lettre* – not least, since it participated so publicly in the process described by Benedict Anderson's analysis of print culture and the latter's role in shaping national »imagined communities«. In his study of nationalism, Anderson notes that the bourgeoisie achieved solidarities on an essentially imagined basis through the printed word (Anderson, 77). He subsequently remarks that as far as the polyvernacular inter-European dynastic Empires were concerned »power and print-language mapped different [even if not always exclusive] realms« (Anderson, 77). This lack of a one-to-one correlation between nation and language can also be applied to the pre-1815 »imagined Germany« described by Staël and her cultural adversaries, Betty Gleim, Esther Gad, and Caroline von la Motte Fouqué.[1] The nominal *Heiliges Römisches Reich Deutscher Nation* [Holy Roman Empire of German Nations] had, after all, been abolished by Napoleon in 1806, and the *Deutscher Bund* [German Confederation] resulting from the Vienna Congress in 1815 would prove to be inadequate in providing a new and effective national structure.[2] Indeed, Gleim, Gad, and la Motte Fouqué take on their »correction« of Staël's representation of Germany, motivated by the anxiety that Staël's »false« construct of *Deutschtum* (based on her reading writers as diverse as Schlegel, Herder, Kant, Novalis, and Goethe, among others) will nonetheless supplant the »true« Germany, even among Germans themselves. Gleim writes: »Fern bleibe denn Alles von uns, was die Einheit und Reinheit unsers Wesens stören, was den Sieg der Wahrheit in uns aufhalten, was uns verhindern könnte, zur rechten Selbsterkenntnis und Selbstachtung zu kommen« (Gleim 1814, viii) [All that might disturb the unity and purity of our being should be kept at a distance from us – as should all that might stop the triumph of truth in us or hinder us from proper self-knowledge and self-esteem]. Gad, for her part, argues that few outside Germany are able to understand German and that, as a result, French opinions, like those represented in *De l'Allemagne*, end up having more currency (if less value) than German ones (Gad, iv, 44). In effect, by taking on the debate about German culture publicly, both seem to recognize intuitively the link between print culture and national identity described by Anderson.

The focus of this chapter is on the question of how Staël sets out to describe a nation that did not exist politically, and of how in 1814 – after the wars of liberation had pushed the Napoleonic forces across the Rhine – Betty Gleim, Esther Gad, and Caroline von la Motte Fouqué undertake a defence of this imaginary Germany. Staël's account of her impressions during her exile in 1803 and then again in 1807–08 in Germany – imposed on her by Napoleon[3] – covers a lot of ground. She takes on a summary of German literature, philosophy, and religion, which is preceded by an initial section focusing more generally on the Germans and their customs. Interspersed between the chapters dealing with geographically-motivated cultural differences (Southern Germany, Austria, Vienna, North Germany, Saxony, Weimar, Prussia, and Berlin), one finds numerous chapters devoted to descriptions of German society, including universities as well as other educational institutions, conversation, and language – not to mention the particularity of the German literary style.

Staël associates a blend of positive and negative traits with the German language. For her, the primitive (though thoughtful) quality of the German language is seen to be a result of its stiffness, inexperience, and obscurity: »[…] on ne s'en est guère servi ni dans la société, ni en public […] l'on risque de prendre des lueurs pour des vérités quand les formes mêmes du langage sont obscures«. [one has hardly made use of the language in society or in public […] one runs the risk of mistaking glimmers of light for truths when even the linguistic forms themselves are obscure] (Staël, I: 198-99). In contrast to Caroline de la Motte Fouqué's agenda of proposing how a (feminine) form of sociability might shape a German (national) identity, as Silke Arnold-de Simine argues in the next chapter, Staël's own experiences in Germany actually leads her to discredit German *Geselligkeit.* In her chapter, »Des moeurs et du caractère des Allemands«, Staël dismisses German interiority as a space of passivity marked by beer, stoves, and tobacco smoke (Staël, I: 60), and in her report on Viennese sociability, she mocks the daily, mind-numbing routine of endless aristocratic *dîners* (Staël, I: 90). Moreover, Staël's dismissive chapter on women ends up overshadowing the rest of her study – at least for her three critics. She notes that German women tend to be less timid than their English counterparts, only to add that the reason for this is the general lack of (superior) men in society who might establish high standards by which to judge them. She also notes the lack of rapid wit and intellectual fire in German women, concluding: » [...] ce genre de plaisir ne se rencontre guère que dans les sociétés de Paris les plus piquantes et les plus spirituelles«. [this kind of pleasure can only be found in the most piquant and witty societies of Paris] (Staël, I: 67).

Staël's emphasis on *conversation* – as constitutive of French cultural identity – is hardly her invention, of course. The apogee of the practice of conversation as a key component of French society is generally considered to be the seventeenth century, where the ideal of *honnêteté classique* [neo-Classical courtesy], understood to be the balance of sociability and individuality, could be achieved. Emmanuel Godo notes in his *Histoire de la conversation* that 17th-century French practices of conversation allowed otherwise incompatible opposites to converge. The desire to express one's individuality was not considered the antithesis of the decision to comply with social norms: »La règle à laquelle on consent à se soumettre balise un espace de sociabilité où peut surgir le *style* [...]« [The conventions to which one submits willingly mark out a kind of sociability where *style* can emerge] (Godo, 83). The speaker can demonstrate his/her individual mastery of the social rules as virtuosity or play. Moreover, as Maurice Magendie notes in *La politesse mondaine et les théories de l'honnêteté en France au XVIIe siècle* (1925), the fascination with the *salons* or, indeed, with the popular topos of the idyllic, fictional Arcadia can be read as the quest for ideal spaces for conversation – where one might avoid the twin extremes of the solipsism of solitude and the tyranny of the (ambitious, unpolished) crowd at Court (Godo, 85).

When one considers the French practice of conversation at the beginning of the 19$^{th}$ century – especially, in conjunction with Mme de Staël – the issue becomes a little murky. Already in 1761 Rousseau had denounced the hypocrisy and personal vanity of *salon* practices, which, to his mind, transformed conversation into a superficial play of masks. Later, the Revolutionaries signaled through their use of words unacceptable to the code of *bienséance* their break with the conversational tradition of *l'Ancien Régime*. At the turn of the 19$^{th}$ century – in counterpoint to the Revolutionary rejection of codes of sociability – the art of conversation becomes for the aristocratic *émigré* community a marker of nostalgia for bygone times and practices.

Staël's own privileging of *conversation* should not be read, however, as a sign of her affiliation with her reactionary aristocratic compatriots. On the one hand, her own *salon* broke with the pleasure-oriented dictates of 18th-century conversation, as d'Alembert defined these under the heading of *conversation* in *l'Encyclopédie* (1754).[4] By incorporating explicitly political discussions (which focused, for instance, on the necessity of convoking the *Etats Généraux*), Mme de Staël and her *salon* broke with the 18th-century code of propriety. Still, one can recognize in Staël's descriptions of conversation in *De l'Allemagne* the intense nostalgia of an expatriate – exiled, in contrast to her reactionary contemporaries, by Napoleon rather than by the Revolutionaries of the Terror.[5]

La Motte Fouqué, Gad, and Gleim's defence of German *Geselligkeit*[6] in the face of this rich heritage of *conversation* attempts to make a case for the value of German cultivation (*Bildung*). In her response to Staël's judgement, *Über deutsche Geselligkeit, in Antwort auf das Urtheil der Frau von Staël* (1814), Caroline von la Motte Fouqué first experiences a shamed silence in the face of the »foreign image« of her own culture before she recognizes that it is primarily language itself that guarantees the authenticity of cultural difference (6-7). Her insight allows her (with a certain sense of relief) to lay the groundwork for challenging Staël's definition of Germanness: »Die Sprache war die gewaltige Scheiderin, die das besondere von dem Allgemeinen trennte, und jedem seine Stelle anwies« [Language was the powerful divider that separated the particular from the general and directed each to his/her place] (La Motte Fouqué, 8). In fact, la Motte Fouqué as well as her two »compatriots« draw primarily on their own linguistic groundedness as a means to discredit Staël's text.

Defensiveness is the dominant tone in all three of the pamphlets, and the three writers each set out to undermine the primacy of French culture as one of the key strategies in order to justify the worth of German society. The easiest approach is, of course, to discredit the personal authority of Mme de Staël as privileged symbol of French culture. Caroline von la Motte Fouqué notes, for instance, that Mme de Staël has not been able to experience German culture, since her attitude vis-à-vis her powerful mind, her preconceptions, and her language create a French vacuum around her which surrounds her even as she travels physically through Germany (La Motte Fouqué, 10-11). Esther Gad, on the other hand, structures her pamphlet around the contradictions inherent in *De l'Allemagne* and lingers particularly on the disadvantages associated with the pleasures of French society. Whereas Staël in her German exile laments the lack of witty conversation so typical for her of French sociability, Gad mocks the emptiness of such pleasure, turning Staël's words against her. Gad first quotes Staël: »Alle Classen in Frankreich fühlen ein Bedürfnis zu sprechen. Worte werden daselbst nicht blos als ein Mittel betrachtet, um sich Gedanken, Gefühle, Geschäfte mitzutheilen, sondern sie sind ein Instrument auf das man spielt [...]« [All classes in France feel the need to speak. Words are not simply considered a means to communicate thoughts, feelings, and affairs. Instead, they are an instrument on which one plays]. Gad goes on to conclude: »Aber eine solche immerwährende Musik, so angenehm sie auch für den seyn mag, der sie selbst macht, würde gewiß bald die Ohren ruhiger und ernsthafter Menschen betäuben« [However, such continual music – no matter how pleasant it might be to him who produces it – would soon deafen the ears of calm and serious people] (Gad, 59). Indeed, Gad's emphasis on the many self-contradictions within Staël's text are used to show up the inadequacy of her rival's methodology as well as to undermine the validity of cultural stereotypes imposed on German identity.

In her quest to lay bare the presumed incoherence of *De l'Allemagne*, Gad juxtaposes Staël's surprise over the level of learnedness among all classes of Germans with her hypothesis about their supposed anxiety about being ridiculed by French wit, in order to draw attention to the incompatibility of the two ideas; to Gad's mind, thoughtful individuals – by virtue of their learnedness – are ostensibly above the fear of mockery (Gad, 41-2). Second, she counters Staël's critique of German women as sentimental with her own anecdote highlighting French women's affectations (Gad, 25-27). Where Staël sees an over-enthusiastic and thus oppressive civility in German women, Gad cautions against confusing an anecdote with an essential national characteristic (Gad, 28). Most interestingly, she turns Staël's criticism that Germany lacks a cultural center such as Paris on its head:

> Wenn Schriftsteller und Künstler so zerstreut in einem Reiche leben als in Deutschland, so werden ihre Werke allgemein bekannt und beliebt. Kenntnisse werden auf mannigfaltige Wege durchs ganze Land verbreitet, und Bildung und Vervollkommnung bezeichnen ihren Lauf [...] Wenn aber der Urquell alles Wissens in einer Hauptstadt eingeschlossen bleibt, dann zeigt sich eine Geistesarmuth in entfernten Provinzen [...].
>
> [If (indeed) writers and artists are so scattered throughout a realm as they are in Germany, their works are generally known and loved. Knowledge is dispersed in many ways throughout the land, and education and perfectability characterize its

development… If however the original source of all knowledge is trapped within a capital city, then a spiritual and intellectual impoverishment manifests itself in the distant provinces] (Gad, 68).

Both Gad and la Motte Fouqué posit a more profound form of German sociability in contrast to what they identify as the empty pleasure of French conversation. Esther Gad concludes her pamphlet by contrasting the painful spur of satire with a milder form of reasoning, more inclined to dispense truths and promote intellectual development (Gad, 156). For la Motte Fouqué, less passionate in her condemnation of Staël than her counterparts, German conversation transcends the theatrical art of dueling inherent in French interactions [»die theatralische Fechtkunst«] by emphasizing reciprocity [»Hören und Gehörtwerden«], honesty, and the desire to communicate (La Motte Fouqué, 13, 33). Nonetheless, she takes to heart Staël's criticisms of German society, even concluding that Staël's misperceptions are in part generated by a split within German consciousness: »Kurz, es ist keine frei herausgebildete Einheit in der Lebenssprache. Wir schwenken zwischen Feierlichkeit und Trivialität, zwischen Verkünstelung und unerzogener Natur« [In short, there is no freely developed unity in the vital language. We oscillate between ceremoniousness and triviality, between artifice and uneducated nature] (La Motte Fouqué, 29). According to la Motte Fouqué, German culture is still a (linguistic) project; she argues that writers need to develop literary forms in order to liberate German society from the desire to imitate its French neighbor, that is, to encourage the use of German in social exchanges: »Die unnatürliche Verkennung unsrer selbst hat uns zu fremden Gefangenen gemacht. Wir haben den Gebrauch eigner Glieder verlernt, und bewegen uns leichter mit erborgten Stützen« [The unnatural ignorance/misrecognition of ourselves has transformed us into foreign prisoners. We have forgotten how to use our own limbs and can move more easily when using borrowed supports] (La Motte Fouqué, 30).

Betty Gleim's response to *De l'Allemagne* is the most vehement of the three, colored, as it is, by her experience of Bremen's occupation by Napoleon's forces between 1806-1813. Whereas Bremen had initially maintained privileged relations with France in order to protect its trade interests – refusing to join the *Norddeutsche Bund,* for instance – the French occupation led to the loss of both political autonomy and economic stability.

Gleim's *Randzeichen zu den Werken der Frau von Staël über Deutschland* takes the form of »notes in the margins«, which does seem to prevent her from constructing an alternative definition of Germanness. In fact, the structure of her text reveals that her defence takes place on the level of textual authority. Gleim cites passages directly from Staël's work, generally both in German and in French, in order to draw attention to Staël's contradictory claims, her negligent use of language or inadequate knowledge of German culture. She writes as a schoolmistress, proofreading Staël's work and taking her to task for her »errors« of judgment as these impact on three main areas: German history; language; and literature.[7] In fact, the most striking image she uses in order to discredit Staël is a mechanical one that undermines both her Swiss-French counterpart's knowledge and humanity:

»Und so ist es denn vollkommen erklärlich, daß sie in ihrem Buche zuweilen erinnert an das akustische Kunstwerk, genannt das unsichtbare Mädchen. Die Metallkugel tönt Manches von dem, was in sie hineingesprochen ist, halb, verworren, und als Mißlaut zurück«

[And thus it is absolutely explicable that she reminds (the reader) sometimes of the acoustic mechanism known as the invisible girl. The metal ball echoes back some of what is spoken into it only in half-measures, in confused, displeasing sounds] (Gleim 1814, vii).

For Gleim (as for Gad and la Motte Fouqué), it is particularly the French language that blocks Staël from being truly able to express herself and, indeed, to comprehend the German state of being.

Gleim argues – in contrast to Caroline von la Motte Fouqué – that German culture (including the language) has very clear characteristics; it is hardly a work-in-progress. Gleim sets out to assert a connection between *Sprachgeist* [linguistic essence] and *Volksgeist* [cultural/national essence] (Gleim 1814, 101) by analyzing very specific aspects of the German language. She notes that: the multiple consonants and scientific grammar are ciphers for precision of thought (Gleim 1814, 40-41); the predominance of the *Periode* [the complex sentence] is associated with syntactical liberty (Gleim 1814, 38); and the use of directional particles and word combinations allows for concision, daring, and freedom of expression (Gleim 1814, 122-23). Whereas Staël associates stiffness (and incomprehensibility) with the use of inversions and nominal declensions, Gleim assembles an arsenal of critics (including the French intellectuals la Harpe and Diderot) in order to assert instead the poetic richness and aesthetic freedom of the German language.[8] Gleim concludes that the German language allows for greater versatility in thought and vision. In fact, while commenting on Staël's impatience with inversions and nominal declensions, Gleim throws into relief two of her rival's presumed faults. Firstly, she criticizes Staël's inability to move beyond *one* language: »sie kennt nur Einen Wohllaut in der Sprache, Eine Gattung, Einen Ausdruck der Leidenschaft« [she knows only One pleasant sound in language, One genre, One expression of passion] (BG, 273, 243)]. Secondly, Gleim attempts to explain Staël's dissatisfaction with the German language on the grounds that the latter has difficulty in valuing linguistic freedom after having been constrained by narrow (French) rules and a clumsiness born of inexperience [BG,100].

There is no doubt that *De l'Allemagne* is sprinkled with evaluations of German sociability that are not always complimentary.[9] Nonetheless, Staël's text takes on several projects – not simply one that might assert (explicitly or not) the superiority of French culture. *De l'Allemagne* is, of course, much more than simply a »faithful« portrait of the German population of the early 1800s. The chapter on »Classical and Romantic Poetry« makes it quite clear that Staël is also engaging in the *querelle des anciens et des modernes*,[10] and that she is establishing her solidarity with the »Moderns«, especially in light of her critique of »taste« and literary conventions and her emphasis on the perfectibility of the Romantic tradition (Staël, I:214).[11] Most importantly, this initiation of the French reader into German culture serves a goal that moves beyond purely national interests. Staël urges her contemporaries to engage seriously with the literary and philosophical writings of their German neighbours, »ces hommes les plus instruits et les plus méditatifs de l'Europe« [these most educated and thoughtful men of Europe]. She adds:

»Il se pourrait qu'une littérature ne fût pas conforme à notre législation du bon goût, et qu'elle contînt des idées nouvelles dont nous puissions nous enrichir en les modifiant à notre manière. C'est ainsi que les Grecs nous ont valu Racine, et Shakespeare plusieurs des tragédies de Voltaire«

[It could be that a literature might not correspond to our rules of good taste but that it might contain new ideas which can enrich us when we transform them in our own manner. This is how the Greeks yielded us Racine and Shakespeare (yielded us) several tragedies by Voltaire] (Staël, I:48).

In fact, her belief in the importance of cross-cultural intertextuality manifests itself again in her chapter on German universities, where she extolls the virtues of studying foreign languages.[12] Paradoxically, defining what is particular to German culture contributes then to the project of cultural intertextuality and ultimately dismantles the clearcut distinctions between the different nations.[13]

Suzanne Nash's insightful reading of the political subtext in *De l'Allemagne* highlights the fact, moreover, that Staël's choice of Germany as the *patrie de la pensée* [land of thought] with no firm political contours functions primarily as a counterpart to Napoleon's nationalism, which supplanted the Revolutionary brand of Republican patriotism (Nash, 19). Nash's analysis throws into relief how the Napoleonic political program is deeply antithetical to Staël's own political ideology:

»I mean by 'nationalism' a specifically nineteenth-century phenomenon that fuses nationality (a cultural group speaking the same language and sharing the same customs) with patriotism, ie: loyalty to a sovereign political state. It is a condition of mind in which loyalty to the ideal of one's national state, belief in its mission and its intrinsic excellence takes precedence over all other loyalties. Mme de Staël's concept of nationhood was different. It derived from the popular revolutionary point of view that a ›nation‹ was not based on ethnicity but on a shared commitment to individual freedom and the common good as opposed to privilege and particular interests«. (Nash, 19)

According to Nash, Staël was attracted to the »disunity, cultural diversity, and permeable boundaries« of the Germany of 1803 as a means to reject both the Napoleonic conflation of nationality with patriotism as well as the branch of German Romanticism »connect[ing] spirituality with unconscious, ancestral, or mystical origins« (Nash, 26, 30).[14]

The analysis of German philosophical thought marks the clearest example of Staël's study of what for her is the »quintessentially German« characteristic – *intériorité* or reflection – and she chooses Kant as the key representative of the new, progressive philosophy in Germany (Staël, II: 128,138). On the one hand, her preoccupation with German *intériorité* allows her to confront head-on a troubling, paradoxical feature of German society. Although she notes a connection between the political fragmentation of Germany and the »peaceful anarchy« of individualism, the freedom of literary and metaphysical opinions (Staël, I: 59), she is also concerned by the curious contradiction in the German character in its »audacity of thought« but submissiveness in practice (Staël, I: 63). She points out: »Tout voir et tout comprendre est une grande raison d'incertitude; et l'énergie de l'action ne se développe pas que dans ces contrées libres et puissantes où les sentiments patriotiques sont dans l'âme comme le sang dans les veines [...]« [To see all and understand all leads to uncertainty; and the energy of action can only develop in free and powerful countries where patriotic feelings are in the soul as blood flows in the veins] (Staël, I: 64). For Staël, the philosophical turn toward interiority needs to be supplemented by political and religious institutions. A predominantly private sociability leads to troubling complacency, an even slavish deference to (corrupt) power. Staël goes on to conclude, then, that the new German philosophy is unable in itself to form a nation. Only a government can stimulate the »moral electricity« that all citizens might feel (Staël, II: 177,178).

On the other hand, she makes use of her study of Kant in order to draw attention to the political potential of Kantian idealism in debunking materialist theories which, she argues, lead to relativism and fuel rampant individualism [*l'intérêt personnel*]. Most interesting is her demystification of »national interest« as a disguised form of the pursuit of personal advantage. She points out:

> »Quand une fois l'on s'est dit qu'il faut sacrifier la morale à l'intérêt national, on est bien près de resserrer de jour en jour le sens du mot nation, et d'en faire d'abord ses partisans, puis ses amis, puis sa famille, qui n'est qu'un terme décent pour se désigner soi-même«
>
> [When one tells oneself that one must sacrifice morals to national interest, then one is close to limiting the meaning of the word nation and equates it first with one's supporters, then one's friends, then one's family, which is only a decent term for designating oneself] (Staël, II: 194).

The »national« ideal that Staël proposes instead of self-interestedness is (an innate) justice, since for her the integrity of principles, indeed, human perfectibility, is of greater value than the (merely temporal) interests of a people. »L'individu et la société sont responsables, avant tout, de l'héritage céleste qui doit être transmis aux générations successives de la race humaine« [The individual and society are above all responsible for the celestial heritage that must be transmitted to successive generations of the human race] (Staël, II: 188). Once again, a purely »national« frame of reference is supplanted by a more global project.

Indeed, it should be noted that Staël's exposition of Kant's three critiques carefully locates his theories within the context of a European philosophical tradition; Staël is intent on describing Kant as a reader of other philosophies, attempting to resolve the »inadequacy« of Locke's materialist philosophy of the senses and of Descartes' and Leibniz' idealist (and mathematical) theories (Staël, II: 128). Whereas for Staël Locke's approach leads to an abdication of the individual's free will in favor of a relativism based on circumstance,[15] Kant foregrounds the principles inherent in the self (space, time, causality, possibility, necessity and, most importantly, conscience) as the basis of the individual's freedom and subsequent accountability for his/her actions (Staël, II: 135).

The disjunction between Staël's *De l'Allemagne* and her three German-speaking critics is somewhat surprising perhaps, considering the many different points of intersection that seem to prepare the ground for solidarity between the four women – not least, the denunciation by all four of Napoleon's politics. All carve out a space for themselves, able to write publicly without having to adopt the mask of domestic fiction[16] and all focus on the tight weave between language and cultural identity, even if – as Anderson points out – the link between nation defined as territory and as language is historically an arbitrary one. All share a fascination with Enlightenment ideals, valuing, in particular, intellectual autonomy made possible through the practice of reading. Gleim's commitment to the education of women is followed by la Motte Fouqué's preoccupation with the effects of intellectually stimulating works (La Motte Fouqué, 1), and Esther Gad's pamphlet undertakes the intellectual demystification of cultural stereotyping. Indeed, one would expect mutual respect – especially between Fouqué and Staël. As Silke Arnold-de Simine points out in her chapter on »Napoleon, the Museum, and Memory Politics«, four years after Staël's death, Fouqué also highlights the importance of a national identity that might avoid xenophia and chauvinism through the promotion of social, cultural, and scholarly exchange between different regions of Europe – a practice she sees exemplified by the the Middle Ages. And yet, the potential for solidarity implicit in Staël's ideal of cultural *métissage* or mixing – supported by the practice of reading – is overshadowed for all three German writers by her critique of the pleasure to be experienced in German society.[17]

The experience of *Aneinandervorbeireden* [speaking past one another] can, of course, be dismissed simply as rivalry, as an expression of Gleim's, Gad's, and la Motte Fouqué's sense of personal and cultural inferiority vis-à-vis Madame de Staël and French society. It could also be motivated, perhaps, by the historical context. In 1814, the fate of the Napoleonic forces is still in the balance, the ultimate defeat occurring, of course, only in 1815.

Equally important, it seems to me, is the asymmetry that results from this scene of reading. Staël uses the othering of Germany in order to construct both a utopian *patrie de la pensée* and a counterpoint to Napoleon's France, defining (and improving) her own cultural identity against the nebulous contours of her neighbour.[18] For Gleim, Gad, and la Motte Fouqué, that project of identity – despite its many positive characteristics – transforms German culture into a text to be deciphered. The authenticity of their culture is defined for them in *De l'Allemagne*, thus transferring the authority over Germanness from those experiencing it to those observing and naming it. In fact, this process represents, especially for Gleim, a form of internal invasion [»Fern bleibe denn Alles von uns, was die Einheit und Reinheit unsers Wesens stören [...] könnte«] [All that might disturb the unity and purity of our being should be kept at a distance from us] (Gleim 1814, viii). It seems to parallel, in part, the French occupation that her native Hanseatic city of Bremen experienced from 1806 until 1813. The three German critiques of *De l'Allemagne* can thus be read as attempts to reestablish textual and linguistic authority over one's own location. In these three accounts, the insistence on the complex superiority of the German language, rendering even the physical experience of German sociability opaque to outsiders, can then be understood as an expression of the effort to reclaim one's own authority as ultimate reader of her own culture.

–Bowling Green State University, Ohio

## Notes

All translations in this paper are my own.

1 Betty Gleim (1781–1827) was first and foremost a pedagogue, founding the first girls' school in her native city, Bremen, in 1810. Strongly influenced by Pestalozzi's pedagogical writings, she published extensively on the subject of women's education, noting in her *Erziehung und Unterricht des weiblichen Geschlechts* (1810): »Von [der] Beschaffenheit [der Frauen] hängt das Wohl und Weh, die Veredlung oder das Verderben des Ganzen ab; wie sie sind, wird das Menschengeschlecht sein«. (Gleim 1810, II: 153) At the end of her educational treatise she claims her place in public discourse by asserting tongue-in-cheek: »Die Frauen regieren die Welt, mögen dies die Männer hören oder nicht« (Gleim 1810, II: 150). Josephine Zimmermann documents Gleim's contact with the leading politicians of Bremen: »Sie bespricht dann in ihrem Brief mit Senator Smidt die Schulverhältnisse Bremens, macht Vorschläge zur Verbesserung des Schulwesens [...] Nach dem Briefe vom 6.12.1815 aus Mannheim zu schließen, ist Smidt auf die Vorschläge Betty Gleims eingegangen«. (Zimmermann, 30). – Esther Gad (also known as Lucie Domeier) was born in Breslau in 1767. She is associated with the *Jüdische Freischule* in Berlin and responded publicly to Campe's text on

female learning. Gad's critique of Campe's Rousseauist argument focuses on three aspects: 1) if men are able to juggle multiple social functions, women should be able to take on more than simply the role of wife, housewife and mother; 2) women's physical weakness justifies all the more the necessity of allowing them to develop their intellectual abilities; 3) one can recognize the *mauvaise foi* in husbands' tendency to satirize women's learning, on the one hand, while continually attempting to educate their spouses. Also known for her correspondance with Jean Paul, Rahel Varnhagen, and Henriette Herz as well as travel accounts and essays, Gad emigrated to London after 1800 and died in 1833. – Finally, Caroline de la Motte Fouqué (1773–1831) from Nennhausen (Brandenburg) was a prolific (Royalist) writer of Romantic texts (*Ritterromane*, for instance).

2 »It is certainly true that the Confederation failed to create genuinely ›national‹ institutions. The Act of 1815 had left open a number of important issues, including joint defence policy, the creation of a unified economic area within the Confederation, the legal status of the Jews and constitutional reform«. (Clark, 43)

3 Pierre Miquel writes in the chapter, »Bonaparte, consul de la République française«, in his *Histoire de la France. De Vercingétorix à Charles de Gaulle*: »Au début de 1802, le Premier consul décida de se débarrasser des libéraux irréductibles, qui le raillaient dans les salons parisiens, le brocardaient à l'Institut de France, et gênaient le travail législatif. [...] Tout ce qui gênait le Premier consul était réputé ›jacobin‹« (Miquel, 294).

4 D'Alembert writes: »[il faut] se souvenir que la conversation est un délassement, et qu'elle n'est ni un assaut de salle d'armes ni un jeu d'échecs [...] [il ne faut point] s'emparer seul et avec tyrannie de la parole; [...] n'y point avoir le ton dogmatique et magistral [...]« [one must remember that conversation is an experience of leisure, that it is neither a fencing match nor a game of chess [...] one must not monopolize the conversation tyrannically [...] nor use a dogmatic and magisterial tone [...]]. This passage is quoted in Godo, 165.

5 A contemporary's description of Staël's *salon* captures the intensity of that pleasure – »the second language of face, voice, and gesture« – associated with this »French« form of sociability. In her *Histoire des salons de Paris*, Mme d'Abrantès (1784–1838) describes Mme de Staël within the context of her own salon: »Ses bras et ses mains, ses épaules, son port de tête, gagnaient beaucoup à être agités, tandis qu'elle parlait, et, comme toutes les femmes, elle ajoutait cette manière de plaire aux yeux, au charme captivant de la parole dans une telle bouche« [Her arms and hands, her shoulders, the way she held her head were enhanced by her movements when she spoke, and like all women, she added to the captivating charm of words uttered by such a mouth this manner of pleasing the eyes] (Godo, 187).

6 Geselligkeit is linked etymologically with Geselle, and the Kluge Etymologisches Wörterbuch provides the following description: »Soziativbildung zu Saal als ›jmd., der im gleichen Haus (Saal) wohnt‹, dann verallgemeinert zu ›Gefährte‹ und schliesslich [...] festgelegt auf ›Handwerksgeselle‹« (262). The term Saal is explained in the following terms: »›Herberge, Speisezimmer‹. Das Wort bezeichnet ursprünglich den Innenraum des Einraumhauses. Aussergermanisch vergleichen sich l. solum ›Boden‹, lit. sala ›Dorf‹, akslav. Selo ›Acker, Dorf‹ (in den slavischen Sprachen von einem *sedlo- ›Siedlung‹, das zu sitzen und siedeln gehört, nicht überall deutlich zu scheiden. Weitere Herkunft unklar« ( 612).

7 Henning concludes: »On a toujours l'impression, lorsqu'on lit ses réfutations pointilleuses, qui ne sont souvent que de simples négations, qu'elle tâche de se débarrasser de la conscience d'une certaine infériorité de l'esprit allemand en comparaison de celui des autres nations, et que, plus sûre de ses arguments, elle aurait éprouvé moins vivement le besoin de les défendre« (Henning, 194).

8 La Harpe's quotation about German inversions reads: »[...] cette libre disposition de mots, arrangés de manière à faire valoir toutes les parties de la phrase, à la couper, à la suspendre, à les opposer, à les rassembler, à attacher toujours l'oreille et l'attention, sans que cette composition artificielle laissât le moindre nuage dans l'esprit« (Gleim 1814, 97).

9 Mona Ozouf, for instance, notes in the chapter »Germaine ou l'inquiétude« in her book *Les mots des femmes*: »Il n'est donc pas mauvais pour une femme de naître allemande. Elle trouve chez les hommes plus de sentimentalité et de sérieux qu'en Italie, et se sent moins réléguée qu'en Angleterre. Mais, cette fois encore, de tels avantages ont un prix: l'absence de séduction sociale, l'austérité, la séparation des hommes de savoir et de cour, qui fait ressembler l'Allemagne plutôt à une université qu'à un salon [...] le manque de grâce, la rigidité, un mortel esprit de sérieux« (Ozouf, 128-29).

10 Lilian Fürst's 1977 study of French and German Romanticism in terms of a dynamics of counterpart is worth mentioning here: »Both Lessing and Mme de Staël were motivated by a disturbing awareness of the `dégradation actuelle' [...] of their respective literatures, and both were in search of the best means of improvement. [...] Both also implied new standards in literary criticism in their admission of the emotional effect of art, [...] in their questioning of the absolute validity of the three unities in drama, and in their conviction that genius towers above any rules. [...] In the place they hold and the function they fulfil within their own literatures the *Hamburgische Dramaturgie* and *De la littérature* form a counterpart to each other. The thirty odd years dividing them are an early instance of the time-lag that casts its metaphoric shadow over Franco-German relationships from Pre-romanticism onwards« (Fürst, 17). Also see p. 2 for a description of her comparative methodology focusing on counterparts understood to be an »analysis of polarity« alongside an analysis of affinity.

11 Ian Henning's study of *De l'Allemagne* elucidates the need to distinguish, of course, between the various strands of Romanticism which Staël acknowledged and those from which she distanced herself (and which distanced themselves from her).

12 »[...] le sens d'une phrase dans une langue étrangère est à la fois un problème grammatical et intellectuel. [...] [L'enfant qui traduit] s'essaie tout seul avec les difficultés que lui présentent deux langues à la fois, il s'introduit dans les idées successivement, compare et combine divers genres d'analogies et de vraisemblances; et l'activité spontanée de l'esprit, la seule qui développe vraiment la faculté de penser, est vivement excitée par cette étude [...] [sans laquelle] il serait borné toute sa vie au cercle de sa propre nation, cercle étroit comme tout ce qui est exclusif« (Staël, I: 141). – Both Henning's study and Suzanne Nash's excellent article on *De l'Allemagne* also draw attention to the importance of cultural diversity and transculturation in Staël's work.

13 It is ironic, in this context, to consider that Staël's use of *conversation* as a marker of a particularly *French* character can itself be read as a particularly rich example of *métissage* – even pointing back to the dialogues and banquets of Antiquity. Emmanuel Godo notes: »Le XVIe siècle est, en Europe, le siècle où naît l'idée de conversation. [...] Converser apparaît, dans des sociétés qui s'engagent dans la pacification des moeurs, comme le

moyen adéquat pour dégager un espace heureux et promouvoir des relations humaines saines exemptes de violence [...] La Renaissance humaniste pressent, à la relecture des textes fondateurs de l'Antiquité, que la conversation, loin d'être une pratique superficielle et superflue, peut être un instrument de construction d'un bonheur« (Godo, 41). For Godo, Erasmus, Castiglione, and Montaigne are three key examples of Renaissance *European* theoreticians of the art of conversation.

14 Nash skillfully connects the different topics analyzed by Staël: »The narrative logic of Mme de Staël's invention of Germany as a model of national virtue for the French depends upon a rhetorical structure which does not call attention to itself as such. Germany, poetry, genius, women, chivalry, and philosophical idealism are all deftly, as if naturally, connected within one coherent semantic field to justify, paradoxically, her non-traditional, post-revolutionary project « (Nash, 30).

15 »Si le hasard de la naissance et de l'éducation décidait de la moralité d'un homme, comment pourrait-on l'accuser de ses actions« (Staël, II, 100)?

16 »More often than not, however, the women writers address public concerns obliquely through their depictions of the family. As Lynn Hunt has observed, 'most Europeans in the eighteenth century thought of their rulers as fathers and of their nations as families writ large.' In her view, the Revolution involved killing the father-king and replacing him with a band of brothers in the collective imagination of the French people. Conservative German writers countered with images of benevolent patriarchs whose happy private lives legitimized dynastic authority in the state. German liberals, on the other hand, linked the abuse of paternal authority in the home to corruption in other authority figures, including decadent aristocrats and captains of industry. [...] In fact, German domestic fiction is often at its most political when portraying the dynamics of family life« (Kontje, 10-11). The link between domestic fiction and politics has also been analyzed by Nancy Armstrong and Doris Kadish, among others.

17 In Gleim's account, we do also find a preoccupation with transcultural exchanges. Within the intracultural context, while noting that the purest German is spoken in Lower Saxony, where one writes presumably as one speaks, Gleim explains this purity in paradoxical terms: »Nicht also in Obersachsen [...] wird das reinste Deutsch gesprochen, wenn man auf die Geschichte Rücksicht nehmen will, sondern in Niedersachsen, wo sich die Volkstämme immer reiner erhalten, die sich dort stark vermischt« (Gleim 1814, 91). The virtues of cultural (or rather tribal) mixing do not extend for her, however, to the intercultural context. – In fact, Gleim attempts to demonstrate the universality of the German language: its presumed ability to translate every foreign form in its most minute detail and palest nuance (Gleim 1814, 164); its ability to comprehend all intellects [Geist]; its status as the true *Allsprache* – »auf diese Art nicht nur der europäischen, sondern auch der amerikanischen Nachtigall gleichend, die außer ihrer eigenen Melodie, auch die Melodien des gesammten Vogelchors nachzusingen vermag« (Gleim 1814, 124). For Gleim, the transcultural borrowing is meant to reach its climax in German culture, which leads to the paradoxical conclusion that it is precisely the invisible (if not inaudible) nation, which is posited as the new model of culture – one that is, albeit, inimitable by outsiders.

18 Daniel Cohn-Bendit and Thomas Schmid write: »Man definiert sich selbst und gewinnt Kontur, indem man sich von anderen abgrenzt [...] Das gilt meist für *beide* Seiten« (Cohn-Bendit and Schmid, 322).

## Works Cited


Anderson, Benedict. *Imagined Communities, Reflections on the Origin and Spread of Nationalism.* London: Verso, 1982, 2001.

Armstrong, Nancy. *Desire and Domestic Fiction. A Political History of the Novel.* Oxford: Oxford UP, 1990.

Baumgartner, Karin. »Defining National Identity: Caroline de la Motte Fouqué Responds to Madame de Staël's De l'Allemagne«. *Colloquia Germanica* 35 (2002): 59-73.

Bredin, Jean-Denis. *Une singulière famille. Jacques Necker, Suzanne Necker et Germaine de Staël*. Paris: Fayard, 1999.

Clark, Christopher. »Germany 1815–1848: Restoration or Pre-March«. *Nineteenth-Century Germany. Politics, Culture and Society. 1780–1918.* Ed. John Breuilly. London: Oxford, UP, 2001: 40-65.

Cohn-Bendit, Daniel & Schmid, Thomas. *Heimat Babylon. Das Wagnis der multikulturellen Demokratie.* Hamburg: Campe, 1992.

*Etymologisches Wörterbuch der deutschen Sprache.* Ed. Friedrich Kluge. New York: de Gruyter, 1989.

Fürst, Lilian. *Counterparts: the Dynamics of Franco-German Relationships, 1770–1895.* Detroit: Wayne State University Press, 1977.

Gad, Esther. *Kritische Auseinandersetzung mehrerer Stellen in dem Buche der Frau v. Staël über Deutschland.* N.p: 1814.

Gleim, Betty. *Erziehung und Unterricht des weiblichen Geschlechts.* Bremen: Heyse, 1810.

Gleim, Betty. *Randzeichen zu den Werken der Frau von Staël über Deutschland.* Bremen: Heyse, 1814.

Godo, Emmanuel. *Histoire de la conversation.* Paris: PUF, 2003.

Gutwirth, Madelyn. A. Goldberger, K. Szmurlo. *Germaine de Staël. Crossing the Borders.* New Brunswick: Rutgers UP, 1991.

Henning, Ian. *L'Allemagne de Madame de Staël et la polémique romantique.* Genève: Slatkine, 1975.

Kadish, Doris. *Politicizing Gender. Narrative Strategies in the Aftermath of the French Revolution.* New Brunswick: Rutgers UP, 1991.

Kontje, Todd. *Women, the Novel, and the German Nation 1771–1871. Domestic Fiction in the Fatherland.* Cambridge: Cambridge UP, 1998.

Miquel, Pierre. *Histoire de la France. De Vercingétorix à Charles de Gaulle.* Paris: Fayard, 1976.

Motte Fouqué, Karoline de la. *Über deutsche Geselligkeit*, in *Antwort auf das Urtheil der Frau von Staël*, 1814.

Nash, Suzanne. »Nationalism and Cultural Diversity in Mme de Staël's De l'Allemagne«. In *Kaleidoscope. Essays on Nineteenth-Century French Literature in Honor of Thomas H. Goetz.* Edited by G. Falconer & M. Donaldson-Evans. Toronto: Centre d'Etudes Romantiques Joseph Sablé, 1996: 15-34.

Ozouf, Mona. *Les mots des femmes. Essais sur la singularité française*. Paris: Gallimard, 1995.

Staël, Germaine de. *De l'Allemagne, Tomes I & II*. Paris: Garnier-Flammarion, 1968.

Szmurlo, Karyna. *The Novel's Seductions. Staël's* Corinne *in Critical Inquiry*. Lewisburg: Bucknell UP, 1999.

Zimmermann, Josephine. *Betty Gleim [1781–1827] und ihre Bedeutung für die Geschichte der Mädchenbildung*. Diss. Phil. Köln, 1926.

# Napoleon, the Museum, and Memory Politics in Caroline de la Motte Fouqué's *Geschichte der Moden* (1829–30)

*Silke Arnold-de Simine*

One of the most prolific and popular writers of her time in Germany, Caroline de la Motte Fouqué (1775–1831), has become in the present all but overshadowed by her better known husband Friedrich.[1] Her production rate, which only decreased during the Wars of Liberation, kept pace with the explosive growth of the German literary market (Kontje 96). She published at prestigious publishing houses, such as Cotta and Hitzig, and was widely read and acknowledged by contemporary writers such as Goethe or Friedrich Schlegel as an author of the so-called ›middle sphere‹ (*mittlere Sphäre*). But at the time of her death her literary contributions had already gone out of fashion.

Her estate *Schloß Nennhausen* and her Salon in Berlin were meeting places for philosophers and writers of the Romantic School, such as the brothers Schlegel, Eichendorff, E.T.A. Hoffmann, Ludwig Tieck, Clemens Brentano, Jean Paul, Adalbert von Chamisso, Johann Gottlieb Fichte and others. Through her husband and these writers, Fouqué[2] was introduced to the ideas of Romanticism. The literary work of her husband can be seen as symptomatic for the then prevalent nostalgia for the past incited by the rediscovery of the Middle Ages and its related idea of a national unity. Fouqué herself, in her *Briefe über Berlin* [Letters on Berlin] (1821), drew upon the ideal of the Middle Ages in order to reject a notion of national identity based on xenophobia and chauvinism, reminding her readers that these were times of fervent social, cultural, and scholarly exchange between different regions in Europe. In her opinion, stable personal and collective identities could only be developed through interaction and exchange, which meant that a secure and independent national identity had to be based on both respect of and for one's neighbours. However, during the Wars of Liberation, such sentiments had been swept away by a militant patriotism which dominated in the German states which were fighting against Napoleon, a patriotism which had been – at times – also shared by Fouqué.

Fouqué had first-hand experiences with the effects of the Napoleonic Wars – a trying, perilous time for her and her family: her husband and her two sons had answered the Prussian call to arms in 1813 and were sent to battle. She was forced to quarter French soldiers at her estate, and she witnessed the French pillage of the countryside after Prussia's defeat at Jena in 1806. As a status-conscious noblewoman who believed in the god-given monarchic order she was deeply opposed to the idea of a violent revolution, although she was by no means a reactionary and acknowledged the need for changes in the feudal system.

Many of her historic novels set in revolutionary or Napoleonic times[3] can be read as an ongoing commentary on the contemporary political situation in France and Germany. However, *Edmund's Wege und Irrwege* [Edmund's Ways and Meanderings] (1815) is the only one that concentrates on the situation in Germany during the Wars of Liberation. Additionally, this novel served as an open vehicle for ideological propaganda. Here, as is the case in all of her historical novels, she aimed to vitalize (contemporary) history: »So *verlebendigt* sich Geschichte in den Schicksalen der Figuren, die gewissermaßen wie aus einem ›historischen Museum‹ erweckt auftreten« (Vollmer 115). The plot, a mixture of history and fiction, fact and fantasy, depicts Napoleon's reign as sinful, even demonic, an insult to the virtuous and fair land of Germany. Her protagonist suffers greatly from an empty, stagnant present condition so that he is compelled to seek refuge in the past. This, however, proves not to be a feasible solution; Edmund feels even more alienated and distraught than before. The message is clear: Salvation only can be found in the heroic, patriotic action that faces the problems of the present and accepts responsibility.

However, Fouqué's texts are by no means simple propaganda against Napoleon in the service of the Prussian state. On the contrary: she was a fierce critic of the Prussian government. Following its defeat in 1806/07, Prussia had strengthened its economy – one that still heavily relied on the exchange of goods and services – in order to facilitate the payment of monetary retribution to France. Fouqué deplored the »agrarian reforms that introduced the free transfer of property for leading to the disintegration of the social fabric of the state.« (Baumgartner 1999a, 184) She lamented the fact that the aristocracy was trying to hang on to its privileges while denying its responsibility towards society as a whole. But instead of placing her hopes on bourgeois male institutions, she advocated »a revival of the Prussian state through a (feminized) aristocracy.« (Baumgartner

1999a, 29) Fouqué hoped that with the end of Napoleon's reign an individual and national awakening would occur. However, in the Restoration period that followed the Wars of Liberation her hopes died: The old order was restored after 1815 and demands for the promised national unity were increasingly seen as subversive.

For some, the call for national unity was not only a response to the Napoleonic threat, but also a means to replace an absolutist particularism with a politically unified republic. The Carlsbad Decrees (1819) were imposed to fight against these tendencies. All hopes for a unified nation which was already restricted to the realm of culture and language, suffered another setback by the institution of drastic censorship laws. In this context, literature gained an important role in the search for national identity during and after the Napoleonic Wars, and not only male writers were engaged in this task. As Todd Kontje has pointed out, »[n]ascent nationalism confronts the cosmopolitan legacy of the Enlightenment as authors use their novels to explore conflicting models of collective identity, and to rethink gender roles within these imagined communities.« (Kontje 97)

In Fouqué's novels up to the 1820s, which are concerned with the French Revolution, politics and war,, the protagonists are often men who play an active role in the public sphere, men who are the agents of change. However, in her historical novels her focus is clearly on women as subjects of history who insist on their right to participate in the political discourses – sometimes even in the political actions – of their time. In Fouqué's opinion, the future of a united Germany was not only fought out on the battlefields, but it also had to be formed through an inner process of maturity which is gained by open-mindedness and free discourse between the sexes and the nations and which had to be established within the minds of all people (Baumgartner 2002, 65). Karin Baumgartner states:

»Nach Fouqué hat die politische Malaise, die zur Französischen Revolution, zur Napoleonischen Machtübernahme und zur Restauration geführt hat, ihren Ursprung in der Unfähigkeit der Männer, die Welt als ein Organisch-Ganzes zu erfassen, das nur durch gegenseitige Abhängigkeit von Frauen und Männern, Bauern, Adeligen und Bürgern lebensfähig ist.« (Baumgartner 1999b, 95)

[According to Fouqué, the political malaise that led to the French Revolution, Napoleon's seizure of power, and the Restoration was caused by the inability of men to conceive the world as an organic whole, one that is viable only through mutual interdependence of woman and men, of farmers, nobles and bourgeois.]

Fouqué pursued this thought openly and actively in her journalistic work in which she also discussed the role of women in the process of defining a national identity. Kontje, Baumgartner and Müller-Adams[4] have explored Fouqués' efforts to develop »a theory of national identity based on the concept of sociability« (Baumgartner 2002, 68), which would enable women to contribute to the political sphere and to the nation-building process through institutions such as the Salon, in which women and men, aristocrats and bourgeois could meet on equal terms and exchange ideas in semi-public surroundings. But the Salons saw their decline at the beginning of the nineteenth century. New cultural institutions such as academies and societies for reading and debating were created in which these bourgeois forms of assembly and discussion could be practised. Most of them excluded women, who were, however, permitted to visit museums, one of few public arenas in which they could participate (Bennett 29). Even if Fouqué did not explicitly identify the institution of the museum as a public sphere in which women could act, she certainly made use of the discoursive strategies which were developed by the museums to vindicate the compilation of the material remnants of the past as national heritage: »For Fouqué both women and the aristocracy symbolize her nation's connection to its heritage [...], and they both guarantee Prussia's stability for the future.« (Baumgartner 1999a, 241) While Fouqué's solutions for the political future of Prussia were obviously out of line with the spirit of her time, her practice of establishing tradition through the processes of musealisation – a way of holding on to the past while simultaneously letting it go – was highly contemporary.

Many of the great nineteenth-century European museums open to the public were founded at the time of the Revolutionary and Napoleonic Wars. They constituted a reaction to the vandalism and iconoclasm of the French Revolution. Representational objects were destroyed due to their association with the tyranny of the monarchy and the idolatry of the church. At the same time, however, the memorials began to be perceived as an integral part of a nation's history: It became impossible to imagine a new cultural identity without recourse to them. As Hans Belting observes, the desecration of Notre-Dame had hardly taken place when the Louvre was opened to the public (Belting 654).[5] The paradoxical flip-side of the destruction was the conscious preservation of the remains in museums.

Alexandre Lenoir collected the first monuments for what was to become the Musée des Monuments Français. According to his *Description historique et chronologique des Monuments de Sculpture, réunis au Musée des Monuments Français* (Paris 1806), he cherished »that famous revolution [...] which has established a new order of things founded on reason and justice« because he ascribed to it »the bringing together of the monuments that I have the privilege to exhibit to friends of order and of the fine arts.« (Quoted in Haskell 241) The religious objects which Lenoir saved from the destruction were exhibited in a dissolved Augustinian monastery. Deprived of their original context and therefore – in the eyes of the revolutionaries – also of their propagandistic function, they were presented in chronological order according to the historical epochs to which they belonged. This modern form of presentation, the *galleria progressiva*, enabled the public to appreciate them not only as objects of art but also as pars pro toto of the successful progress of civilization (Grasskamp 22-23 and 25). The Louvre (opened in 1793) and the Musée des Monuments Français (opened in 1795 and later renamed Musée de la Monarchie Française) are among the first museums in a modern sense: Their primary function as public institutions was not to impart knowledge for an exclusive and elitist audience but rather to preserve a national and collective heritage in the newly established concept of ›patrimoine‹ (Fliedl 117-18). This enlightened concept, which secularized churches and opened palaces to the public by turning them into museums, effectively placed the museum in the tradition of institutions connected to political power and religious reverence.

Until 1682 when Louis XIV departed to Versailles, the Louvre had been a royal residence. As *Musée Français* it was opened to the public in 1793, exhibiting former royal collections of painting and sculpture. Napoleon Bonaparte moved into the adjoining *Tuileries* in 1800 and after he had crowned himself emperor, the galleries were renamed the *Musée Napoléon*. During his reign he commissioned the renovation and extension of the Louvre and received important visitors, such as foreign ambassadors, in the Great Gallery, the place which also served as the setting for his marriage to Marie-Louise. Napoleon did his best to reinterpret this relatively new bourgeois public sphere as his representational realm (Grasskamp 33).

The artistic loot Napoleon brought home from his campaigns in Europe and Egypt was paraded through Paris in triumphal processions and afterwards exhibited in the Louvre. The museum was a place to celebrate Napoleon's deeds by marvelling at the cultural treasures of countries to which Napoleonic France had proved itself superior. It was the place where his greatness as a military leader and statesman could impress as many of his subjects as possible. The museum was instrumental in establishing a sense of national history, identity and superiority in the symbolic sphere and in counterbalancing the radical changes which took place in the socio-political realm.

The twenty-six years between the French Revolution in 1789 and Napoleon's final defeat at Waterloo was a time of massive historical change, one which ushered in the idea of a new era and at the same time provoked a yearning for a past that seemed so abruptly and irretrievably lost. Many German castles were used as quarries in order to finance Napoleon's costly military campaigns. This was perceived as a sellout of national monuments which stood for a lost German identity and the German ruin became the symbol of the oppressed German country (Bühlbäcker 59). The destruction which coincided with Napoleonic secularization was manifold. One prominent example was the dissolution of the monasteries which were turned into factories or barracks with all liturgical artwork sold or melted down (Calov 75 and 81). Bourgeois collectors such as the brothers Boisserée or Ferdinand Franz Wallraf became interested in the so-called Old German School of painting (*altdeutsche Maler*), that was ignored by the French conquerors. They saved many ecclesiastical panels, which would otherwise have been used as firewood, shutters or for similar purposes. By doing so they established the basis for many future art galleries such as the *Alte Pinakothek* in Munich (Grasskamp 78).

As critical as Fouqué was about the sudden and violent destruction of the old order, she was certainly convinced that society was not a static entity and that evolutionary change through reforms was inevitable. She showed understanding for sentimental feelings for the past, something she saw no reason to deny, but she realized that they had to find a new place in the ever-changing fabric of society. In *Ruf an die deutschen Frauen* [A Call to German Women] (1813) Fouqué seems to partake in patriotically tinged nostalgia, when she deplores changes in the German national character resulting from French influence. Fouqué maintains that for the sake of their children, German women should guard their traditions of language, dress, and »einfache edle Haltung« [simple noble bearing]. (Hofacker 78)

But she is equally aware that a balance has to be found between the acknowledgement of tradition and the reform of society in respect to a rising bourgeoisie. As Kontje observes:

»With this insight into time's relentless advance, Fouqué identifies an ambivalence that will remain at the heart of her subsequent treatments of the Revolution and its aftermath: while she condemns the Revolution as an unnatural aberration in the order of things, she nevertheless accepts historical change as inevitable and irrevocable [...] The question for the conservative aristocrat, then, will be how to preserve or rejuvenate old values in a new era without clinging rigidly to an outmoded vision of the past, or surrendering completely to the fashion of the present.« (Kontje 99).

One solution to this dilemma can be found in the process of musealisation which situates something clearly in the past while continuing to value, preserve and integrate it into an historic narrative that connects to the present. The practices of musealisation are not restricted to the institution of the museum; these discoursive modes can be transferred to other cultural and artistic realms such as literature. Fouqué made use of the discourses of museal preservation as they were established in the wake of the French Revolution and pursued under Napoleon. Nevertheless she distanced herself from the instrumentalisation of these museal practices for the purpose of legitimizing stately power and superiority. No longer was this power seen as the result of a transcendental order but as the necessary outcome of a continual historical development that was represented as a narrative unity – ›unified history of the nation‹ (Baumgartner 1999a, 138).

In pursuing the work on ›her-story‹, Fouqué neither aims for consistency nor does she valorize art and hoarded wealth as signs of dominance over foreign countries and cultures. Fouqué does not concentrate on outstanding historical figures; she does not perceive history as a series of momentous political and intellectual events and acts of heroism (Arnold-de Simine 391). She rather regards history from the vantage point of quotidian female life, emphasizing easily overlooked long-term developments and foreign influences on mentality as they are mirrored in this sphere. »[S]he reads the historiography of her time for gaps and elisions of pertinent information, such as women's participation in historical events. By privileging non-traditional accounts such as mythologies or memoirs, the author constructs a [different] version of history.« (Baumgartner 1999a, 27) In her discussion of Madame de Staël's *De l'Allemagne* (1810, German translation *Über Deutschland*, 1814), she agrees with some of de Staël's negative evaluations of German cultural life, but reproaches the French author for the general lack of insight into German culture and mentality resulting from her stance of superiority including the fact that she spoke French with the Germans she met and disregarded the historical dimensions of the situations she encountered while on her travels through Germany. According to Fouqué, the malaise de Staël witnessed stemmed from

»a lack of German pride in its heritage and culture as evidenced by the lack of a national language, of national culture and of a unifying political and cultural center.« (Baumgartner 1999a, 255)

This essay aims to take a closer look at the role Fouqué attributes in her journalistic writing, in particular in her essay *Geschichte der Moden*, to the diverse perspectives of communicative and cultural memory as opposed both to the official and more monological attitude of history and to strategies of museal preservation. Fouqué addresses questions of tradition and heritage in her texts on cultural history, such as her *Geschichte der Moden, vom Jahre 1785 bis 1829, als Beitrag zur Geschichte der Zeit* [History of Fashion, from 1785 to 1829, as a Contribution to the History of the Age], which appeared anonymously in twenty installments between the 11th of December, 1829 and the 6th of February, 1830 in the popular *Morgenblatt für gebildete Stände* (1807–1865) - a daily newspaper dealing with every aspect of social and cultural life except politics. The text was published separately in 1830, and was also included in the posthumously printed *Der Schreibtisch, oder alte und neue Zeit, ein nachgelassenes Werk* [*The writing desk, or old and new times, a posthumous work*].

Annegret Pelz and Elisa Müller Adams have demonstrated that Fouqué uses *Der Schreibtisch* to establish a private museum (Pelz 233), a museum of her authorship (Müller-Adams 2001/2002, 79). The desk is, just like the museum or the archive, a repository from which the past can be retrieved, where documents have accumulated as objects. These documents are remains of the past which, on the one hand, trigger memories simply through their rediscovery as objects, while on the other hand they tell stories about the past in a very literal way. In the rediscovery and the reorganisation of the manuscripts, the tasks of a museum or an archive are imitated: Some texts are discarded, others are chosen for transmission, purposefully collected, filed, preserved, arranged and exhibited. They are equally used for a representational, legitimizing function in Fouqué's own life and work as they are supposed to portray a bygone age. As Fouqué writes in her introduction, it is a reflection on the personal life of the 69-year-old author and on an entire epoch, both of which can be seen as nearing their end:

»Das alte Jahr ist abgelaufen. Drei Decennien liegen hinter uns. Das Rad der Zeit rollt weiter. Wir schließen ab mit der Vergangenheit. Noch einmal sieht der Schreibende zurück! Erinnerungen! euch grüßt mein feuchtes Auge. Ihr allein bleibt, und bewahrt, was der rastlose Sinn kaum beachtet.« (Fouqué 1833, no page number)

[The old year has come to an end. Three decades lie behind us. The wheel of time rolls on. We are done with the past. Once again, the writer looks back! Memories! My dampened eye greets you! You alone remain and preserve that which restless sense barely notices.]

Fouqué thus consciously ties her work to the evolution of the modern memory venue *par excellence*: the museum. And by highlighting the object status of the texts she also engages in a competition between the memory medium that is the written text, based on words, and the memory medium that is the museum, based on objects. She imitates the spatial layout of the museum by structuring the chapters according to the desk cases in which the documents are stored. Nevertheless the spatial order follows the chronological order in that the documents are arranged according to their date of origin, covering the years from 1785 to 1829.

This period is perceived as a time of crisis, characterized not so much by continual change, but by a chaotic fluctuation of trends, trends which do not simply replace each other but rather converge:

»Der herrschende Ton des Tages verklingt niemals absolut, so wenig wie der Wurf und die Falten einer abgeworfenen Mode sich beim Beginn der neuen spurlos fügen wollen. Deshalb ist es so übel nicht, einmal einen ganzen Zeitabschnitt zu überschauen, damit man sieht, wie alles *Untereinander* und mit der Gegenwart zusammenhängt.« (Fouqué 1833, 27)

[The dominant tone of the day never fades away completely, and as little do the warp and the folds of an outmoded style yield completely to the fashion of the day. It is thus hardly a vain endeavor to survey an entire period at once, so that one may see how all things relate *among themselves* and to the present time.]

In ordering these trends into a coherent chronological narrative in which cause and effect are highlighted, Fouqué aims to stabilize a collective, national identity which is perceived as threatened and unstable. Fouqué thereby follows the paradigm shift from the atemporal spatiality of curiosity cabinets of the Renaissance to the historical perception that characterized the (natural) history and art museums of the nineteenth century:

»Entsprechend dem Museumsgedanken der Zeit, in dem jeder Raum in chronologischer Abfolge so eingerichtet werden sollte, daß er den Charakter des Jahrhunderts, dem die Gegenstände entstammen, neu erstehen ließ, geben die einzelnen ›Text-Fächer‹ die darin gespeicherte Erinnerung nur fragmentarisch frei.« (Pelz 241)

[In accordance with the conception of the museum of the time which dictated that each chronologically ordered room be arranged in such a way that it reproduces the character of the period from which the objects were derived, the individual ›text-compartments‹ uncover the memory stored within them in a merely fragmentary way.]

In her essay on the *Geschichte der Moden,* Fouqué drew not only on her private memories but also on collections of authentic documents such as letters and surveys of the development of fashion. The term ›fashion‹ is thereby not restricted to attire. Fashion is, in Fouqué's words, the »Physiognomie des Augenblicks [...] welche in der wechselnden Art und Weise, die sie annimmt, Mode genannt wird und als solche sowohl Kleidung als Ansichten, sowohl gaukelnde Tändeleien als Gesinnungen beherrscht.« (Fouqué 1833, 63) [The physiognomy of the moment, which in the modality of change it assumes is named fashion and as such controls dress as well as opinion, trifling flirtations as well as personal dispositions]. This broad definition of fashion was pioneered by the *Journal des Luxus und der Moden.* Established by Friedrich Justin Bertuch in 1786, it ran until 1827 and dealt with every aspect of the ever-changing outer appearance of people's lives, establishing itself as one of the most successful journalistic enterprises of its time. It concerned itself with »clothes, books, daily activities, and morals in addition to contemporary political changes.« (Baumgartner 1997, 228) The journal itself contributed to the accelerated pace of fashion change by communicating to the reader the latest styles from Paris via coloured fashion plates. Fouqué was probably the first who wrote a coherent narrative on bygone fashion, using these plates (*Kupferstiche*) to illustrate cultural phenomena of the past.[6] In so doing, she does not only rely on the medium of text, but rather incorporates images in order to convey a vivid impression to her readers.

Fouqué pays »particular attention both to changes the French Revolution brought to the dress code and behavior of the lower nobility and the upper middle classes [...] and to the changes that eventually affected the political, intellectual, and cultural situation in Fouqué's native Prussia.« (Baumgartner 1997, 215)

She discusses the changes in fashion under the premise that they are indications of changes in mentality mirrored in various forms of social life (Kabus 50). It becomes obvious through her recollections that her contemporaries did not necessarily take much notice of the outstanding achievements of their time, be it the literature of Goethe and Schiller or the politics of the day, but rather concentrated on everyday matters such as dress, interior decoration and architecture, which seemed closer to their heart. For those looking back to that time to investigate its concerns, it appears that the seemingly trivial ones probably reveal more about people's life at the time: »Es gibt in dem Sinne nichts absolut Unwichtiges.« (Fouqué 1833, 25) [In this sense, there is nothing of absolutely no importance.] Fouqué reads, for example, the return of the corset, passé forty-five years earlier, as a clear indication of the onset of the Restoration period.

Fouqué investigates the dynamic between the ability of the individual to exert influence on his/her time and the disposition of being influenced by it: »Der Mensch bildet die Atmosphäre *außer* sich, und diese bedingt die Fähigkeit des Bildens *in ihm*.« (Fouqué 1833, 27) [The human being forms the atmosphere *external* to him-/herself, which in turn conditions his/her ability of *internal* formation.] She presents the development of history as a series of nexuses of vaguely interdependent factors and strives to visualize it through private recollections of the more sensual aspects of everyday life and fashion. By doing so she anticipated museal developments of the late twentieth century, as can be seen in museums of local and everyday history which also aim to transform communicative into cultural memory.

Some of the trends Fouqué remembers were themselves modelled on examples from bygone epochs: Inspiration for dresses, for example, was drawn from well-known historical figures such as Mary Stuart or Jane Gray. The French Republic drew their political ideals from the tradition of the ancient Greeks and Romans. Fashion, however, was not so much interested in ideals as in design; people referred to statues in order to reconstruct the ancient look: »[E]he man es geträumt, sahe sich ein lebendes Geschlecht in bewegliche Bilder antiker Museen umgeschaffen.« (Fouqué 1833, 69) [Before one had even dreamed of the possibility, a living generation saw itself transformed into mobile images of ancient museums.]. Greek, Roman and Egyptian stylistic features were often imitated and combined in one outfit. This form of pastiche, which saw these cultures as mere suppliers of period styles, is based on a museal appropriation of foreign epochs and cultures in which they are uprooted from their religious and ideological contexts and incorporated in a contemporary culture only as purely aesthetic phenomena: »Mit je größerem Triumph die Pariser Italiens Kunstschätze bei sich aufgestellt hatten, mit je regsamerer Eile trugen sie das Fremde auf sich über.«[7] (Fouqué 1833, 69) [The greater the triumph with which the Parisians had amassed the artistic treasures of Italy, the more urgent the haste with which they adopted things foreign.].

The same goes for the bourgeois interior, which through the »democratization of collecting« (Maleuvre 115) became a private museum where the bibelot was the equivalent of the museumized work of art. Fouqué reflects on this process and its implications. She bemoans the fact that the nineteenth century seems to abandon all aspirations of originality and that its creativity is restricted to mimeticism that results in historical and aesthetic alienation.

»Selbst das Lallen barbarischer Kunst, in grimmiger Verzerrung, lieferte Heiligen- und Götzenbilder aus Japan, der Tartarei und Kamtschatka, die neben guten Copieen aus der deutschen und italienischen Schule, neben Bronze- und Alabaster-, Perlemutter- und Elfenbein-Uhren, Klingeln, Schaalen, Vasen und Schreibzeug auf den Tischen der Damen standen und ein Haupterforderniß eleganter Zimmerverzierung ausmachten. Diese Tische [...] erinnerten zu sehr an Boutiken, um dem Wohnzimmer, oder dem Schreibcabinet angemessen zu sein. ›Man bewahre hier‹, hieß es ›eine Menge lieber Andenken‹. Wenn die Erinnerung indeß schon einen Wegweiser brauchte um sich zurecht zu finden, so blieb das fremde Auge ganz verwirrt daran, und sah eigentlich *nichts*, da es zu Vielem und zu Vereinzeltem begegnete.« (Fouqué 1833, 122)

[It was even the incoherent babble of barbarian art, in its gruesome distortion, which provided saintly images and idols from Japan, Tartary and Kamchatka, which, alongside good copies from the German and Italian schools, alongside clocks, bells, scarves, vases and writing utensils of bronze and alabaster, nacre and ivory, constituted a main requirement of elegant interior decoration. These tables [...] reminded one too much of boutique shops to be appropriate for the drawing room or the writing chamber. ›Here we keep‹ one was told ›many personal souvenirs‹. If, however, even memory needed a signpost to find its way, then the unaccustomed eye must have become utterly confused and in the end perceived nothing since it met only with objects too many and too diverse.]

The image of the bourgeois home is suffused with nostalgia and is supposed to provide a sentimental connection between the objects displayed and their owner. But, according to Fouqué, the trinkets, ornaments and intricate inlay work fail to provide a sense of orientation and identity because they themselves are rootless and indifferent to their origins and provide only an artfully constructed not a genuine connection to the past.

The fact that, among many other possible aspects of everyday-life, Fouqué chose to centre her essay around the topic of fashion – considered at the end of the eighteenth and the beginning of the nineteenth century as a feminine realm -, indicates that she wanted to authorize a female voice and perspective in a discourse on historicity, which had been seen as a (male) academic discipline. She differs from official historiography in concentrating on the spheres of fashion and lifestyle, thereby illustrating how new social structures became typified by new forms of dress and habit. By doing this, she reveals that the ›private is political‹ and that efforts to separate a female private from a male public sphere are not only illusionary but also disadvantageous for society as a whole. She establishes a form of writing that fuses political analysis, literary/cultural history and the seemingly trivial concerns of everyday life.

The fashion journal, the department store and the museum can be seen as feminine realms deployed for reformatory purposes and for a civilizing effect: They provided models of bourgeois lifestyles. They also allowed for cross-class and cross-gender forms of social contact, albeit under the condition that everyone follows a strict code of fashionable dress and proper conduct. It was an environment of education and instruction which endeavored to improve tastes, values and norms of conduct by setting standards and encouraging mimetic practices. Fouqué reflects on the museum and the museal practices that developed in the wake of the French Revolution and the Napoleonic Wars in order to develop a literary program fuelled by the notion of a »national identity based on the concept of sociability«, one which would not only include women, but also give women the lead in constructing a collective identity. She thus negates the ideological instrumentalization of the museum as a legitimation of (male) state power as it developed under Napoleon. In her *Geschichte der Moden*, she projects an alternative path, a multiperspective everyday history which highlights communicative and cultural memory, a perspective on the past which the institution of the museum would only acquire at the end of the twentieth century.

–Birkbeck, University of London, UK

Translations of German quotes in this article have been provided by Eric Kuchle, Heidelberg. I would like to thank him also for his careful editing of the English style of the text.

## Notes

1 She wrote over one hundred works in twenty-five years, among these were twenty novels, sixty novellas or short stories, and twenty-one nonfiction pieces on cultural history for women. Cf. Hofacker.

2 The name Fouqué always indicates Caroline Fouqué.

3 *Magie der Natur. Eine Revolutionsgeschichte* (1812), *Das Heldenmädchen aus der Vendée* (1816), *Lodoiska und ihre Tochter* (1820), *Die beiden Freunde* (1824), *Memoiren einer Ungenannten* (1831).

4 Cf. her 2003 monograph, *»daß die Frau zur Frau redete«. Das Werk der Caroline de la Motte Fouqué als Beispiel für weibliche Literaturproduktion der frühen Restaurationszeit.*

5 See his statement, »[a]ls man den Louvre eröffnete, hatte man gerade die Kathedrale Notre-Dame entweiht« (Belting 654).

6 See Fouqué 1988, 173.

7 In Germany, the ›Revolutionary‹ or ›Napoleonic‹ style came into vogue. Notwithstanding its ideological implications it was propagated by Bertuch, and even those who disagreed with its political ideals nevertheless imitated the fashion. Cf. Fouqué 1833, 58: »Selbst während unsere Truppen gegen die dreifarbige Fahne zogen, und tausend blutige Opfer im Kampfe gegen die Neuerer fielen, verschmähete die wechselnde Mode die tricoloren Stoffe und Bänder nicht, die uns Paris herüberschickte. Die verrufene Farbenmischung hatte darum nicht weniger Reiz. Man fand es piquant sie zu tragen.«

## Works Cited

Arnold-de Simine, Silke. *Leichen im Keller. Zu Fragen des Gender in Angstinszenierungen der Schauer- und Kriminalliteratur (1790–1830).* St. Ingbert: Röhrig, 2000.

Baumgartner, Karin. »Through the Eyes of Fashion: Political Aspects of Fashion in Caroline de la Motte Fouqué's Geschichte der Moden, vom Jahre 1785 bis 1829: als Beytrag zur Geschichte der Zeit.« *The Germanic Review* 72/3 (1997): 215-230.

Baumgartner, Karin. *›She passes judgement as would a man.‹ Political Discourse in the Novels of Caroline de la Motte Fouqué.* Diss. Washington University, St. Louis, Missouri, 1999.

Baumgartner, Karin. »Möglichkeiten weiblicher Geschichtsschreibung? Einige Gedanken zu Caroline de la Motte Fouqués ›Das Heldenmädchen aus der Vendée‹ (1816)«. *Jahrbuch der Fouqué-Gesellschaft Berlin-Brandenburg* (1999): 78-97.

Baumgartner, Karin. »Defining National Identity: Caroline de la Motte Fouqué Responds to Madame de Stael's *De l'Allemagne*«. *Colloquia Germanica* 35/1 (2002): 59-73.

Belting, Hans. »Das Museum. Ein Ort der Reflexion, nicht der Sensation«. *Merkur. Deutsche Zeitschrift für europäisches Denken* 8 (2002): 649-662.

Bennett, Tony. *The Birth of the Museum. History, Theory, Politics.* London and New York: Routledge, 1995.

Bühlbäcker, Hermann. *Konstruktive Zerstörungen. Ruinendarstellungen in der Literatur zwischen 1774 und 1832.* Bielefeld: Aisthesis, 1999.

Calov, Gudrun. *Museen und Sammler des 19. Jahrhunderts in Deutschland.* Berlin: de Gruyter, 1969.

Fliedl, Gottfried, ed. *Die Erfindung des Museums. Bürgerliche Museumsidee und Französische Revolution,* Wien: Turia & Kant, 1996.

Fouqué, Caroline de la Motte. *Geschichte der Moden, vom Jahre 1785–1829. Als Beitrag zur Geschichte der Zeit.* After the original 1829-30 edition. Ed. Dorothea Böck. Berlin (DDR): Union, 1987 [Neudruck Hanau: Dasien, 1988].

Fouqué, Friedrich de la Motte ed. *Der Schreibtisch oder alte und neue Zeit.* Ein nachgelassenes Werk von Caroline, Baronin de la Motte Fouqué. Köln: Bachem, 1833.

Grasskamp, Walter. *Museumsgründer und Museumsstürmer. Zur Sozialgeschichte des Kunstmuseums.* München: Beck, 1981.

Haskell, Francis. *History and Its Images. Art and the Interpretation of the Past.* New Haven: Yale University Press, 1995.

Hofacker, Erich P. Jr. »Caroline de la Motte Fouqué (1774–1831)«. *German Writers of the Age of Goethe.* Ed. James Hardin and Christoph E. Schweitzer. Detroit: Gale Research, 1989: 78-83.

Kabus, Petra. »Caroline de la Motte Fouqué (1775–1831). Fächer eines ›Schreibtisches‹. Zu den Beziehungen verschiedener Textarten in ihrem Werk.« *Vom Salon zur Barrikade. Frauen der Heinezeit.* Ed. Irina Hundt. Mit einem Geleitwort von Joseph A. Kruse. Stuttgart, Weimar: Metzler, 2002: 47-59.

Kontje, Todd. *Women, the Novel, and the German Nation (1771–1871). Domestic Fiction in the Fatherland.* Cambridge: Cambridge University Press, 1998.

Maleuvre, Didier. *Museum Memories. History, Technology, Art.* Stanford, CA: Stanford University Press, 1999.

Müller-Adams, Elisa. »›Wie das Leben so in lauter kleine Welten zerfällt.‹ Caroline de la Motte Fouqués ›Fragmente aus dem Leben der heutigen Welt‹ (1820)«. *Jahrbuch der Fouqué-Gesellschaft Berlin-Brandenburg* (2001/2002): 75-93.

Müller-Adams, Elisa. *›daß die Frau zur Frau redete‹. Das Werk der Caroline de la Motte Fouqué als Beispiel für weibliche Literaturproduktion der frühen Restaurationszeit.* St. Ingbert: Röhrig, 2003.

Pelz, Annegret. »Der Schreibtisch. Ausgrabungsort und Depot der Erinnerungen«. *Autobiographien von Frauen. Beiträge zu ihrer Geschichte.* Ed. Magdalene Heuser . Tübingen: Niemeyer, 1996: 233-246.

Vollmer, Hartmut. »›Die Wahrheit bleibt das Höchste‹. Die historischen Romane Caroline de la Motte Fouqués.« *Geschichten aus (der) Geschichte. Zum Stand des historischen Erzählens im Deutschland der frühen Restaurationszeit.* Eds. Norbert Otto Eke and Hartmut Steinecke. München: Fink, 1994: 109-141.

# Belated Nineteenth-century and Twentieth-century opposition: Lessons of Nationalism

# The Triumph of Moderation? The »Wars of Liberation« in the Writing of Louise von François

*Caroline Bland*

»Jahrtausende vergehen, ehe solch eine gewaltsame Natur der Zeit begegnet, in welcher sie sich entfalten darf; aber auch dann nur als Flugstern am eignen Unmaß und Uebermaß zu Grunde zu gehn«. (*Geschichte der preußischen Befreiungskriege in den Jahren 1813 bis 1815*, 23)

[Millennia will go by before such a mighty nature meets the time in which it can flourish, but even then it will perish like a shooting star from its own immoderation and excess.]

Such was Louise von François's judgement of Napoleon in the history of Prussia's »wars of liberation« which she published in 1873. François was born in 1817, two years after the triumph of the European coalition over Napoleon, yet the man himself and his legacy in the German states are a recurrent theme in some of the key texts in her œuvre. Napoleon's hold on the European imagination is readily apparent in both popular and high culture throughout the whole nineteenth century and beyond.[1] For German patriots the enduring tensions between France and Prussia perpetuated the need to resist his influence and commemorate those who had defeated him, a political discourse from which it has often been assumed that women were largely excluded. This article will demonstrate that Louise von François (1817–1893) was engaged in this political tradition, both in her portrayal of Napoleon as a reckless tyrant who had to be resisted for the benefit of ordinary citizens throughout Europe, and in her presentation of Prussia as the state destined to lead the German peoples to unity, nationhood, and self-determination. Her enthusiasm stemmed partly from resonances between the »wars of liberation« and François's own family history, and partly from her subscription to the liberal nationalist project which sought to legitimise Prussia's growing hegemony amongst the German states. François was born and lived for most of her adult life in Saxon territory, which had become part of Prussia only once the Saxon state was partitioned in 1816.[2] Her work bears witness to her identification with both German states and also the conflict which this »mixed heritage« entailed on account of Saxony's former alliances with France against Prussia. Furthermore, her father's family was of Huguenot origin, and one can detect a natural sympathy with France in her writing, which produced a more nuanced image of the French than one might expect to find in the work of a self-confessed »deutsche Patriotin« [German patriot].[3] These conflicts of identity necessarily colored her historical and fictional accounts of the »wars of liberation« and merit further investigation, although they remain a secondary theme in the current analysis.

Louise von François achieved some recognition in her own lifetime as a realist author of the historical mode and, unlike many women writers of the nineteenth century, she has never quite disappeared from the established literary canon since her death, even if her status within it has been very marginal. Regarded for a long time as being rather conservative, it is only in the past twenty years that literary historians have begun to reassess her work and point to some more radical subtexts within it.[4] These studies have concentrated largely on her use of irony and invention of eccentric figures to question women's status and the »caste« mentality affecting relations between the bourgeoisie and the nobility. Most recently, Thomas C. Fox has considered the political implications of the »cross-gendering« of some of her characters.[5] There has also been an interesting psychological reading of her biography by Linda Kraus Worley (1989), which reassesses the role of literature in a life which was long regarded as the perfect example of nineteenth-century women's capacity for renunciation. François's body of work consists of over twenty-five short stories, three novels – *Die letzte Reckenburgerin* (*The last von Reckenburg*, 1871), *Frau Erdmuthens Zwillingssöhne* (*Mrs Erdmuthe's Twin Sons*, 1872) and *Stufenjahre eines Glücklichen* (*Life Stages of a Happy Man*, 1877) – several short pieces in magazines and a history of the »wars of liberation«.

In this chapter I shall be analyzing François's contribution to the »unfolding narrative of nation-building« (Sheehan 58) in which the »wars of liberation« were a pivotal episode, using these three texts: the short story *Fräulein Muthchen und ihr Hausmeier* (*Miss Muthchen and her Steward*, 1859), the novel *Frau Erdmuthens Zwillingssöhne* (*Mrs Erdmuthe's Twin Sons*, 1872) and the historical study *Geschichte der preußischen Befreiungskriege in den Jahren 1813 bis 1815* (*History of the Prussian Wars of Liberation*, 1873). *Fräulein Muthchen und ihr Hausmeier*, set in 1813, connects the marriage prospects of the young Saxon heiress, Erdmuthe von Kettenloß, with the liberation of the German states since she promised her late father only to marry a free German who had participated in this fight. Erdmuthe is introduced to a patriotic Saxon student, Hermann Wille, by some local notables whose coach he shares while returning home from Leipzig. Inspired by Erdmuthe and her even more fervently patriotic steward, Hermann volunteers to fight for Prussia in the battle of Groß-Görchen. He loses an arm but is nursed back to health by Erdmuthe and returns to the Prussian ranks in time for the Battle of the Nations at Leipzig. When Hermann returns from this victory, Erdmuthe marries him, and thus fulfills her promise to her father. The novel *Frau Erdmuthens Zwillingssöhne* was not published until 1872, but François herself dated its writing to the late 1850s.[6] It is closely related in subject matter to the short story *Fräulien Muthchen.*[7] Erdmuthe von Kettenloß appears here as Erdmuthe von Fels, the heiress to the Arnheim estate in the Saxon heathland and the last in the line of the von Fels family. Her marriage (in the mid-1780s) to Raul von Roc, son of an old family of Huguenot origin, produces twin sons: Hermann, the first-born, is blond and sturdy, and shares his mother's quiet patience, while Raul is dark-haired, passionate, and quickly bored. As an adolescent Raul hears of his paternal roots in Provence and decides he is a Frenchman, unlike his very clearly »German« brother. On their way home from the tour of Italy which completes their education in 1805, the brothers witness the arrival of Napoleon's army in Vienna; Raul is thrilled by this first glimpse of his »compatriots« but the same incident begets a fierce German patriotism in Hermann. After this their paths diverge: Raul sees Europe's future in Napoleon's hands and serves him in the Saxon army (from 1806 allied with France), while Hermann bears arms for Prussia to deliver the German states from French domination. The brothers' final meeting is in 1813 on the battlefield of Dennewitz close to their home, where Hermann witnesses Raul's death. The third text I will discuss, *Geschichte der preußischen Befreiungskriege in den Jahren 1813 bis 1815* (1873), in some editions bears the subtitle »Ein Lesebuch für Schule und Haus« [A Reader for Home and School] which suggests that it was intended as a textbook or simple reference work to familiarize subsequent generations with this defining moment in Prussian-German history.[8] The *Geschichte* is an accessible and detailed account, written in a lively style which is not afraid to use vivid military clichés, such as battles resulting in »Ströme von Blut« [rivers of blood] and generals rushing through »wildesten Kugelregen« [a hail of bullets] (*Geschichte* 58 and 67). Apart from the opening section, which discusses the

Prussian reforms arising from the defeat at Jena and briefly characterizes Friedrich Wilhelm III, Napoleon and Alexander I of Russia, François concentrates almost exclusively on the military action with very little analysis of the politics and diplomacy which informed the various alliances and strategic decisions. Since François was predominantly a writer of fiction it is not surprising that little critical attention has been paid to this popular history, but its more detailed depiction of Napoleon is a useful counterpart to the aforementioned fictional texts and attests more clearly to François's judgement of the French Emperor. My analysis of the texts outlined above will focus on three aspects: François's presentation of Napoleon; the opposing images of German heroism she creates; and, finally, the role women play in her depiction of the years 1813–1815.

## Napoleon

From the founder and protector of the French Empire, to the »Little Corporal« championing the cause of the ordinary man, from the »demon« to the determined and lucky opportunist, Napoleon aroused a variety of strong emotions amongst the people of Europe. Even after his death in 1821, he continued to act as a repository for the hopes and fears of both the weak and powerful, and his image continued to be reproduced everywhere, from vast canvases of battle scenes to the most lowly snuff-box, from epic historical novels to the cheapest chapbook verse.[9] In the German states, particularly, his impact had been profound and not entirely negative. There had been many who welcomed Napoleon as a defender of progress during his lifetime and who were grateful to him long after his death for the territorial, constitutional, and legislative changes he had introduced.

Even though François's own patriotic politics determined a negative attitude to Napoleon, she reflected a wide range of German reactions to him in her work. Descriptions of rapturous Saxon welcomes for the impassive Napoleon are recorded in her letters to Conrad Ferdinand Meyer, in the story *Fräulein Muthchen* and in the *Geschichte der preußischen Befreiungskriege*, referring to his passage through Saxony after the Treaty of Tilsit (July 1807), to his victory at Dresden (August 1813) and the mistaken anticipation of a French victory at Leipzig (October 1813).[10] In these passages she did not investigate motives but rather suggested a simple identification between the Saxon people and their victorious ally, at times when Prussia's fortunes seemed uncertain. However, the short story *Fräulein Muthchen* offers some striking cameo appearances for Napoleon, allowing the main characters to give voice to their personal reactions to him. A political justification for supporting Napoleon is offered by the *Hofrat* (court official) in this text, who justifies his fanatical enthusiasm for the hero he compares to Alexander, Caesar and Charlemagne, on the grounds of progress. He claims that Napoleon, who has already abolished the Holy Roman Empire with its host of petty rulers, may well be the Germans' best chance to become united and, eventually, free »sobald eine weniger starke Hand als die seine die Zügel der Weltherrschaft nicht mehr festzuhalten vermöchte« [as soon as a weaker hand than his can no longer keep hold of the world] (*Fräulein Muthchen* 271). The *Hofrat* sees Napoleon as a Titan »der die Geschichte dieses Jahrhunderts auf seinen Schultern trägt« [who carries the history of this century on his shoulders] (*Fräulein Muthchen* 269), an epithet used with some irony by the narrator Gottlieb Bleibtreu in *Frau Erdmuthens Zwillingssöhne*, echoing decades of comic mileage from the contrast between Napoleon's influence and his diminutive size.[11]

The *Hofrat*'s firm belief in the ability of Great Men to determine the course of history by giving »dem formlosen Brei der Völkermassen Gestalt und Richtung« [[by] forming and directing the shapeless mess of peoples] (*Fräulein Muthchen* 269) is juxtaposed with the nationalist liberal hopes of the patriotic student, Hermann Wille, who predicts that the German people will liberate themselves. The patriotic logic of the text and the implied reader's knowledge of history vindicate the position of Hermann and his future wife, Erdmuthe, as far as Napoleon's defeat is concerned. But Hermann's hope that the Germans will become »ein Volk« [one people] (*Fräulein Muthchen* 269) is also alluding to the liberal hopes of national unification as yet unrealised in 1859. In this connection, it is worth considering the extreme patriotism of the steward, who is an obviously comic figure. Many jokes are made about the steward's admiration for the ancient Teutons and the archaic »teutonisation« of his speech, especially his doomed attempts to reverse the widespread adoption of French terms into military vocabulary (*Fräulein Muthchen* 296). It is illustrative of François's plea for moderation even in the pursuit of national identity, that she examines such divergent opinions in this »heitere Szene«) [humorous scene] from the »Heldendrama« [heroic drama] of 1813 (*Fräulein Muthchen*

325). Of the range of Saxon opinion presented here – pro-Napoleonic (in word or action), diplomatic neutrality, straightforward German patriotism, a rejection of Prussia for a stronger anti-French ally, and extreme »teutonizing« – it is the latter which is depicted as the most ridiculous and may be read as François's humorous riposte to the tendential patriotic literature of the 1840s. Placing literature in the wider discourse on nation, however, this text, with its exploration of a range of positions on the national question and their expression in small details such as the steward's attempts at linguistic »purification«, shows how historical fiction could juxtapose shades of difference in the debate in a fashion that would be impossible in a factual history. At the same time, François's close adherence to the facts, such as the incorporation of real battles and historical personages into her fiction, suggests that she intended it to have a didactic and/or political function.

Within *Fräulein Muthchen*, the steward's extreme Germanness also has the function of showing the more ›natural‹ and moderate patriotism of Hermann Wille and Erdmuthe von Kettenloß to its best advantage.[12] As the hero and heroine of this tale, their reactions to Napoleon are of the upmost importance. Hermann's faith in the concept of the German nation implies his moral superiority to Napoleon, whom he regards to be of dubious nationality and lacking respect for the national pride of others:

»De[r] gewaltige[ ] Italiener, der das einst grimmig gehaßte Frankenreich zum Fußschemel seines ehrgierigen Dranges gemacht hatte, um nun von dort aus, soweit seine Arme greifen konnten, alles, was Vaterlandsliebe heißt, im Herzen der Völker zu ersticken, wie er diese Liebe in seinem eigenen Herzen erstickt hatte, auf daß er der werde, der er geworden war«. (*Fräulein Muthchen* 324)

[The mighty Italian who had turned France, the country he once hated fiercely, into the footstool of his glory-seeking ambitions, in order […] to suffocate everything patriotic in the hearts of the peoples, as he had suppressed this love in his own heart, so that he might become the person he had become.] (*Fräulein Muthchen* 324)

François frequently emphasises Napoleon's Italian (Corsican) origin, thus making a distinction between the more honourable French and their untrustworthy Emperor. Hermann's description of Napoleon as the »Italian« naturally brings to mind the ancient Germanic victory over a seemingly invincible enemy. The Italianate imagery is also found in Erdmuthe's account of seeing Napoleon during his retreat from Russia in December 1812, when she compares his impassive demeanour to that of a marble statue. For Erdmuthe it is Napoleon's inhumanity which is most shocking: »Aber mich erbarmte des Mannes, der den grausigen Untergang einer Million von Menschenleben auf seinem Gewissen hatte, und ich flehte zu Gott, daß er seiner Seele gnädig sein möge« [I felt pity for the man who had the horrifying end of a million men's lives on his conscience and I beseeched God that He might take mercy upon his soul]. (*Fräulein Muthchen* 299) Thus Erdmuthe's moral superiority over Napoleon is also established, since he appears unmoved by the terrible fate he had inflicted on so many of his own troops, while she turns her home into a hospital for wounded soldiers, regardless of which side they fought on.

Napoleon is more of a shadowy presence in *Frau Erdmuthens Zwillingssöhne* since the peace-loving pastor (and narrator), Gottlieb Bleibtreu, is reliant upon the accounts of others for his impressions. Through the narrative device of letters, it is the opinions of Napoleon's own soldiers which come to the fore in this novel. Napoleon's capacity to inspire great loyalty is reflected in the figure of Raul. A Frenchman by choice and temperamentally also inclined to excess, Raul outlines Napoleon's plans for a trail of imperial conquest, eventually leading to victory over England via the subjugation of India, with his leader's own »ruhmgeblendeten Blicken« [glory-dazzled eyes] and, rather implausibly despite his time at Napoleon's court in Paris, »mit dessen eignen späterhin kundwerdenden Worten« [almost with his own, later infamous, words] (*Frau Erdmuthens* 200-201). Raul's faith in Napoleon is unbroken even by his own experiences in Moscow, where he is saved from death only by a chance encounter with a German family. He is finally disabused of his enchantment just hours before his death, when he hears the Emperor blaming heavy French losses in the battle of Dennewitz on the cowardice of their Saxon allies. Betrayed – like the rest of his Saxon compatriots – by his idol, Raul at last seeks reconciliation with his German brother on his deathbed.[13]

A different perspective is offered by the letter of an actual Frenchman and exiled Royalist, initially reconciled to his homeland by Napoleon's new court and remodelling of the army. This French officer curses his leader during the winter campaign of 1812 in Russia, claiming that those he had elevated to power would turn against this »gewissenloser Menschenschlächter« [butcher of humanity with no conscience] and predicting that Napoleon would end his days »verlassen von aller Welt, als flüchtiger Abenteurer« [abandoned by the world as an adventurer on the run] (*Frau*

*Erdmuthens*, 303-304). This prediction is rendered more plausible since the reader, already acquainted with the officer's wife and daughter, knows that the officer himself is a life-long adventurer and optimist.

The charges raised against Napoleon in the earlier fictional texts reach their culmination in François's pen portrait of him at the beginning of the *Geschichte der preußischen Befreiungskriege.* Claiming that his startling career has been unique in the history of the world, she sums up his all-consuming appetite for power:

»Alle Schranken, alle heilig gehaltenen Rechte der Völker fallen vor seiner Allgewalt. Die Theilung der Welt kann seinem Stolze nicht mehr genügen; er will nur Vasallen des allein gebietenden Frankreich und einen Napoleon als dessen Herrn. Nicht nur was Menschenkraft, auch was die Natur, was der Raum ihm entgegenstellen, verschwindet vor seiner wahnsinnigen Gier. [...] So rüstete er sich denn zu einem Weltenzuge, der Mann mit der kleinen gedrungenen, bürgerlichen Gestalt und dem marmorgelben, marmorkalten stolzen Cäsarenangesicht; mit dem kochenden italischen [sic] Blut und der schwindelnden französischen Einbildung; der Mann mit dem Greifenblick und der Greifenklaue, der als Gesetz nur die Gewalt und als Pflicht nur den Ruhm anerkennt, der Wohl die Unordnung zu zerstören, aber keine dauernde Ordnung an ihrer Stelle zu gründen verstanden hat«. (*Geschichte* 22-23)

[All barriers, all the rights held sacred by the various nations collapse in the face of his omnipotence. The partitioning of the world is no longer enough to satisfy his pride, he will not rest until all are vassals under the sole command of France with Napoleon as its master. Not only the obstacles created by human strength, but also those of nature and distance disappear in the face of his deluded greed. [...] So he armed himself for a world-wide campaign, the man with the short and stocky bourgeois figure and the imperial visage as cold and pale as marble; with the seething Italian blood and the breathtaking French arrogance; the man with the eyes and grip of a bird of prey, who recognises only the law of violence and the duty of glory, who certainly knew how to destroy chaos, but who was incapable of establishing any lasting order in its place.]

In this indictment of Napoleon, François combines the moral defects of egotism, megalomania, and inhumanity with stereotypical French and Italian national characteristics.[14] This suggests a greater willingness on her part to acquiesce to widespread German prejudices in the wake of 1871, perhaps with an eye to her readership.[15] Nevertheless she does acknowledge his organisational and tactical abilities as well as his capacity to inspire great admiration and loyalty in his soldiers (*Geschichte* 33, 34, 132, 174), although this he ultimately betrays by leading them on hopeless campaigns »um eines Wahnes von Ehre willen, um den Wunderglauben an seinen Stern«

[for the sake of the chimera of honour, of his miraculous belief in his own destiny] (*Geschichte* 174). This same vanity leads him to abandon honesty if it is not in his interest or where it would require him to admit having made a mistake (*Geschichte* 129). By contrast the French soldiers, despite being the enemy, are described as »löwengleich [...] sich geschlagen« [having fought like lions] (*Geschichte* 129) and she praises many of the French generals for their bravery in battles on difficult enemy territory.[16] To conclude, François's image of Napoleon is remarkably consistent throughout these three publications and she presents immoderate ambition and pride as his defining features.[17] François depicts Napoleon as a threat to the principles she expounded and defended in her work as a whole, namely brotherly love and the duty of the individual to work towards a common purpose.

## German heroes

»Die Zeit heroischer Tyrannen ist abgelaufen. [...] Von heute ab wird allein das Volk seine Geschichte machen, deren Jahrbücher werden sich füllen mit wohltätigem Wirken und freie Fürsten über freie Völker regieren«. (*Fräulein Muthchen* 269)

[The age of heroic tyrants is over [...] from now on the people alone will make their own history, their annals will be filled with actions that benefit all and free princes will rule over free people.]

Hermann Wille's view of the future of Germany echoes François's own liberal position: she places no individual German hero figure against Napoleon, but rather sees him opposed by all freedom-loving Germans, who will subsequently determine their nation's future. François espoused the liberal *kleindeutsch* (or Prussian-led) perspective on German history, in which nationalism was to save the German peoples from particularism.[18] Not only Prussians, but also many other Protestant Germans saw the Prussian state, especially since its reforms, as the natural leader and unifier of the German peoples and the power with which all free Germans should identify. The inclusive nature of the Prussian »people's army« founded upon universal conscription in March 1813 to fight the »war of liberation« was a vital aspect of the liberal identification with Prussia as the nation's saviour (Hagemann 188-89). In her account François leaves aside the issue of conscription to emphasize a universal recognition of a duty that had to be and was fulfilled with many sacrifices and great bravery on the part of the ordinary soldiers, who were often ill-equipped and had the minimum of training (*Geschichte* 42-44). This aspect of the history is part of the text's didactic function, which at times is very explicit: »Ja, viele Wunden haben in dieser Zeit geblutet, viele Thränen sind geflossen: aber es ist ein hoher Segen, in solcher Zeit gelebt zu haben, und wehe dem Enkel, dem ihre Erinnerung nicht zum Segen würde!« [Yes, many wounds bled at this time and many tears flowed, but it is a great blessing to have lived through such an era and woe betide the grandchild who draws no advantage from this memory!] (*Geschichte* 142)

Despite this acknowledgement of the ordinary footsoldiers, the heroic warriors who feature in *Fräulein Muthchen* and *Frau Erdmuthens Zwillingssöhne* are of officer status, since here, as elsewhere in her fiction, François's main interest is in the bourgeoisie or nobility. This liberal view of the »wars of liberation«, which acknowledges the »people's« contribution but does not use it as the main focus of the narrative, also fits in with the dominant realist aesthetic connected with the historical novel in the mid-nineteenth century. Uta Schuch categorizes both *Fräulein Muthchen* and *Frau Erdmuthens Zwillingssöhne* as examples of fashionable and tendentious historical novels and notes that François adhered to the exhortations of her realist contemporaries, such as Alexis, Scheffel, and Riehl that the historical novel could best bring an era to life by focusing on the life of typical individuals than on prominent historical figures (Schuch 88 and 90). This tenet of bourgeois realism also corresponded to the mid-century liberal political aims of national unification and carefully delineated democracy (Fox 110; Schuch 91). In a letter to Conrad Ferdinand Meyer, François explained – albeit in hindisght – her motivation for writing *Frau Erdmuthens Zwillingssöhne* and the military history: the memories of the liberation campaign were almost »wie mit dem Schwamme ausgelöscht« [wiped away] but »es regte sich ein gewisses Bedürfen [...] dieselben aufzufrischen« [one felt a certain need to refresh them] perhaps because of a »ein Vorspuken nahender Thaten« [premonition of deeds about to be done].[19] This comment reveals clearly her proximity to the school of liberal historians whose interpretation of the past was governed by the political needs of the present.[20] Again François is more explicit about such intentions in the *Geschichte der preußischen Befreiungskriege*, where her conclusion notes that the actions of 1813 to 1815 had borne fruit generations later when a united Germany had once again »sich des Feindes von Neuem erwehrt« [warded off the enemy] with »dem Drange von 1813« [the urgency of 1813] and resurrected »die erloschene

Kaiserkrone des deutschen Reiches« [the crown of the German Empire] (*Geschichte* 296).

Indeed it is the Prussian Generals, whose popularity persisted into the Imperial era, who are the stars of François's history. The liberation campaigns of Friedrich Wilhelm von Bülow (1755–1816) and Gebhard Leberecht von Blücher (1742–1820) were waged close to their retirement from active service and François is at pains to point out the advantages of their age in terms of experience and moderation, compared to Napoleon's relative youth and over-ambitious campaigning. Bülow is characterized as: »ein preußisches Herz bis auf den Grund: so tritt er, nahe dem Greisenalter, aus der Verborgenheit hervor, schreitete von Gelingen bis zum Triumph, um erst von der Nachwelt in seinem vollen Heldenwerthe gewürdigt zu werden« [a Prussian soul to the core: he was almost an old man when he stepped out of obscurity, striding from success to triumph, and his true heroism was only recognised by posterity] (*Geschichte* 30), while Blücher's vitality, thirst for adventure, and determined spirit are contrasted with his age, since he is repeatedly referred to as »old Blücher«. Blücher, who came by the name of »Marschall Vorwärts« [Old Forwards] during this campaign, is the most colorful character in the *Geschichte* on account of his turbulent military career, his love of high living, and his terse pronouncements (cf. *Geschichte* 47-48). Yet even here, the quality François highlights most memorably is his fairness and ability to put the greater good before his personal reputation. This is exemplified towards the end of the Battle of the Nations, when Blücher gave up a lot of his troops the command of Bernadotte, the Crown Prince of Sweden, so foregoing the honor of being in command during the decisive battle. This »Opfer der Selbstüberwindung [...], welches gleich einem Sieg in seinem Ehrenkranze leuchtet« [act of self-control [...], shines like a victory in his wreath of honor] (*Geschichte* 176) and stands out against the repeated incidences of Napoleon searching for scapegoats to save his reputation when he had made the wrong decision.

The German military leaders play a much more visible role than the King himself in François's *Geschichte der preußischen Befreiungskriege*. François was a great admirer of Friedrich II (»the Great«), and she begins and ends her history of the »wars of liberation« by recalling the last words of his will: »möchte das preußische Reich in höchster Blüthe dauern bis an das Ende der Tagen« [may the Kingdom of Prussia continue to flourish until the end of time] (*Geschichte* 1). Her presentation of Friedrich Wilhelm III is, however, ambivalent. Born in 1769, just twelve days before Napoleon, in many ways Friedrich Wilhelm serves as a positive foil to the megalomania of the French leader. Thus although François is not entirely uncritical of his hesitations and vacillations, she presents them as arising from essentially positive character traits. Her defence of him begins with the claim that he had taken to heart the last advice given to him by Friedrich II: »Wolle niemals *mehr* scheinen als du bist« [Never try to appear *better* than you are] (*Geschichte* 5):

»[er] zeigte immerdar *weniger* als er war und verstand. Gottesfürchtig und von reiner, schlichter Sitte, ernsten, in sich gerichteten Sinnes, karg und kurz in Worten, von majestetischer Gestalt und Haltung, fühlte er sich *wohl* berufen für ein Regiment, aber für ein väterlich still wirkendes Regiment, und sah sich mit Widerwillen in den Zeitlauf ungeheuerlicher Strömungen fortgerissen.«

[[…] for ever afterwards he revealed *less* than he actually was and comprehended. God-fearing and of pure and simple habits, of a serious, inward-looking disposition, frugal and brief in his speech, with a majestic figure and bearing, he *certainly* felt called to govern, but in a paternalistic, quietly effective fashion. It was with reluctance that he saw himself swept along by the awful currents of his times.] (*Geschichte* 6; François's emphasis)

However, her ambivalence is apparent, since Friedrich Wilhelm scarcely appears after the introductory part of the text and before citing and commenting on the dramatic reaction to Friedrich Wilhelm's speech »An mein Volk« [To my People] in March 1813, she notes that it was written by »einem der wärmsten ostpreußischen Patrioten« [one of the warmest East Prussian patriots], the state official von Hippel (*Geschichte* 41).

The weak paternal influence of Friedrich Wilhelm III in leading his people finds its counterpart in the numerous absent and deceased fathers in François's fictional texts.[21] François adopts contemporary rhetoric when she describes Friedrich Wilhelm's inability to unite the various German states against France before 1813 as a failing which has to be atoned for.[22] The result of this failing was civil war (»Brüderkrieg«) which François addresses through the motif of actual brotherly conflict in her work, although in each of the texts considered here François stopped short of depicting a scene in which biological brothers do have to fight one another.[23] In the closing scenes of *Frau Erdmuthens Zwillingssöhne* Hermann von Fels finds Raul surrounded by Prussian soldiers and about to take his own life. Hermann is able to prevent the suicide yet his brother still collapses, his constitution weakened by years of fighting and recent remorse for the rivalry in politics and love with his brother. The idea of brothers in conflict is also found in *Fräulein Muthchen,* as Hermann Wille's brother fights (and dies) under the Saxon General Thielemann with the French, while Hermann joins the Prussian side and loses his arm fighting a German soldier in the opposing army. Although Napoleon is not responsible for the differences between the brothers he certainly exacerbates them and allows them to find potentially bloody expression. Of course the metaphor of the family extends to the incipient nation; it is already far from harmonious collective, but Napoleon exploits the differences between the German states to extend his power in Central Europe. Schuch describes the twin brothers in the novel, with their typical German and French »national traits« as being mere representatives of these nations, rather than differentiated individuals (Schuch 59). While one can agree with her assessment of the »functional« nature of these characters, the Saxon location of the story is of great importance since the brothers' conflicting political allegiances reflect the divisions within Saxony to an extreme degree: Hermann not only fights for Prussia but also joins the *Tugendbund,* Raul not only fights with the Saxons allied to France, but also deserts the Saxon army to fight with the French when Saxony intermittently joins Prussia. The resolution of the text – Raul is broken by his adventures with the French and disputes with his brother, while Hermann mourns his brother but strides away on »die befreiende Bahn« [the path of liberation] together with the Prussian army (*Frau Erdmuthens* 503) – is also a resolution to the long-term crisis of identity, afflicting Saxony. Hermann, with his patient temperament and steadfast personal and political loyalty is the epitome of moderation. His patriotism is innate and unswerving. Hermann loves his fatherland »wie einer den Vater liebt, welchen Gott ihm gegeben hat« [as one loves the father we are given by God], whereas Raul »erkor sich ein Heimatsland wie ein schönes Weib« [chose his homeland like a beautiful woman] (*Frau Erdmuthens* 199). Hermann thus embodies many of the virtues invoked in the contemporary national discourse as typical of the German man: he is »loyal«, »honorable«, »valorous« and »honest« (Hagemann 185). With this narrative of the feuding and eventual reconciliation between German brothers, François was contributing to a history of the German nation in which the shared aspects of culture heritage and future destiny were often overshadowed by short-term political and territorial disputes. Her theories about the relationship between Saxony and Prussia, discussed briefly in the *Geschichte,* are illustrated at length in this novel about dissimilar twins, whose mother has for them both the same vision of a future in Prussia's safe hands, despite their differences in temperament and ambition. The desirability of Erdmuthe's vision is emphasised at the end of the text by the pastor-narrator's sermon on the occasion of Raul's burial. He invokes a time of universal brotherhood, where emnity between the nations will be resolved by understanding and Christian love. Although François expresses her nationalist sentiments in a stronger and more militant fashion appropriate to the context of the *Geschichte der preußischen Befreiungskriege*, her horror of bloodshed is apparent in both texts.[24] Most important of all is her assertion at the end of the history that, in order for nations to be stable and prosperous, »alle Bürger« [all citizens] have to obey their duty to the national cause (*Geschichte* 296).

## Women

To what extent does François's notion of citizenship apply to women? Overwhelmingly the narrative position adopted in the texts considered here is male-gendered. In *Fräulein Muthchen,* the omniscient narrator privileges the male perspective and has only a limited view of the Erdmuthe's desires and expectations, in part to maintain the narrative tension until the end of the story, but partly because seeing Erdmuthe's attractions from a male perspective is important for the appreciation of the romantic subplot. *Frau Erdmuthens Zwillingssöhne* does have an identifiable (male) narrator, the pastor Gottlieb Bleibtreu. The *Geschichte der preußischen Befreiungskriege* appears, to judge from the immediacy of its style, to be based on the letters and memoirs of some of the leading military commanders, as well as histories of the conflict.[25] Necessarily the male perspective is privileged here too, with the contributions of Prussian women being mentioned on only three occasions. The first of these is in the Spring of 1813 as Prussia struggled to equip its *Landwehr* [universal militia] (Hagemann 180) with the aid of voluntary contributions. François includes some well-worn anecdotes about golden wedding rings being exchanged for iron ones and of the poor woman who sacrificed her only asset, her thick golden hair, for the campaign. François also mentions that »mehr als *eine* Jungfrau focht tapferen Muthes in der Reihen der Freiwilligen« [more than one maiden who fought bravely in the volunteer ranks] but concludes:

»Aber was bedeutet das Opfer dieser Einzelnen, deren Andenken sich erhalten hat, gegen die Hingebung der Ungezählten, die den Gatten, den Sohn, oft den letzten und einzigen, den Versorger des Heerdes und den Liebling des Herzens, mit freudigem Stolz sich dem Tod für das Vaterland weihen sahen? Es war eine Zeit des Selbstvergessens und der starken Liebe«. (*Geschichte* 44)

[What does the sacrifice of these individuals, whose deeds are still remembered today, count for when compared to the devotion of the countless number who saw their husband, their son, often their youngest or only child, their provider and the darling of their hearts, dedicate himself with joyful pride to die for the fatherland? It was a time of self-forgetfulness and strong love.]

François emphasizes self-sacrifice in the patriotic cause as the paramount virtue here. The courage of those women who actually bore arms is not denied but, because they were exceptions, this also counts for little in terms of their actual achievement or as examples for later generations to follow; François reads their actions as largely symbolic, on a par with the woman who sold her golden hair. She leaves aside the issue of women acting beyond their gendered role to emphasize their more realistic contributions to the effort of liberation, namely those of support and sacrifice, as an example for later generations. The topos of the armed woman does appear, however, in *Fräulein Muthchen.* Even after the young Erdmuthe, frequently referred to as an amazon, has wielded a sword to defend her steward, the suggestion that she might have used it against Napoleon is dismissed as a joke in very poor taste: »Und was bliebe denn euch Männern, wenn die Weiber eure Tyrannen meuchlings ermorden wollten?« [And what would there be left for you men to do, if women were to assassinate your tyrants?] (*Fräulein Muthchen* 299). Her comment suggests both that violence does not befit a woman and that to attack the unarmed Napoleon would be a treacherous murder, rather than an honorable defeat in battle.

The only prominent woman mentioned in the *Geschichte der preußischen Befreiungskriege* is Queen Luise of Prussia (1776–1810), but only in the introductory section since the history really focuses on 1813-15. It is Luise who warns against Prussia's complacency after Friedrich II's achievements, and the tragedy of her death served as »ein Stachel der Rache gegen den Gewalthaber, der sich nicht gescheut hatte, die tiefgebeugte Frau mit Hohn und Verleumdung zu verfolgen« [a spur of revenge against the despot, who was not ashamed to mock and slander this woman bowed with grief] (*Geschichte* 7).

In the fictional texts François indicates the significance of the female figures by their title roles (*Fräulein Muthchen und ihr Hausmeier* / *Frau Erdmuthens Zwillingssöhne*), yet there is little attempt to develop them fully as characters. We have a very limited view of the young Erdmuthe's hopes and feelings in *Fräulein Muthchen*, for example, while her more mature counterpart in *Frau Erdmuthens Zwillingssöhne*, from the rather restricted perspective of her friend Bleibtreu, is limited to little more than the hopes and fears of a mother whose sons (and husband) go to war. The strangely two-dimensional quality of these women is by no means typical of François's characters, who are, even at their most positive, studies in human frailty. This leads me to a reading of the two Erdmuthes as intentionally symbolic embodiments of abstract qualities, rather than realistic figures. Indeed, the descriptive name »Erdmuthe« (»earth« and »courage«) lends itself to further interpretation,[26] although descriptive names are a favorite stylistic device of François's, generally employed as an ironic comment on the family background of a figure, as well as their personal attributes. With the name »Erdmuthe« François follows this humorous pattern, leavening ponderous and inevitable associations with »Mother Earth« by attributing the choice of name to the rather eccentric and isolated father-figures and further lightening the tone with ironic linguistic play on German names (and abstract nouns) based on the short noun *Mut* (»courage« but also »spirits« or »mood«).[27] However, the comic element does not ultimately detract from the serious exemplary purpose of the Erdmuthe figures. Both women embody the qualities of quiet courage, upstanding morality, innate motherliness,[28] and a capacity for mourning and honoring the memory of the fallen. In others, particularly men, they inspire ardor for the patriotic cause and hope for the future, which is vital for the morale of those fighting for liberation and working towards a better peace. According to Karen Hagemann's analysis of patriotic literature at the time of the »wars of liberation«, these were qualities frequently ascribed to German women by contemporaries. Rather than mere commonplaces of the gender-specific and nationally specific discourse of patriotism, Hagemann asserts that the women's role of sacrifice, mourning, and commemoration »was the necessary precondition for both men's individual ›valour‹ and the nation's collective capacity to conduct war« (Hagemann 195). In these war-time fictions by François, the figure of Erdmuthe is the central point to which the male warriors are drawn, seeking her encouragement and her approval before battle and finding healing or a peaceful death in her care afterward.

Erdmuthe the Saxon noblewoman, in both her younger and older reincarnations, is a personification of the state of Saxony and of the more noble qualities of its people (but *not* of its ruling house). Despite being landowners and members of the aristocracy, their households and bearing have all the hallmarks of positive bourgeois simplicity which distinguishes them from the more frivolous aristocrats, of whom François disapproves.[29] Erdmuthe's lands are trampled and occupied by invading armies, she lacks the strength (but not the will) to defend herself, and what she needs is protection from the male German warrior, who will bear arms on her behalf and secure her possessions for her offspring. The analogy between Erdmuthe and Saxony is quite explicit in *Fräulein Muthchen*, where Erdmuthe's vow only to marry a free and valiant German provokes a lively discussion amongst three men with very different political positions: the pro-Napoleonic *Hofrat*, the lawyer, who defends the King of Saxony's attempts to remain neutral and the passionately patriotic student. In *Frau Erdmuthens Zwillingssöhne*, the mother Erdmuthe (Saxony) has given birth to both a convinced French ally and a determined »German« patriot, who sees Saxony's destiny only achieved via an alliance with Prussia.

In each of the Erdmuthe tales it is a sword-bearing Hermann, crucially a Saxon who supports the Prussian-German cause and refuses to ally with France, whom she rewards with her loyalty and a share of her wealth.[30] Most importantly perhaps, despite her unswerving loyalty to the Prussian-German cause, the figure of Erdmuthe has a reconciliatory function, nursing wounded soldiers, regardless of their nationality or allegiance in both texts. While demonstrating the steadfastness in the face of war praised by François in the *Geschichte der preußischen Befreiungskriege*, the heroines of these stories look forward to the prospect of peace and reconciliation between peoples.

A brief glance at other texts by François reveals that the schematic figure of Erdmuthe is by no means typical of her female characters.[31] Erdmuthe represents a specifically Saxon and female response to the French attack on her homeland, which identifies Saxony's interests with those of Prussia. She becomes a maternal inspiration for male warriors and almost a female allegory of the homeland. This renders her more powerful than gendered social norms would normally permit, yet ultimately she remains limited in her ability to act as an individual and is dependent upon the male liberator who is linked with Prussia. Thus François resolves the conflict of Saxon versus Prussian identity, which is implicit in much of her work, by the visions of redemption and future unity in these texts. In *Frau Erdmuthens Zwillingssöhne*, after losing both her Huguenot husband and the son who has inherited French characteristics, Erdmuthe is left with her first-born son, Hermann, a Saxon who is fighting with the Prussians for the liberation of Germany. Similarly in *Fräulein Muthchen*, Erdmuthe marries the Saxon student (also named Hermann) she has inspired to fight for liberation, in preference to the Prussian general who changed his allegiance to Russia in despair at his country's apparent acquiesence to Napoleon. Erdmuthe's choice of husband in *Fräulein Muthchen*, the injured but victorious Hermann, is underscored by the symbols which surround her chance meeting with Napoleon, under the oak tree on the *Hünengrab* (barrow). Both tree and ancient grave recall the ancient Teutons' struggle against the Roman invaders, the conquering empire reincarnated in France, which is further emphasized in this text by references to Napoleon's Italian origins: »Unter der ehernen Imperatorenstirne mit Falkenblicken den Schauplatz kommender Taten erspähend, der marmorbleiche Italiener Auge im Auge dem blühenden, deutschen Mädchen« [under the brazen imperial brow the eagle eye surveyed the scene of future battles, the Italian, pale as marble, face to face with the fair German maiden] (*Fräulein Muthchen* 278). Erdmuthe's function as a personification of Saxony is obvious here: she uses the barrow as a vantage point and during the meeting with Napoleon holds fast to an ancient oak tree, a survivor of the primeval forest, which served as a symbol of the area while pointing with her right arm towards the northerly side of the valley, a place which Hermann Wille identifies as the hill of Roßbach, scene of a Prussian victory over the French during the Seven Years' War.

## Conclusions

At first glance the heroines of the texts considered here seem to offer little inspiration for feminist scholars, trapped as they are in a series of essentialist assumptions about femininity. However, a reading of them as female personifications of Saxony at a crucial moment in German history reveals their power as female counterparts to the martial male with whom

François tended to identify (Worley 1989). In the wider context of historical literature narrating Germany's path to unification, we can certainly regard François herself as a woman against Napoleon. Her resistance took place in a specific liberal framework, and she makes a strong case for the peaceful coexistence of useful citizens as the bedrock of progress and strength of the nation, by contrasting this with the egotism of the tyrant who »makes history« only by destroying countless lives. As such, the fictional texts can be regarded as narratives of defining moments on the way to German national unity. However, there is evidence that, given its eventual publication date of 1872, *Frau Erdmuthens Zwillingssöhne* was read as a triumphalist account of German virtue and courage overcoming French superficiality and treachery. This is undoubtedly why it appealed to the publishers of the *Deutsche Romanzeitung* in 1872 and why the novel received renewed critical attention under National Socialism. A careful reading of the text suggests that it is not a chauvinistic anti-French novel, but an examination of characteristics which Germans needed to develop to mature into a peaceful and stable nation. There is also evidence in the historical account for such a viewpoint. One could argue that François was exploiting her knowledge of and keen interest in the »wars of liberation« by seizing this opportune moment to publish a textbook. However, there is also evidence in her presentation of these events that she felt the swift victory against France in 1870–1871 had lead to too much self-assurance, a return to the complacency which Queen Luise had criticised and a slackening of the devotion to duty François deemed so essential a feature of being Prussian and now German. Its primary function was to recall the earlier sacrifices and commemorate them as well as continuing her defence of moderation, found in the earlier texts, where the excesses of Napoleonic ambition are contrasted with careful husbandry of strength and resources advocated by Erdmuthe and Hermann. The key aspects to be gained from all three texts are: firstly François's liberalism, viewing citizens as the catalyst of history, as the creators and guarantors of the nation, rather than the great individual; secondly the texts' reflection of the complexities of François's identity, especially since she suggests a set of characteristics which she deems »German«, but could equally be seen as Saxon or Prussian attributes, or indeed a combination of the two; and finally, her presentation of women's role in the nation-building process and by extension, Louise von François herself as a »woman against Napoleon«, a female writer who for reasons both political and national chose to write about the struggle against Napoleon and use it as a backdrop for her prophetic fictions of German identity.

–University of Sheffield, UK

## Notes

1 See Alexander for a recent study of the changing image of Napoleon in the 19th and 20th centuries.

2 She was born in Herzberg and lived mostly in Weissenfels an der Saale; today both towns are in the federal state of Sachsen-Anhalt.

3 Cf. François's letter to Conrad Ferdinand Meyer of 16 October 1881 (Bettelheim 26).

4 For a recent survey of modern François criticism see Fox 128.

5 See Fox. Ruth Ellen Boetcher Joeres also discusses cross-gendering in François in her book, *Respectability and Deviance* (280-86).

6 Cf. letter to C.F. Meyer, 17.12.1885 (Bettelheim 181). This letter contradicts Thomas Fox's assumption (based on the date of publication [1872]) that the novel was written during the Franco-Prussian war of 1870-71. Cf. Fox 122.

7 Uta Schuch maintains that one can regard the short story as a precursor and/or a simplified version of the novel (Schuch 88). The term precursor is problematic, however, since it is difficult to attach specific dates to the writing of *Frau Erdmuthens Zwillingssöhne.*

8 According to Emil Staiger's »Vorwort« to the 1954 edition of *Frau Erdmuthens Zwillingssöhne*, this *Geschichte der preußischen Befreiungskriege* was used as a textbook (Lehrbuch) in Prussian officer training academies (François 1954, 11). See also Staiger's 1954 article on Louise von François in the *Neue Schweizer Rundschau.* In the »Volks-Ausgabe« [People's Edition] I have used, key dates are printed in the margins together with the dates of birth and death for major figures, but there is no index or other bibliographical apparatus.

9 Alexander offers many examples in the chapters on »Nineteenth-century Literature and Art« and »Popular Culture« in his monograph, *Napoleon.*

10 *Fräulein Muthchen* 298, *Geschichte* 114 and 168, letters to C. F. Meyer (Bettelheim.25), *Frau Erdmuthens* 381-82.

11 Napoleon's »short, stocky figure« is emphasized in *Fräulein Muthchen* (278) and in the *Geschichte* (23).

12 As with many of François's characters, their positive attributes are also denoted in their names, which imply soldierliness and resolution, courage and liberty respectively (cf. Fox 130) whilst the steward's even more improbable name, Polykarpus Storch, merely increases his comic potential by emphasising his huge appetite and angular frame.

13 The attack on Saxon virtue after Dennewitz is described by François in her history of the wars as a »lügenhafte Beschimpfung« [mendacious slander] (*Geschichte* 141) and the main reason why Saxony sought to end its alliance with France at the earliest opportunity, which in her judgement was one of the worst consequences of the defeat at Dennewitz for Napoleon.

14 The problem of nationhood for Italy is not discussed.
15 Schuch has demonstrated François's awareness of fashions in the literary marketplace regarding fictional texts (106-107). The early 1870s was clearly an opportune moment for a publication such as this military history.
16 Other positive depictions of the French in François's fiction include Madame Barbe, the sutler, in *Frau Erdmuthens Zwillingssöhne* and Duke of Crillon in *Der Posten der Frau* (*A Woman's Post*, 1857/1881).
17 Some passages in *Frau Erdmuthens Zwillingssöhne* are very similar to sections of the history, suggesting that François was either recycling earlier descriptions or that she revised the novel just before publication in the light of her work on the history.
18 There is no direct reference to the work of Johann Gustav Droysen, but it seems likely that François was familiar with Droysen's *Vorlesungen über das Zeitalter der Freiheitskriege*, first published circa 1845, cf. Sheehan 48. For example, she expresses similar views to Droysen on the settlement of 1815 as a missed opportunity for Prussia at the end of *Geschichte der preußischen Befreiungskriege* and this disappointment is reflected in her novel *Stufenjahre eines Glücklichen* (1877). A useful comparison of Droysen's liberal view with that of the more conservative Leopold von Ranke is provided in Georg Küntzel's introduction to Ranke's *Zwölf Bücher Preußischer Geschichte* (CII – CIII).
19 Letter to C. F. Meyer, 17.12.1885 (Bettelheim 181).
20 On the liberal historians of this era, see for example, Wirsching.
21 To some extent this reflects François's personal experience: her own father died when she was in infancy, her stepfather was a long-term invalid who lost his sight at an early stage and a guardian, who was supposed to look after the family finances, lost most of her inheritance, causing her to break off her marriage plans.
22 Cf. *Geschichte* 7, 44; for examples from contemporaries of the wars, see Hagemann 187.
23 Again, there is a parallel in François's family history, since two of her uncles had fought at Dennewitz, with one changing from the Saxon to the Prussian sides at the last moment before the battle (letter to C. F. Meyer, 17.12.1885 [Bettelheim 180-81]).
24 Though not at times bereft of a certain grim humour in the comments of the maverick army surgeon, François's descriptions of battlefields emphasise the human cost of war, and even in the *Geschichte der preußischen Befreiungskriege*, each battle scene closes with a reminder of the number of lives lost by each of the combatant groups.
25 There are no sources cited in the edition I have used. A good recent survey of primary source material and nineteenth-century accounts of Napoleon's German campaigns is available in Michael V. Leggiere's book, *Napoleon and Berlin* (356-60).
26 Many critics have commented on this. For the most recent discussions of the significance of names see Schuch 58 and Fox 116-17.
27 See *Fräulein Muthchen*, 291, 329 and 330. The conceit about names ending in »Mut« in the short story is found for names beginning with »Gott« in the novel. Here too, because the contrast between French and German characteristics is addressed more explicitly, Erdmuthe's family name is von Fels and she marries a nobleman of French extraction called, de Roc, to emphasise the essentiality of their ›national‹ characteristics, which prove so fateful for their sons.
28 Cf. examples in *Frau Erdmuthens* 44, 180, 266.
29 Bourgeois simplicity was frequently cited as one of the positive qualities of the Prussian royal family. François describes the King living »in bürgerlich stiller Beschränkung, ein

Vorbild jener reinen Familientugend, auf welche in erster Ordnung die Dauer der Völker gegründet ist« [in quiet bourgeois simplicity, an example of that pure family virtue, which ensures above all else the longevity of nations] (*Geschichte* 6). See also Hagemann 194 for other contemporary references. On class-specific norms in François's work see Laane 97-100.

30 After Raul senior's death, it is Hermann who helps his mother to run the estate and they make a joint will.

31 One thinks particularly of Eberhardine in *Die letzte Reckenburgerin* and several of the figures in *Stufenjahre eines Glücklichen.*

## Works Cited

Alexander, Robert S. *Napoleon*, Oxford: Oxford University Press, 2001.

Bettelheim, Anton (ed). *Louise von François und Conrad Ferdinand Meyer: Ein Briefwechsel*, Berlin: Reimer, 1905.

Boetcher Joeres, Ruth Ellen. *Respectability and Deviance. Nineteenth-Century Women Writers and the Ambiguity of Representation*, Chicago: University of Chicago Press, 1998.

Fox, Thomas C. »A Woman's Post: Gender and Nation in Historical Fiction by Louise von François« in Todd Kontje (ed), *A Companion to German Realism, 1848-1900*, Rochester, NY: Camden House, 2002: 109-131.

François, Louise von. *Die letzte Reckenburgerin*, in *Deutsche Romanzeitung*, Berlin 1870.

François, Louise von. »Fräulein Muthchen und ihr Hausmeier« in Louise von François: *Ausgewählte Novellen.* (Gesammelte Werke 4) Leipzig: Insel, 1918. Abbreviated as *Fräulein Muthchen.*

François, Louise von. *Frau Erdmuthens Zwillingssöhne.* Roman. Vorwort Emil Staiger.Zürich: Manesse, 1954 . Abbreviated as *Frau Erdmuthens.*

François, Louise von. *Geschichte der preußischen Befreiungskriege*, Berlin 1873. Abbreviated as *Geschichte.*

François, Louise von. *Stufenjahre eines Glücklichen.* Leipzig, 1877.

Hagemann, Karen. »A Valorous *Volk* Family: The Nation, the Military, and the Gender Order in Prussia in the Time of the Anti-Napoleonic Wars, 1806-15« in Ida Blom, Karen Hagemann and Catherine Hall (eds): *Gendered Nations. Nationalisms and Gender Order in the Long Nineteenth Century*, Oxford: Berg, 2000: 179-206.

Laane, Tiiu van. »Comic Mirrors and Sociological Implications in Louise von François'ss Narratives« in Ginette Adamson and Eunice Myers (eds): *Continental, Latin-American and Francophone Women Writers*, Vol 4, Lanham MD: Rowman & Littlefield, 1998: 95-107.

Leggiere, Michael V. *Napoleon and Berlin. The Napoleonic Wars in Prussia, 1813*, Stroud /Oklahoma: Tempus, 2002.

Ranke, Leopold von. *Zwölf Bücher Preußischer Geschichte*, Edited by Georg Küntzel, 3 volumes. Munich: Drei Masken, 1930.

Schuch, Uta. *»Die im Schatten stand«. Studien zum Werk einer vergessenen Schriftstellerin: Louise von François*, Stockholm: Almqvist & Wiksell, 1994.

Sheehan, James J. »State and nationality in the Napoleonic period« in John Breuilly (ed), *The State of Germany*, Harlow: Longman, 1992: 47-59.

Staiger, Emil. »Louise von François und ihr Roman Frau Erdmuthens Zwillingssöhne«, in: *Neue Schweizer Rundschau*, 21 (Juni 1954): 89-100.

Wirsching, Andreas. »Liberale Historiker im Nachmärz: Georg Gottfried Gervinus und Heinrich von Sybel« in Helmut Koopmann and Michael Perraudin (eds): *Formen der Wirklichkeitserfassung nach 1848. Deutsche Literatur und Kultur vom Nachmärz bis zur Gründerzeit in europäischer Perspektive I*, Bielefeld: Aisthesis, 2003: 147-166.

Worley, Linda Kraus. »Louise von François (1817–1893): Scripting a Life« in Ruth-Ellen Boetcher Joeres and Marianne Burkhard (eds): *Out of Line/Ausgefallen: The Paradox of Marginality in the Writings of Nineteenth-Century German Women*, (Amsterdamer Beiträge zur Germanistik Vol 28), Amsterdam: Rodopi, 1989: 161-86.

# Fighting Napoleon – Loving the French. Friedrich Spielhagen, *Noblesse oblige* (1888)

*Jeffrey L. Sammons*

One of the corollaries of Friedrich Spielhagen's notoriously rigid and prescriptive narrative theories is a rejection of the genre of the historical novel. It follows logically on the insistence that fictional characters must be modeled on persons one has known.[1] One cannot, after all, have personally known the figures of the past: »Einem Wallenstein, einer Maria Stuart, einem Götz, einem Egmont sind doch ihre Dichter im Leben nicht begegnet; ein Ingo und Ingraban; ein Richard Löwenherz und Ivanhoe haben doch nie zu ihrem Bekanntenkreise gehört« (Spielhagen, *Am Wege*, 105) [Their authors never met in life a Wallenstein, a Maria Stuart, a Götz, an Egmont; an Ingo and Ingraban; a Richard the Lion-Hearted and Ivanhoe have never belonged to their circle of acquaintance]. How, then, can the author form them realistically? There is, however, considerable incongruence between Spielhagen's theories and his creative practice, which is fortunate, for it is difficult to see how his imaginatively vigorous and reasonably literary novels could have been written at all under the yoke of his rules. Among these productive incongruities is the circumstance that he wrote two historical novels, *Deutsche Pioniere* [German Pioneers], concerning the resistance of German settlers in New York in an episode of the French and Indian War in 1753, written on the threshold of the Franco-Prussian War in 1870, and *Noblesse oblige* of 1888, which takes place during the French occupation of Hamburg.[2]

Spielhagen's novels are densely plotted and full of detail, therefore difficult to summarize conveniently. I will try to abstract the main line of the story. The latter novel begins in October 1812, when Napoleon is still sending back his falsified reports from the Russian campaign. The central figure is the twenty-three-year-old beauty Minna Warburg, whose Belgian mother has died and whose father is a quondam senator, though he is not from one of the established families, and a luxury-loving but failing businessman on the verge of bankruptcy.[3] Minna has engaged herself to the

Marquis Hypolit Drouot d'Héricourt, currently serving as a captain in the *Grande Armée*. But Warburg is determined to block this union, not because he has any patriotic objection to a French son-in-law, but because he desperately wants Minna to marry Theodor Billow, a selfish and unfeeling businessman still prosperous because he is partly based in London.[4] Warburg has therefore suppressed Minna's letters to Hypolit and his to her, so that each, while still in love with the other, feels abandoned. Warburg is uncomfortable about this behavior but feels he has no choice. In the course of time Minna reads in the newspaper of the marriage of a Hypolit d'Héricourt; Hipolyt has explained in one of the suppressed letters that this was a relative of a similar name; she, however, left without this information, now feels irretrievably abandoned and begins to accommodate herself to the idea of sacrificing herself to the disagreeable Billow to rescue the family. Minna's brother Georg, two years younger, who has an almost incestuous bond with his sister, has been conscripted against his will into Napoleon's army; her blithe, seventeen-and-a-half-year-old sister Johanna supports the Billow project because she hopes her beau, the young Swedish businessman Oskar Sandström, can obtain employment with him.

Minna, who is loved and admired by everyone except her father, her sister, and Billow, has a number of supportive friends. Among them is the enterprising publisher Friedrich Perthes, one of a small minority of middle-class patriots who were actually active and took up arms, and who at intervals offers Minna wise counsel (on Perthes' historical role see Hagemann). »Minna kannte nichts Verehrungswürdigeres, als diesen frommen, weitschauenden, begeisterten Mann« [Minna knew nothing more venerable than this pious, far-sighted, enthusiastic man], though she finds him too cautious (Spielhagen, *Noblesse oblige*, 193). Another friend is the elderly emigré physician Dr. Boutin, whose feelings of displacement in exile express themselves in a cynical, materialistic attitude that, in turn, masks great kindness and generosity (Boûtin, incidentally, was the maiden name of Spielhagen's French-descended wife). A third is the Jewish banker Samuel Hirsch, whose connections among relatives and associates are more reliable than the mails, so that he is able to give early notice of the disaster of the Russian campaign before the arrival of the famous Bulletin no. 29. When Georg deserts from Napoleon's army after Borodino, Hirsch has him passed around from one Jewish family to another until he reaches Billow's estate in Holstein, thus safely on Danish territory. Hirsch also secretly relieves Warburg's worst financial difficulties and later he and Dr.

Boutin are the only two men who attend the funeral of the ostracized bankrupt.

Billow has given refuge to Georg because, although he fears Minna, he lusts after her and, understanding that he can possess her only by marrying her, pursues a policy of helpfulness to the family, getting Hirsch, who has been arrested for possessing letters from Russia, out of prison with a bribe, and offering Sandström a position in London. In anticipation of a double marriage, he holds a lavish party in his manor house with its inscription *Noblesse oblige*, employed in the novel, as Spielhagen's titles often are, as a leitmotif in significant and often ironic contexts. Minna has by now accepted her fate; she considers suicide before her wedding but decides that it would be too easy (235). After the marriage she enrages Billow by trying to inspire him to a shared spirit of patriotism and civic duty, apparently in lieu of sexual relations.[5] Billow regards patriotism as tiresome nonsense, and is further enraged when the now fervently nationalistic Georg endangers Billow's Danish employees and his own safety by taking part in the uprisings against the French in the city; Georg's father is also annoyed and disowns him. Billow escapes the situation by departing for London, instructing Minna to take care of the estate in a way that makes her feel like his housekeeper. In Hamburg Minna faces down the governor general Louis-Nicolas Davout (spelled »Davoust«, as he often was at the time), to get her father, who is one of forty businessmen taken hostage to guarantee payment of French demands, released, and as a result she is assigned to forced labor on the fortifications, from which she is rescued by Hypolit, now a colonel returned from a diplomatic mission in Vienna. He is seriously wounded when he duels with and kills a lascivious officer who has been stalking and threatening Minna. Hypolit and Minna untangle their misunderstandings with one another, as she realizes that it must have been her father who suppressed their correspondence.

Apparently Minna and her husband have had some sexual congress, for she has discovered herself to be pregnant. She is ashamed at having betrayed her lover and wonders if she can love a child who resembles the despised father, but develops maternal feelings at the birth of the baby, which she announces to him. But she loses the baby to scarlet fever transmitted by the children of some of the poor and ill to whom she has given refuge when they were expelled by the French from the city. Billow meanwhile has replied to the news of the birth of his son with a pompous and hectoring letter in which he tells Minna that he will raise the child entirely according to his principles without sentimentality like love of one's neighbor whether the boy likes this strict discipline or not, and that she is to have nothing to say about it (398-99). Disgusted, Minna renounces Billow and returns to the ruined city, now in the grip of the second, punishing occupation; she finds her friends Boutin and Hirsch have died, but she tries to organize nursing care for the ill in her home, aware that Billow would be enraged if he were to know of it. The way seems open to a renewed relationship with Hypolit after a divorce, but she begins to have difficulties with the aristocratic assumptions of his relatives, and Georg, whose experiences have turned him into a raging nationalist and who, in his incestuous attachment, has always been jealous of Hypolit, insults him and Minna in public, declaring that a German officer cannot have the beloved of a Frenchman as a sister. Hypolit challenges him to a duel, Minna forbids it; Hypolit asserts that Germans are a barbaric people, causing Minna to renounce him.[6] Meanwhile Billow, who does not know of his son's death, announces his imminent arrival from England. Minna, thinking she should make another attempt with him, goes to meet him. His ship arrives in a raging storm; Billow is seen clinging to the rigging; Hypolit, who has followed Minna, loses his life in an unsuccessful attempt to rescue him. The novel ends with an overview of later years: Minna is living alone in the manor house, supporting herself with the income of a small inheritance while employing the larger revenues of the estate exclusively in the service of the needy. The aristocrats look askance at her and her way of life, but she is beloved by the little people, who think if they had her as the ruler of Holstein they would not need the duke.

For all that Spielhagen complained that the historical novel was born in the library, with characters that were »Statuen, welche die Wissenschaft in einer bestimmten Stellung ausgemeißelt hat«[7] [statues that scholarship has carved into a particular posture], he closely conformed *Noblesse oblige* to the historical record. The novel is mapped on the external chronology of events from the reports of the disintegration of Napoleon's campaign to the popular rebellion against the French customs officials in February 1813; its suppression by the Danish troops summoned by General Jean-François Carra (here »Cara«) St. Cyr; the departure of the French and »liberation« of the city by the Cossack commander Friedrich Karl von Tetttenborn in March; the formation of the patriotic *Hanseatische Legion* [Hanseatic Legion] and *Bürgergarde* [Civil Guard], relatively feeble forces whose middle and merchant class volunteers were more concerned to suppress popular uprising from below than antagonize the French;[8] the violent reoccupation of the city by Davout at the end of May, a spring and summer that brought »die schwarzen Winterwolken einer Tyrannei, wie die Welt sie so furchtbar kaum zum zweiten Mal gesehen« (286) [the black winter clouds of a tyranny so terrible as the world has hardly seen a second time]; his demand for forty-eight million francs, resulting in the taking of merchants as hostages and a raid on the deposits of the bank; the crushing burdens of conscription, quartering of troops and officials in private houses, and house searches for contraband; the forced labor, including women and children, on fortifications; the expulsion on Christmas Eve of several thousand poor and ill inhabitants, of whom more than a thousand died; and the total ruin of the city, occupied by Davout even after Napoleon's abdication until May 1814 (Loose, 418-29; Klessmann, 311-85). The characterizations of the ferocious if personally incorruptible Davout and the unreliable, self-aggrandizing Tettenborn correspond to the historical record up to the present day.[9] A number of historical figures among the patriots play recognizable background roles, such as the physician and local historian Jonas Ludwig von Hess, the lawyer Ferdinand Beneke, and the artisan-class roofer and especially competent leader of men, David Christoph Mettlerkamp.

With such fidelity to the record it is evident that Spielhagen must have had specific sources, but it is not easy to be sure what they were. In the case of the earlier historical novel, *Deutsche Pioniere*, dealing with an episode in the North American theater of the Seven Years War obscure not only in Germany, only one source is probable: the first and only volume of Friedrich Kapp's history of the German immigration (Kapp). The occupation of Hamburg, »[d]as Jahr der gewaltigsten Ereignisse« [the year of the mightiest events], as the narrator puts it (Spielhagen, *Noblesse oblige*, 372), left a much vaster and long remembered record.[10] The first liberation of 1813 was celebrated in an increasingly nationalistic and, eventually, monarchist spirit at twenty-five year intervals for a century.[11] Whether in 1888 Spielhagen would have had time to make use of Adolf Wohlwill's compact account of the events, intended for school use, is uncertain ([Wohlwill]).[12] Given the prominence of Perthes, it is likely that Spielhagen was acquainted with the biography written by his son; although the first and most relevant volume had been published as long ago as 1848 (Perthes), a sixth edition of the evidently widely-read work had appeared as recently as 1872. Much in the novel seems to reflect this account. Spielhagen takes over, with somewhat less emphasis, Perthes's view, possibly heightened by his son, that the particular cause of Hamburg was subordinate to that of the nation; Minna, too, deplores the lack of focus on national liberation. The stress in the biography on the Christian piety of Perthes and his wife Karoline leaves traces in the novel, but they are diluted, in keeping with Spielhagen's militantly antireligious attitude. In addition, he quite likely knew Karl August Varnhagen von Ense's by now famous *Denkwürdigkeiten des eignen Lebens* [Memoirs of My Own Life], of which a third edition had appeared in 1871; Varnhagen had woven into the second volume his earliest publications on the occupation of Hamburg and on Colonel Tettenborn. However, Varnhagen's heroic account of Tettenborn, under whom he had served, is more positive than the portrayal in the historical record otherwise or in Spielhagen's novel,[13] in which Varnhagen makes a cameo appearance (Spielhagen, *Noblesse oblige*, 239).

Apart from the source question, there are two aspects worthy of consideration. One is the placement of a courageous and active female figure at the center of the narration. It is true that her courage flags sometimes, and on several occasions she is on the verge of suicide. At one point she contemplates a portion of poison she has taken from her brother's supply, as she considers her position as the wife of a traitorous coward, but when she looks from her balcony at the caravans of the poor, weeping refugees, she determines to submerge her misery in the larger catastrophe and smashes the vial (284-85). Throughout she tries to numb her suffering with active public concern; when Perthes wants to take her with his family to refuge with Count Adam von Moltke, she insists she must stay and meet her responsibilities (283). Later, Dr. Boutin, sensing her depression, confirms her pregnancy in order to make it clear to her that she must not die (343-44). Her independent positions grate on others, who, like her father and her sister, find her arrogant, but the narrator credits her with »ihrem kraftvollen Hirn« (287) [her powerful brain]; it is also stressed in several places that she is physically strong. During her time as mistress of Billow's manor she entertains the Swedish crown prince (Jean Bernadotte, later King Karl XIV) and Tettenborn, who admire her with empty phrases; her housekeeper thinks she is superhuman (374-76).

The women in Spielhagen's fiction, from the outset often lively and sometimes erotically vibrant, evolve over the course of his career to increasing independence of judgment and action. Although he does not engage the women's emancipation movement except for fleeting allusions, he appears to develop a sensibility parallel to it.[14] The development can be illustrated by looking back at *Deutsche Pioniere*. The armature of the novel is the love story of the German settler Lambert, who rescues the beautiful Katherine, an immigrant orphaned in transit, by paying her indenture. Katherine is a competent and courageous woman who fends off the advances of Lambert's infatuated brother and assists during the French siege by, for example, loading the guns, but her role remains subordinate and ancillary to that of the men.[15] But Minna, like many of Spielhagen's women, wishes she were a boy so that she could act like her brother (64). Perthes praises her: »Ach, welche Wonne ist es, mit einer Frau reden zu dürfen, wie mit einem Manne, während es so viele Männer gibt, denen man stundenlang Vernunft umsonst predigt!« (182-83) [Oh, what a joy it is to be able to speak with a women as with a man, while there are so many men to whom one preaches reason for hours in vain!]. He urges her to express her opinions even when they do not agree with his; »Minna machte von dieser Erlaubnis in bester Form den ausgiebigsten Gebrauch. Dabei stellte es sich denn wiederholt heraus, daß sie, die Unerfahrene, Weltfremde, als sei sie mit Seher- und Prophetengabe ausgestattet, die gegenwärtige Lage richtiger verstanden, das Kommende klarer vorausgeschaut hatte als er« (183) [Minna made the most extensive use of this permission in the best way. It then repeatedly appeared that she, the inexperienced woman, as though she were furnished with the gift of a seer and prophet, foresaw the current situation more clearly than he]. As in numerous places in Spielhagen's fiction, men seem to need quite a lot of sustaining; Minna muses that women must be brave so as not to undermine men in crisis (180-81). In the face of her strength Billow, like many of Spielhagen's male figures, develops sexual timidity.

Minna's conscientiousness appears often to be an expression of religious belief; she is inclined not only to service but to contrition, frequently feeling that she has failed in her duty. But, after having survived so many horrendous experiences, her recognition of the treachery of her father undermines her faith: »Das ist die Gerechtigkeit des Himmels: ein Vater betrügt schamlos sein Kind; dann wird das arme Geschöpf mit der Not der Ihren gemartert und in Verzweiflung gejagt; zuletzt, um das Opfer sicher zu haben, schlägt es ein Dämon mit Blindheit! Und da spricht man von einem allbarmherzigen Gott!« (340) [That is the justice of heaven: a father shamelessly betrays his child; then the poor creature is martyred with the suffering of her people and driven to desperation; in the end, in order to secure the sacrifice, a demon strikes her with blindness! And they speak of an all-merciful God!]. Hypolit, too, it turns out, has lost his faith (341). By Spielhagen's principles these are steps in the direction of maturity.

Minna's sense of self also has a literary dimension. Spielhagen's practice, especially in the later novels, to employ literary works as background reference in a way tending toward a primitive intertextuality has, to my knowledge, never been adequately perceived. In the case of *Noblesse oblige*, the background work is Rousseau's *Julie, ou la nouvelle Héloïse*, to which Minna recurs at intervals throughout the novel. In several places passages are quoted verbatim, including one where Julie applies her eloquence to dissuading St. Preux from a duel with Edouard, which Minna reads by Hypolit's side when he is lying in a fever from his wound incurred in the duel with the officer who beleaguered her (363-64; cf. Part 1, Letter LVII, Rousseau, 155-56). A letter of Hypolit to Minna, read by her father, is a fairly good imitation of St. Preux's epistolary style in the early part of Rousseau's novel (Spielhagen, *Noblesse oblige*, 9-15); when Minna reads the recovered letters, she thinks: »Welch herrlichste poetische Ergüsse, als wären sie aus Rousseaus geweihter Feder geflossen« (353) [What magnificent poetic outpourings, as though they had flowed from Rousseau's sacred pen]. Warburg derives his daughter's high-mindedness from Rousseau, which she acknowledges to be the case (42-43). *La nouvelle Héloïse* is also Hypolit's favorite book, although he warns her that it is not appopriate reading for young girls (146). The book was still regarded as scandalous at this time, and Minna is uncomfortable about her attraction to it, but she keeps reading »in dem entsetzlichen Buche« [in the horrible book], at first naively, as she makes identifications with her own situation:

»Und das war nicht St. Preux, das war nicht Julie d'Etange, das war Hypolit d'Héricourt, das war sie selbst! Das Weltkind Claire mit ihrem Lachen und Weinen in einem Atem, das war nicht die von der Heldin »unzertrennlichen Kousine«, es war leibhaftig ihre Schwester Johanna; der Baron, der das Glück seiner Tochter den eigenen Interessen so resolut zum Opfer bringt, – es war ihr leibhaftiger Vater!« (147-48).

[And it was not St. Preux, it was not Julie d'Etange, it was Hypolit d'Héricourt, it was herself! The worldly child Claire with her laughter and weeping in one breath, it was not the heroine's »inseparable cousin«, it was her sister Johanna in person; the baron who so resolutely sacrifices his daughter to his own interests – it was her father in person!]

Already she sees that not all the correspondences are exact, but they seem to impose obligations on her:

»Und wenn Theodor Billow und Monsieur de Volmar noch so himmelweit verschiedene Naturen sein mochten, – in dem einen Umstande glichen sie sich völlig: sie begehrten, sie nahmen ein Mädchen zur Gattin, von dem sie wußten, daß es einen andren liebte, für sie im besten Falle nie etwas anderes empfinden würde als Achtung und Freundschaft! « (148)

[And even if Theodor Billow and Monsieur de Volmar might be such enormously different personalities – in one circumstance they resembled one another completely: they desired, they took a girl as a wife of whom they knew that she loved another, would at best never feel anything for them other than respect and friendship!]

But it is not only Billow who does not resemble the model, and, in fact, in no way deserves respect and friendship; Warburg turns out to be morally far inferior to Julie's stern but ultimately authoritative father, nor does the shallow Johanna much resemble the wise and stable Claire. The novel is not a model but an occasion for thoughtful consideration. Minna says to herself that if she had given herself to Hypolit as Julie did to St. Preux, she would never have become the wife of another, »und hätte er tausendmal die Philosophie und die Tugenden des Herrn von Volmar besessen!« (148) [and though he had possessed a thousand times the philosophy and the virtues of Monsieur de Volmar!]

It would go too far to claim Spielhagen as any sort of feminist, but he portrays women, to a degree unusual in his time, as strong, smart, capable of sexual initiative, and longing for equality with men. They are often central figures like Minna, and his last novel, *Frei geboren* (Born Free, 1900), has a female first-person narrator, very unusual among male writers in the Victorian age. In 1929, the feminist Dr. Ella Mensch, who was one of the first German women to earn a Ph.D. (in 1886 at the University of Zurich, the only institution where it was then possible), and who had become Spielhagen's admirer and correspondent, certified: »In ihm haben wir den ersten ausgesprochen modernen Romanschriftsteller [...], der sehr eingehend sich mit dem Wesen der Frau und seinen verschiedenen Typen befaßt hat« (Mensch, 16) [In him we have the first distinctly modern novelist [...] who concerned himself very thoroughly with the nature of women and its various types].

*La nouvelle Héloïse* was perceived at that time as a French product, so that Minna's fascination with it, along with her love for Hypolit, shows her located between the French and German cultures, or, in her personal formation, attempting to bridge them. This brings us to the other point of interest: the novel's perspective on patriotism and nationalism. In these matters, too, one can detect an evolution in the author, from the national-liberal convictions of his origins to skepticism tending to dismay toward the realities of the Wilhelminian Reich. Once again we may look back for contrast at *Deutsche Pioniere*, which, for all that it takes place in New York State, is the most emphatically nationalistic of all of Spielhagen's works (it is also, in my opinion, the weakest of his novels, but that is not the point here). It was written in the atmosphere of rising tension leading up to the Franco-Prussian War, and in it the Germans are innocent, peaceful farmers threatened with death and destruction by the barbaric and belligerent if cowardly French *Erbfeind* [hereditary enemy]. Katherine declares their struggle »ein ehrlicher Kampf für Haus und Hof, für Leib und Leben! derselbe Kampf in anderer Form, der ihren alten guten Vater mit seiner ganzen Gemeinde aus Deutschland vertrieben!« [an honorable struggle for home and hearth, for body and soul! the same struggle in another form that drove her old, good father with his whole community out of Germany!]. A patriarchal old farmer remembers when »die fränkischen Wölfe« [the Frankish wolves] murdered his family and burned their house in Heidelberg in 1689, and he renews his curse on the »Henker und Mordbrenner« [hangmen and murdering incendiaries] (Spielhagen, *Deutsche Pioniere,* 455, 500).

One might think that *Noblesse oblige* would offer an occasion for a continuation of this spirit. The occupation of Hamburg, especially the second one under Davout, may have been the most dreadful experience the German people endured in the Napoleonic era. Not all contemporaries failed to perceive the advantages of Napoleonic government: the reform and rationalization of law and administration, the partial leveling of class discrimination, the steps taken toward Jewish emancipation, but these positive features were submerged in the miseries of conscription, taxation, censorship, arrests and forced labor, the violent destruction of economic life at every level, and the clear evidence that the Empire was bringing not revolutionary emancipation but tyranny and ruthless exploitation in the sole interest of what we would today call a colonial power. Georg, who says he never hated the French until his experiences with them in Hamburg (228-34), illustrates how Napoleon came to be a major progenitor of the fervent nationalism and anti-French chauvinism that was to accompany Germany's formation as a nation and rise to a world power. Anniversaries of Hamburg's first liberation in 1813, including those of 1888, were increasingly celebrated in this spirit. One might easily imagine Spielhagen replicating it in his novel. That he does not do so is another indication of his increasing inability to get with the program after 1871.

*Noblesse oblige* comes between two critical sociopolitical novels, *Was will das werden?* [What Meaneth This?, 1887] and *Ein neuer Pharao* [A New Pharaoh, 1889], the latter of which, as I have commented, »indicates Spielhagen's further dissociation from the Reich« (Sammons, *Friedrich Spielhagen*, 220). In the former, the protagonist's former teacher sadly sees the Franco-Prussian War as

»eine traurige Notwendigkeit. Ich schäme mich nicht, weiter zu sagen: ich liebe Paris, in welchem ich ein köstliches Studienjahr verbrachte; ich liebe das schöne sonnige Frankreich; ich liebe die Franzosen, denen wir, als dem älteren, vielleicht dem geistvolleren Kulturvolke, man mag sagen, was man will, für unsre Bildung Unendliches zu verdanken haben würden. Nun ist diese Quelle intellektueller und ästhetischer Labung für uns verschüttet auf wer weiß wie viele Jahre!« (Spielhagen, *Was will das werden?*, 336)

[a sorrowful necessity. I am not ashamed to say further: I love Paris, in which I spent a lovely student year; I love beautiful, sunny France; I love the French, to whom, as the older, perhaps more brilliant cultural nation, say what one will, we would owe infinitely much for our culture. Now this wellspring of intellectual and aesthetic refreshment is obstructed for us for who knows how many years!]

*Noblesse oblige* is in this sequence. There is, to be sure, nothing euphemistic about the portrayal of French atrocity: the fearsomely harsh Davout, the lascivious officer who besets Minna, the corrupt, bullying customs officials, the crude soldiers driving the forced laborers. Since Minna must acknowledge all this, her enduring love for the French officer puts her into a bitter bind. Thus her first reaction to the news of the defeat of Napoleon, whose adjutant Hypolit has become, is painful anxiety: »Waren doch die siegreichen französischen Fahnen das Symbol ihres persönlichen Glücks gewesen, wie das Unterliegen derselben die Besiegelung ihres Unglücks« [After all, the victorious French flags had been the symbol of her personal happiness, as their defeat are the seal of her unhappiness]. But her beloved »war und blieb doch immer der Feind ihres Vaterlandes« [was and remained, still, the enemy of her fatherland]. Thus she herself is a tool, against her will and instincts, of Napoleon's atrocities. The only solution is contrition and service in imitation of Christ, »die Buße für das Verbrechen an ihrem Volke, ihrer Familie, das sie hatte begehen wollen, dessen erste Stadien sie bereits durchmessen« (Spielhagen, *Noblesse oblige*, 105-06) [atonement for the crime against her people, her family, that she had wanted to commit, whose first stages she had already crossed].

The overall tone of the novel is one of discouragement. No aspirations are fulfilled. There is here no celebration of liberation. German leadership, anxious about unleashing popular forces, was dilatory about confronting Napoleon. Perthes, like many liberals, frets that Friedrich Wilhelm III »ist einmal ein Kunktator« [is once and for all a *cunctator*]; he wants the princes to lead. But Minna does not want to wait for princes, thinking to herself: »Wenn wir harren wollen, bis alles auf dem Papier in Ordnung ist und die Fürsten ihre Siegel darunter gedrückt haben, wird die rechte Stunde nie schlagen« (184-86) [if we want to delay until everything is order on paper and the princes have affixed their seal to it, the right hour will never strike]. With the exception of Perthes and his brave comrades, the burghers of Hamburg, far from being patriotic or yearning for the national cause, are, like Minna's father, timid and servile, thinking only of their own advantage; they waste no time in reversing the Napoleonic reforms and restoring the good old system (cf. Stieve). The narrator observes that the people are already being cheated in Frankfurt after the Battle of Leipzig (Spielhagen, *Noblesse oblige*, 372). If Georg's fanatic nationalism, although understandably motivated, leads to a breach with and public insult of his splendid sister, it cannot be an acceptably humane position. Despite the turns of plot, the hope of a union of Hypolit and Minna, is, as she herself suspects early on, »eine Schimäre« (105) [a chimera], and this failed liaison is a synecdoche for the larger cultural estrangement deplored in the preceding novel. She tells Hypolit she has concluded that one cannot get free of the fetters of the national identity into which one is born; [16] Dr. Boutin believed he had become a German, but dreamed and thought in French »und blieb in seinem Herzen Franzose« (446-47) [remained in his heart a Frenchman]. At the end of the novel, Minna, rereading Hypolit's letters, comes across this passage:

»Das ist die entsetzliche Barbarei, zu der wir unsre Feinde gezwungen haben, und durch die sie uns wiederum zur Begehung von Greueln zwingen, die sonst ungeschehen geblieben wären. Oh, meine geliebte Freundin, mir stockt das Herz, denke ich dieses verderblichen Zirkels, der sich durch die Jahrtausende der Geschichte schlingt! Wird denn nie die Zeit kommen, in welcher der Mensch des Vorrechts, durch die Gabe der Vernunft geadelt zu sein vor aller Kreatur, voll wird genießen; den Pflichten, die aus diesem höchsten Adel fließen, frei und fröhlich wird genügen: ein Mensch wird sein können, ohne daß man im Namen der Familienliebe, der Wohlfahrt des Vaterlandes, der Ehre der Nation Unmenschliches von ihm fordert? Wird sie niemals kommen, diese Zeit?«

[That is the dreadful barbarism to which we have forced our enemies, and with which they force us, in turn, to atrocities that otherwise would not have happened. Oh, my beloved friend, my heart stops if I think of this vicious cycle that winds through the millennia of history! Will then the time never come when the human being will fully enjoy the privilege of being ennobled with the gift of reason beyond all creatures, will freely and cheerfully fulfill the duties that flow from this highest nobility, will be able to be a human being without brutalities being required of him in the name of love of family, the welfare of the fatherland, the honor of the nation? Will it never come, this time?]

To which Minna whispers to herself: »Niemals, geliebter Freund [...], niemals!« (506) [Never, beloved friend [...] never!].

However, this was not to be Spielhagen's last word in the matter. Three years later, in 1891, he turned the novel into a stage play, *In eiserner Zeit* [In Iron Times]. Spielhagen's dramas are much less important than his novels; his understanding of the requirements of the stage led him to escalate the melodrama about which critics of his novels have always complained. The counterpart to Minna Warburg, here named Charlotte Wilbek, is less of a heroine than a victim, and she does commit suicide. Hypolit's counterpart, named Gaston, Marquis von Ormand, is executed a quarter hour before the French finally give up the city. However, a Huguenot, Barbeyrac, who is Charlotte's tutor, is more foregrounded as a bicultural figure than Dr. Boutin in the novel. He has apparently overcome Dr. Boutin's fractured identity and makes the cosmopolitan, internationalist hope more explicit: »ich bin ein Franzose, den das Schicksal zu einem Deutschen gemacht hat; ich bin ein Deutscher, der ein Franzose geblieben ist« [I am a Frenchman whom fate has made into a German; I am a German who has remained a Frenchman]. As for the conflict with Napoleon, it is »ein blutiger Schein, der uns die ewige, sonnenhafte Wahrheit verhüllen will, daß die Brüderlichkeit der Individuen, wie der Völker Endzweck der Menschheit, Ziel ihrer Geschichte, und Liebe der heilige Urgrund ist, in dem sie unerschütterlich wurzelt« [a bloody illusion that tries to obscure the eternal, sunbright truth that the brotherhood of individuals as of the nations is the ultimate purpose of mankind, goal of its history, and love is the sacred foundation in which it is unshakably rooted]. He has the last word in the tragedy, undoubtedly addressed to Spielhagen's contemporaries: »[...] ich höre einen Jubelsang durch die Ferne der kommenden Jahrhunderte. Er schallt zum Himmel empor von der Erde, die keine sich hassenden Völker mehr kennt, – nur Menschen – Menschen nach dem Ebenbilde Gottes, der die Liebe ist«[17] [...] I hear a song of jubilation through the distances of the coming centuries. It resounds up to heaven from the earth that no longer knows nations hating one another – only human beings – human beings made from the image of God, who is love].

By the time of *Noblesse oblige*, Spielhagen's literary reputation was in serious decline among the critics and tastemakers of the Wilhelminian Reich. The novel's alternative treatment, in 1888, of the saga of the »liberation« of Hamburg shows in what ways he became estranged from the main line of public opinion.

–Yale University

## Notes

1 Spielhagen, Beiträge, 180; *Am Wege*, 96-97. On his literary theories, see Rebing; Sammons, Friedrich Spielhagen, 52-69.

2 In Sammons, *Friedrich Spielhagen*, xviii, I claimed that the given date of 1888 was in error because I found an entry in the *Gesamtverzeichnis deutschprachigen Schrifttums* indicating a first edition of 1882; I am now persuaded that the entry in GV is an error and that 1888, the seventy-fifth anniversary of the first liberation of Hamburg, is correct.

3 Many Hamburg businesses, including well-established ones, had been driven to bankruptcy by Napoleon's Continental blockade and the exclusion of the city, even though it had been made a department of the Empire, from the French tariff system. See Schmidt, pt. 1: 634-35.

4 Some Hamburg businessmen were able to preserve and even increase their wealth because of holdings in England and other foreign places. See Schmidt, pt. 1: 666-67.

5 This is only implicit but plausible because the sexless, »white« marriage or the denial of sex for one purpose or another by a wife or mistress is a recurrent motif in Spielhagen's novels. See Sammons, *Friedrich Spielhagen*, 141-42.

6 Duels in Spielhagen's novels are always deplorable affairs and often end sadly. See Sammons, Friedrich Spielhagen, 102-07.

7 Spielhagen, *Aus meiner Studienmappe*, 263, n., quoting Berthold Auerbach; Spielhagen, *Beiträge*, 16.

8 The Hamburg council had Napoleon's »victory« in Moscow celebrated with a Te Deum long after his retreat began (Loose, 122-23).

9 The most pejorative characterization of Tettenborn I have encountered is Klessmann's, 324: »ein unangenehmes, eitles Großmaul und militärisch ein Hanswurst« [an unpleasant, vain braggart and militarily a clown].

10 A bibliography of contemporary and nineteenth-century sources fills sixty-two pages (Schmidt, pt. 2: 117-78).

11 On this point and on historical matters in general I am especially grateful for the advice of Professor Katherine B. Aaslestad of West Virginia University, who has allowed me to

read her forthcoming paper (»Collective Memory«) and chapters of her forthcoming book (*Place and Politics*).

12 As the title indicates, the pamphlet must have appeared in March. The introduction (3) notes that the celebration could not be held owing to the death of Wilhelm I on March 9 and because of further worries, no doubt referring to the illness of Friedrich III, who lived on until June. Wohlwill published supporting documents in the March issue of *Mittheilungen des Vereins für Hamburgsche Geschichte*, 11, No. 3 (1888): 185-95. Wohlwill's nationalistic tone, characteristic of the time, is considerably modified by Spielhagen, as we shall see.

13 See the commentary to Varnhagen von Ense, 782, 844. On Varnhagen and Tettenborn, see Feilchenfeldt, 88-116. Pickett, 34-37.

14 See the chapter »Women, *Femmes fatales*, Love, and the Erotic« in Sammons, *Friedrich Spielhagen*, 136-52.

15 She may be descended from the sister of the protagonist in Charles Sealsfield's *Nathan, der Squatter-Regulator*, with which Spielhagen was acquainted. She, too, serves bravely during a siege, loading the guns, but remains subordinate. See my forthcoming essay, Sammons, »Die Verteidigung«.

16 The liaison also encounters class problems; Hypolit's relatives assume that, in the event of a marriage, Minna would turn Catholic, which she surely would not do, and she is warned of the certain hostility of Hypolit's mother, a fierce royalist whose husband had been guillotined in the Revolution. This may appear as a distraction from the national issues – I myself feel that Spielhagen need not have made Hypolit a marquis – but class barriers are a preoccupying concern in his fiction from the beginning to the end of his career. They are rarely overcome by love.

17 Spielhagen, *In eiserner Zeit*, 74-75, 139. Davout is here spelled »d'Avoust«, perhaps as an indication of his pretensions to Napoleonic aristocracy as duke of Auerstädt and prince of Eckmühl.

## Works Cited

Aaslestad, Katherine B. »Collective Memory and National Identity: Remembering the Wars of Liberation in Hamburg.« *Central European History* (2005; forthcoming).

Aaslestad, Katherine B. *Place and Politics: Local Identity, Civic Culture, and German Nationalism in North Germany during the Revolutionary Era.* Boston: Brill, 2005 (forthcoming).

Feilchenfeldt, Konrad. *Varnhagen von Ense als Historiker.* Amsterdam: Erasmus, 1970.

Hagemann, Karen. »Die Perthes im Krieg. Kriegserfahrungen und -erinnerungen einer Hamburger Bürgerfamilie in der ›Franzosenzeit.‹« *Eliten im Wandel. Gesellschaftliche Führungsschichten im 19. und 20. Jahrhundert.* Ed. Karl Christian

Führer, Karen Hagemann, and Birthe Kundrus. Münster: Westfälisches Dampfboot, 2004: 72-101.

Kapp, Friedrich. *Geschichte der deutsche Einwanderung in Amerika*, vol. 1: *Die Deutschen im Staate New York bis zum Anfang des neunzehnten Jahrhunderts.* Leipzig: Quandt & Händel, 1868.

Klessmann, Eckart. *Geschichte der Stadt Hamburg.* 2nd ed. Hamburg: Die Hanse, 2002.

Loose, Hans-Dieter, ed. *Hamburg: Geschichte der Stadt und ihrer Bewohner.* Ed. Werner Jochmann and Hans-Dieter Loose, vol. 1: *Von den Anfängen bis zur Reichsgründung.* Hamburg: Hoffmann und Campe, 1982.

Mensch, Ella, ed. *Er lebt noch immer! Ein Spielhagen-Brevier.* Leipzig: Staackmann, 1929.

Perthes, Clemens Theodor. *Friedrich Perthes Leben. Nach dessen schriftlichen und mündlichen Mittheilungen.* 3 vols. Hamburg and Gotha: Perthes, 1848–55.

Pickett, Terry H. *The Unseasonable Democrat: Karl August Varnhagen von Ense (1785–1858).* Bonn: Bouvier, 1985.

Rebing, Günter. *Der Halbbruder des Dichters. Friedrich Spielhagens Theorie des Romans.* Frankfurt am Main: Athenäum, 1972.

Rousseau, Jean-Jacques. *La nouvelle Heloïse. Œuvres complètes*, vol. 2. Ed. Bernard Gagnebin and Marcel Raymond. [Paris]: Gallimard, 1964.

Sammons, Jeffrey L. »Die Verteidigung des Blockhauses dreiunddreißig Jahre später : Streiflichter auf Friedrich Spielhagens *Deutsche Pioniere* « (forthcoming in the papers of the Olomouc Sealsfield conference).

Sammons, Jeffrey L. *Friedrich Spielhagen: Novelist of Germany's False Dawn.* Tübingen: Niemeyer, 2004.

Schmidt, Burghart. *Hamburg im Zeitalter der Französischen Revolution und Napoleons (1789–1813). Teil 1. Darstellung; Teil 2. Kommentierte Übersicht über Literatur und Quellen.* Hamburg: Verein für Hamburgische Geschichte, 1998.

Spielhagen, Friedrich. *Am Wege. Vermischte Schriften.* Leipzig: Staackmann, 1903.

Spielhagen, Friedrich. *Aus meiner Studienmappe. Beiträge zur litterarischen Aesthetik und Kritik.* Berlin: Verein für Deutsche Litteratur, 1891.

Spielhagen, Friedrich. *Beiträge zur Theorie und Technik des Romans.* Leipzig: Staackmann, 1883.

Spielhagen, Friedrich. *Deutsche Pioniere. Ausgewählte Romane*, 2nd ser., vol. 2. Leipzig: Staackmann, 1891.

Spielhagen, Friedrich. *In eiserner Zeit.* Leipzig: Staackmann, 1891.

.Spielhagen, Friedrich. *Noblesse oblige. Ausgewählte Romane*, 3rd ser., vol. 2. Leipzig: Staackmann, 1892.

Spielhagen, Friedrich. *Was will das werden?*, pt. 1, *Ausgewählte Romane*, 3rd ser., vol. 4. Leipzig: Staackmann, 1892.

Stieve, Tilman. *Der Kampf um die Reform in Hamburg 1788–1842.* Hamburg: Verein für Hamburgische Geschichte, 1993.

Varnhagen von Ense, Karl August. *Werke*, vol. 2: *Denkwürdigkeiten des eignen Lebens, Zweiter Band (1810–1815)*. Ed. Konrad Feilchenfeldt. Frankfurt am Main: Deutscher Klassiker Verlag, 1990.

[Wohlwill, Adolf]. Die Befreiung Hamburgs am 18. März 1813. Verfaßt und herausgegeben im Auftrage des Comités für die Märzfeier 1888. Hamburg: Diedrich, [1888].

# Growing into a Nation: Queen Luise and the Lessons of Nationalism in Adolescent Fiction for Girls

*Jennifer Drake Askey*

This article explores a unique aspect of the nineteenth-century cult of Prussian Queen Luise (1776–1810). By the end of the nineteenth century the Prussian bourgeoisie celebrated Luise – the mother of Emperor Wilhelm I – as the paragon of German womanly virtue and as a secular Prussian saint. She symbolized the noble German spirit laid temporarily low by Napoleon's France and her early death was transformed in poetry and song to a rallying cry for revenge against the French. The adoration of Luise found expression at the highest levels of the government and in art, music, and literature. Luise's literary legacy will be the focus of this analysis; specifically, how stories of Luise's life guided young female readers in Wilhelminian Germany in their attitudes towards German culture and national belonging. I contend that historical novels centered on Luise's life story, as well as popular biographies, encourage a gender-appropriate emotional nationalism in their young readers. Literary encounters with Luise also teach young women to recognize the seductions of France and to resist them by calling upon Luise's memory. The story of Luise, Prussian saint and *Landesmutter*, edifies and educates young women in nationally appropriate ways. Historical novels that feature her rely upon familiar tropes of the fairy tale and the coming of age story to shape adolescent fantasy in a nationally productive manner.

Wulf Wülfing outlines the mythologizing of Luise's biography that occurred over the course of the nineteenth century. The Luise myth, Wülfing argues, functioned socio-politically within the Prussian nation and the emerging German empire, and functioned semiotically within the narration and artistic presentation of Luise's biography (234). He demonstrates how Luise's biography is divided into phases, each serving a distinct social and political function for the formation of a positivist teleological national history (such as »1. Phase: 1770–1806: ›Verbürgerlichung‹ des Hofes« [Bourgeois Transformation of the Court], »2. Phase: 1806–1815: ›Erwachen‹ einer Nation« [National Awakening], and »3. Phase: 1815–1870: Konsolidierung der Nation« [National Consolidation]). Within these phases, her biography is broken down even further into stations, similar to stations of the cross, where the Prussian patriot can pause and reflect and be edified (235). This pattern is at work in the historical novels for young women I wish to examine here: Elisabeth Halden's *Königin Luise* (*Queen Luise*, 1893) and Brigitte Augusti's *Die Erben von Scharfeneck* (*The Heirs of Scharfeneck*, 1889). In these texts, a young female protagonist becomes a companion to Queen Luise and experiences these phases and stations of Luise's life at the queen's side. The young protagonist becomes both teacher (of the reader) and student (of Luise) of the gendered, emotional lessons of German history.

As part of a longer project (Askey 2003), I have examined the relationship between popular literature, such as Halden's and Augusti's historical novels, and the curriculum of the Prussian *Töchterschule*, or girls' school. There I demonstrate that the curriculum of the girls' school, as well as the narrative strategies of popular historical fiction for young women, aim to foster an emotional relationship between the ideal reader/pupil and the state, symbolized by Queen Luise, by relying on conventions of romance and domesticity that underwrote gender roles in nineteenth-century Germany. Biographies of significant figures in German history thus featured prominently in school texts for girls' schools: descriptions of Friedrich II from Gustav Freytag's *Bilder aus der deutschen Vergangenheit* (*Pictures from the German Past*) and first-hand stories of Friedrich Wilhelm III and Queen Luise's court from the lady-in-waiting Countess Voss and the court bishop Rulemann Friedrich Eylert make regular appearances in girls' readers (see Paldamus, Kippenberg). Popular novels such as Halden's and Augusti's were often commissioned by the same publishers that published school textbooks, so it does not surprise that these authors employed strategies for creating a successful historical novel that reflected the pedagogical goals of the girls' school: the creation of nationally-minded, self-sacrificing German women. Given, however, that these novels were popular literature, intended for entertainment as well as edification, they also offered their young readers a chaste and civically productive outlet for fantasy. It is at this intersection of fantasy and national duty that the story of Luise took on its particular power.

The juvenile historical fiction of Brigitte Augusti and Elisabeth Halden belonged to a large genre of popular, liberal fiction in the spirit of the family periodical *Die Gartenlaube* (*The Garden Bower*). The ornate design of the books, as well as the publisher's information inside the covers, indicates that these novels were intended to be given as gifts to young women by family and other well-meaning adults. One can picture a young lady receiving the five volumes of Augusti's *An deutschem Herd* [sic] (*At the German Hearth*) on the occasion of her confirmation. As works of edification, as well as education, these novels introduced young women to events and figures in German history and, more importantly, provided a national narrative of female involvement and belonging that reflected the goals and aspirations of the German middle class. The story of Queen Luise proved irresistible as historical material: her biography provided romance and fairy tale, adventure and calamity. Luise personified the charming child, the beautiful queen, the doting wife and mother. The nineteenth-century narrative of her life emphasized her bourgeois credentials, as it were: her domesticity, her motherhood, her loyalty as wife and mother, and her commitment to the middle-class standards of cultural self betterment. Her early death lent a romantic, fairy-tale aspect to her story and the entire Luise narrative was intensified by the persistent threat from Napoleon's France. In Luise girls' educators found the ideal vehicle for conveying the lessons of nation and gender to the young women of the German empire.

Brent Petersen writes in *History, Fiction, and Germany: Writing the Nineteenth-Century Nation* about the symbolic importance of Luise for novelists and historians narrating the history of Germany in what is sometimes referred to as the long nineteenth century. In his analysis of historical novels by Wilibald Alexis, Luise Mühlbach, and others, Petersen demonstrates the breadth of exposure middle-class Germans would have had to the historical and legendary Luise throughout the nineteenth century and the central role of her life story in crafting the national myth of Germany's tragic fall at the hands of Napoleon and its triumphant rebirth with the rise of the bourgeoisie and the nation state. Summarizing the national utility of Luise's biography for novelists and historians, he writes:

> »Part of the attraction of Queen Luise was the ease with which her persona could be used to invoke continuity with the past. As Treitschke put it, ›she lives on in the memory of her thankful people, a luminous figure who pointed the way for combatants in our war of liberation shimmering high up in the heavens‹«. (173)

The era of the Wars of Liberation is a constitutive one for the nationalist ideology of late nineteenth-century Germany and Luise functions synecdochally for Germany in that time of suffering.

Petersen correctly demonstrates that both authors of historical fiction and historians concurred that there existed a personal link between Luise and the people. This personal connection, in turn, enabled authors to show that Luise »helped enable the popular uprising of 1813, saving the Prussian state from Napoleon and thereby paving the way for German unification« (174). In historical fiction and biography written expressly for young women at the end of the nineteenth century, this personal connection between the queen and her subjects is all-important. It not only bolsters the popular liberal contention that true Germanness was embodied in bourgeois values, but also reinforced for young readers the ideal emotional relationship they should have with the state.

Adolescent fiction and biographies of Luise for young women sought to recreate the relationship between the queen and her early-nineteenth-century subjects and to capture the spirit of Luise's time. The Napoleonic occupation and subsequent wars against France functioned as the crucible of the German nation in the historical rhetoric of the Wilhelminian era. By identifying with the struggles and fears of Luise and her subjects, these late-nineteenth-century readers participate emotionally in the creation and consolidation of the German nation and develop a sense of what kind of role they, as women, are to play in their national community.

This emotional investment in Germany takes several guises in fiction for girls: the romantic encounter with national significance; the development of a mature gender sensibility; and a commitment to German cultural production. The two novels discussed here each feature a fictional protagonist: a young lady who becomes a companion to Luise. These figures function as ideal vehicles for reader identification and provide the author with a means to articulate the characteristics of her model reader. By introducing a young woman much like the target audience of their fiction into Luise's life story, Augusti and Halden show how the average girl can become more and more like the German feminine ideal not only by aspiring to be like Luise – by making the attitudes towards family, state, and responsibility that Luise reflected in her own life their own – but by adopting the emotional attachment to the state, its representatives, and its welfare exhibited by the middle-class characters that populate these Luise stories and spend time at the queen's side.

The final volume of Brigitte Augusti's series, *The Heirs of Scharfeneck*, chronicles the story of Gabriele von Fiedler as she learns lessons about becoming a German woman at Luise's side. Gabriele's family, at home in rural Thuringia, occupies a nexus of sorts for the articulation of feminine German national identity in the early nineteenth century. Girls' education, the Revolution in France, the domestic and political values of the nobility, and the proper attitude for women to possess towards politics, war, and revenge intersect in discussions at the Scharfeneck estate.

Young Gabriele's German spirit faces challenges on many fronts. Her Aunt Arabella wants to send her to a francophone boarding school, to rescue her from a certain future as a social oddball. Her brother's new French wife, Marie, rails against the family estate as a provincial backwater with no culture, no entertainment, and no reason for existing. Most important, however, Count le Malthême, a French nobleman on the run from the Terror in France, arrives at the estate and threatens to steal Gabriele's heart. He arrives at the estate one winter's day, suffering and cold, and the ladies of the house invite him in and nurse him back to health. Gabriele, in particular spends hours a day reading to him, taking walks with him in the garden, and listening to him tell of his beautiful, tragic queen, Marie Antoinette.

Gabriele romanticizes her role as the count's caretaker. Her thoughts are occupied with him and his fate even when she should be focusing on her lessons in school. Of all the things she loves about spending time with him, however, she loves most of all the opportunity to hear him talk about his »schöne, unglückliche Königin« (41) [beautiful, unhappy Queen]. He had been a page at Marie Antoinette's court and sings praises of her beauty and grace to Gabriele, his captive audience. An anticipated encounter with Luise brings Gabriele's infatuation into check. Alone and preparing to go visit Luise in nearby Hildburghausen, Gabriele reflects more negatively on the count, his nature as a man, and his actions. In particular, she asks herself: »War es heldenhaft, auf jeden Versuch, seine angebetete Königin zu befreien, von vornherein zu verzichten?« (48) [Was it heroic to refuse, categorically, any possible attempt to free the queen he worshipped?]

When she arrives in Hildburghausen and is reunited with Luise, Gabriele's sudden change of heart regarding the count begins to make sense. Luise's influence on the impressionable protagonist is significant and obviously has made itself known even before Gabriele's departure. When she explains her confusion regarding the count to Luise, the princess interprets it for her, providing a commentary on masculinity and nationhood that Gabriele and the readers alike should take to heart.

»Ich glaube, ich verstehe dein Gefühl ganz gut, du Teure; dieser liebenswürdige Graf scheint mir mehr ein Held von Worten und Gefühlen, als von der That zu sein. Was ist es aber, was uns bei einem echten Manne unwiderstehlich fesselt und uns Achtung abnötigt? Doch zumeist die mannhafte Thatkraft.« (50)

[I believe I understand your feelings quite well, my dear; this charming count appears to me to be more a hero in words and feelings but not in deed. What is it about a *real* man, however, that grips us and demands our admiration? Most of the time it is [his] masculine will to action.]

Without saying it directly, Luise uses phrases and concepts to explain Gabriele's sudden ambivalence towards the count that suggest definitions of manhood and national belonging. The man of action, the reader understands, will most likely be German, while the man of ideas and flights of fancy will turn out to be French. The count, Luise agrees, is most likely a fine person, but he does not possess the qualities that would endear him to a German woman like Gabriele or her. Luise contrasts her impression of the count with the admiration she feels for the future Prussian king, Friedrich Wilhelm III. She also tells Gabriele

»Man spricht viel Gutes von den Prinzen, besonders der Kronprinz hat sich durch seinen reinen Sinn, sein edles Streben große Anerkennung bei den Besten seiner Umgebung erworben. Solche Männer, die Redlichkeit und Kraft in sich vereinen, thun unserer Zeit not, und ich preise Preußen glücklich, das in seinem Hohenzollernstamm so würdige Fürsten besitzt.« (50)

[People say many good things about the princes; the Crown Prince [the future Friedrich Wilhelm III] in particular has earned the admiration of the best people in his circle through his pure spirit and his noble striving. Men such as these, in whom power and honesty are united, are sorely necessary in this day and age and I deem Prussia fortunate to have such worthy men in the house of Hohenzollern.]

In this analysis of masculinity and patriotism, Luise reveals the nature of her personal interest in the political arena, which could easily serve as a blueprint for the type of historical and political involvement deemed appropriate for German women in the nineteenth century. Recognizable from the pedagogical discussions surrounding the proper methodology for teaching young women history, Luise's interest in the public sphere and matters of state is limited primarily to an interest in the men who are actively engaged in national business.

For the didactic purposes of historical fiction the message is clear: the monarch and his successor, who enjoy their positions by the grace of God, also are the kind of men who faithfully incorporate and represent Prussia and the values of their subjects. This was the legacy of Friedrich II, whose popularity in Prussia persisted well into the nineteenth century and the reign of Friedrich Wilhelm III and Luise. The contrast, then, that Augusti (and other Luise biographers and novelists) illuminates between the Prussian royal household, with its bourgeois values and its purported domesticity, and the French »upstart« emperor, Napoleon, couldn't be starker.

*The Heirs of Scharfeneck* contains several episodes that reveal the nature of female political involvement or interest in the greater affairs of the nation. These episodes clearly delineate appropriate and inappropriate female emotional involvement in politics and set up Luise, as well as Frau von Fiedler, Gabriele's mother, as examples of how women should relate to the public sphere. When news of revolutionary activity in France reaches the remote Scharfeneck estate via the newspapers, the family assembles around the dinner table to hear the news read aloud.

»Alle blickten gespannt auf den Sprecher, das Thema erregte bei jedem das lebhafteste Interesse; denn so selten man sich im allgemeinen mit Politik befaßte, und so wenig die spärlichen Zeitungen für Verbreitung solcher Kenntnisse thaten, so waren doch die Ereignisse in Frankreich zu gewaltig, um sie unbeachtet zu lassen.« (24)

[Everyone looked eagerly at the reader; the topic interested everyone immensely; although they did not generally deal with politics and the rare newspaper did little to educate them along those lines, the events in France were too enormous to ignore.]

This passage reveals the essential ground rules for the group of patriotic German women that form the centerpiece of Augusti's novel. Before Augusti narrates the events taking place in France, she must tell her readers that Frau von Fiedler and her family live a rural life completely cut off from the court and the social obligations and influences thereof. She, and by association her daughter and her female companion Maria, do not pay attention to politics. The same is said of Queen Luise during Napoleon's successful creation of the *Rheinbund*: »Die Königin ist außer sich; so wenig sie sich sonst um Politik bekümmert – sie sagt, sie habe als Gattin und Mutter nähere und heiligere Pflichten zu erfüllen –, so leidet doch ihr deutsches Herz bitter unter dieser Schmach.« (104) [The Queen is beside herself; as little as she concerns herself with politics – she says she has more pressing and more holy duties as wife and mother –, her German heart suffers bitterly because of this disgrace.]

Political events affect women, these passages suggest, and provide them with the opportunity to reveal their patriotism through gender-appropriate responses. Frau von Fiedler, confronted with the grisly reality of the Terror in France, clutches her hand to her heart. Luise, upon learning that a sizeable amount of the former Holy Roman Empire of the German Nation has put itself under the protection of Napoleon, »suffers« as if she had been physically wounded.

Gabriele, more than the royal children, becomes the object of Luise's pedagogical efforts. But the lessons Luise has to teach Germany's children are, it appears, difficult to absorb in the face of historical reality. The historical record indicates that Luise died in 1810, at the age of thirty-four, from a chronic lung ailment. Biographies – and hagiographies – of the queen immediately interpreted her death, however, as the direct result of the Napoleonic occupation of Prussia: by taking Jena, then Berlin, and finally Magdeburg from her, Napoleon had robbed her not only of her home. He had subjected her to such physical and emotional privation that her death could easily be interpreted to have come at his hands. Augusti's narrative echoes the memoirs of Countess Voss and numerous adulatory biographies of Luise when she has Gabriele recount in a letter to her mother,

»Mein armer König! Was muß er empfunden haben, als er im letzten Frühjahr in Dresden erscheinen und Napoleons ergebenen Diener spielen mußte! Als der herzlose Mann ihn mit der Frage empfing: Sie sind Witwer? Wahrlich, er konnte es ganz genau wissen, daß er selbst der Mörder unserer Engelskönigin war, daß nur seine Bosheit und Tücke ihr das schöne Herz gebrochen hatte!« (178-9)

[My poor King! What must he have felt last spring in Dresden when he had to make an appearance and play Napoleon's faithful servant! As that heartless man saw him and asked, You are widowed? Indeed, he should know perfectly well that he himself murdered our angelic queen; that only his malice and spite broke her lovely heart!]

Gabriele personalizes political relations between Prussia and France and turns them into a family drama between Bonaparte and the Hohenzollern family. This personalization reflects the pedagogical priorities of girls' political education in Augusti's era but also leads into dangerous emotional and political territory for Gabriele. She does not react appropriately to Luise's death. She does not clutch her hand to her heart as her mother would have done; she feels personally wounded, like Luise did when she heard of the formation of the Rheinbund, but unlike Luise, Gabriele initially yearns for revenge.

Gabriele eventually softens her tone, which reflects both a general nineteenth-century trend and a specific, gendered response to political events. Non-fictional Germans certainly shared Gabriele's belligerent anti-French attitude – the songs of the Wars of Liberation testify to that – but this was seen by many as not consistent with Luise's own values. While it remains appropriate to question the motives of neighboring France, even to wish for its defeat on the battlefield, Gabriele's lingering personal anger and desire for revenge are decidedly unfeminine and inappropriate for her. She realizes the error of her thinking in a moment before Rauch's sculpture of the late queen that decorates her sarcophagus in the mausoleum in Charlottenburg and tells her

»›O meine Luise, [...] deinem Vorbilde bin ich nicht gefolgt, als ich mein Herz dem Haß und Rachedurst öffnete; vor dir hätte ich nur lernen können, zu dulden und zu tragen, zu vergeben und zu hoffen, und alles dem gerechten Richter anheimzustellen‹«. (239).

[›O my Luise, [...] I did not follow your example when I opened my heart to hate and vengeance; from you I could only have learned to bear and to tolerate, to forgive and to hope, and to leave everything to the heavenly judge.‹]

Although historical fiction like Augusti's certainly aimed to incite an emotional nationalist response from its young readers, this author as well as the others who wrote for a female audience was at pains to ensure that the historical and political education they were providing in their texts was appropriate for young women. Augusti expressly refutes the lust for revenge, as well as other passions, in her novels and shows characters turning intense feelings into a nationally useful state of mind.

Luise stories such as Augusti's demonstrate that emotional connections between women and the state should not be confined to women like Luise, who represents the state. Rather, the intertwining pedagogical and social discourses of politics, romance, history, legend, and nation cooperated in encouraging this sort of identification on the part of all middle-class women. Schools, churches, and the family library all created and reinforced a pattern of identification with and affection for the German nation and an understanding of their role as women in it. By directing the attention of women and girls towards the personalities, character traits, and physical descriptions of national heroes and leaders, literature and formal education created an atmosphere in which a woman was expected to respond emotionally rather than rationally or politically to events of national importance.

This relationship of women to politics emphasizes the passivity and emotionality of German women. It encourages them to view their familial relationships in light of their national significance but not to undertake political action on behalf of their patriotic convictions. Upon meeting Count Malthême years later when accompanying Luise to Tilsit and discovering the count is an officer in Napoleon's guard, Gabriele rejects his offer of friendship and even marriage. Here, she revisits the seductiveness of her youthful friendship with the Count, rejecting the earlier appeal of the French aristocrat in favor of the earnestness and seriousness of her current duties as Luise's companion and loyal German woman.

»›Einst, wäre es Ihnen nicht schwer geworden, das unerfahrene Kind für sich zu gewinnen, aber damals wollten Sie nur das vermeintliche, reiche Erbe erwerben; das thörichte, kleine Herz galt Ihnen nichts. Jetzt liegt zwischen dem Günstling des Kaisers Napoleon und der Freundin der Königin Luise eine Kluft, die durch nichts auszufüllen ist; nie könnte ich daran denken, dem Feinde meines Vaterlandes meine Hand zu reichen.‹« (150)

[›Once it would not have been difficult for you to win the inexperienced child over, but back then you only wanted the supposedly rich inheritance; the foolish little heart meant nothing to you. Now there is a gulf between the favorite of Emperor Napoleon and the friend of Queen Luise that cannot be bridged. I could never think of giving my hand to my Fatherland's enemy.‹]

Women, in other words, should represent the values and priorities of their nation but primarily by reflecting national values in their interpersonal relationships. Gabriele, along with myriad fictional women who populate nationally-minded novels of the period, learns to find emotional fulfillment by aligning the desires of her heart with the supposed needs of her country.

Since, in the nineteenth century, success for women of Gabriele's class resided solely in the acquisition of an appropriate husband, the lessons about love and the feminine role in courtship and marriage that Augusti weaves into her tale were of critical interest – and importance – to her young readers. In Gabriele's case, her seduction by Count Malthême, though not complete, stands in for the seductiveness of all things French: the supposed gaiety of aristocratic life at Versailles, the odd combination of loose morals (as far as the Germans were concerned) and rigid propriety that characterized family relationships, and – very important for young women – fashion and style.[1] Augusti's readers learn that young women are educated differently in France. Furthermore, Gabriele's encounters with her French sister-in-law, Marion, teach her that the propriety and family loyalty that are the norm for a German woman might not be so common on the other side of the Rhine.

By following Luise's guide, Gabriele learns to tend to her heart and emotions in a nationally significant way. She sees her own desires in the designs of patriarchy and has found fulfillment in self-denial and living for other. Sacrificing any personal desire for family or home, Gabriele follows her friend Luise into a cold and unfriendly exile. She has followed Luise's lead not only in self-sacrifice for the national cause, but also by consciously rejecting the temptations of France and defining herself as a German woman. In this respect, Gabriele goes through a maturation and development similar to the development of the national idea in the nineteenth century. The promise and the loathing inspired by the French Revolution, the exuberance of the Wars of Revolution, and finally the mature and self-confident empire are echoed in Gabriele's own emotional development. Luise's pupil matures into the ideal German woman, worthy of continuing Luise's legacy.

Gabriele's development reflects Wülfing's final stage of the Luise myth: National Consolidation. The novel shows Gabriele united with her king and aware of the special, civilizing mission of the German middle class, which represented the special destiny of Germany in Europe. As a figure of identification, Gabriele shows readers that even girls, who do not receive a share of the attention and glory reserved for the men in their families and community in times of national need or crisis, can integrate their own experiences and perceptions into what was generally perceived as history, i.e. the lives and actions of statesmen, kings, and warriors.

Elisabeth Halden's historical novel, *Queen Luise* (1893), covers much the same time period and events as Augusti's *Scharfeneck* and also features a young protagonist who serves as a primary vehicle for reader identification. As with Gabriele, young Johanna's story is about a young girl who grows into a woman at Luise's side. The productive fantasy of bringing one's personal desires into harmony with the perceived needs of the nation is the same in both novels. But whereas Gabriele's romantic encounter in *The Heirs of Scharfeneck* provides August with an opportunity to articulate the temptations of France and structure a patriotic and emotional rejection of the same, Johanna's story is a positive model for young romance. In the figure of Johanna are combined the ideal female qualities of loyalty to family and state, knowledge and appreciation of German literature and culture, and a patriotic German heart that seeks its mate.

The creation of a protagonist who is Luise's official reader allows Halden to emphasize girls' cultural education. By showing Luise engaged in the project of middle-class self betterment – reading German literature and history, learning about Germany's destiny in Europe and her place within that national community – Halden doubles up on the lessons of nation and female identity in her narrative. Luise reading, Luise being read to by a daughter of the middle class, and Luise and the women in her circle discussing German literature all provide an opportunity to witness the manner in which the bourgeoisie constructed their social class and their national identity along cultural lines. With the ascension of the middle classes to political and economic authority in Germany, educated writers and readers could easily begin to insert themselves and their middle-class values and experiences into the life stories of kings and queens. Reader identification with Queen Luise was not merely a matter of allowing young female readers a fairy-tale fantasy story in which they, as in their childhoods, played the role of the princess or queen. It was also a matter of reminding them that they, as middle-class girls, had much in common with the most exemplary Queen in the Hohenzollern dynasty, that their values and life experiences were the same, and that this consistency over time constituted much of the foundation upon which Germany as a cultural and national entity rested. Reading literature, Queen Luise's experiences show the young readers of her biographies, was one of the primary ways in which a German woman could demonstrate her emotional involvement in her nation and its history.

The text shows both Luise and Friedrich Wilhelm and Johanna and her betrothed, Pastor Hillern, articulating their love for each other though an appreciation of German literature. Pastor Hillern, in very Rousseauean fashion, gives young Johanna reading lists. He tells her that, although she certainly is free to enjoy *Götz*, Klopstock's odes, and Schiller's *Don Carlos*, these works might be too mature for her. He suggests instead that she read Voß's »dear Luise« and Goethe's *Hermann and Dorothea* (39). In a passage cribbed from Eylert's court history, Friedrich Wilhelm exclaims upon first seeing Luise, »Sie, oder keine sonst auf Erden!« [she, or none other on this earth!], a verse from Schiller's *Die Braut von Messina* (*The Bride of Messina*). Both of these romantic relationships, then, participate in the common nineteenth-century discourse insisted that classical German authors – Schiller and Goethe, Herder and Jean Paul – wrote works that not only entertained and edified, but that also expressed the deepest truths of German nature and revealed the essence of the German character. It is especially telling that *The Bride of Messina* was first published in 1803, a full ten years after Luise and Friedrich Wilhelm first met and fell in love. The memoirs of Eylert and Voss, as well as the biography of Luise published by her friend Caroline von Berg in 1814, contributed to both the mythologizing of Luise and to the conflation of the national historical narrative-represented by the King and Queen – with the narrative of German cultural supremacy constructed around the works of German classicism.

Halden's narrative of Luise and Johanna's literary activity features the pair reading classical German literature, as well as popular histories that help them locate themselves and their tumultuous political era within a broader narrative of German cultural history. Friedrich Adami, whose 1868 biography of Luise serves as an obvious source for many fictional treatments of her life, praises Luise's ability to relate literature to her life, to absorb from Goethe and Schiller and others lessons about her own nature as a German and a woman. He instructs his readers, »Und Alles, was sie las und hörte, fruchtete ihr: denn durch die eigenthümliche Art, wie sie Schrift und Rede in sich aufnahm, verwandelte sie Alles gleichsam in ihren Geist« (85) [Everything that [Luise] read and heard bore fruit for her: for due to the characteristic manner in which she took in the written and spoken word, it was all converted, as it were, in her mind]. Adami, and Halden with him, do not specifically tell their readers what Luise's »characteristic manner« of reading was, but they certainly imply that she selected her texts well and used them to their intended purpose – to edify and educate and, importantly, to enter into a state of emotional patriotism. The reading list Halden provides covers fiction, poetry, and works of history, each read according to its usefulness for the queen's present situation or state of mind.

Armed with Schiller's *Wilhelm Tell* and historical works, Luise and Johanna are well-equipped to withstand the tribulations visited on them by Napoleon. During negotiations in Tilsit with Napoleon, Johanna »las ihr Schillers Wilhelm Tell in diesen ernsten Tagen vor, und oft mußte sie eine Stelle voll vaterländischer Begeisterung und leidenschaftlicher Freiheitsliebe wiederholen, weil sie der Königin so ganz aus dem Herzen kam« (101) [read to her from Schiller's *Wilhelm Tell* during these serious times, and she often had to repeat a passage full of patriotic enthusiasm and passionate love of liberty, because these seemed to come straight from the queen's heart]. *Wilhelm Tell*, one of the most frequently read classics in girls' schools, serves here as a connection between the world of Queen Luise and its values and the world of the later nineteenth-century middle-class girls. By showing Luise and Johanna reading Schiller and using his play to articulate their own hopes for Germany in the face of Napoleon's occupation, Halden provides her ideal readers with a pattern for national involvement that transforms the limitations of the traditional, receptive female role in public discourse into an activity – reading – that constitutes and consolidates certain notions of national community and belonging.

Reading German classics and popular histories not only prepares these women for their encounter with Napoleon by reminding them of both the progress of German civilization and the remarkable qualities of German men and women. Reading in and of itself, as demonstrated by Luise, contributes to that very cultural progress. Luise, and women who share her cultural values and assumptions, takes responsibility for learning and preserving German culture. She will pass these values on to her children even in the face of the virtual disintegration of sovereign German lands. At one point in Halden's narrative, Luise tells Friedrich Wilhelm that reading German literature is her way for making up for a Francophone education. »Was an dem Kinde versäumt wird, das muß die Frau nachholen. Ich will eindringen in das deutsche Geistesleben, seine Dichter sollen mich in das Wesen des deutschen Volkes einführen.« (61) [What the child neglected must be made up by the woman. I want to penetrate into the intellectual life of Germany; his poets will introduce me to the nature of the German people.] As articulated by Luise, the knowledge and proper use of German literature and cultural history guarantees the preservation of preservation of German culture and furthers the progress of German history. Napoleon, in this narrative, represents merely a blip on the German historical radar. Luise represents the link between Germany as it existed before Napoleon's occupation and the German Empire at the end of the century. In the mythologizing narrative of her life, her role as reader, preserver, and supporter of German literature lends her the cultural authority that makes her role as historical bridge possible.

The young readers of Halden and Augusti's fiction see their education, their family's cultural values, and their relationship to the broader national community reflected in these stories about Luise's life. In reading about figures such as Johanna and Gabriele and the lessons they learn from Luise, these young readers learn to make sense of history and make sense of their role as middle-class German women. They learn that their emotional and intellectual life is not inconsequential to their national community. Rather, the timeless qualities that characterize them, as well as their ancestor Luise, provide the necessary congruity between generations of Germans. The role of the young woman, perched on the cusp of motherhood and home life, is to ensure the continuity of German culture by way of guaranteeing the continuity of the ideal of the German woman.

The Luise myth was a crucial component of the narrative of German national history in the nineteenth century. As Brent Petersen, Wulf Wülfing, and Günter de Bruyn have discussed, Luise represented an easily idealized, non-political link to a pre-Napoleonic German past, upon which the generation of Empire could draw in creating their positivist, nationalist narrative of German civilization.[2] I contend that the utility of the Luise myth for encouraging women – especially young women – to identify emotionally with the national project is an equally important and as yet unexamined aspect of that myth's power. Through carefully constructed stories that capitalize on Luise's bourgeois appeal and the qualities that made her the figure of an ideal German woman, authors such as Augusti and Halden incorporate young women's stories into the national narrative.

The gendered nationalist discourse that informs Augusti and Halden's fiction suggests to the reader that their role in holding up Germany –comprised as it is of seemingly small domestic acts such as reading, displaying loyalty to one's family, and raising children – is critically important to the cultural mission of Germany within Europe. In particular, by aligning their hearts with the nation, by choosing romantic alliances that reflect national cultural values, girls have a significant opportunity to participate in the building and consolidation of the German nation.

–Kansas State University

## Notes

All translations in this paper are my own.

1 The appearance of Malthême in the narrative is borrowed from one of Augusti's sources, Gustav Freytag's *Die Ahnen* (*The Ancestors*), where a French branch of the family also features prominently. However, Augusti's treatment of the count in *The Heirs of Scharfeneck* differs from Freytag's narrative in her instrumentalization of Malthême as a representative for the negative qualities of the French.

2 The authors of popular nineteenth-century fiction for girls were, of course, not the first to narrativize Luise's life story in the service of the Prusso-German national telos. In fact, the mythologizing of Luise as an angel for the Prussian cause began during her lifetime. See: Novalis, *Glaube und Liebe oder der König und die Königin* (1798); Kleist, *Prinz Friedrich von Homburg* (1810), and »An die Königin von Preussen (zum 10. März 1810)«, and Theodor Körner, »Vor Rauchs Büste der Königin Luise« (1812).

## Works Cited


Askey, Jennifer. The Girl's Library: Nationalism, Popular Literature, and Girls' Education in Wilhelminian Germany. Diss. Washington University, St. Louis. 2003.

Augusti, Brigitte [Auguste Plehn]. *Die Erben von Scharfeneck. Bilder aus der Zeit der Königin Luise.* 2nd ed. Vol. 5. *An Deutschem Herd. Kulturgeschichtliche Erzählungen aus alter und neuer Zeit. Mit besonderer Berücksichtigung des Lebens der deutschen Frauen.* Leipzig: Ferdinand Hirt & Sohn, 1889.

De Bruyn, Günter. *Preußens Luise. Vom Entstehen und Vergehen einer Legende.* Berlin: Seidler, 2001.

Halden, Elisabeth [Agnes Breitzmann]. *Königin Luise.* Berlin: Verlag von Hermann J. Meidinger, 1893.

Paldamus, Friedrich C. *Deutsches Lesebuch. Nach Maßgabe der Bestimmungen von vom 31. Mai 1894 für höhere Mädchenschulen.* Frankfurt/M: Moritz Diesterweg, 1903.

Petersen, Brent. *History, Fiction, and Germany: Writing the Nineteenth-Century Nation.* Detroit: Wayne State University Press, 2005.

Wülfing, Wulf. »Die Heilige Luise von Preußen. Zur Mythisierung einer Figur der Geschichte in der deutschen Literatur des 19. Jahrhunderts«, *Bewegung und Stillstand in Metaphern und Mythen. Fallstudien zum Verhältnis von elementarem Wissen und Literatur im 19. Jahrhundert.* Eds. Jürgen Link and Wulf Wülfing. Stuttgart: Klett-Cotta, 1984. 233-73.

# Thwarted Enemy. Eros and Self-Assertion in Gertrud Kolmar's Poem Cycle *Napoleon und Marie* (1920–21)

*Barbara Besslich*

At the beginning of the 20th Century, the subject of Napoleon was a popular one in German literature. And among the German literature dedicated to Napoleon from this time, very little of it can be said to be anti-Napoleonic. Whereas both journalists and poets during the Wars of Liberation demonized Napoleon as the Antichrist and the progeny of hell, he was only rarely seen as a national enemy in German literature after 1821. For 19th–century Germans, Napoleon became the focus of epigonal longings, evoking a past greatness that transcended the restrictions of nationality. He had already become a paragon of the autonomous, self-creative genius for German poets. Heinrich Heine praised him as the »weltlichen Heiland« [worldly savior]; Goethe named him a »Kompendium der Welt« [compendium of the world]; Friedrich Hebbel saw himself in a dream as Napoleon's valet; Nietzsche designated him as the »Synthesis von Unmensch und Übermensch« [synthesis of brute and *Übermensch*];[1] and a less sophisticated strand of Nietzsche reception thought to have found in him the historically realized »Übermensch«.

In the 20th Century, Napoleon gradually became woven into a German national mythology. The circle around Stefan George celebrated him as a great man of action and propagated the astonishing notion of a »Wesensgleiche von Napoleon und den Deutschen« [essential similarity between Napoleon and the Germans] (Vallentin, *Napoleon und die Deutschen* 9f). By the 1920s critics of such acts of appropriation of an historical figure were already mocking the way their contemporaries represented »Napoleon I. als Nationalhelden der Deutschen« (Napoleon I as the national hero of the Germans; Hegemann, *Napoleon oder »Kniefall vor dem Heros«*, unpaginated dedication page). Thus many texts devoted to Napoleon managed to achieve the paradoxical status of being German nationalist, critical of France, and inspired by Napoleon at the same time.[2] Beyond this unambiguously heroicizing, nationalistic appropriation of Napoleon, one finds in German Expressionism a more complex Napoleon-inspired literature, one that demonizes the Emperor and antagonizes bourgeois Wilhelminian hero worship. Early Expressionist drama de-idealizes Napoleon – but it does not demythologize him; he rather becomes resuscitated as a myth, albeit one with a negative bent. For the Expressionist poet Georg Heym, Napoleon represented the perfect vehicle to catapult himself out of Wilhelminian *ennui*, and to conjure up an elementary kinesis through his Napoleonic projection. Heym found inspiration in Napoleon as the representative of the extraordinary and the extreme. Napoleon became the catalyst for a heroic vitalism; he became the anti-bourgeois *par excellence*. His deviation from social, political and moral norms and his final failure in 1815 are ultimately what made him so alluring and »heroic« in the Expressionistic sense. It is the image of the haughty, power-obsessed Napoleon which interested Expressionism, the man who, in his self-overestimation, hurls himself from the *juste milieu* into a vitalism of extremes. Here, the degree of extremism counted for more than any actual success. In the wake of Heym's lyric poetry and Hermann Essig's drama *Napoleons Aufstieg* [The Rise of Napoleon], Napoleon became a subject suitable for treatment by the literary avant-garde (Besslich 2002). Heym's sonnet cycle *Mont St. Jean* stylizes battle as the encapsulation of intensified living. Even in his Napoleon-related texts from before 1914, Heym was already rehearsing the glorification of the war to come. Gertrud Kolmar's poem cycle *Napoleon und Marie*, with its labored emphasis on victimhood and self-sacrifice, also reveals a profound longing for heroism and for an intensive participation in a great moment in history. From this perspective Kolmar's work approaches the kind of demonization of Napoleon found in Expressionism. However, Kolmar paints a much more ambivalent portrait of Napoleon than Heym, one presented to the reader from the vantage point of his thwarted enemy: Marie Walewska.

## Gertrud Kolmar and Napoleon

In the poem cycle *Napoleon und Marie*, the young Gertrud Kolmar traces the relationship between Napoleon and the Polish countess Marie Walewska back to its beginning in 1807. The date of origin of the cycle is still disputed; while Johanna Woltmann dates the cycle at 1912 (cf. Woltmann, *Gertrud Kolmar* 68), the commentator of the Göttingen edition of Kolmar's works, Regine Nörtemann (Kolmar, *Das lyrische Werk* 122), insists on a later period between 1920–1921. The German-Jewish lyric poet Gertrud Kolmar (1894–1943) was 27 years old in 1921, and had by then already published a volume of her poetry.

Napoleon himself does not have a voice in Kolmar's work; only through the retrospective gaze of his thwarted enemy Marie does one receive accounts of respective stages of their encounter. The cycle places an initial stress upon the difficult process of establishing a rapport (*Die Alte hat das Kästchen heimlich hergestellt, Murat, Das Zeichen, Stolz, Im Morgen*) [*The Old Woman Put the Box here in Secret, Murat, The Sign, Pride, In the Morning*], whereupon it recalls love in stormy times (*Geschichte, Das Schwertlied, Die Sterne*) [*History, The Song of the Sword, The Stars*], directs the reader's attention to marginal figures (*Junot, Rustan*), and finally conjures darkly prognostic images of Napoleon's fall (*Nichts, Irgendwo in Rußland*) [*Nothing, Somewhere in Russia*]. From Marie's perspective, the »Rollengedichte« [role poems] show both how the Polish nobility exerted its influence at the beginning of the affair and Marie's initial antagonism. Antipathy to politics is transformed into an erotic fascination with Napoleon's »Lippen, die vernichteten, mich küßten« (Lips that annihilated, kissed me).[3] Marie's initial aristocratic pride in the face of the »upstart« Bonaparte must be given particular consideration in the present analysis. Psychological introspection reveals the contradiction between amorous inclination and political duty; the exaggerated gestures of victimhood and self-sacrifice betray a longing for heroism and for greater participation in a momentous time: »O, ein Mann sein! Ja, ein Held! « [Oh, to be a man! Yes, a hero!].[4]

Not untouched by the Expressionism of her time, Kolmar shared the fascination for Napoleon as a subject of heroic lyricist poetry with Georg Heym, whose sonnet cycle *Mont St. Jean* depicts the battle of Waterloo as the end of an age of heroes. Kolmar had already written a sentimental poem entitled *St. Helena* in 1910, at the early age of 15.[5] Whereas Heym chose the field of battle as his poetical backdrop, Kolmar reflects – both in her *St. Helena* poem and in her *Napoleon und Marie* cycle – the vitalistic longing engendered in lean times for the private realm. However, Marie's look at politics from inside the boudoir also reflects a time of pervasive politicization in which the Polish nobility attempted to exert its influence on the Emperor by amorous means outside of the framework of political institutions.

The poem cycle *Napoleon und Marie* represents the transition between the conventionality in form and content of the incipient phase of Kolmar's lyrical production to the idiosyncracy characteristic of her literary output of the late 1920s and the 1930s, with its suggestive metaphors and hymnic tones.[6] With *Napoleon und Marie*, Kolmar turned from autobiographically inspired lyric poetry to historical subjects. But whereas her poetic treatment of Robespierre in later years represents a direct confrontation with the political realm, in *Napoleon und Marie* the political is mediated by the private; from the intimate viewpoint granted by Marie, the political situation remains unclear.[7] What begins as a fierce confrontation with the usurper Napoleon becomes pacified into profuse lyricism. Some poems simulate lyricized journal entries, while others take on features characteristic of the ballad. Kolmar shows the utmost virtuosity in her juxtaposition of varying verse forms and in her arrangement, in abrupt alternation, of dreamy tercets (*Im Morgen*) [*In the Morning*] and martial stanzas (*Das Schwertlied*) [*The Song of the Sword*]. Though in terms of content certainly pro-Napoleonic, the enthusiasm expressed in these stanzas is nevertheless indebted to Theodor Körner's lyric poetry of the Wars of Liberation. As a result of the inherent tension between form and content thus produced, the war poems manifest in poetic form the antagonism between loving devotion and political self-assertion. Even the title of Kolmar's *Schwertlied* bears a direct allusion to Körner's own *Schwertlied.* The following analysis will address the question of how to characterize the intertextual relationship between these two poems more closely.

The encounter between Marie Walewska and Napoleon was already a popular literary subject. Before Gertrud Kolmar's poem cycle, Karl Biesendahl had based a tragedy on the same topic, and both Willy Rath and Anton Strambowiski would write Walewska-based dramas after her.[8] Later, the Hollywood film *Conquest* (1937), which also portrayed the amorous episode, would achieve popularity because of its casting of Greta Garbo as Marie. As early as 1920, a German film based on the same subject had already been made by Otto Rippert, entitled *Gräfin Walewska. Napoleons Liebe* [*Countess Walewska. The Love of Napoleon*] and starring Rudolf Lettinger as Napoleon. Whether or not Gertrud Kolmar knew this film is a matter of conjecture.[9]

## Marie's Defence: Feminine Pride, Aristocratic Resentment, and Contempt for the Revolution

The young Polish countess Maria Walewska met Napoleon in Warsaw in the year 1807, and after her initial resistance to his advances, they had an affair. The Poles desired the establishment of an independent Polish state; in Maria Walewska they saw a way to exert influence on the Emperor to this end. Napoleon himself, however, had no interest in an independent Polish state (Lefebvre, *Napoleon* 228f). The relationship between Napoleon and Maria Walewska lasted approximately three years. They met in Paris in 1808 and in Austria in 1809. In 1810, Maria bore Napoleon a son.[10] In the following one and a half years, Maria Walewska lived in France, whereupon she returned to Poland in 1812 in order to be near Napoleon during his Russian military campaign, although she actually had very few further opportunities to see him. In 1814, she visited him once more on Elba, and in 1816, she was married to her second husband Count Ornano. She died in 1817 at the age of 31.

Kolmar probably drew her sources from the memoirs of Napoleon's valet (Wairy, originally published in 1830) and from Frédéric Masson's work *Napoléon et les Femmes* (originally published in 1894). In his account, Masson gives the impression that Marie Walewska's involvement with Napoleon was a politically calculated act in the service of the Polish people.[11] It is from his studies that Kolmar drew the anecdote relating how Napoleon had a pearl necklace sent to Marie along with the message that putting on and touching the necklace during a soirée would be the signal for her consent to a love affair. This situation forms the thematic basis for the first three poems of the cycle. The first poem (*Widmung* or *Die Alte hat das Kästchen heimlich hergestellt*) [*Dedication* or *The Old Woman Put the Box here in Secret*], which contains four stanzas, presents Marie upon receiving the jewelry box. While the first stanza focuses on the bearer of the gift (»die Alte«) [The Old Woman] and the last stanza makes a transition to Marie's husband, the two middle stanzas express Marie's thoughts relating to the Emperor's gift itself (*Die Alte hat das Kästchen heimlich hergestellt* 201):

Auf samtnem Grund ein zartes zwiegeschlung'nes Band:
Ich liebe Perlen sehr. Ich lieb' ihr weiches Rinnen.
Sie flossen fein und leicht durch meine weiße Hand,
Sie rieselten herab wie köstlich kühler Sand
und krochen träge hin wie kleine Spinnen.

Dann möcht' ich träumen, denn ich lächelte: »Despot!
Du sendest mir die Tränen, die dein Schwert vergossen.«
Das rote Sammetkissen schien mir blutig rot.
Ich lächelte im Traum; auch ich war ja bedroht:
glänzt so das Blut, das deiner Gier geflossen?

[Upon a velvety base a delicate double-coiled band:
I love pearls dearly. I love them flowing smooth.
They ran smartly and easily through my white hand,
They trickled down like cool priceless sand
and crawled off languidly like little spiders.

Then I'd like to dream, for I'd smiled: »Despot!
You send me the tears your sword spilled.«
The red velvet pillow seemed blood red to me.
I smiled in my dream; even as I was also threatened:
Does the blood gleam so, which flowed for your greed?]

The regularly flowing structure of the iambic pentameters and hexameters, interwoven both through cross rhymes and envelope rhymes, imitates the »zwiegeschlung'ne[] Band« [double-coiled band] (v. 6) of the necklace, which both fascinates Marie and makes her shudder at the same time. The comparison of the pearls with »little spiders crawling off lazily« (v. 10) relativizes the affirmation expressed in the previous simile (»wie köstlich kühler Sand« [like cool priceless sand] (v. 9)) and lends particular plasticity to the ambivalence of Marie's feelings. She perceives the attempted seduction as a threat. Marie's apostrophe to Napoleon (v. 11f) adopts the traditional pearls-as-tears trope in order to transform it to »Tränen, die dein Schwert vergossen« [tears your sword spilled] (v. 12). Marie thus embeds Napoleon's courtship in an imagery of war, one that increases in intensity when the »rote Sammetkissen« [red velvet pillow] appears to her to be »blutig rot« [blood red] (v. 13), which evokes the blood of Napoleon's victims in battle. Already here, the concluding question: »Glänzt so das Blut, das deiner Gier geflossen?« [Does the blood gleam so, which flowed for your greed] (v. 15) suggests a Marie Walewska who, by virtue of her rhetorically placed question, attempts to liberate herself from the spell of seduction cast upon her. The last verses of the first poem show Marie's incipient self-alienation, when she »[sich] selbst den Tag nicht mehr im Spiegel an[sah]« [looked at herself in the mirror no more that day] (v. 19).

Still, Marie is capable of coming back to reason and shielding herself against the imperious gestures on the part of the courting Napoleon. *Das Zeichen* [*The Sign*] , the third poem of the cycle and, with its 175 verses, also the longest, affords the reader a look at Marie's inner conflict. Whereas the first poem, consisting of four equal stanzas of five verses each (all in regularly declining, mostly six-footed iambic meter), formally reproduces the external calmness of the represented events, *Das Zeichen*'s stanzaic irregularity and rhymelessness (as well as the reduction of its verses to five feet) already indicate the internal agitation of the speaker. Marschall Duroc informs Marie of the Emperor's expectation that she lay her »rechte Hand zum Herzen« [right hand on her heart] upon the pearl necklace as a sign of her consent to the liaison (*Das Zeichen* 203). In her indignation, Marie rebuffs this request; in a monolog set apart in quotation marks, whose blank verse dramatizes the lyrical scene, she presents herself as the aristocratic enemy of the parvenu Bonaparte (*Das Zeichen* 203):

Und ich riß aus samt'nem Schrein die Kette,
Seine Kette, Seine schöne Gabe,
Warf sie wild, gleich gift'ger, ekler Natter
In den Winkel. »Mag ein Dieb sie finden!
Denn die Frauen Polens, edle Frauen
– Mag ihr Sinn auch tanzen – nein, sie gleichen
Nimmer noch den Dirnen Deiner Hauptstadt,
Die zu kaufen sind um Perlenschnüre!
Ob der Herr der Christenheit dich salbte,
Ob vor Deinem kleinen schwarzen Hute
Uralt gold'ner Kronen Glanz erblaßte,
Ob dir tausend gunstbegier'ge Schreiber
Tausend Reihen hoher Ahnen malen –
Als Napoleon bleibst du Bonaparte:
Erbe und Genoß der Königsschlächter,
Pöbelliebling, Held der Soldateska,
Roher Kriegsmann stets von nied'ren Sitten,
Ohne Maß und Feinheit, ohne Anstand:
Nein, dem stolzen Adel der Laczinski
Und dem alten Adel der Walewski
Darf dein neues Blut sich nie vermischen!

[And from the velvety shrine I pulled the chain,
His chain, his beautiful gift,
I flung it fiercely into the corner,
Like it were a viper, poisonous, repulsive.
»May a thief find it!
For Poland's women, noble women,
– May their senses also spin – they will never

Resemble the whores in your capital,
Who can be bought for a string of pearls!
If the lord of Christendom anointed you,
If, before your small black hat
The gleam of ancient golden crowns paled,
If a thousand writers craving favor
Painted a thousand ranks of lofty ancestors for you –
As Napoleon you remain Bonaparte:
Heir and companion to slaughterer of kings,
The rabble's darling, hero of the soldiery,
A raw warrior constantly of lower customs,
Without measure and finesse, unmannered:
No, your new blood may never mingle
With the proud nobility of the Laczinskis
With the old nobility of the Walewskis!]

Marie's anger not only reflects the indignation of one whose expected amatory services are to be recompensed materially with jewelry, it also clearly betrays her aristocratic consciousness. The anti-Napoleonic sentiment which Kolmar has Marie express in this poem could also be a reference to the historically verifiable fact that, during her journey to Rome between 1804-1805, Marie had met Madame de Staël, one of Napoleon's bitterest enemies.[12]

Whereas the beginning of the apostrophe to Napoleon engages in national stereotyping by pitting the »Frauen Polens« [Poland's women] (v. 14) against the »Dirnen Deiner Hauptstadt« [the whores in your capital] (v. 16), the reflections which follow reveal Marie's political conviction. Neither the imperial coronation of 1804, in the presence of the Pope, nor the artificial genealogical links forged with clear political intent could impress her. For Marie, even if »[ihm] tausend gunstbegier'ge Schreiber | Tausend Reihen hoher Ahnen malen« [a thousand writers craving favor / Painted a thousand ranks of lofty ancestors (for him)] (v. 21f), no retroactive fabrication of family tradition can belie the truth of his bourgeois ancestry.

Marie is not only concerned in this context with the violation of birth-endowed social status, but also with her own ideological opposition toward revolution. In Napoleon, who stood in military service to the Directory, she sees the »Erbe und Genoß der Königsschlächter« [Heir and companion to slaughterers of kings] (v. 24); Napoleon had, after all, also been responsible for stopping, by order of the Directory, the rebellion of the Paris sections led by royalists in 1795. Marie's hopes of liberating Poland aren't strong enough to displace her aversion to the republic. An antirevolutionary attitude outweighs all nationalistic aspirations. Marie has absolutely no sympathy with the empire's popularist orientation and the military foundations of its rule. She accordingly berates Napoleon as »Pöbelliebling, Held der Soldateska« [The rabble's darling, hero of the soldiery] (v. 25). The »kleine[r] schwarze[r] Hut[ ]« [small black hat] (v. 19) which styled the Emperor as man of the people is, for Marie, no replacement for the traditional insignia of monarchal rule, the »Uralt gold'n[e] Kronen« [ancient golden crowns] (v. 20). His self-coronation is no substitute for the legitimacy granted by divine grace alone. Marie's perception that Napoleon himself is not equal to his assumed rank is succinctly expressed in the way his bourgeois family name is set against the name he used as Emperor: »Als Napoleon bleibst du Bonaparte« [As Napoleon you remain Bonaparte] (v. 23).

## The Napoleonic Liaison as a Sacrifice to the People

Marie is, however, incapable of remaining autonomous in her resistance, being placed under pressure to submit to Napoleon's advances by the Polish nobility who see it as her patriotic duty. More vocal than anybody else in making a case for the liaison with the bourgeois parvenu was Marie's husband, Count Anastasius Colonna-Walewski, whom she coldly and contemptuously names the »Greis« [elderly man] (v. 40). At the time referred to in Kolmar's poem, Count Anastasius Colonna-Walewski was 72 years old, his wife Marie merely 21.

Marie, harassed by the expectations placed upon her, imagines that the soirée, which both Napoleon and Polish royalty hope will cement an amorous bond, is her funeral feast. In Marie's Expressionistic gaze, the other guests metamorphose into grotesque, voyeuristic phantoms: »An langer Tafel schmausten | Farb'ge Schemen, grinsende Gespenste.« [At a long table feast / colorful phantoms, grinning specters.] (v. 57). Though Kolmar's work was normally closer to that of the French Symbolists than that of her German Expressionist contemporaries, she exploits Expressionist imagery in this passage in order to give poetic form to the moment of greatest uncertainty of identity. The ghost metaphor in reference to the gathering of aristocrats is further developed later in the poem: »Um mich neckten sich die flachen Schatten | [...] Lauter zischelten die bunten

Schemen, | Streckten Finger aus mit scharfen Nägeln, | Witterten mir nach mit spitzen Nasen, | Ließen Spott auf mich herniedersausen, | Fein, gleich dünnen Geißeln. Ich empfand sie.« [Flat shadows bantered about me […] Louder hissed the colorful phantoms, / Extending sharp-nailed fingers, / Sniffing me out with pointed noses, / Whipping down ridicule onto me, / Fine, like narrow lashes. I sensed them](v. 110 and 126–130).

Marschall Duroc, constantly trying to persuade Marie, uses rational argumentation as a Frenchman to rouse a feeling of national duty in a Pole. The poem renders Duroc's words in direct speech: »Fühlt Ihr nicht ein Herz, seid Frau, seid Polin – | Und er kommt, um Polen zu erlösen« [Do you have no heart, be a woman, a Pole – /And he's coming to save Poland] (v. 84f). Napoleon's gaze strikes her at this very moment of distress, a gaze which she can hardly elude and which weakens her resistance. Her identity thus destabilized, she finally gives the expected *Zeichen* [*sign*], during which she comments on her own actions in such a way that the speaker and the agent appear as two separate entities:

Und ich sah – und konnte nicht erschrecken,
Eine Hand sich stetig sacht erheben,
Wie aus Marmor, groß, fast übermächtig –
[...]
Zögernd blickt ich auf mich selbst hernieder.
Und ich sah, und konnte nicht begreifen,
Leis am Tischtuch eine Hand sich heben,
Zart und zitternd und der meinen ähnlich,
Sah für ewig, ewig in Sekunden
Meine Hand auf meinem Herzen liegen – –
Dieses ist das Zeichen, das ich liebe. (v. 152–154 and 169–175).

[And I saw – and could not be frightened,
A hand rising steadily gently,
As of marble, great, almost overpowering
[…]
Reluctantly I gazed down upon myself
And saw and could not comprehend,
Softly over the tablecloth a hand rising,
Tenderly and trembling and just like my own,
Saw for ever, for ever in seconds
My hand lying upon my heart.
This is the sign which I love.]

This ego dissociation, in which the observation of one's own actions seems to take place on a plane parallel to, yet independent from, that of the actions themselves, frames the beginning of the affair as a moment in which the individual is determined by the outside world. The thwarted enemy Marie Walewska can no longer uphold her own autonomy and, with the demanded *Zeichen* [*sign*], gives the signal for her own submission to Eros.

The Polish nobility described this self-abandonment as an appropriate sacrifice to the people. The poem *Geschichte* [*History*] records the Old Testament imagery used by a Polish delegation which comes to remind Marie of her patriotic duty. While such imagery may offer increased support for the historical authenticity of the poem cycle,[13] more importantly it anticipates Kolmar's later lyric poetry, with its preoccupation with and confirmation of her Jewish identity. In her poetic treatment of the demands placed on Marie by the Polish aristocracy, Kolmar literarily prefigures her own later conflicts[14] with the subjects of Jewish sacrificial willingness and the search for female identity through self-surrender (*Geschichte,* 212):

Es haben Männer mir den Brief geschrieben
Und Männer schildern Ahasvers Gebot;
Wie dächten sie an stolzer Frauen Lieben,
Was wissen sie von scheuer Frauen Not?

»Sie haßte ihn und schürte seine Triebe,
Sag': als sie schaudernd hinsank – war das Glück?
Nein, ihres Volkes Qual galt ihre Liebe,
Und ihres Volkes Rettung war ihr Glück.«

Ich wusch wie Esther mein Gesicht in Tränen
Und lächelte dem Sieger schmerzlich zu.
Ach, meinem Herzen weint' ich meine Tränen,
Und meinem Lande lächelte ich zu.

[Men wrote me the letter
And men depict Ahasver's commandment;
How would they think of the loves of proud women,
What do they know of the needs of shy women?

»She hated him and spurred his desire,
Say now: as she collapsed shuddering – was that happiness?
No, her love was for the torment of her people
And the salvation of her people was her happiness.«

Like Esther I washed my face in tears

And smiled painfully at the conqueror.
Ah, I cried my tears for my heart
And smiled at my land]

While verses 3-8 and 13-15 reproduce Marie's reflexions, the interposed verses 9-12 cite the letter sent to her by the Polish aristocrats. The Polish delegates, repeatedly anonymized as »Männer« [men] (v. 5, 6) and thereby reduced to their sex, are characterized as aristocrats devoid of understanding. »Ahasvers Gebot« [Ahasver's commandment] (v. 6) refers to the story of Esther, told in the Old Testament book of the same name. In this story Esther, the adopted Jewish daughter of Mardocai, is able to hamper the vesir Haman's plan to murder the Jews, by virtue of the fact that she is wed to the Persian King Ahasuerus (Xerxes). The Poles hope for Marie to exert a similar influence on Napoleon as Esther did on Ahasuerus. They thus seek in Marie an amorously mediated access to the ruler. Marie accepts, stylizing herself as a national martyr and identifying herself with the Jewish sacrificial figure Esther, who risks her own life by appearing unsummoned before King Ahasuerus in order to plead for her people (Esther 4, 11). In 1937, Kolmar would write the poem *Esther*, which portrays Esther as a Jewish sacrificial figure and outsider, problematizing her identificatory function.[15]

## Kolmar's *Schwertlied*: Eros and Politics, Love and War

However, Kolmar depicts this self-sacrificial gesture in a slightly ambivalent fashion. This is shown in the *Schwertlied* [*The Song of the Sword*], which directly follows the poem *Geschichte* [*History*], in which Polish nobility demanded Marie's selfless sacrifical readiness. The *Schwertlied's* three stanzas of seven lines each already imply a formal affinity to the poetry of the Wars of Liberation. Both Max von Schenkendorf's *Jägerlied (Song of the Hunter)* and Theodor Körner's *Lied des Lützowschen Jäger-Corps bei Einweihung der Fahnen* (*Song of Lützow's hunter corps upon the consecration of flags*) used the so-called *Lutherstrophe* of seven lines. Kolmar too chooses a stanza of seven lines, and further intensifies the communicative intertextual reference to Körner's *Schwertlied* [*Song of the Sword*] by naming her own poem *Das Schwertlied* [*The Song of the Sword*].[16] While the metric reference indicates a structural intertextuality which plays with the forms of the pretext,[17] the title *Das Schwertlied* intensifies the intertextual relation in terms of both communicativity and dialogicity: with her womanly *Schwertlied*, Kolmar offers a direct critical response to Körner's manly heroicism. Clothed in the stanzas and titles of German poetry from the Wars of Liberation, her liaison with Napoleon is staged as a private Polish War of Liberation reflecting a desire to participate in world-historical events (*Das Schwertlied*, 213):

Gießt mir Kugeln! Schleift den Degen!
O, ein Mann sein! Ja, ein Held!
Jubelnd einem Los entgegen,
Das ihn krönt, der trotzt und fällt.
Ach, was biegt statt bricht,
Kennt das Wehren nicht,
Nur sein Liebstes wirft es schutzlos in die Welt.

Laßt mich denn zur Lohe fliegen,
Die verbrennt, was sie begehrt,
Kann ich sinken, niemals siegen,
Schmelzt mich tief in euer Schwert!
Seinen ersten Schlag
Weiht dem bessern Tag,
Da ein neues Volk die junge Freiheit ehrt!

[Cast bullets for me! Whet the sword!
Oh to be a man! Yes, a hero!
Rejoicing headlong into a fate
Which crowns the one who defies and falls.
Ah, that which bends instead of breaks
Knows no resistance
Casting its dearest thing defenselessly into the world.

Let me now fly to the blaze
That burns up what it craves
I can sink, never triumph
Melt me deep into your sword!
Its first blow
Dedicate to the better day,
When a new nation honors young freedom!]

While Kolmar's unusual stanza form is reminiscent of a well-known Baroque hymn form, because of its rhyme scheme and the trochaic tetrameter beginning each stanza, the variation in the number of rhymes and the shift to lines of three and six feet in the latter part of each stanza marks a clear difference to the stanza form common to the Baroque.[18]

Marie's readiness to become Napoleon's mistress is described as a military mobilisation and as her part in a manly sword fight; »Schmelzt mich tief in euer Schwert!« [Melt me deep into your sword!] (v. 11), she demands of the Polish delegates. Since her desire for equal participation fails as a result of her sex, exhausting itself finally in the elliptical exclamation »O, ein Mann sein! Ja, ein Held!« [Oh, to be a man! Yes, a hero] (v. 2), she is forced to make do with an amorous mission instead. With this, of course, the Polish conflict with Napoleon no longer limits itself to the political and military domain, but enters new territories. Marie depicts herself in this song as the Polish partisan who uses her femininity, one which »biegt statt bricht« [bends instead of breaks](v. 5), as a weapon. The equivocality and ambiguity of an erotic struggle that presents itself as an interplay between political duty and amorous inclination is also illustrated by the metaphor of the »Lohe« (v. 8); the blaze, symbol for Napoleon's destruction of that which he desires, can also be interpreted as a symbol for a Polish emancipatory struggle that demands Marie's contribution without taking her sensibilities into account.

Körner's *Schwertlied* forms a dialogue between the lyrical ego and his sword, figured as a bride. The battle becomes the longed-for wedding of the lyrical ego to his sword: »Zur Brautnachts-Morgenröthe | Ruft festlich die Trompete; | Wenn die Kanonen schrei'n, | Hol' ich das Liebchen ein. | Hurrah!«[19] (To the wedding night's dawn | The trumpets solemnly call | When the cannons shriek | I will find my sweetheart. | Hurrah!) Kolmar's *Schwertlied* reveals the willingness to enter into a liaison with Napoleon as a feminine War of Liberation for Poland. Both texts thus connect love and war metaphorically. However, while Körner with his lyrical apostrophe represents war as an amorous encounter between the lyrical ego and his (female) sword, Kolmar turns this trope on its head, symbolizing an amorous encounter as a military struggle using a (male) sword. Marie demands: »Schmelzt mich tief in euer Schwert!« [Melt me deep into your sword!] (v. 11).

Whereas Körner's lyrical ego personifies his sword as a woman, Kolmar's Marie objectifies her love as part of a sword brandished in the cause of the Polish War of Liberation. Körner thus depicts war as the setting for love, while Kolmar by contrast depicts love as a military struggle. If one reads Kolmar's *Schwertlied* as, among other things, a dialogical reply to Körner's *Schwertlied*, Kolmar can be seen to complement and correct Körner's model of manly heroicism with her own feminine counter-model. In the figure of Marie Walewska, a longing for heroism becomes tangible, one which manifests itself in two ways: on the one hand, this desire projects itself upon the figure of Napoleon himself, while on the other hand Kolmar's Marie fashions herself as a Polish liberation fighter, albeit one who is doomed to succumb to her amorous combatant: Napoleon.

Gertrud Kolmar's thwarted enemy Marie begins as Napoleon's political adversary who derides him as a product of the revolution and who, viewing him from the perspective of her traditional aristocratic background, harbors contempt for his self-made empire. Despite her political aversion to him, Marie is called in the name of national duty to further the Polish War of Liberation by amatory means; love functions as a political tool where no official channels to the ruler are otherwise open. The private sphere becomes subjugated to the political; it becomes its vehicle. Political opposition, amatory victimhood, and national partisanship intermix and condense in the *Schwertlied* [*The Song of the Sword*], in which Kolmar metaphorically confounds the distinction between love and war and yet remains formally – but only formally – indebted to the tradition of German poetry of the Wars of Liberation.

–University of Freiburg, Germany

This article has been translated by Eric Kuchle, Heidelberg. The translations of the Kolmar poems, as excerpted and quoted, were provided by Eugene Sampson, University of Iowa. No published translation of *Napoleon und Marie* is available.

## Notes

1 Cf. Heine, *Ideen*, 195; Eckermann, *Gespräche mit Goethe in den letzten Jahren seines Lebens*, 159 (16 February 1826); Hebbel, *Tagebücher*, 230 (27 March 1838); Nietzsche, *Zur Genealogie der Moral*, 288.

2 On the construction of the »German Napoleon« and on the later literary comparison between Napoleon and Hitler cf. Besslich, *Der deutsche Napoleon-Mythos*.

3 Kolmar, *Im Morgen*, in: *Das lyrische Werk*, vol. I, 210. In the following, *Napoleon und Marie* will be cited according to this edition; title and page number of the respective poem will be given.

4 *Das Schwertlied*, 213. For more on female self-surrender and readiness to make sacrifices in Kolmar's works cf. Brandt; Colin; Dicks.

5 Cf. *St. Helena*, in: *Das lyrische Werk*, vol. III, 8.

6 For a more detailed discussion of Kolmar's poetics cf. Witte; Mattenklott; Kambas; Völker.

7 For Robespierre's role in Kolmar's poems cf. Bauschinger; Fetscher; Breysach; Huss.

8 Cf. Karl Biesendahl: Der Stern des Korsen. Tragödie in fünf Akten. Berlin 1890; Willy Rath: Maria Walewska. Ein unhistorisches Kammerspiel in drei Akten. Berlin 1931; Anton Strambowski: Die Walewska. Drei Akte mit Vorspiel. Leipzig 1948.

9 Cf. Viviani, »Napoléon vu, entrevu et fantasmé par Hollywood«, in: *Napoleon & le Cinéma* 132ff. For more on Rippert's film cf. Dumont, »Filmographie raisonnée«, in: *Napoléon & le Cinéma* 170.

10 This son of Napoleon, Alexander Walewski, would advance in the Second Empire in 1856 to the position of French foreign minister.

11 For more on the historical figure Maria Walewska cf. Brandys; Dufresne; Sutherland; Aretz; Gläser.

12 Cf. Gläser 217. In the 20th Century, German exile authors identifed themselves with Madame de Staël in the context of literary struggle against Hitler. Ferdinand Bruckner wrote a *Heroische Komödie* (1942) which presented Germaine de Staël as a model for political commitment in anti-Hitlerian exile.

13 Masson, *Napoleon I und die Frauen* 152f. cites the letter of Poland's provisional government to Marie in which the comparison with Ahasuerus and Esther appears as a threatening warning.

14 For a critical angle to the topic cf. Shafi, *Gertrud Kolmar* 21.

15 Kolmar, *Das lyrische Werk*, vol. II, 499.

16 The concept of communicativity used here is that developed in the context of Ulrich Broich and Manfred Pfister's theory of intertextuality. Here, communicativity denotes the degree of consciousness of the intertextual relationship on the part of both author and recipient. Structurality concerns the formal integration of the pretext into the posttext. Dialogicity refers to the semantic and ideological tension between pretext and posttext. Cf. Ulrich Broich, Manfred Pfister.

17 Achim Aurnhammer pursues such structural references to the lyric poetry of the Wars of Liberation in his study of Goethe's *West-östliche Divan* [*West-Eastern Divan*]. Whereas Goethe responded to the poetry of the Wars of Liberation as a contemporary, Kolmar, making use of historical poetic forms, engages over a century later in an intertextual situation. She allows Marie to speak ex post in the 20th Century as a contemporary of Körner.

18 Cf. Frank, *Handbuch der deutschen Strophenformen* No. 7.11, 555f.

19 Körner, *Schwertlied*, in: *Sämmtliche Werke* 32. For more on such models of manliness in texts from the War of Liberation cf. Hagemann.

## Works Cited

Aretz, Gertrude. *Napoleon und Gräfin Walewska.* Wien, Leipzig, Olten: Bernina, 1936.

Aurnhammer, Achim. »Unzeitgemäße Zeitdichtung. Strukturale Intertextualität und latente Gegenwartsbezüge im ›West-östlichen Divan‹«. *Prägnanter Moment. Studien zur deutschen Literatur der Aufklärung und Klassik. Festschrift für Hans-Jürgen Schings*, ed. Peter-André Alt, Alexander Košenina, Hartmut Reinhardt and Wolfgang Riedel. Würzburg: Königshausen & Neumann, 2002: 421–437.

Bauschinger, Sigrid. »Vindication through suffering. Gertrud Kolmar's cycle of poems ›Robespierre‹«. *Transforming the center, eroding the margins. Essays on ethnic and cultural boundaries in German-speaking countries*, ed. Dagmar C. G. Lorenz u. Renate S. Posthofen. Columbia: Camden House 1998: 44–61.

Besslich, Barbara. *Der deutsche Napoleon-Mythos. Literatur und Erinnerung 1800–1945.* Darmstadt: Wissenschaftliche Buchgesellschaft, 2007.

Besslich, Barbara. »L'Empereur zwischen Expressionismus und Exil. Napoleon-Dramen von Hermann Essig, Fritz von Unruh, Walter Hasenclever und Georg Kaiser«. *Jahrbuch der Deutschen Schillergesellschaft 46*, 2002: 250–278.

Biesendahl, Karl: *Der Stern des Korsen. Tragödie in fünf Akten.* Berlin: Lüstenöder, 1890.

Brandt, Marion. »›Opfre ich mich auf schäumender Altars Stufe‹. Über das Bild des Opfers im Werk von Gertrud Kolmar (1894–1943)«. *Jüdische Kultur und Weiblichkeit in der Moderne*, ed. Inge Stephan. Köln: Böhlau, 1994: 173–185.

Brandys, Marian. *Maria Walewska, Napoleons große Liebe. Eine historische Biographie.* Frankfurt am Main: Insel, 1996.

Breysach, Barbara. »›Du mußt dich wandeln!‹ Gertrud Kolmars Gedichtzyklus ›Robespierre‹ zur Diskussion gestellt«. *Apokalyptische Visionen in der deutschen Literatur.* Ed. Johanna Jablowska. Lódz: Wyd. Uniw. Lódzkiego, 1996: 180–192.

Broich, Ulrich; Pfister, Manfred (eds.). *Intertextualität. Formen, Funktionen, anglistische Fallstudien. Konzepte der Sprach- und Literaturwissenschaft, 35.* Tübingen: Niemeyer, 1985.

Colin, Amy. »Macht, Opfer, Selbstzerstörung. Jüdisches Frauenschicksal in Gertrud Kolmars ›Nacht‹«. *Brücken über dem Abgrund. Auseinandersetzung mit jüdischer Leidenserfahrung, Antisemitismus und Exil. Festschrift für Harry Zohn*, ed. Amy Colin. Munich. Fink, 1994. 199–223.

Brown, Clarence (dir.) *Conquest* (USA, 1937; also: *Marie Walewska*). Starring Alan Marshal (as Capt.D'Ornano], Charles Boyer [as Napoleon], Greta Garbo [as Marie Walewska], Reginald Owen [as Talleyrand].

Dicks, Barbara. *Ich bin nur ein Ackerstrauß und halte mich selbst in Händen. Entwürfe von Weiblichkeit bei Gertrud Kolmar.* Trier: Kulturverein AphorismA, 2003.

Dufresne, Claude. *Marie Walewska, l'épouse de Napoléon Ier.* Paris: Pygmalion, 2000.

Dumont, Hervé. »Filmographie raisonnée«. *Napoleon et le Cinéma: Un siècle d'images.* Ed. Jean-Pierre Mattei. Ajaccio: Piazzola, 1998. 151–359.

Eckermann, Johann Peter. »Gespräche mit Goethe in den letzten Jahren seines Lebens«. Goethe, Johann Wolfgang: *Sämtliche Werke nach Epochen seines Schaffens* (Münchner Ausgabe), ed. Karl Richter with the cooperation of Herbert G. Göpfert, Norbert Miller and Gerhard Sauder, v. 19, ed. Heinz Schlaffer. Munich: Hanser, 1986.

Fetscher, Justus. »'Les peuples meurent, pour que Dieu vive'. Gertrud Kolmar's consecration of the protagonists in the drama of the French revolution«. *War, violence and the modern condition*, ed. Bernd Hüppauf. Berlin: de Gruyter, 1997. 317–342.

Frank, Horst J. *Handbuch der deutschen Strophenformen.* Tübingen, Basel: Francke, 1993.

Gläser, Stefan. *Frauen um Napoleon.* Regensburg: Pustet, 2001.

Hagemann, Karen. »*Mannlicher Muth und teutsche Treue*.« *Nation, Militär und Geschlecht zur Zeit der antinapoleonischen Kriege Preußens.* Paderborn, Munich, Wien, Zurich: Schöningh, 2002 (Krieg in der Geschichte, 8).

Hebbel, Friedrich. *Tagebücher.* ibid. *Sämtliche Werke*, Historisch-Kritische Ausgabe, Ed. Richard Maria Werner, Zweite Abteilung, vol. 1 (1835–1839). Berlin: Behr, 1903.

Hegemann, Werner. *Napoleon oder »Kniefall vor dem Heros«.* Hellerau: J. Hegner, 1927.

Heine, Heinrich. Briefe aus Berlin, Über Polen, Reisebilder I/II (Prosa). *Ideen. Das Buch Le Grand, Historisch-Kritische Gesamtausgabe der Werke*, ed. Manfred Windfuhr, vol. 6, ed. Jost Hermand. Hamburg: Hoffmann & Campe, 1973.

Hopkins, Tighe. *The Women Napoleon loved.* Leipzig: Tauchnitz, 1910.

Huss , Abraham. »Zum Bild von Robespierre bei Gertrud Kolmar.« *Widerstehen im Wort. Studien zu den Dichtungen Gertrud Kolmars*, ed. Karin Lorenz-Lindemann. Göttingen: Wallstein, 1996: 88–104.

Kambas, Chryssoula (ed.). *Lyrische Bildnisse. Beiträge zur Dichtung und Biographie von Gertrud Kolmar.* Bielefeld: Aisthesis-Verl, 1998.

Kolmar, Gertrud. *Das lyrische Werk.* Ed. Regine Nörtemann. 3 vols. Göttingen: Wallstein, 2003. The poem cycle »Napoleon und Marie« is cited according to this edition (vol. 1) including the titles of individual poems in italics.

Körner, Theodor. *Sämmtliche Werke.* Ausgabe in einem Band. Leipzig: Reclam, 1869.

Lefebvre, Georges. *Napoleon*, ed. Peter Schöttler, with an epilogue by Daniel Schönpflug. Stuttgart: Klett-Cotta, 2003.

Masson, Friedrich. *Napoleon I und die Frauen.* Transl. by Oscar Marschall von Bieberstein. Berlin: Brandus, 1913 (originally published in 1894).

Mattenklott, Gert. »Gertrud Kolmar. Versuch eines Porträts«. *Kolmar, Gertrud. La Straniera.* Rom: Bulzoni, 1999. 67–89 (Pro forma, 1).

Nietzsche, Friedrich. *Zur Genealogie der Moral.* ibid. *Kritische Studienausgabe in 15 Bde.*, ed. Giorgio Colli and Mazzino Montinari, vol. 5. Munich: Dt. Taschenbuch-Verlag, 1988.

Rath, Willy. *Maria Walewska. Ein unhistorisches Kammerspiel in drei Akten.* Berlin: Vertriebsstelle d. Verb. Dt. Bühnen-Schriftsteller u. Komponisten, 1931.

Rippert, Otto (dir.) *Gräfin Walewska* (Germany, 1920). Starring Rudolf Lettinger [as Napoleon], Hella Moja [as Gräfin Walewska]. Writing credits Paul Georg, Willy Rath.

Shafi, Monika. *Gertrud Kolmar. Eine Einführung in das Werk.* Munich: Iudicum, 1995.

Strambowski, Anton. *Die Walewska. Drei Akte mit Vorspiel.* Leipzig: W. H. Hans Badnitz, 1948.

Sutherland, Christine. *Maria Walewska. Geliebte Napoleons, Gräfin Ornano.* Munich: Callwey, 1981.

Vallentin, Berthold. *Napoleon und die Deutschen.* Berlin: Bondi, 1926.

Viviani, Christian. »Napoléon vu, entrevu et fantasmé par Hollywood«. *Napoleon & le Cinéma. Un siècle d'images.* Ouvrages publié avec le concours de la Direction Régionale des Affaires de Corse, de la Collectivité Territoriale de Corse, du Conseil Général des Hauts-de-Seine et de la municipalité d'Ajaccio. Ajaccio: Piazzola, 1998: 125–135.

Völker, Ludwig. »Formstrukturen als Sinnstrukturen. Der Zyklus als poetische Form im Werk Gertrud Kolmars«. *Vom Gedicht zum Zyklus. Vom Zyklus zum Werk. Strategien der Kontinuität in der modernen und zeitgenössischen Lyrik*, ed. Jacques Lajarrige. Innsbruck, Wien, Munich: Studien-Verlag, 2000: 98–121.

Wairy, Louis Constant. *Napoleon I nach den Memoiren seines Kammerdieners Constant.* Transl. by Oskar Marschall von Bieberstein. 3 volumes. Leipzig: Schmidt & Günther, 1904 (originally published in 1830).

Witte, Bernd. »›Und wir, wir sind geworden durch den Galgen und durch das Rad!‹ Die jüdische Lyrikerin Gertrud Kolmar (1894–1943)«. »*Manche Worte strahlen*«. *Deutsch-jüdische Dichterinnen des 20. Jahrhunderts*, ed. Norbert Oellers. Erkelenz: Altius-Verlag, 1999: 43–60.

Woltmann, Johanna. *Gertrud Kolmar. Leben und Werk.* Göttingen: Wallstein, 1995.

# List of Contributors

*Arnold-de Simine, Silke*, is Lecturer at the Birkbeck College, University of London, after teaching German literature, culture, and film as Assistant Professor of German at the University of Mannheim (Germany). She is the author of *Leichen im Keller: Zu Fragen des Gender in Angstinszenierungen der Schauer- und Kriminalliteratur, 1790–1830* (2000) and is researching the organization of memory in the media of literature, film, and the museum. She is the editor of a volume of essays, *Memory Traces: 1989 and the Question of German Cultural Identity* (2005).

*Askey, Jennifer Drake*, is Assistant Professor of German at Kansas State University. Her dissertation (Washington University, 2003) was titled »Reading as Women, Reading as Patriots: Nationalism, Popular Literature, and Girls' Education in Wilhelminian Germany.« Her research interests include Queen Louisa in all of her incarnations, theories of reading and feminism, nineteenth-century realism and historical fiction, and contemporary German-Jewish literature. She has taught German literature and Women's Studies at the University of Utah, Wesleyan University, and the University of Connecticut.

*Besslich, Barbara*, is Adjunct Associate Professor of German at the Albert Ludwig University of Freiburg (Germany). One of her main fields is ›German Literature and History‹ since the eighteenth century, and her wide range of publications includes the monographs *Wege in den ›Kulturkrieg‹: Zivilisationskritik in Deutschland 1890–1914* (2000), *Faszination des Verfalls: Thomas Mann und Oswald Spengler* (2002), and her extensive study on Napoleon in German literature and memory (*Der deutsche Napoleon-Mythos: Literatur und Erinnerung 1800–1945*, 2006). She has coedited together with Katharina Graetz and Olaf Hildebrand a book on history in post-1989 German literature (*Wende des Erinnerns? Geschichtskonstruktionen in der deutschen Literatur nach 1989*, 2006).

*Bland, Caroline*, is Lecturer in Germanic Studies at the University of Sheffield (UK). She has published several articles on feminist politics and literature in Imperial Germany and co-edited (with Máire Cross) studies on *Gender and Politics in the Age of Letter-Writing, 1750–2000* (2004) and with Elisa Mueller-Adams *Schwellenueberschreitungen. Politik in der Literatur von deutschsprachigen Frauen, 1780-1918* (2007), to be followed by a companion collection on women and the German literary market in the same era. She is currently writing a monograph on gender and national identity in Wilhelminian German women's writing.

*Davidson, Denise Zara,* is Associate Professor of History at Georgia State University, Atlanta. Her book, *France after Revolution: Urban Life, Gender, and the New Social Order* was published by Harvard University Press in 2007. She has also published several highly visible articles on issues of gender and bourgeois provincial sociability in early 19th-century France, including »Women at Napoleonic Festivals: Gender and the Public Sphere during the First Empire« (*French History* 2002) and »Making Society ›Legible‹: People-Watching in Paris After the Revolution« (*French Historical Studies* 2005).

*Guenther, Beatrice,* is Assistant Professor of French Studies at Bowling Green State University. She received her B.A. from the University of Toronto and her Ph.D in Comparative Literature from Princeton University. Her research focuses on constructs of identity – both in terms of gender and transculturation or *métissage* in early nineteenth-century French and German literature; she is especially interested in women's education in post-revolutionary France and Germany. To date, she has published *The Poetics of Death* (1996), a study of the limits of *mimesis* in Honoré de Balzac and Heinrich von Kleist's prose, and she has co-authored *Générations*, a 5th/6th-semester French textbook on oral and written forms of expression. She is currently also working on Francophone culture, in particular, on identity politics in Quebec and the Maghreb.

*Jensen, Heather Belnap,* is an instructor in Art History at Brigham Young University. She has received numerous fellowships to support her research, including a Kress Foundation Travel Fellowship, and is a contributor to the proposed anthology *Vanishing Acts: Women and the Art World in 19th-Century France.* Her dissertation, »*Portraitistes a la plume:* Women Art Critics in Revolutionary and Napoleonic France«, will serve as a basis for a monograph on women artists, critics, and patrons of this formative period.

*Kennedy, Deborah*, is Associate Professor in the Department of English, Saint Mary's University, Halifax, Canada. Her publications include *Helen Maria Williams and the Age of Revolution* (2002) as well as essays on Felicia Hemans, Charlotte Smith, and William Wordsworth.

*Lokke, Kari,* is Professor of Comparative Literature at the University of California, Davis. She is the author of *Gérard de Nerval: The Poet as Social Visionary* (1987) and *Tracing Women's Romanticism: Gender, History and Transcendence* (2004). The latter was awarded the Jean-Pierre Barricelli Book Prize for 2005 by the International Conference on Romanticism. With Adriana Craciun she co-edited *Rebellious Hearts: British Women Writers and the French Revolution* (2001). She has also written articles on the aesthetics of the sublime and the grotesque, Romantic fairy tales, and women poets of the Romantic era.

*Maierhofer, Waltraud,* Associate Professor of German at the University of Iowa, has published widely on narrative prose by German-language authors such as Benedikte Naubert, Goethe, Heinrich Heine, Adele Schopenhauer, Karl Immermann, Karl Gutzkow, Ricarda Huch, Alfred Döblin, Julian Schutting as well as on issues of life writing, auto/biography, and biographical/historical fiction. She is the author of *Hexen, Huren, Heldenweiber: Bilder des Weiblichen in Erzähltexten über den Dreißigjährigen Krieg* (2005). She has also edited the extant letters by painter Angelica Kauffmann (1999, 2001) and published an introductory monograph on to her life and works.

*Potter, Dorothy,* is Associate Professor of History at Lynchburg College, VA. Her publications and presentations at conferences most frequently deal with various aspects of Wolfgang Amadeus Mozart, and/or Anglo-American culture in the 18th through mid-19th centuries. In 2002 she edited the journal of Mary Freman Caesar, the wife of an 18th-century British Member of Parliament; Mrs. Caesar was a strong supporter of the Jacobite cause, and was also a friend of Jonathan Swift and Alexander Pope. In 2005 her essay on the influence of Mozart's music on 19th century Philadelphia culture was published in *Music and History: Bridging the Disciplines.* She has also written several biographical essays on various aspects of Napoleonic Europe.

*Roesch, Gertrud Maria,* is Professor of German as a Foreign Language at the Ruprecht-Karls-University of Heidelberg. Her research focuses on German drama in the nineteenth century, the German novel in the twentieth century; satire and caricature, literature in exile, issues of fact and fiction, and gender studies. Her recent publications include a monograph on *roman à clef* (*Clavis Scientiae: Studien zum Verhältnis von Faktizität und Fiktionalität am Fall der Schlüsselliteratur*, 2004). Together with Corinna Onnen-Isemann she has edited an interdisciplinary volume on sisterhood in literary, psychological, and sociological perspectives (*Schwestern: Zur Dynamik einer lebenslangen Beziehung*, 2005).

*Sammons, Jeffrey L.,* is Leavenworth Professor of German Literature Emeritus at Yale University. He has published primarily on nineteenth-century topics. His most recent books are *Ideology, Mimesis, Fantasy: Charles Sealsfield, Friedrich Gerstäcker, Karl May, and Other German Novelists of America* (1998) and *Friedrich Spielhagen: Novelist of Germany's False Dawn* (2004).

# List of Illustrations



# Acknowledgements

This book grew out of several sessions on women in/on war, women and the nation, and historical fiction at conferences organized by the American Society for Eighteenth-Century Studies, Interdisciplinary Nineteenth-Century Studies, The Group on 18th and 19th-century Women Writers, etc. with additional networking contacts. All the participants helped us to think out the issues, even if their papers and projects are not represented here. To focus on opponents to Napoleon was the idea of Gertrud M. Roesch. Special thanks go to an anonymous reviewer and to John McCarthy for their critical comments and input, as well as to the University of Iowa and to the Ruprecht-Karls-Universität, Heidelberg, for the financial support. We would also like to thank Mary Wheat and Anastasia Novikova for their invaluable help in the preparation of the manuscript. – The contribution by Barbara Besslich has been substantially revised and translated from the corresponding chapter in her book in German, *Der deutsche Napoleon-Mythos. Literatur und Erinnerung 1800–1945* (2006). All other articles are original.